y Tree

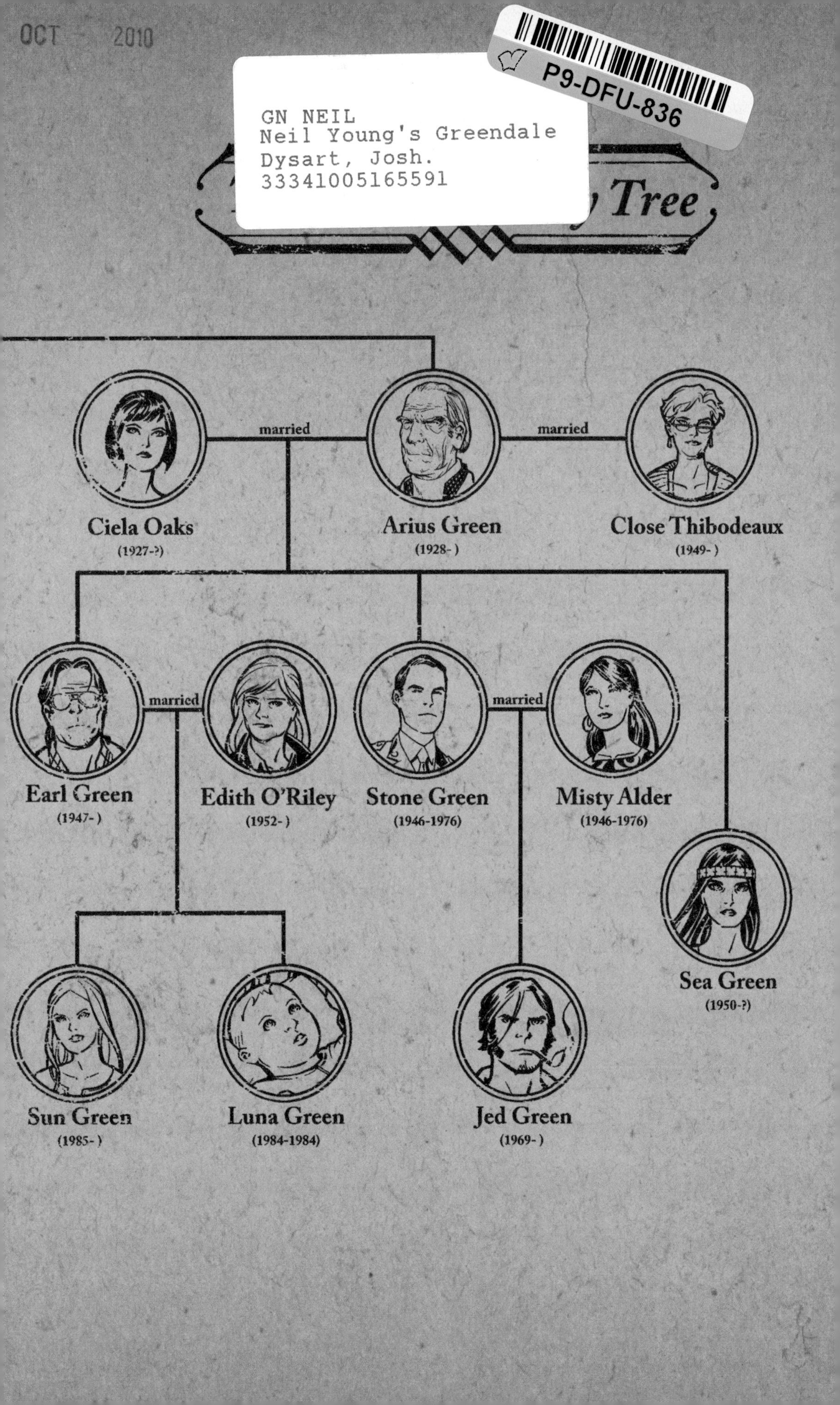
married
married
Ciela Oaks
(1927-?)
Arius Green
(1928-)
Close Thibodeaux
(1949-)
married
married
Earl Green
(1947-)
Edith O'Riley
(1952-)
Stone Green
(1946-1976)
Misty Alder
(1946-1976)
Sea Green
(1950-?)
Sun Green
(1985-)
Luna Green
(1984-1984)
Jed Green
(1969-)

VERTIGO

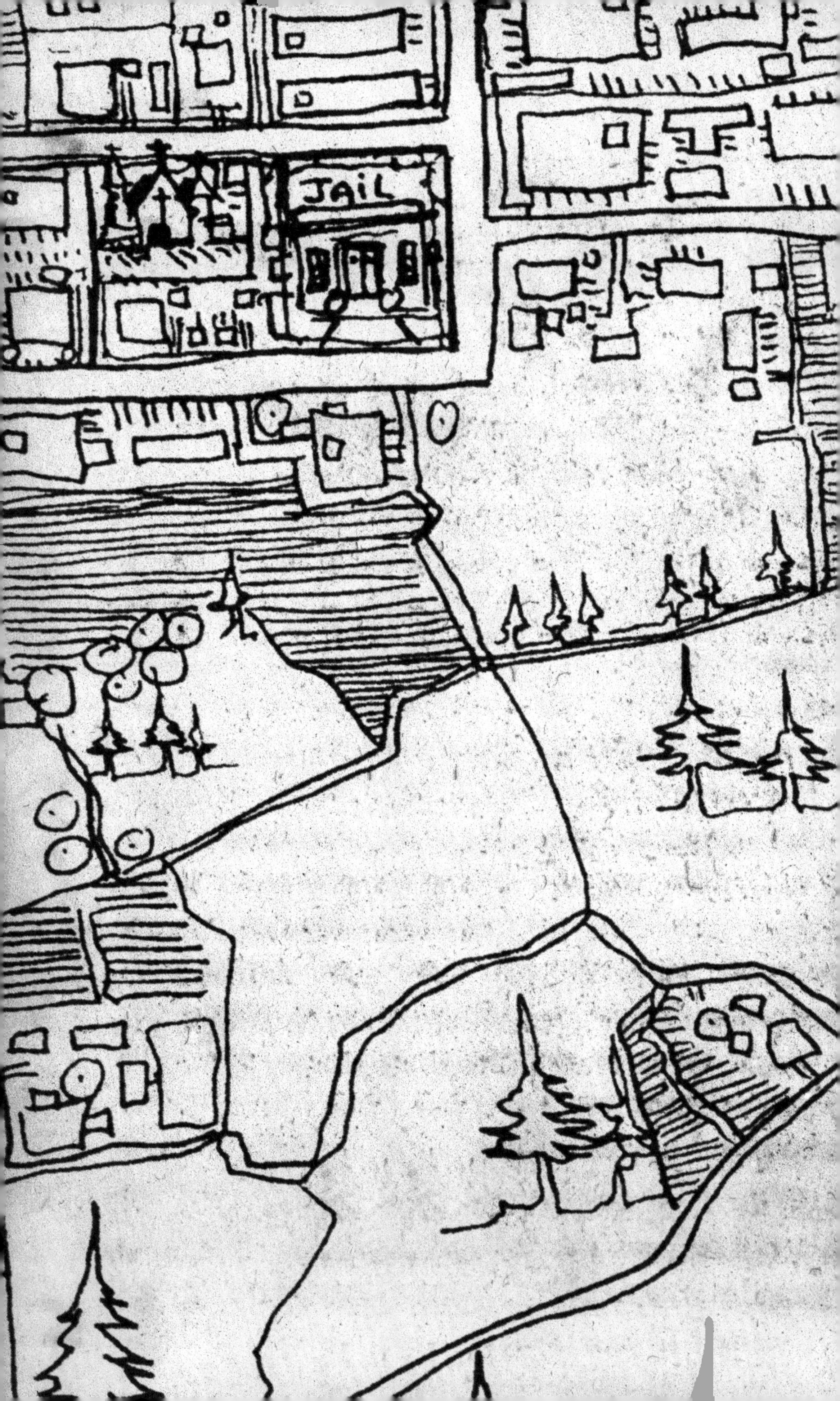
JAIL

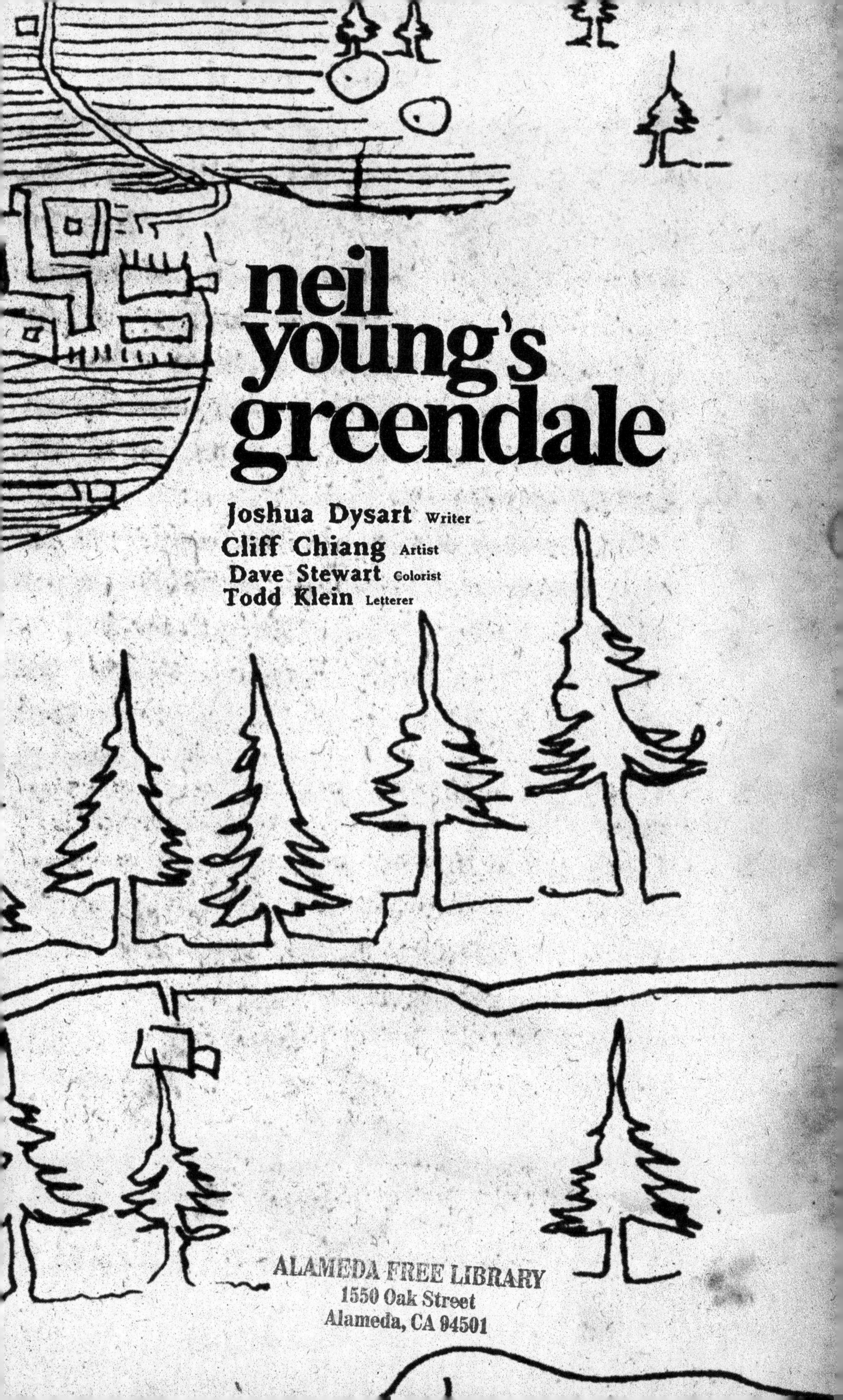

neil young's greendale

Joshua Dysart Writer
Cliff Chiang Artist
Dave Stewart Colorist
Todd Klein Letterer

We're going on a little trip, folks... so, these stories are about a place called Greendale and it's a green dale... there's a lot going on in town. It seems to be a pretty mellow place, really. In town, there's about 20 to 25,000 people and it's not a very big place at all... if there is a huge map, which there is, that just shows Greendale, very little happening over here, there's mountains, and farms, over there, there's an ocean... well, Greendale is a nice town, but it has its quirks...there's a lot going on in Greendale that I don't know about either. Can you imagine? I mean, I made it up and I don't know what the hell is goin' on. So don't feel bad if you feel a little out of it with this. No one really knows...

Neil Young

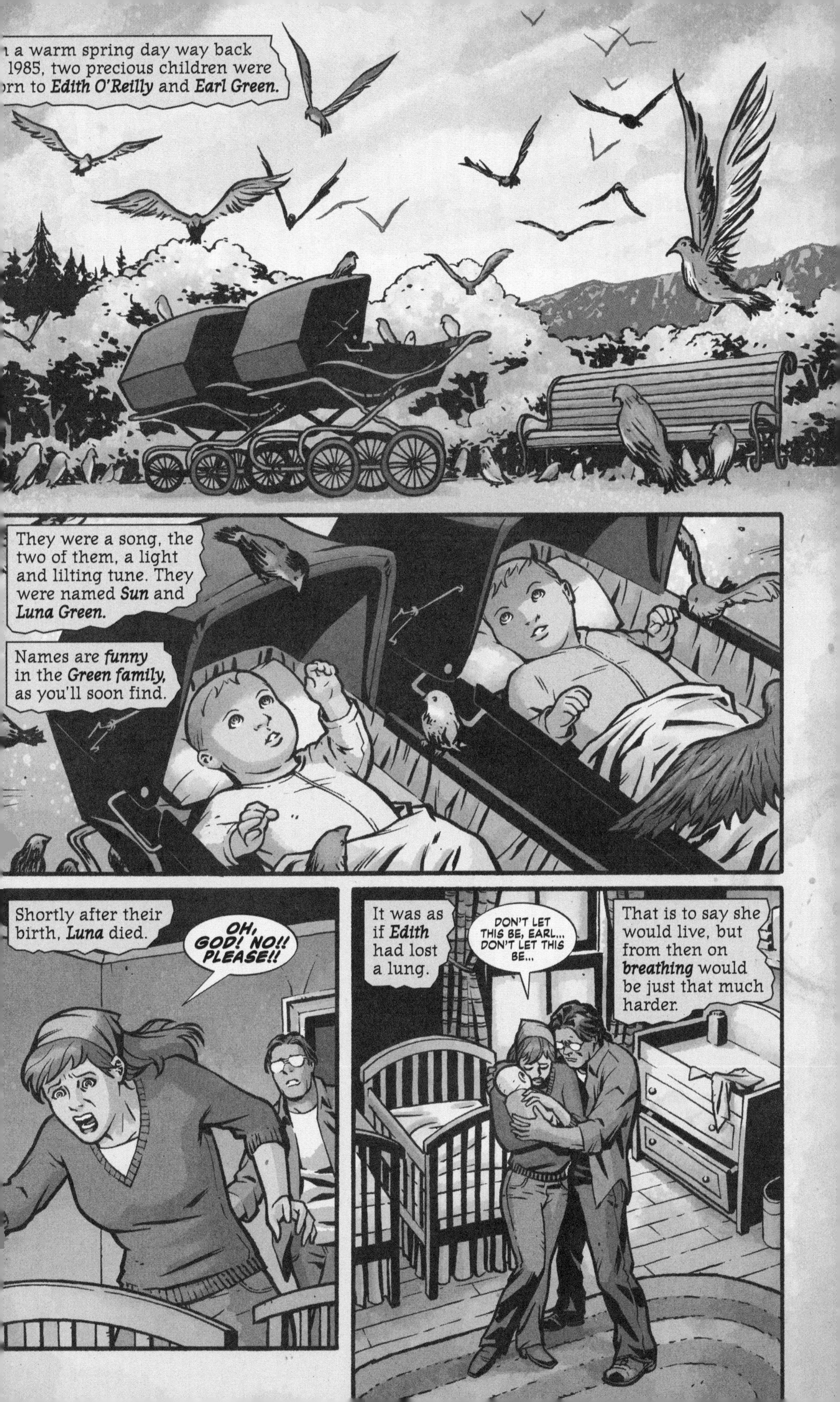

n a warm spring day way back 1985, two precious children were orn to Edith O'Reilly and Earl Green.
They were a song, the two of them, a light and lilting tune. They were named Sun and Luna Green.
Names are funny in the Green family, as you'll soon find.
Shortly after their birth, Luna died.
OH, GOD! NO!! PLEASE!!
It was as if Edith had lost a lung.
DON'T LET THIS BE, EARL... DON'T LET THIS BE...
That is to say she would live, but from then on breathing would be just that much harder.

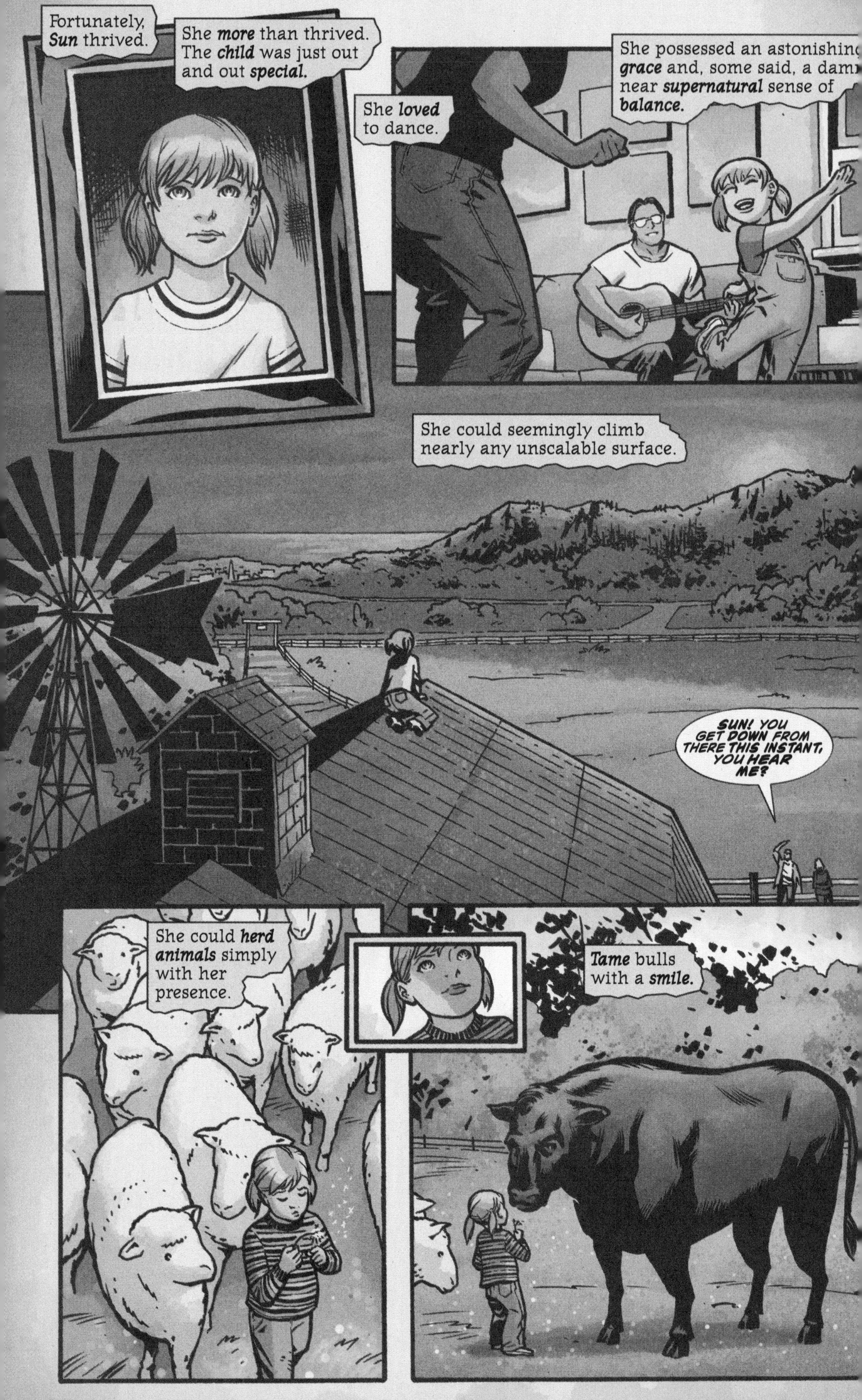
Fortunately, Sun thrived.
She more than thrived. The child was just out and out special.
She loved to dance.
She possessed an astonishing grace and, some said, a damn near supernatural sense of balance.
She could seemingly climb nearly any unscalable surface.
SUN! YOU GET DOWN FROM THERE THIS INSTANT, YOU HEAR ME?
She could herd animals simply with her presence.
Tame bulls with a smile.

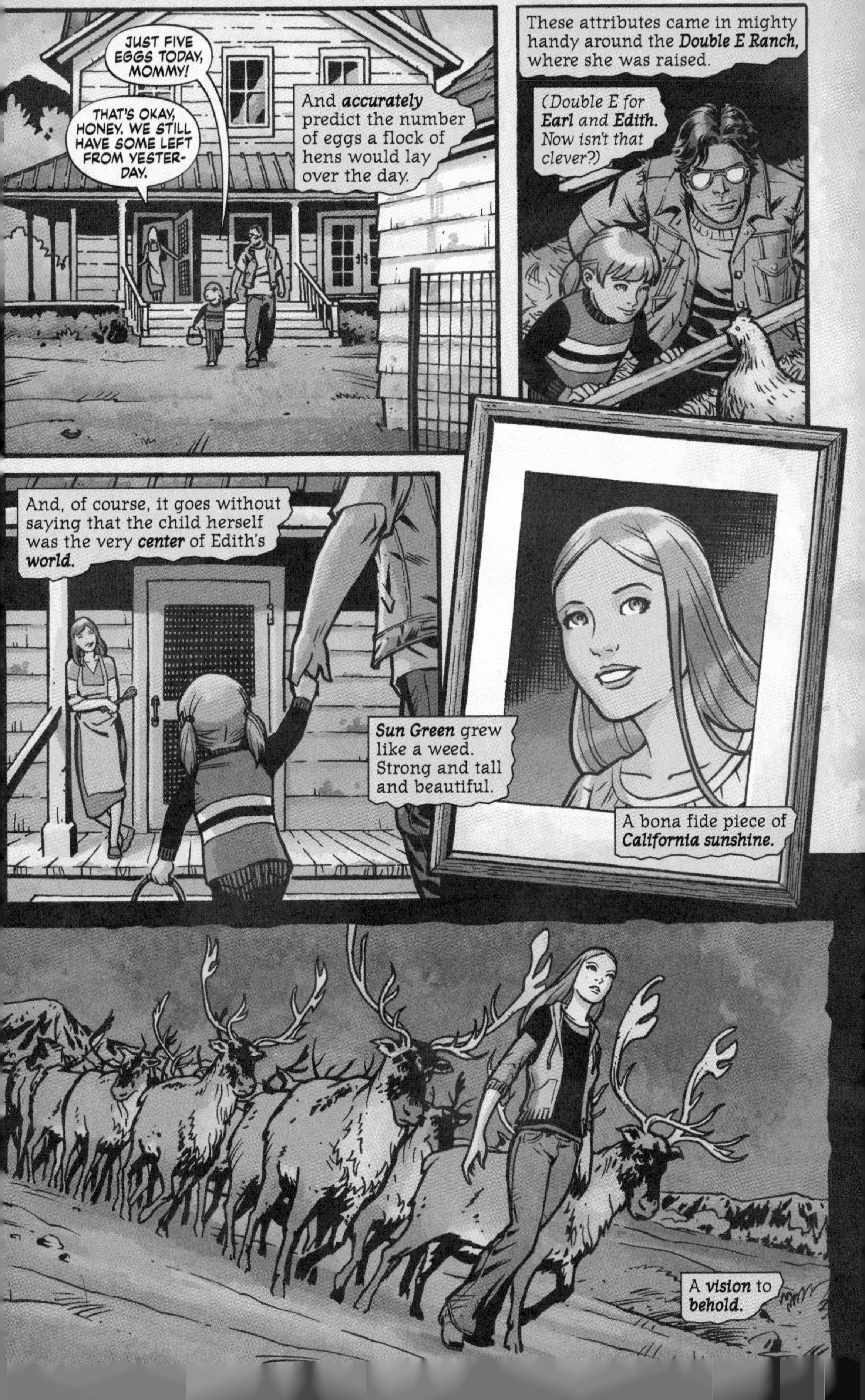
JUST FIVE EGGS TODAY, MOMMY!
THAT'S OKAY, HONEY. WE STILL HAVE SOME LEFT FROM YESTER-DAY.
And *accurately* predict the number of eggs a flock of hens would lay over the day.
These attributes came in mighty handy around the *Double E Ranch*, where she was raised.
(Double E for **Earl** and **Edith**. Now isn't that clever?)
And, of course, it goes without saying that the child herself was the very *center* of Edith's *world*.
Sun Green grew like a weed. Strong and tall and beautiful.
A bona fide piece of *California sunshine*.
A *vision* to *behold*.

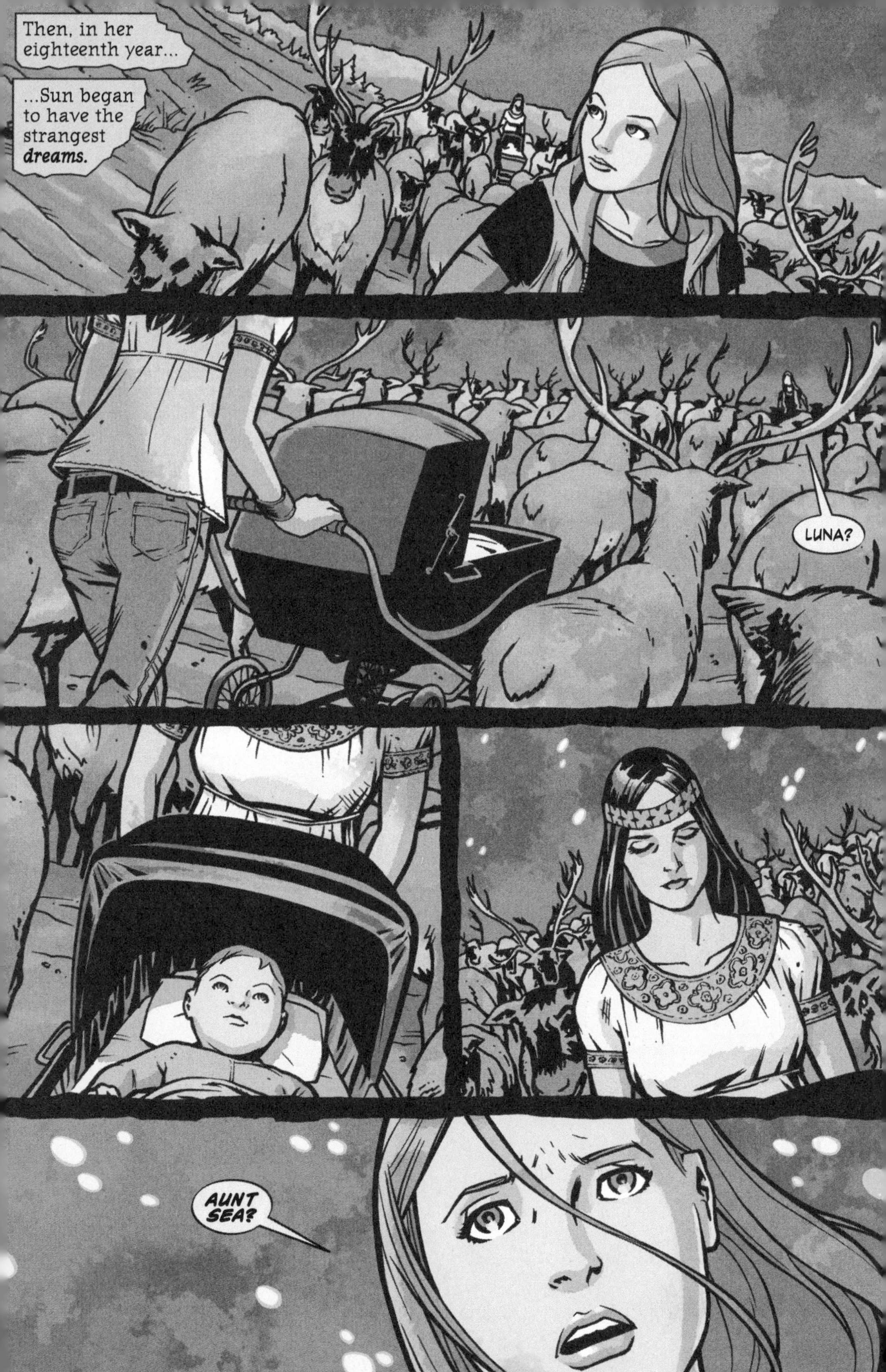
Then, in her eighteenth year...
...Sun began to have the strangest ***dreams.***
LUNA?
AUNT SEA?

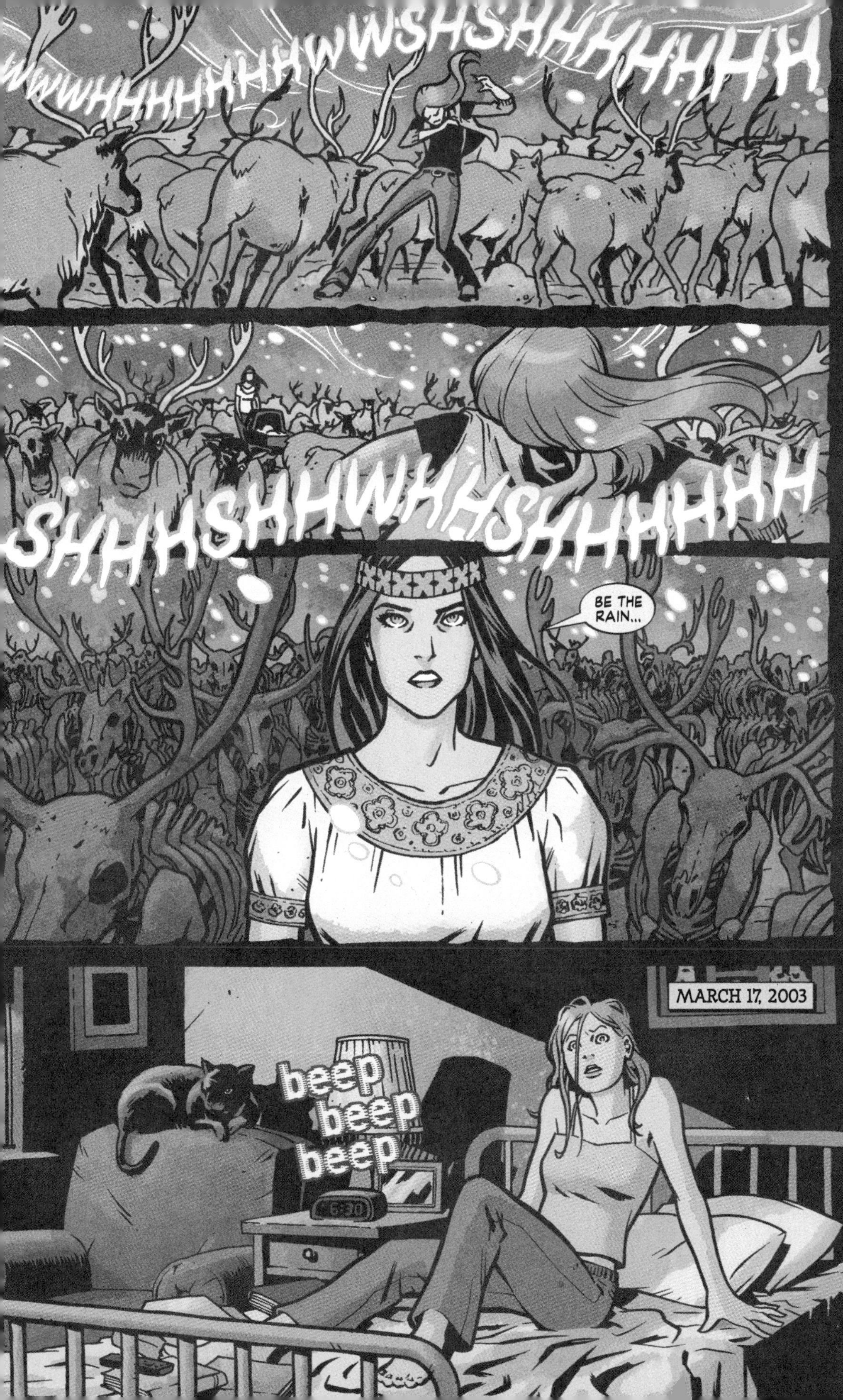

WWWHHHHHHWWSHSHHHHHHHH
SHHHSHHWHHHSHHHHHHH
BE THE RAIN...
MARCH 17, 2003
beep
beep
beep

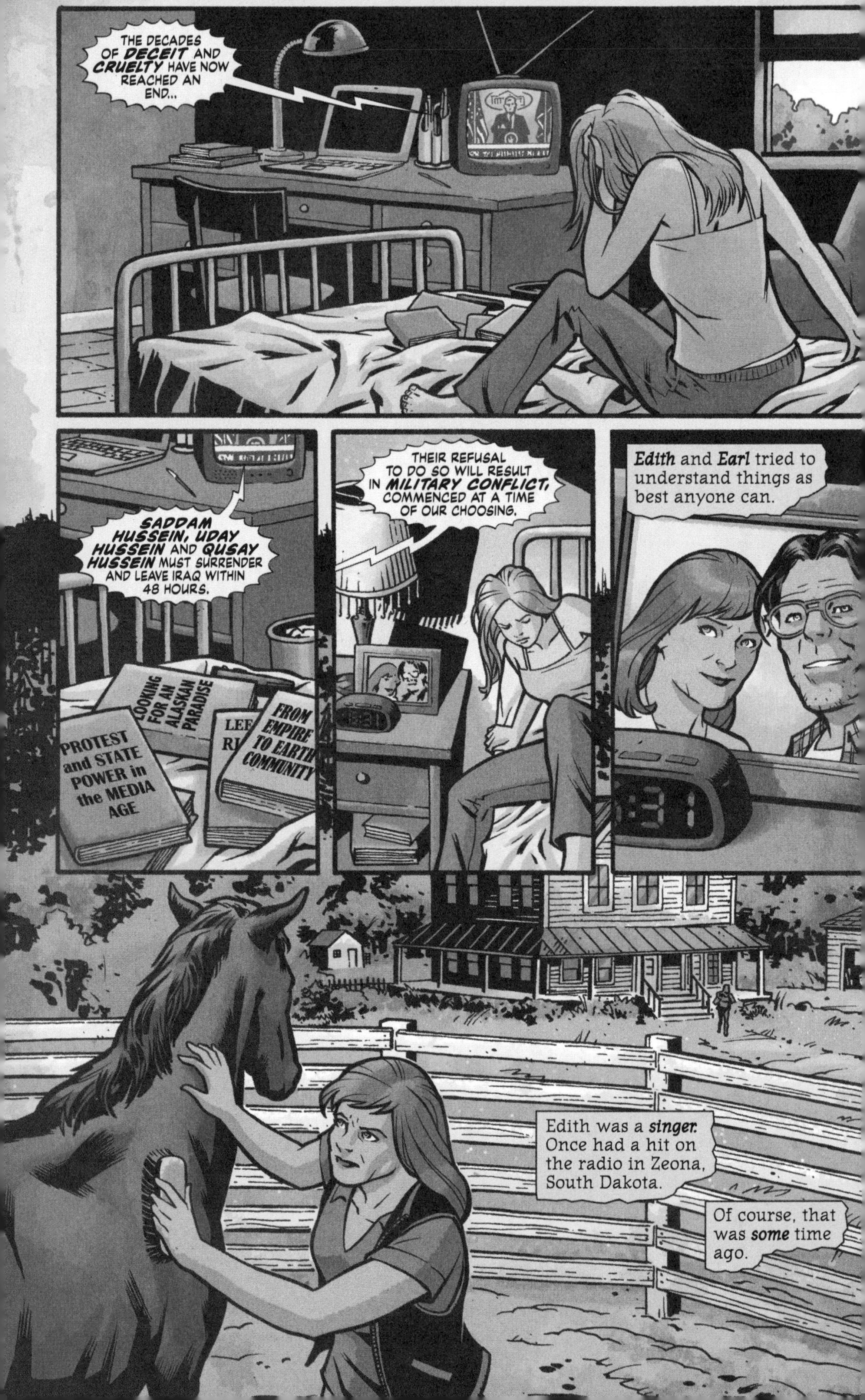
THE DECADES OF DECEIT AND CRUELTY HAVE NOW REACHED AN END...
SADDAM HUSSEIN, UDAY HUSSEIN AND QUSAY HUSSEIN MUST SURRENDER AND LEAVE IRAQ WITHIN 48 HOURS.
LOOKING FOR AN ALASKAN PARADISE
PROTEST and STATE POWER in the MEDIA AGE
FROM EMPIRE TO EARTH COMMUNITY
THEIR REFUSAL TO DO SO WILL RESULT IN MILITARY CONFLICT, COMMENCED AT A TIME OF OUR CHOOSING.
Edith and Earl tried to understand things as best anyone can.
Edith was a singer. Once had a hit on the radio in Zeona, South Dakota.
Of course, that was some time ago.

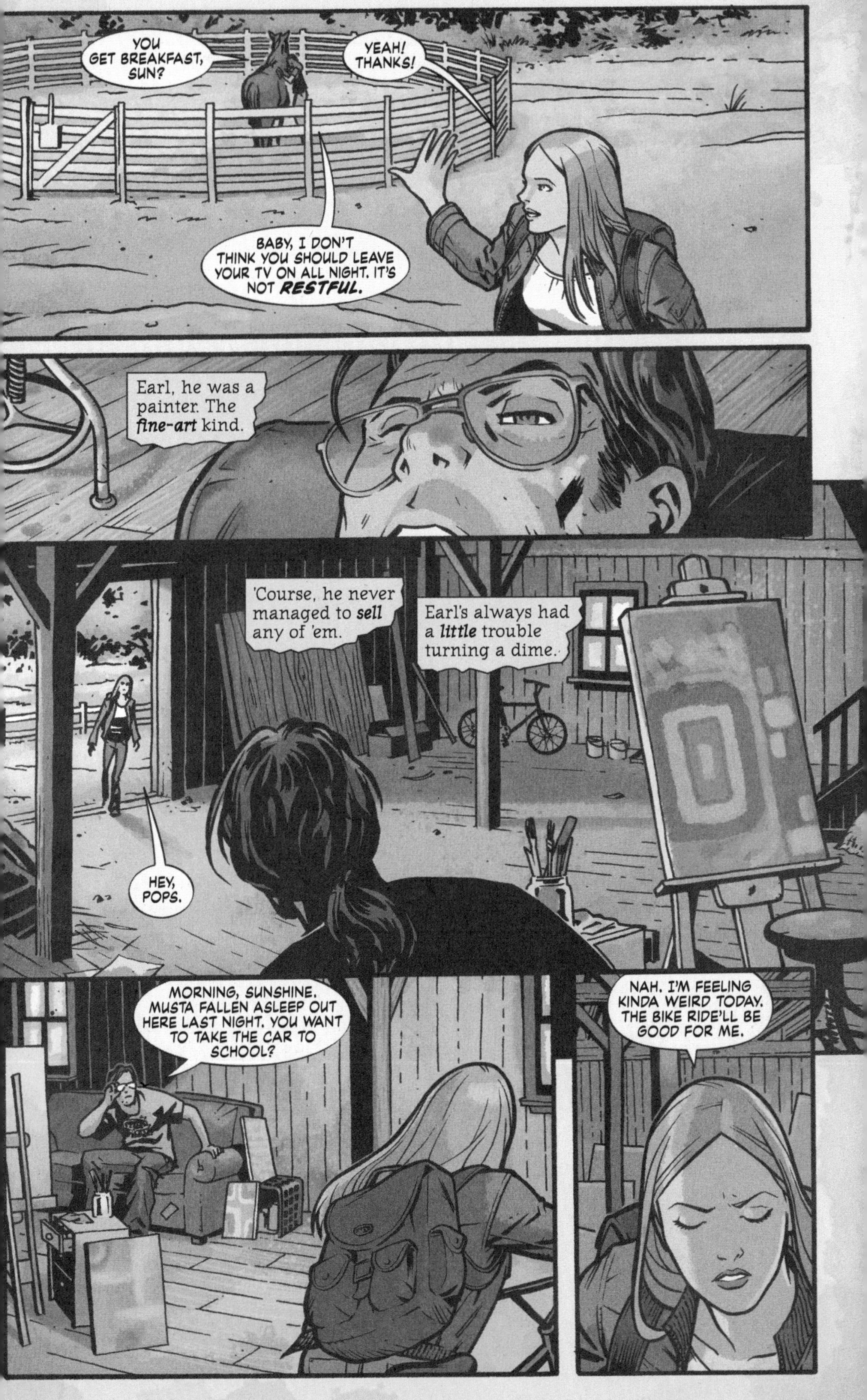
YOU GET BREAKFAST, SUN?
YEAH! THANKS!
BABY, I DON'T THINK YOU SHOULD LEAVE YOUR TV ON ALL NIGHT. IT'S NOT ***RESTFUL.***
Earl, he was a painter. The ***fine-art*** kind.
'Course, he never managed to ***sell*** any of 'em.
Earl's always had a ***little*** trouble turning a dime.
HEY, POPS.
MORNING, SUNSHINE. MUSTA FALLEN ASLEEP OUT HERE LAST NIGHT. YOU WANT TO TAKE THE CAR TO SCHOOL?
NAH. I'M FEELING KINDA WEIRD TODAY. THE BIKE RIDE'LL BE GOOD FOR ME.

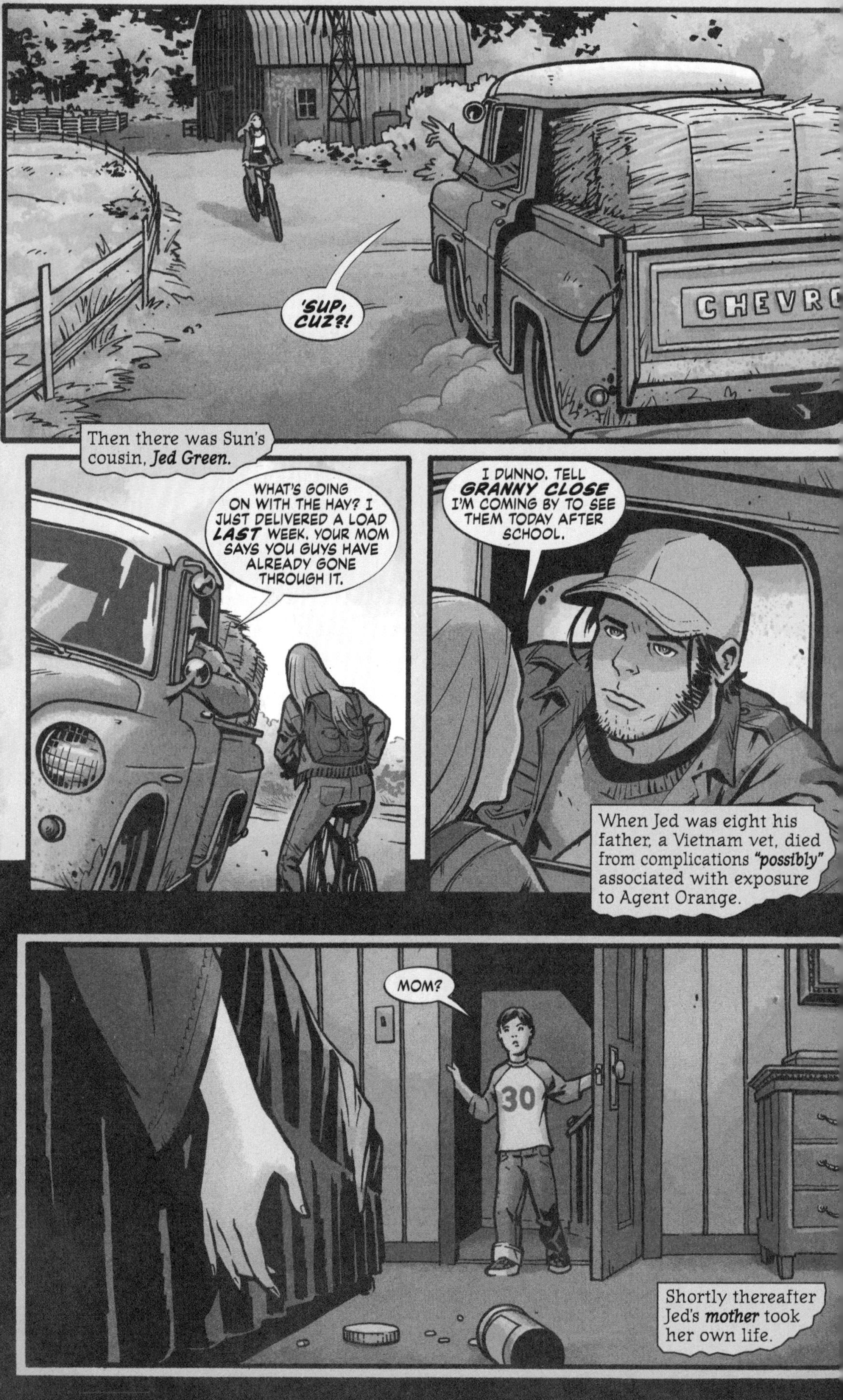
'SUP, CUZ?!
CHEVRO
Then there was Sun's cousin, Jed Green.
WHAT'S GOING ON WITH THE HAY? I JUST DELIVERED A LOAD LAST WEEK. YOUR MOM SAYS YOU GUYS HAVE ALREADY GONE THROUGH IT.
I DUNNO. TELL GRANNY CLOSE I'M COMING BY TO SEE THEM TODAY AFTER SCHOOL.
When Jed was eight his father, a Vietnam vet, died from complications "possibly" associated with exposure to Agent Orange.
MOM?
30
Shortly thereafter Jed's mother took her own life.

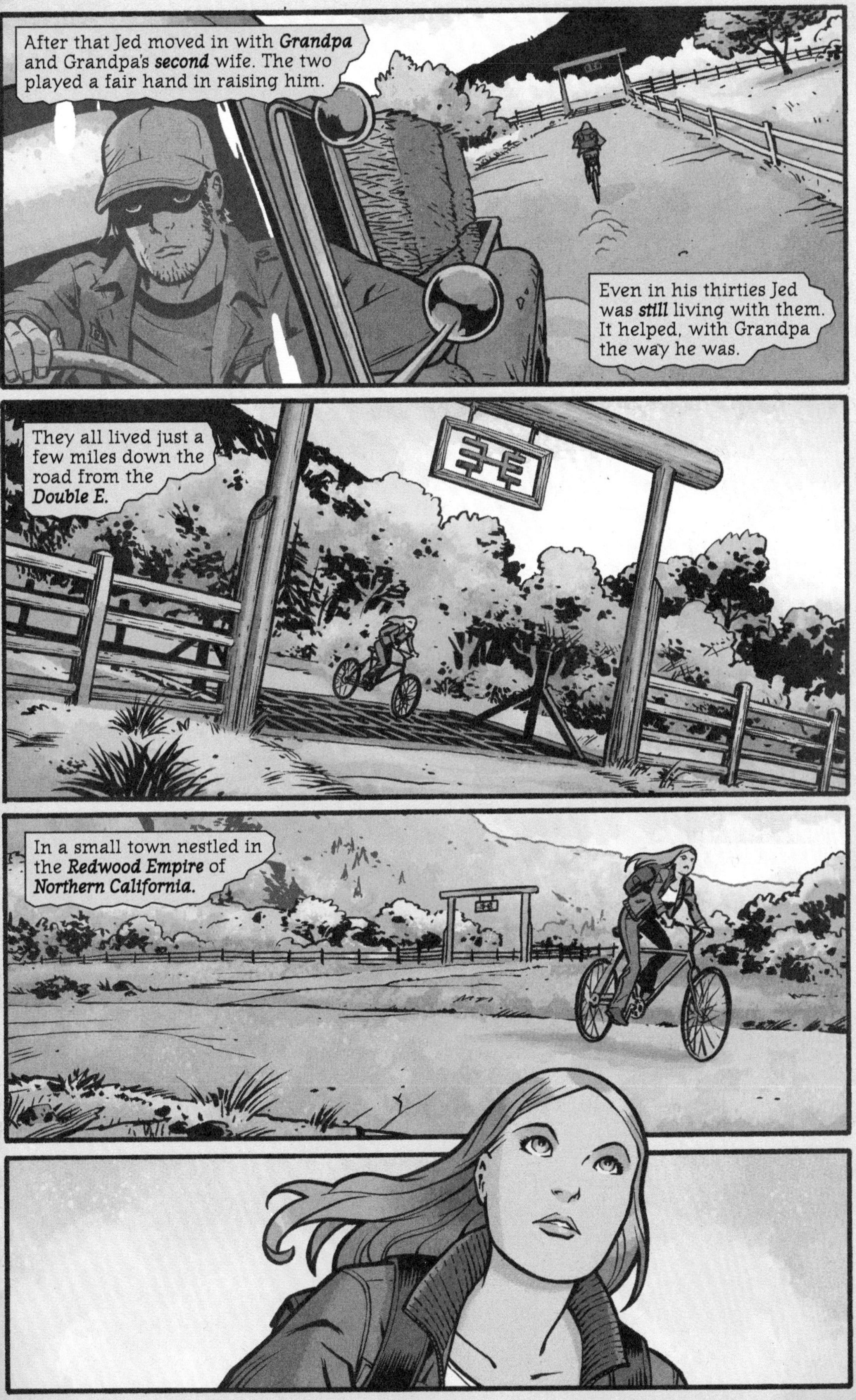
After that Jed moved in with ***Grandpa*** and Grandpa's ***second*** wife. The two played a fair hand in raising him.
Even in his thirties Jed was ***still*** living with them. It helped, with Grandpa the way he was.
They all lived just a few miles down the road from the ***Double E.***
In a small town nestled in the ***Redwood Empire*** of ***Northern California.***

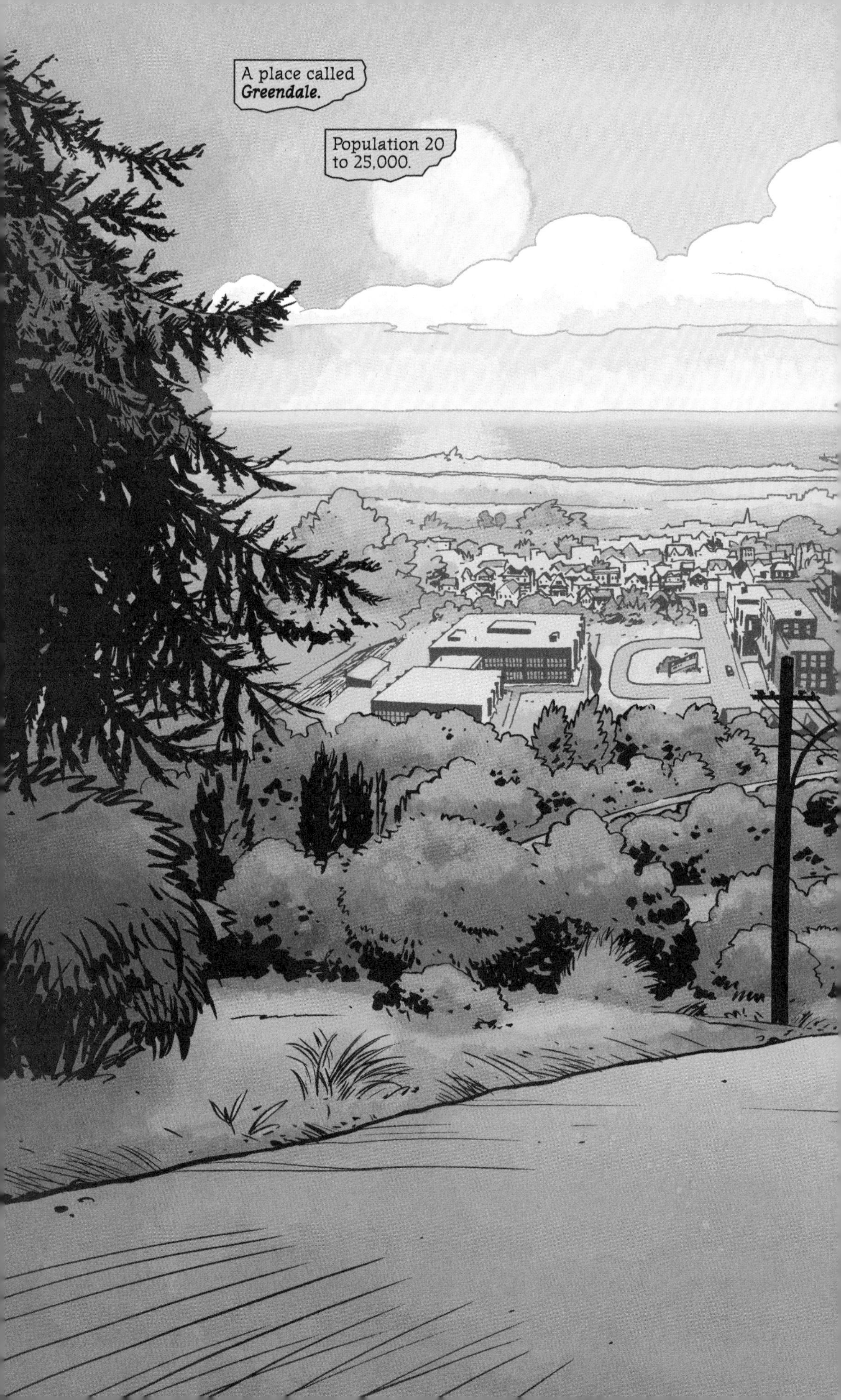
A place called *Greendale.*
Population 20 to 25,000.

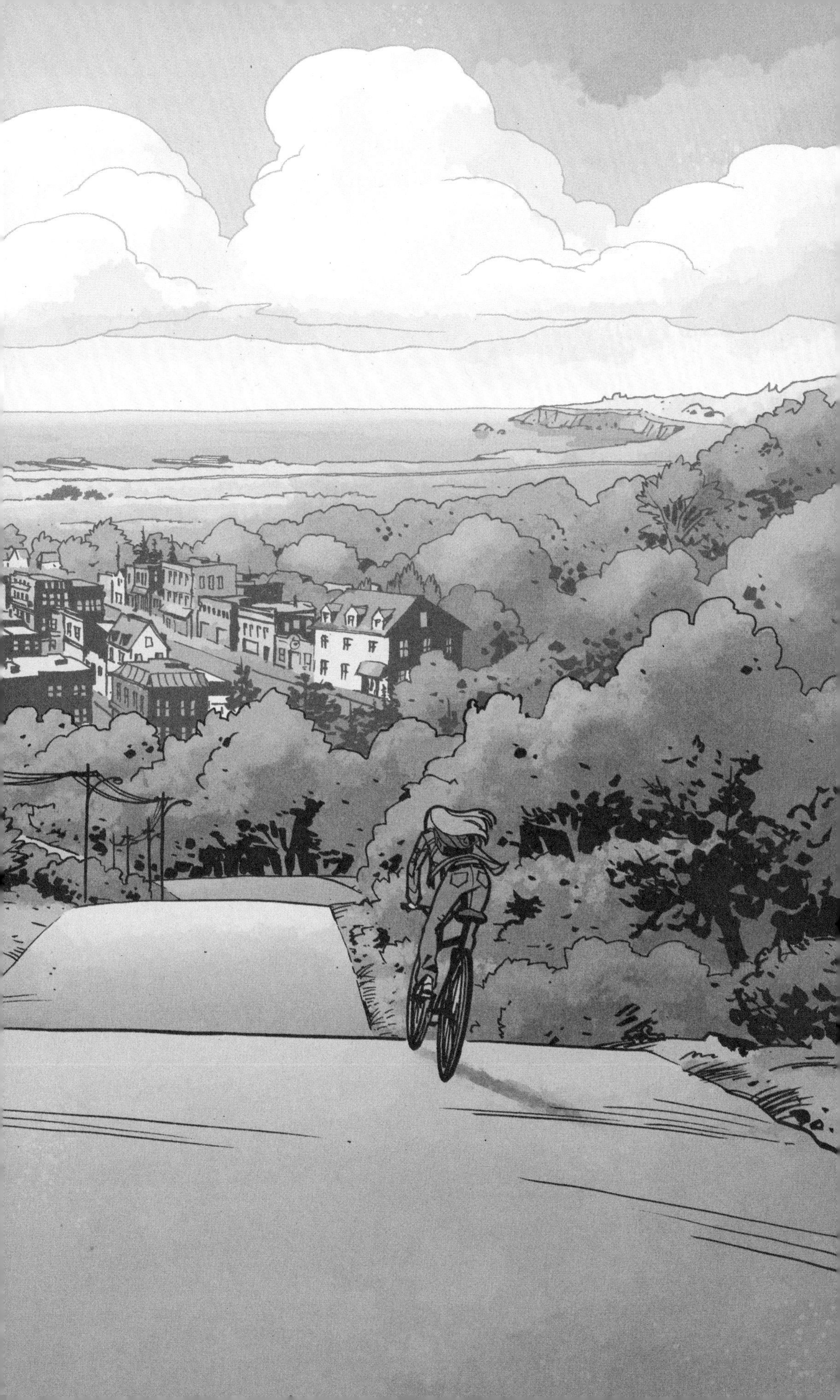

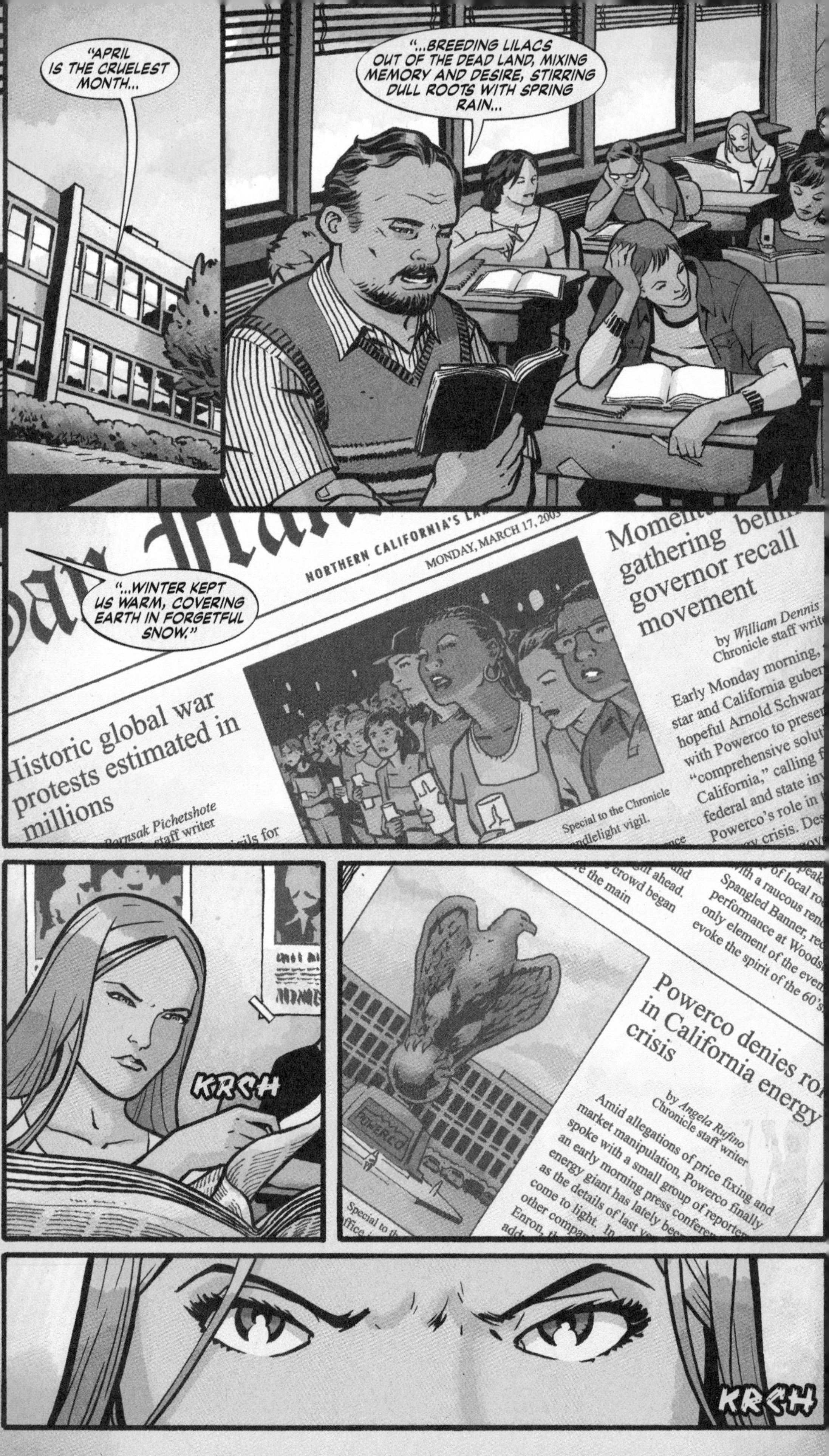
"APRIL IS THE CRUELEST MONTH...
"...BREEDING LILACS OUT OF THE DEAD LAND, MIXING MEMORY AND DESIRE, STIRRING DULL ROOTS WITH SPRING RAIN...
NORTHERN CALIFORNIA'S
MONDAY, MARCH 17,
gathering
governor recall
movement
by William Dennis
"...WINTER KEPT US WARM, COVERING EARTH IN FORGETFUL SNOW."
Early Monday morning,
hopeful Arnold Schwar
with Powerco to prese
"comprehensive solut
California," calling f
federal and state in
Powerco's role in
Historic global war
protests estimated in
millions
Pornsak Pichetshote
Special to the Chronicle
KRCH
Spangled Banner,
performance at Woods
only element of the even
evoke the spirit of the 60's
Powerco denies
in California energy
crisis
by Angela Rufino
Chronicle staff writer
Amid allegations of price fixing and
market manipulation, Powerco finally
spoke with a small group of reporter
an early morning press confere
energy giant has lately bee
as the details of last
come to light.
other compa
Enron,
KRCH

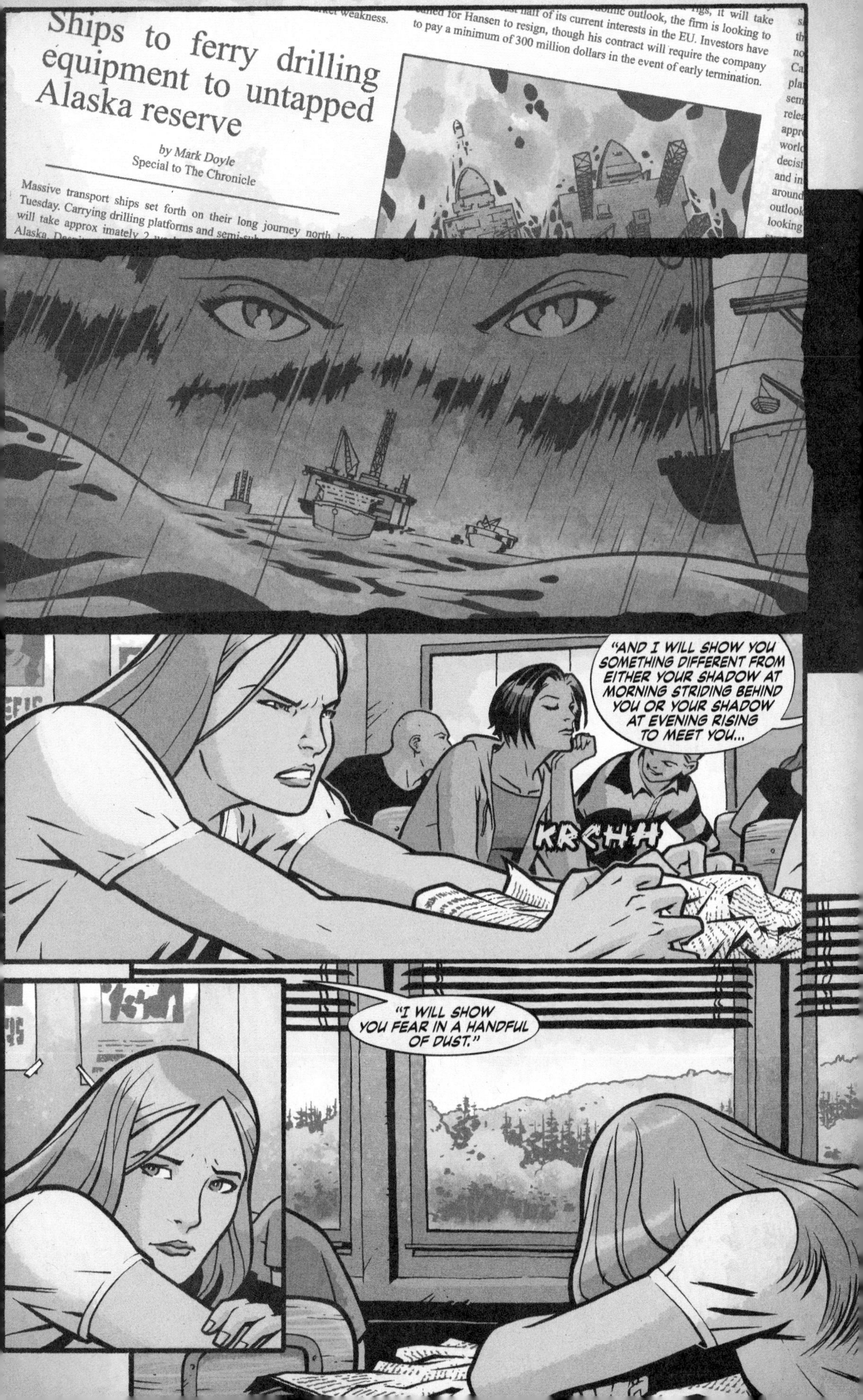

...ket weakness.
Ships to ferry drilling equipment to untapped Alaska reserve
by Mark Doyle
Special to The Chronicle
Massive transport ships set forth on their long journey north last Tuesday. Carrying drilling platforms and semi-sub... will take approx imately 2 ... Alaska...
...rigs, it will take ...half of its current interests in the EU. Investors have called for Hansen to resign, though his contract will require the company to pay a minimum of 300 million dollars in the event of early termination.
...outlook, the firm is looking to
"AND I WILL SHOW YOU SOMETHING DIFFERENT FROM EITHER YOUR SHADOW AT MORNING STRIDING BEHIND YOU OR YOUR SHADOW AT EVENING RISING TO MEET YOU...
KRCHH
"I WILL SHOW YOU FEAR IN A HANDFUL OF DUST."

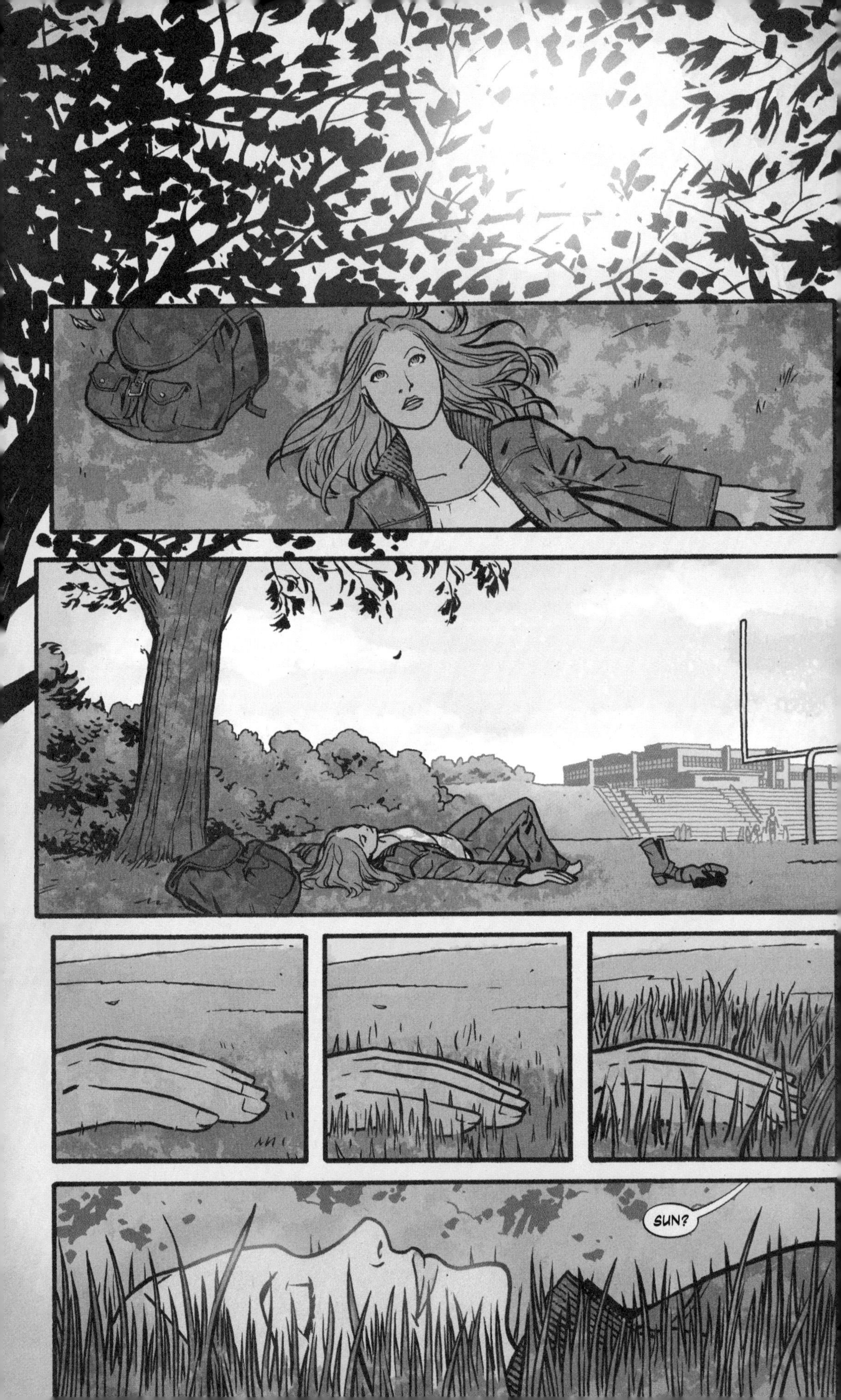
SUN?

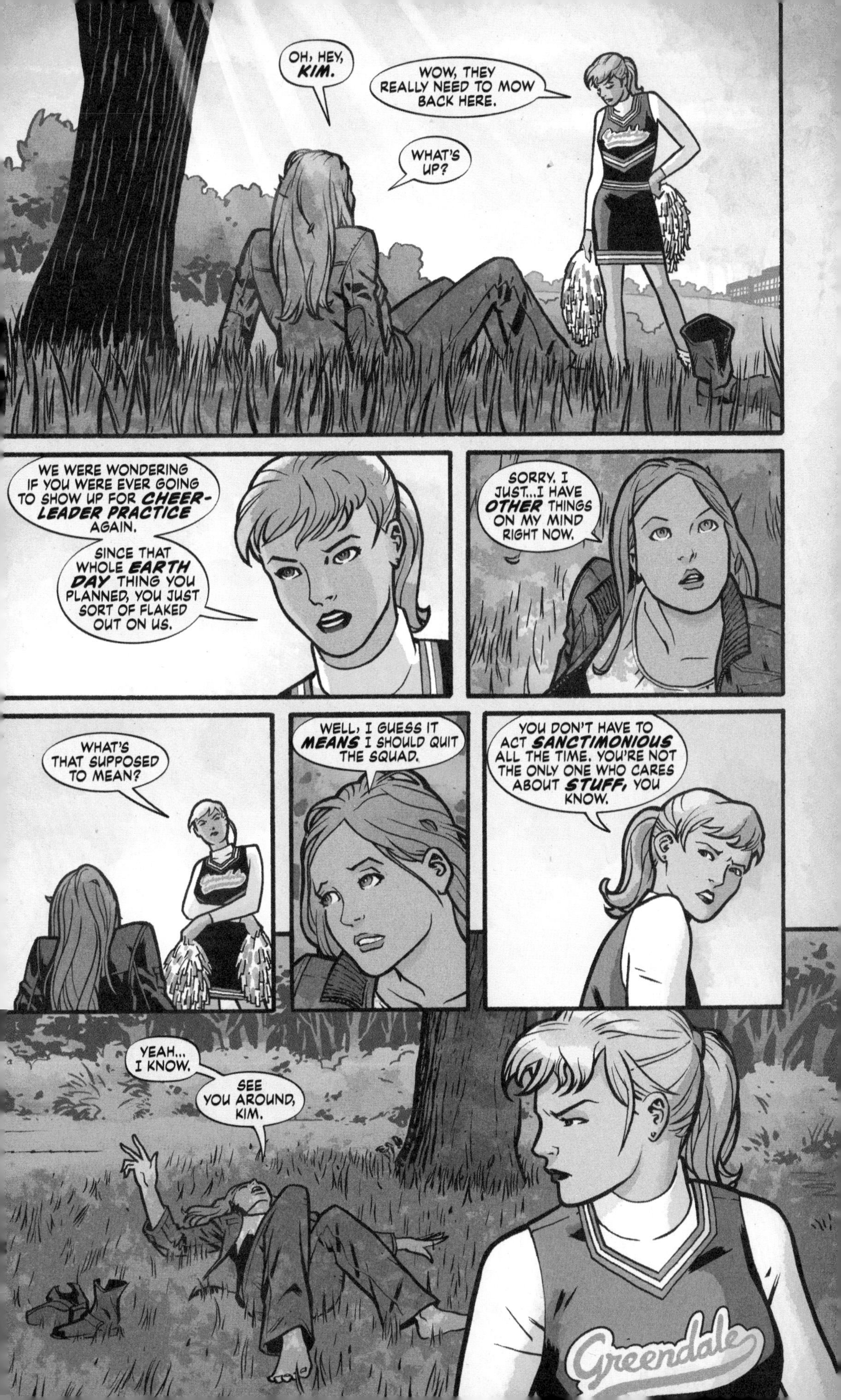

OH, HEY, KIM.
WOW, THEY REALLY NEED TO MOW BACK HERE.
WHAT'S UP?
WE WERE WONDERING IF YOU WERE EVER GOING TO SHOW UP FOR CHEER-LEADER PRACTICE AGAIN.
SINCE THAT WHOLE EARTH DAY THING YOU PLANNED, YOU JUST SORT OF FLAKED OUT ON US.
SORRY. I JUST...I HAVE OTHER THINGS ON MY MIND RIGHT NOW.
WHAT'S THAT SUPPOSED TO MEAN?
WELL, I GUESS IT MEANS I SHOULD QUIT THE SQUAD.
YOU DON'T HAVE TO ACT SANCTIMONIOUS ALL THE TIME. YOU'RE NOT THE ONLY ONE WHO CARES ABOUT STUFF, YOU KNOW.
YEAH... I KNOW.
SEE YOU AROUND, KIM.
Greendale

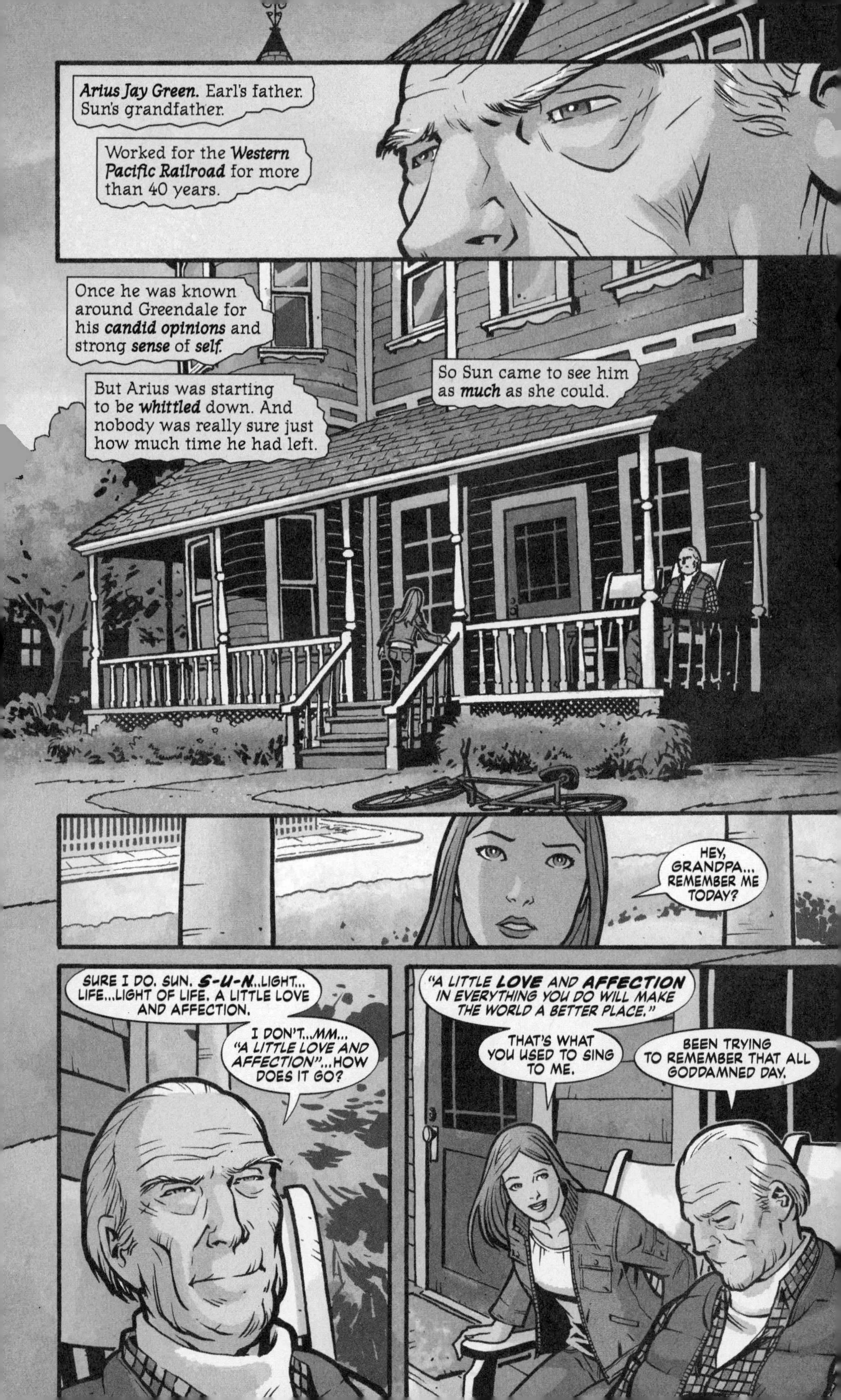

Arius Jay Green. Earl's father. Sun's grandfather.
Worked for the Western Pacific Railroad for more than 40 years.
Once he was known around Greendale for his candid opinions and strong sense of self.
But Arius was starting to be whittled down. And nobody was really sure just how much time he had left.
So Sun came to see him as much as she could.
HEY, GRANDPA... REMEMBER ME TODAY?
SURE I DO. SUN. S-U-N...LIGHT... LIFE...LIGHT OF LIFE. A LITTLE LOVE AND AFFECTION.
I DON'T...MM... "A LITTLE LOVE AND AFFECTION"...HOW DOES IT GO?
"A LITTLE LOVE AND AFFECTION IN EVERYTHING YOU DO WILL MAKE THE WORLD A BETTER PLACE."
THAT'S WHAT YOU USED TO SING TO ME.
BEEN TRYING TO REMEMBER THAT ALL GODDAMNED DAY.

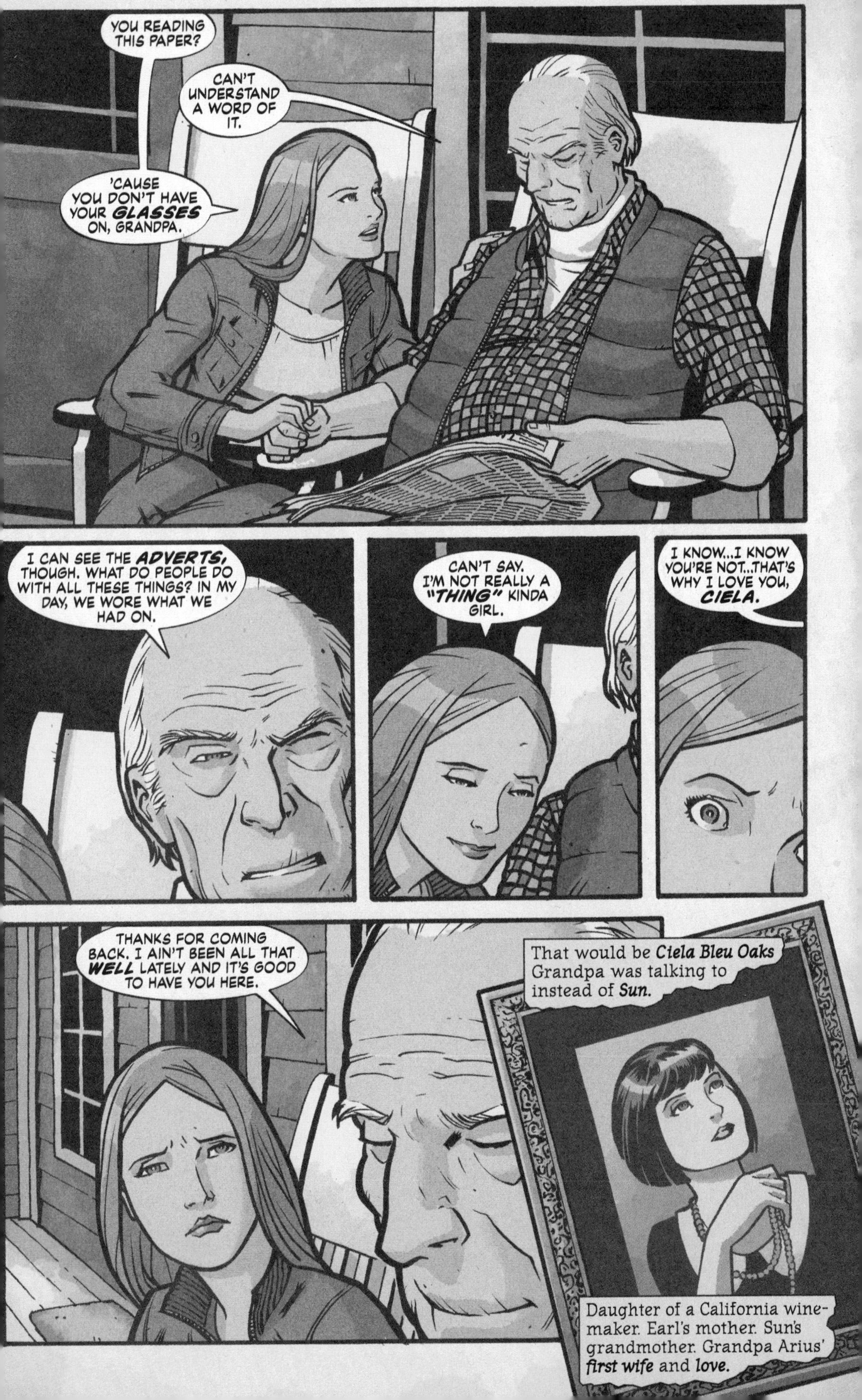

YOU READING THIS PAPER?
CAN'T UNDERSTAND A WORD OF IT.
'CAUSE YOU DON'T HAVE YOUR GLASSES ON, GRANDPA.
I CAN SEE THE ADVERTS, THOUGH. WHAT DO PEOPLE DO WITH ALL THESE THINGS? IN MY DAY, WE WORE WHAT WE HAD ON.
CAN'T SAY. I'M NOT REALLY A "THING" KINDA GIRL.
I KNOW...I KNOW YOU'RE NOT...THAT'S WHY I LOVE YOU, CIELA.
THANKS FOR COMING BACK. I AIN'T BEEN ALL THAT WELL LATELY AND IT'S GOOD TO HAVE YOU HERE.
That would be Ciela Bleu Oaks Grandpa was talking to instead of Sun.
Daughter of a California wine-maker. Earl's mother. Sun's grandmother. Grandpa Arius' first wife and love.

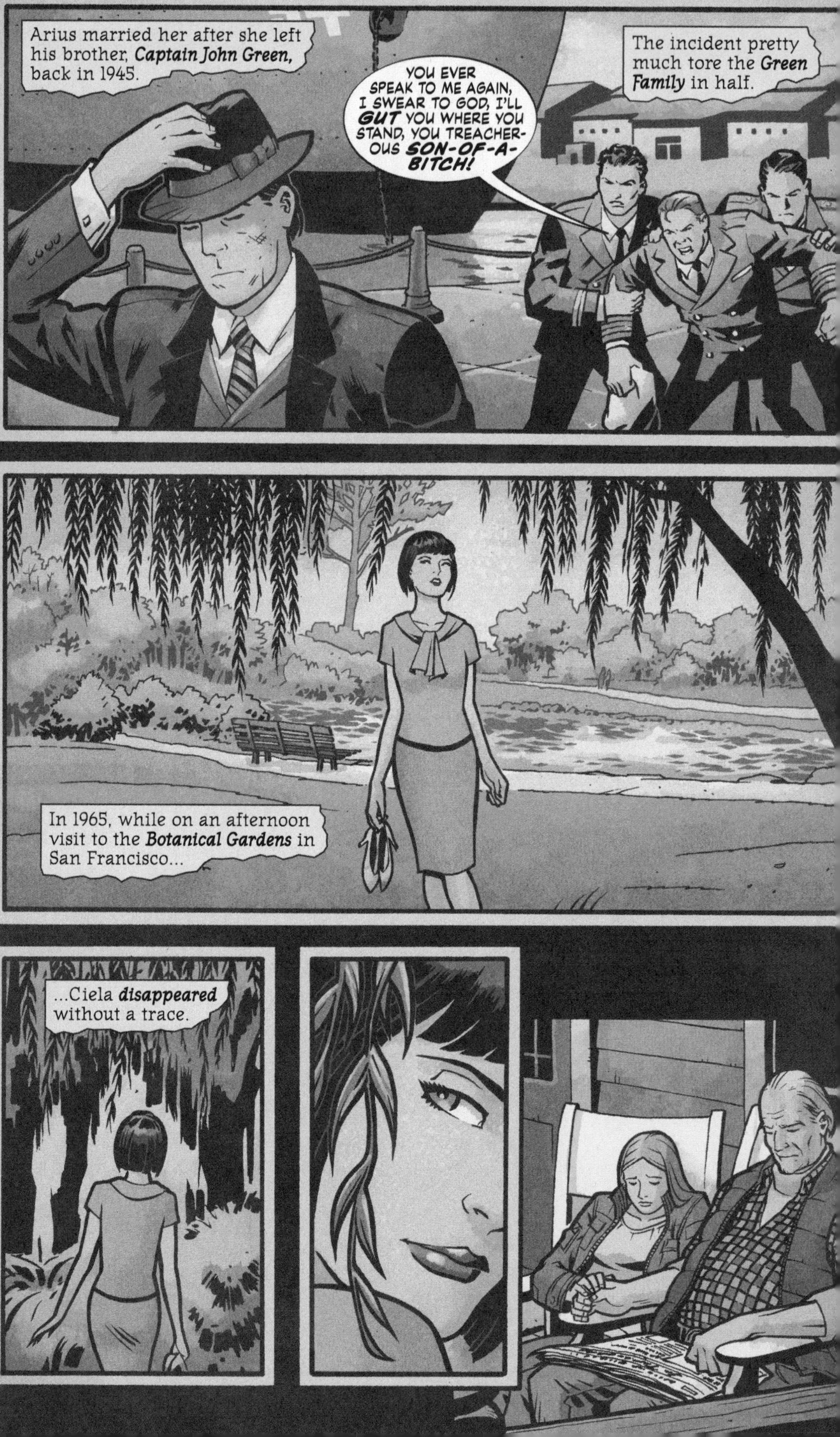
Arius married her after she left his brother, ***Captain John Green,*** back in 1945.
YOU EVER SPEAK TO ME AGAIN, I SWEAR TO GOD, I'LL ***GUT*** YOU WHERE YOU STAND, YOU TREACHEROUS ***SON-OF-A-BITCH!***
The incident pretty much tore the ***Green Family*** in half.
In 1965, while on an afternoon visit to the ***Botanical Gardens*** in San Francisco...
...Ciela ***disappeared*** without a trace.

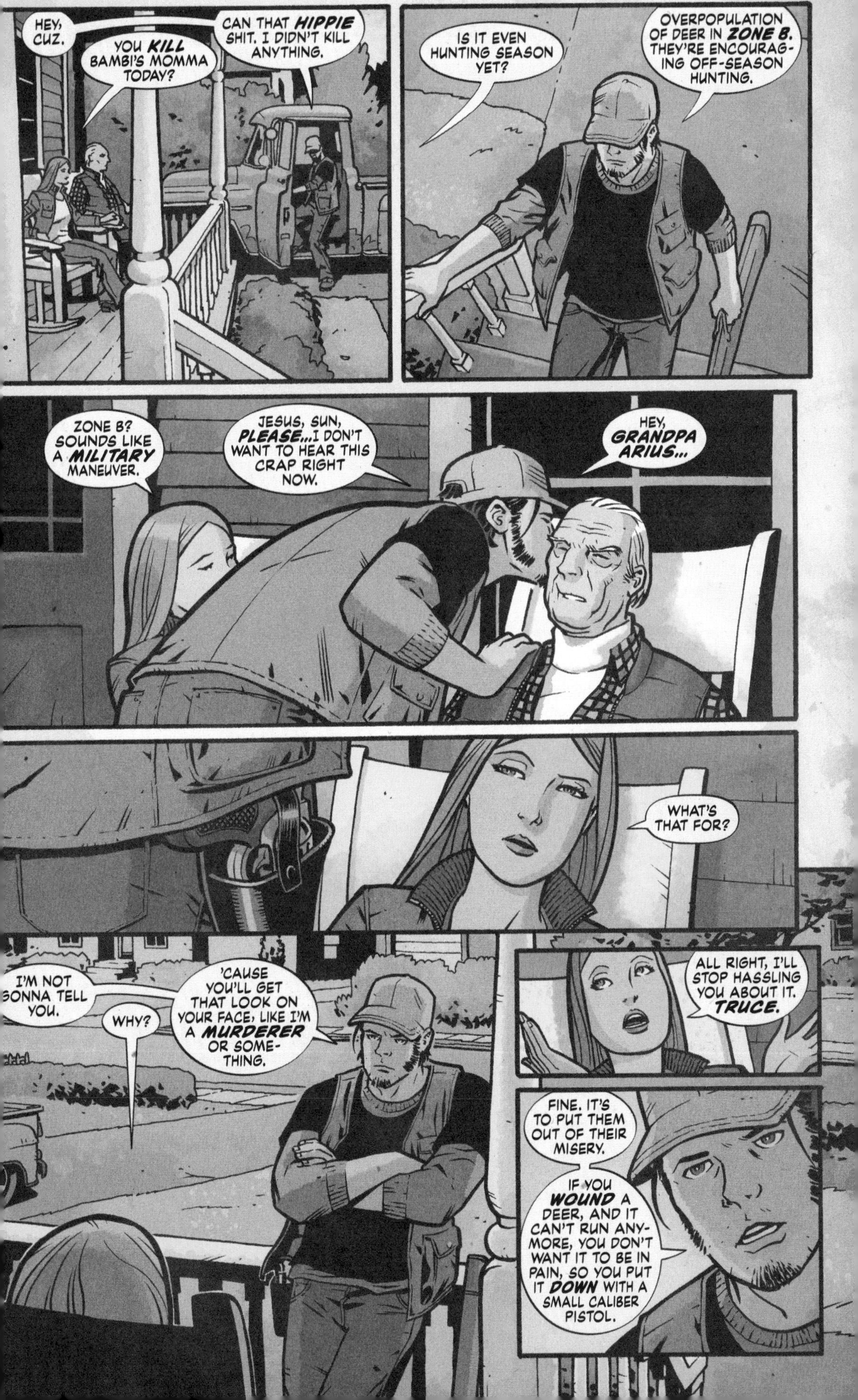
HEY, CUZ.
YOU KILL BAMBI'S MOMMA TODAY?
CAN THAT HIPPIE SHIT. I DIDN'T KILL ANYTHING.
IS IT EVEN HUNTING SEASON YET?
OVERPOPULATION OF DEER IN ZONE B. THEY'RE ENCOURAGING OFF-SEASON HUNTING.
ZONE B? SOUNDS LIKE A MILITARY MANEUVER.
JESUS, SUN, PLEASE...I DON'T WANT TO HEAR THIS CRAP RIGHT NOW.
HEY, GRANDPA ARIUS...
WHAT'S THAT FOR?
I'M NOT GONNA TELL YOU.
WHY?
'CAUSE YOU'LL GET THAT LOOK ON YOUR FACE, LIKE I'M A MURDERER OR SOMETHING.
ALL RIGHT, I'LL STOP HASSLING YOU ABOUT IT. TRUCE.
FINE. IT'S TO PUT THEM OUT OF THEIR MISERY.
IF YOU WOUND A DEER, AND IT CAN'T RUN ANYMORE, YOU DON'T WANT IT TO BE IN PAIN, SO YOU PUT IT DOWN WITH A SMALL CALIBER PISTOL.

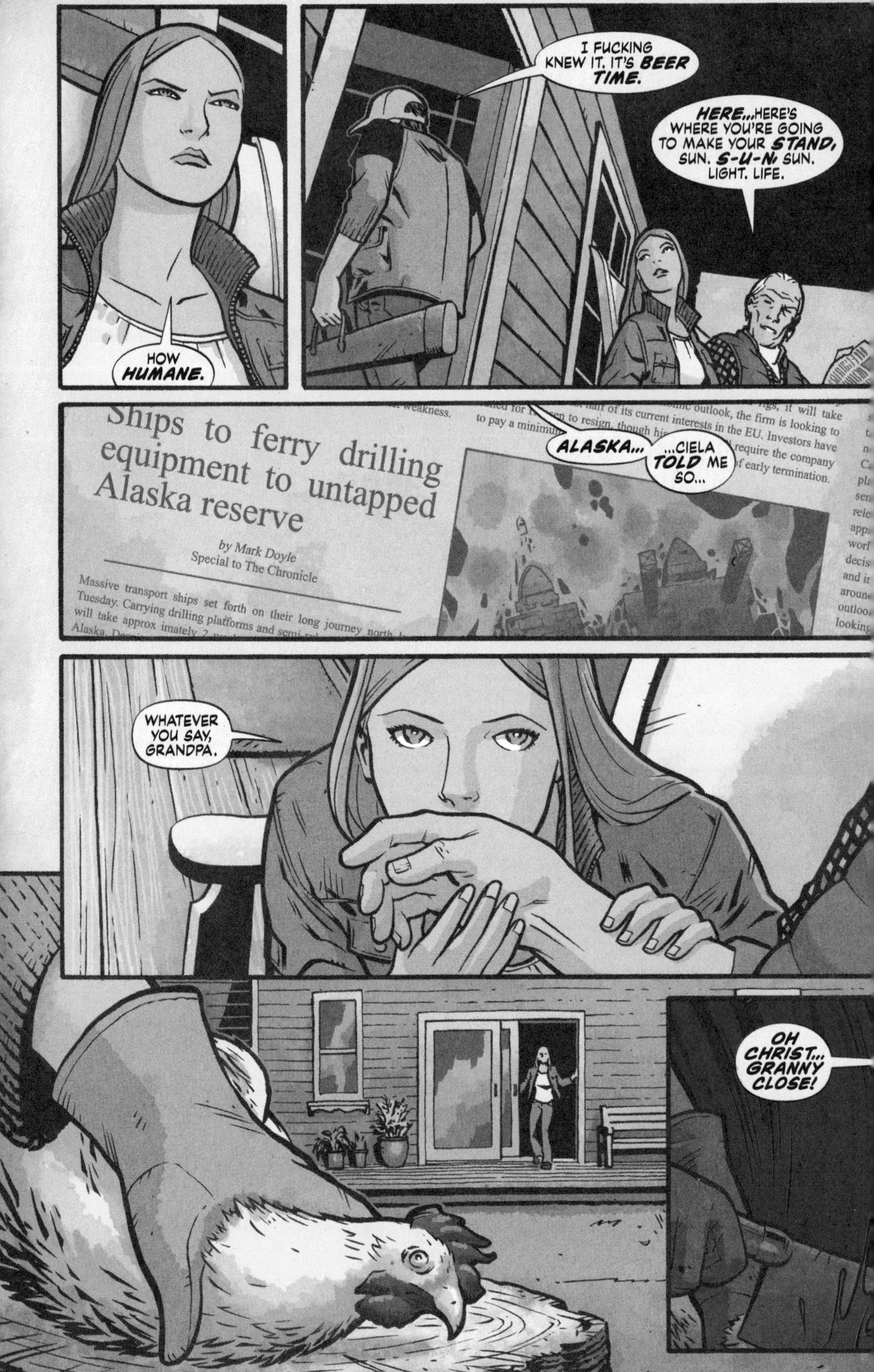
HOW HUMANE.
I FUCKING KNEW IT. IT'S BEER TIME.
HERE... HERE'S WHERE YOU'RE GOING TO MAKE YOUR STAND, SUN. S-U-N. SUN. LIGHT. LIFE.
Ships to ferry drilling equipment to untapped Alaska reserve
by Mark Doyle
Special to The Chronicle
ALASKA...
...CIELA TOLD ME SO...
WHATEVER YOU SAY, GRANDPA.
OH CHRIST... GRANNY CLOSE!

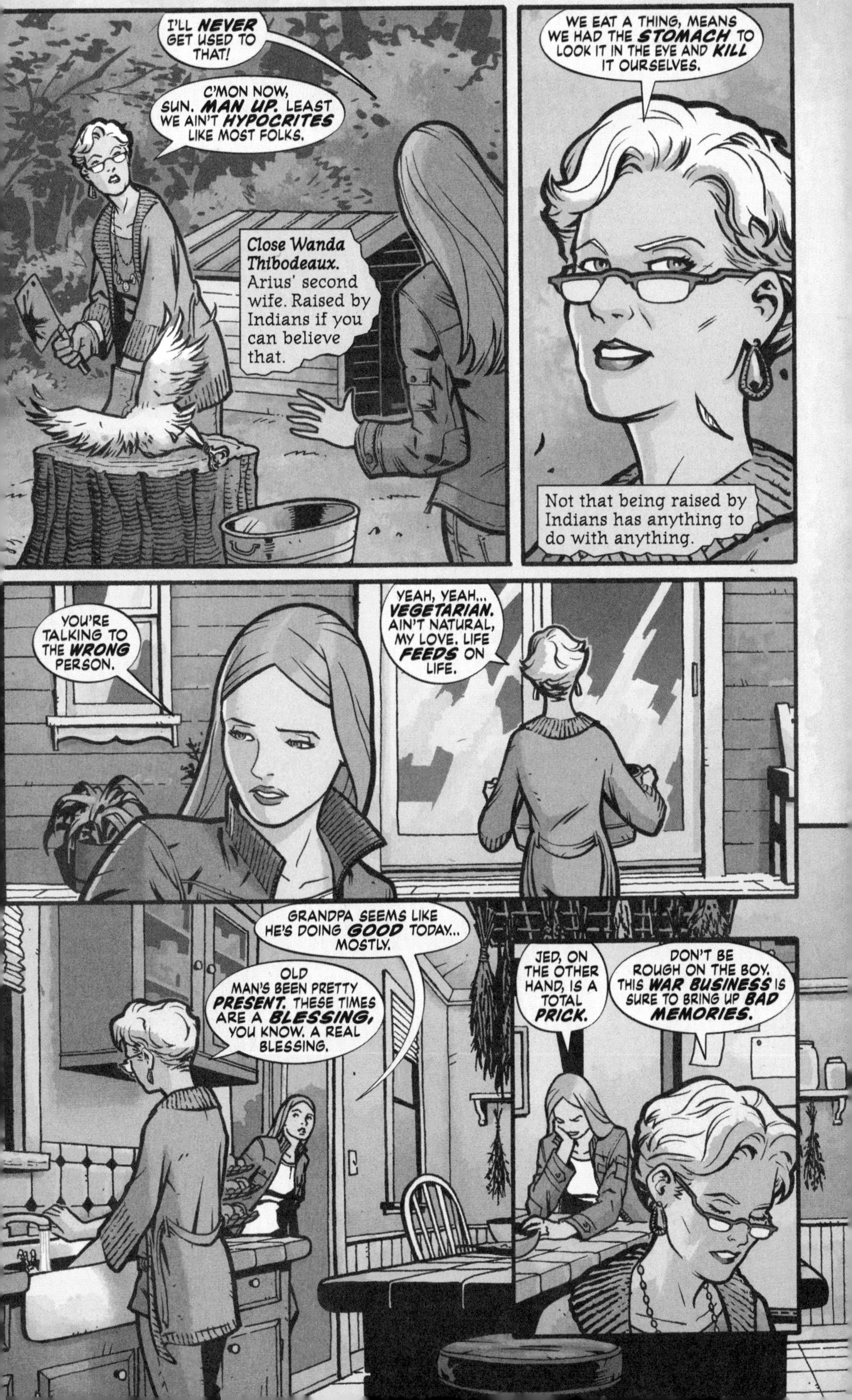
I'LL NEVER GET USED TO THAT!
C'MON NOW, SUN. MAN UP. LEAST WE AIN'T HYPOCRITES LIKE MOST FOLKS.
Close Wanda Thibodeaux. Arius' second wife. Raised by Indians if you can believe that.
WE EAT A THING, MEANS WE HAD THE STOMACH TO LOOK IT IN THE EYE AND KILL IT OURSELVES.
Not that being raised by Indians has anything to do with anything.
YOU'RE TALKING TO THE WRONG PERSON.
YEAH, YEAH... VEGETARIAN. AIN'T NATURAL, MY LOVE. LIFE FEEDS ON LIFE.
GRANDPA SEEMS LIKE HE'S DOING GOOD TODAY... MOSTLY.
OLD MAN'S BEEN PRETTY PRESENT. THESE TIMES ARE A BLESSING, YOU KNOW. A REAL BLESSING.
JED, ON THE OTHER HAND, IS A TOTAL PRICK.
DON'T BE ROUGH ON THE BOY. THIS WAR BUSINESS IS SURE TO BRING UP BAD MEMORIES.

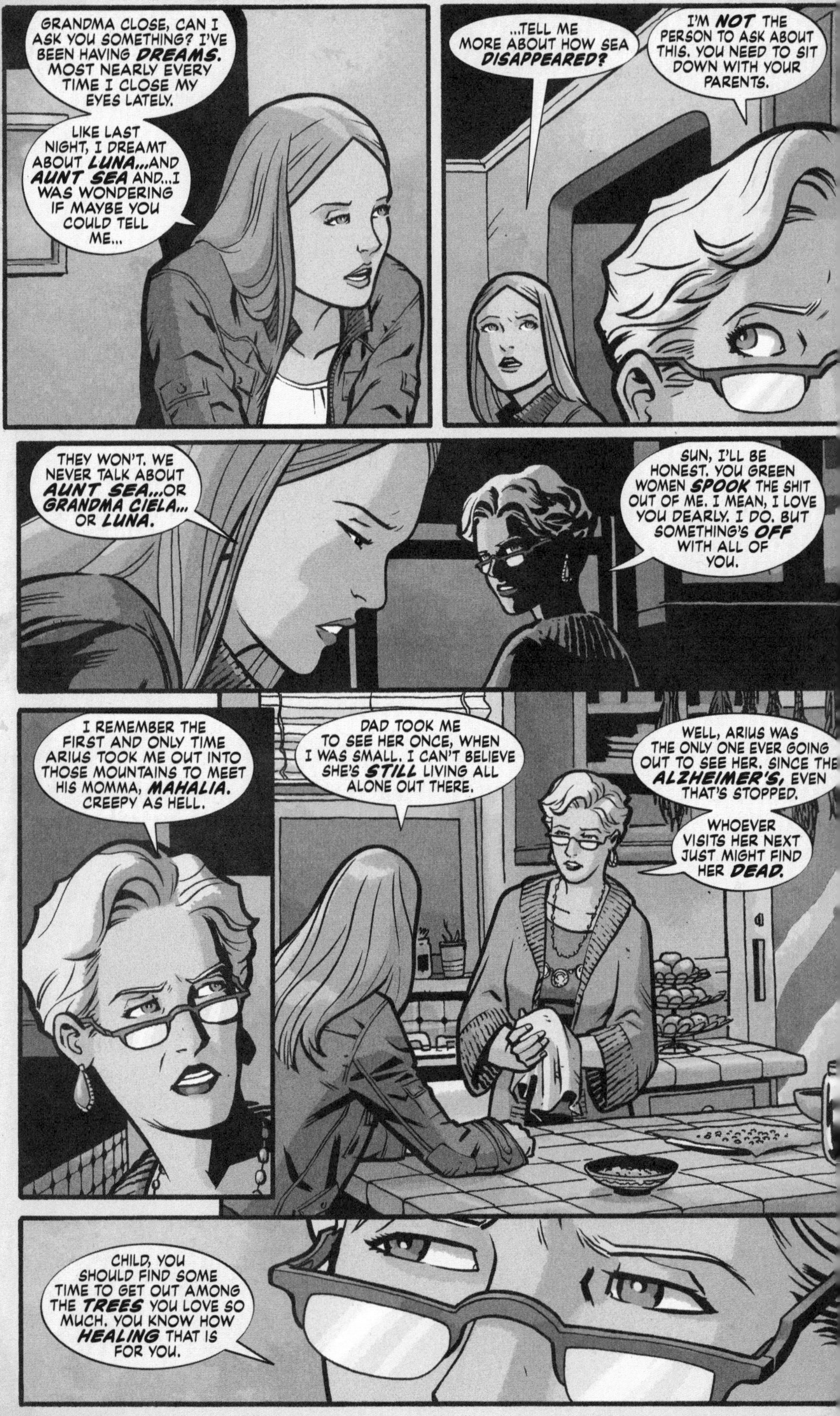
GRANDMA CLOSE, CAN I ASK YOU SOMETHING? I'VE BEEN HAVING DREAMS. MOST NEARLY EVERY TIME I CLOSE MY EYES LATELY.
LIKE LAST NIGHT, I DREAMT ABOUT LUNA...AND AUNT SEA AND...I WAS WONDERING IF MAYBE YOU COULD TELL ME...
...TELL ME MORE ABOUT HOW SEA DISAPPEARED?
I'M NOT THE PERSON TO ASK ABOUT THIS. YOU NEED TO SIT DOWN WITH YOUR PARENTS.
THEY WON'T. WE NEVER TALK ABOUT AUNT SEA...OR GRANDMA CIELA... OR LUNA.
SUN, I'LL BE HONEST. YOU GREEN WOMEN SPOOK THE SHIT OUT OF ME. I MEAN, I LOVE YOU DEARLY. I DO. BUT SOMETHING'S OFF WITH ALL OF YOU.
I REMEMBER THE FIRST AND ONLY TIME ARIUS TOOK ME OUT INTO THOSE MOUNTAINS TO MEET HIS MOMMA, MAHALIA. CREEPY AS HELL.
DAD TOOK ME TO SEE HER ONCE, WHEN I WAS SMALL. I CAN'T BELIEVE SHE'S STILL LIVING ALL ALONE OUT THERE.
WELL, ARIUS WAS THE ONLY ONE EVER GOING OUT TO SEE HER. SINCE THE ALZHEIMER'S, EVEN THAT'S STOPPED.
WHOEVER VISITS HER NEXT JUST MIGHT FIND HER DEAD.
CHILD, YOU SHOULD FIND SOME TIME TO GET OUT AMONG THE TREES YOU LOVE SO MUCH. YOU KNOW HOW HEALING THAT IS FOR YOU.

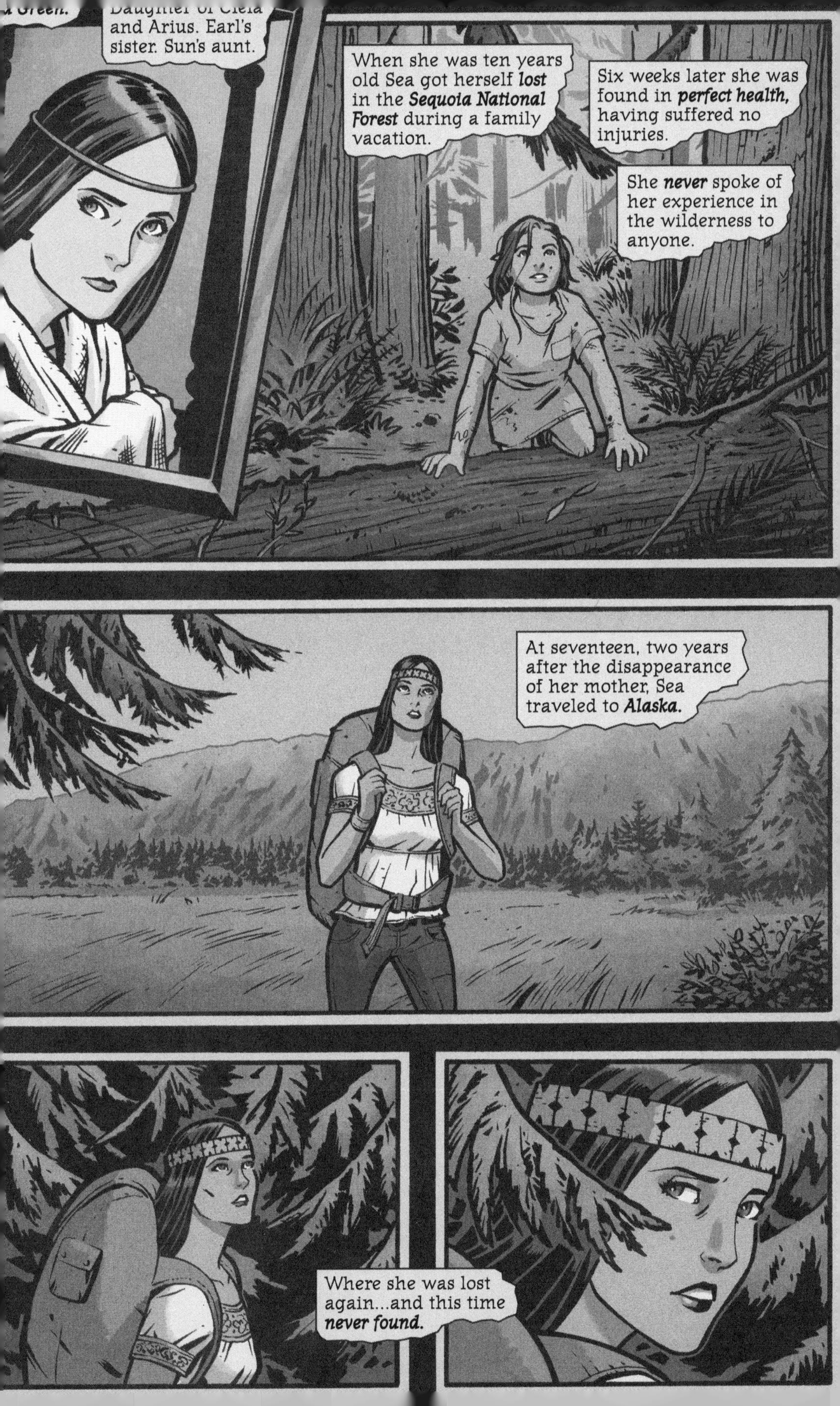

and Arius. Earl's sister. Sun's aunt.
When she was ten years old Sea got herself *lost* in the *Sequoia National Forest* during a family vacation.
Six weeks later she was found in *perfect health,* having suffered no injuries.
She *never* spoke of her experience in the wilderness to anyone.
At seventeen, two years after the disappearance of her mother, Sea traveled to *Alaska.*
Where she was lost again...and this time *never found.*

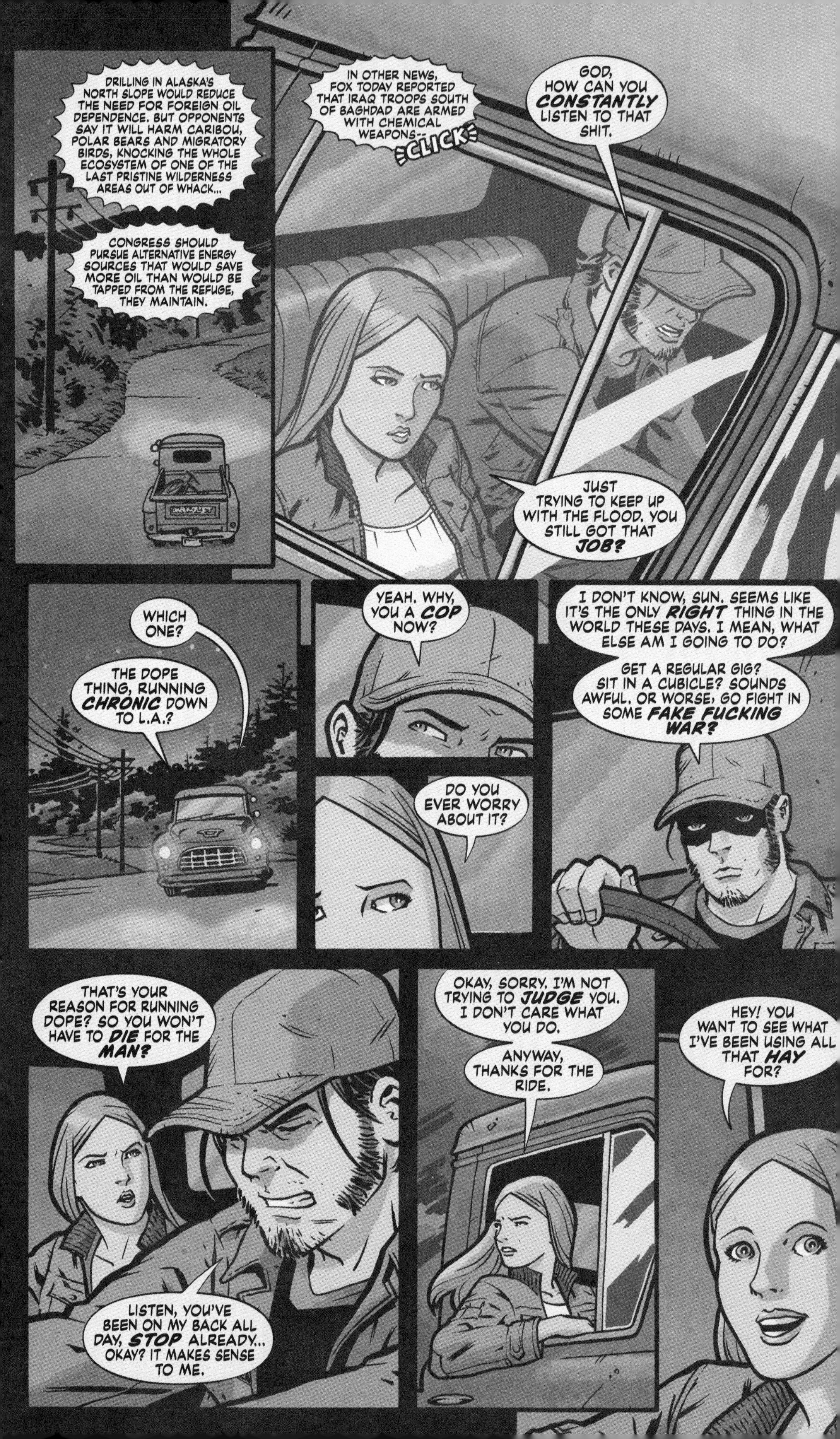
DRILLING IN ALASKA'S NORTH SLOPE WOULD REDUCE THE NEED FOR FOREIGN OIL DEPENDENCE. BUT OPPONENTS SAY IT WILL HARM CARIBOU, POLAR BEARS AND MIGRATORY BIRDS, KNOCKING THE WHOLE ECOSYSTEM OF ONE OF THE LAST PRISTINE WILDERNESS AREAS OUT OF WHACK...
CONGRESS SHOULD PURSUE ALTERNATIVE ENERGY SOURCES THAT WOULD SAVE MORE OIL THAN WOULD BE TAPPED FROM THE REFUGE, THEY MAINTAIN.
IN OTHER NEWS, FOX TODAY REPORTED THAT IRAQ TROOPS SOUTH OF BAGHDAD ARE ARMED WITH CHEMICAL WEAPONS--
CLICK
GOD, HOW CAN YOU CONSTANTLY LISTEN TO THAT SHIT.
JUST TRYING TO KEEP UP WITH THE FLOOD. YOU STILL GOT THAT JOB?
WHICH ONE?
THE DOPE THING, RUNNING CHRONIC DOWN TO L.A.?
YEAH. WHY, YOU A COP NOW?
DO YOU EVER WORRY ABOUT IT?
I DON'T KNOW, SUN. SEEMS LIKE IT'S THE ONLY RIGHT THING IN THE WORLD THESE DAYS. I MEAN, WHAT ELSE AM I GOING TO DO?
GET A REGULAR GIG? SIT IN A CUBICLE? SOUNDS AWFUL. OR WORSE, GO FIGHT IN SOME FAKE FUCKING WAR?
THAT'S YOUR REASON FOR RUNNING DOPE? SO YOU WON'T HAVE TO DIE FOR THE MAN?
LISTEN, YOU'VE BEEN ON MY BACK ALL DAY, STOP ALREADY... OKAY? IT MAKES SENSE TO ME.
OKAY, SORRY. I'M NOT TRYING TO JUDGE YOU. I DON'T CARE WHAT YOU DO.
ANYWAY, THANKS FOR THE RIDE.
HEY! YOU WANT TO SEE WHAT I'VE BEEN USING ALL THAT HAY FOR?

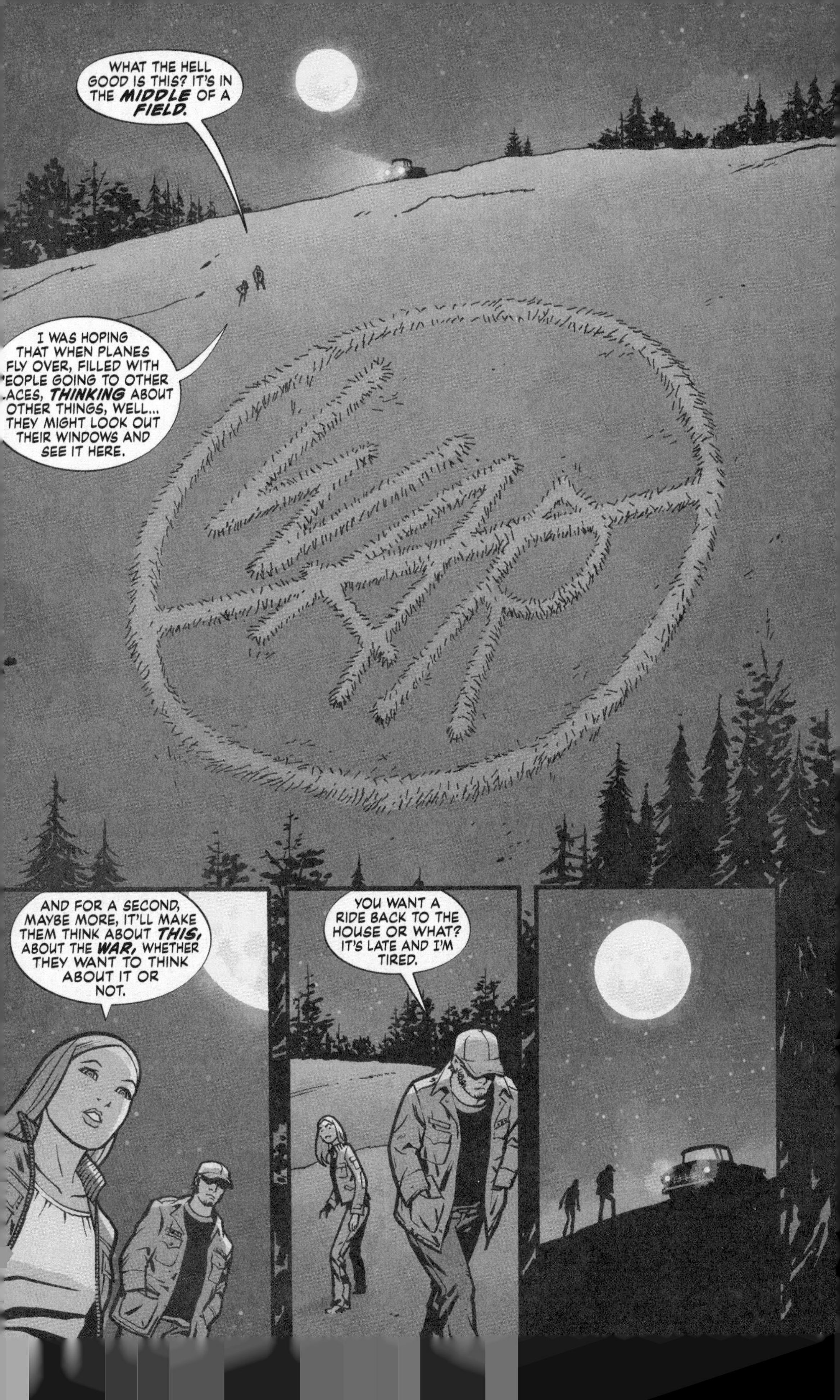
WHAT THE HELL GOOD IS THIS? IT'S IN THE MIDDLE OF A FIELD.
I WAS HOPING THAT WHEN PLANES FLY OVER, FILLED WITH EOPLE GOING TO OTHER ACES, THINKING ABOUT OTHER THINGS, WELL... THEY MIGHT LOOK OUT THEIR WINDOWS AND SEE IT HERE.
AND FOR A SECOND, MAYBE MORE, IT'LL MAKE THEM THINK ABOUT THIS, ABOUT THE WAR, WHETHER THEY WANT TO THINK ABOUT IT OR NOT.
YOU WANT A RIDE BACK TO THE HOUSE OR WHAT? IT'S LATE AND I'M TIRED.

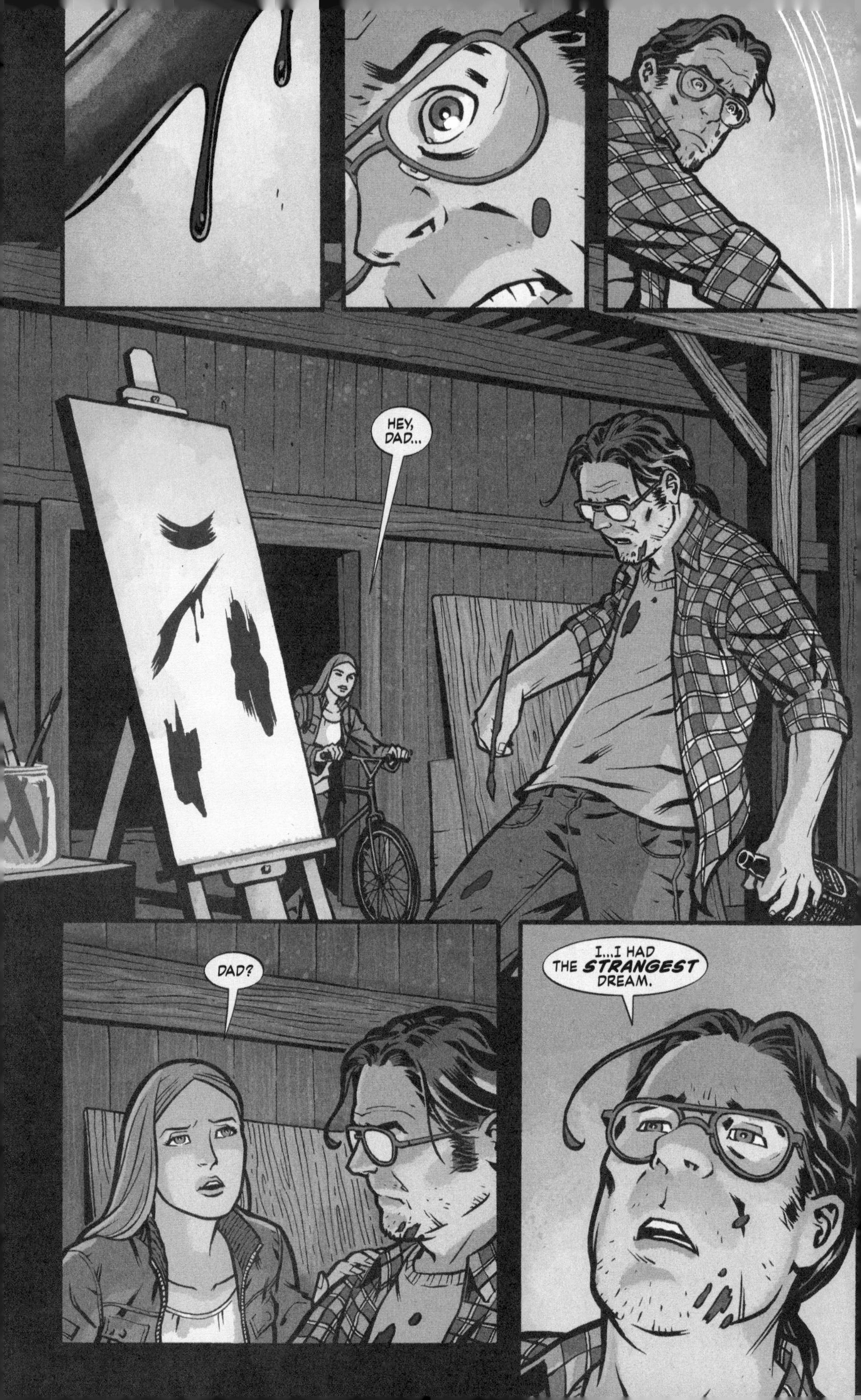
HEY, DAD...
DAD?
I...I HAD THE STRANGEST DREAM.

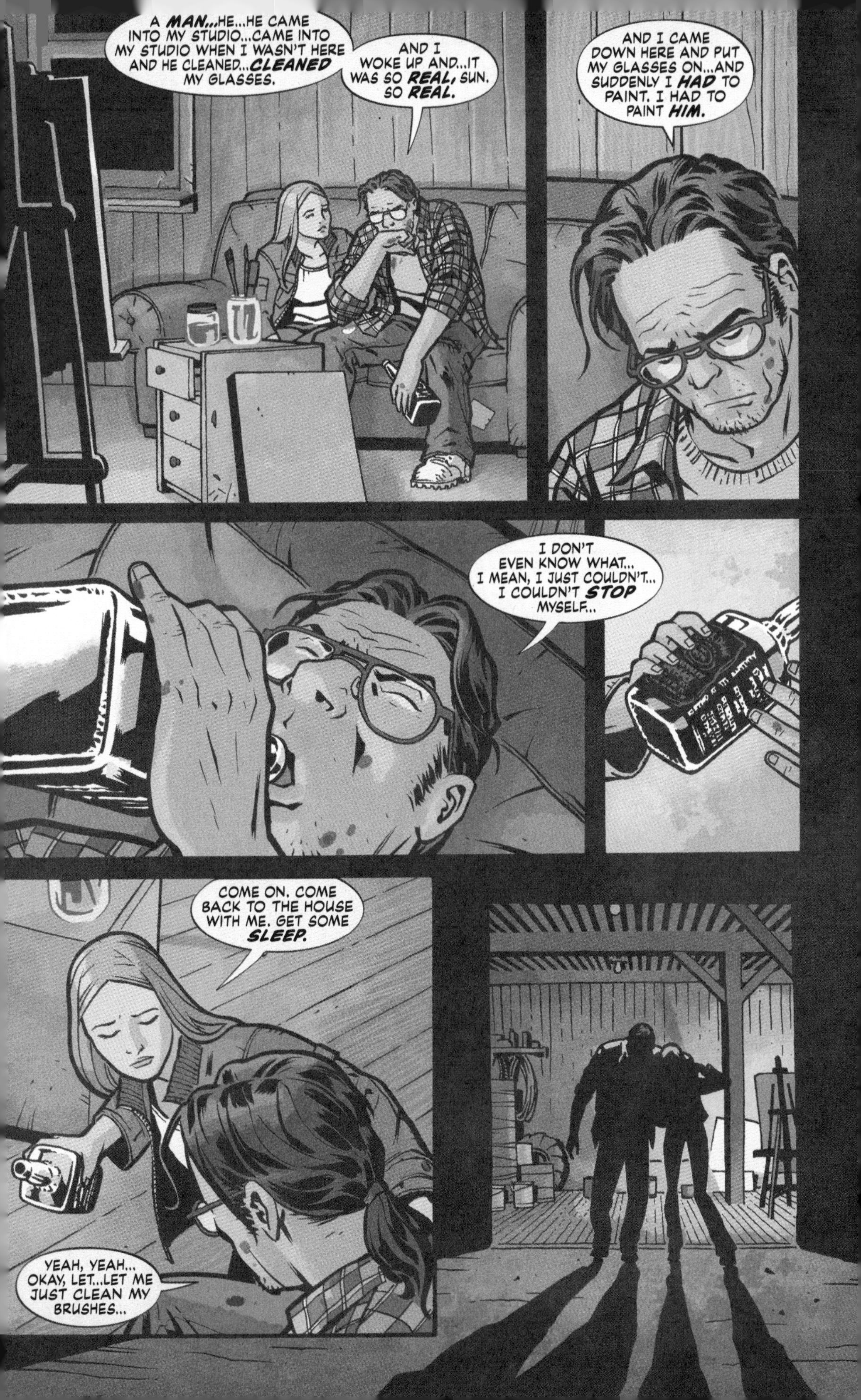
A MAN...HE...HE CAME INTO MY STUDIO...CAME INTO MY STUDIO WHEN I WASN'T HERE AND HE CLEANED...CLEANED MY GLASSES.
AND I WOKE UP AND...IT WAS SO REAL, SUN. SO REAL.
AND I CAME DOWN HERE AND PUT MY GLASSES ON...AND SUDDENLY I HAD TO PAINT. I HAD TO PAINT HIM.
I DON'T EVEN KNOW WHAT... I MEAN, I JUST COULDN'T... I COULDN'T STOP MYSELF...
COME ON. COME BACK TO THE HOUSE WITH ME. GET SOME SLEEP.
YEAH, YEAH... OKAY, LET...LET ME JUST CLEAN MY BRUSHES...

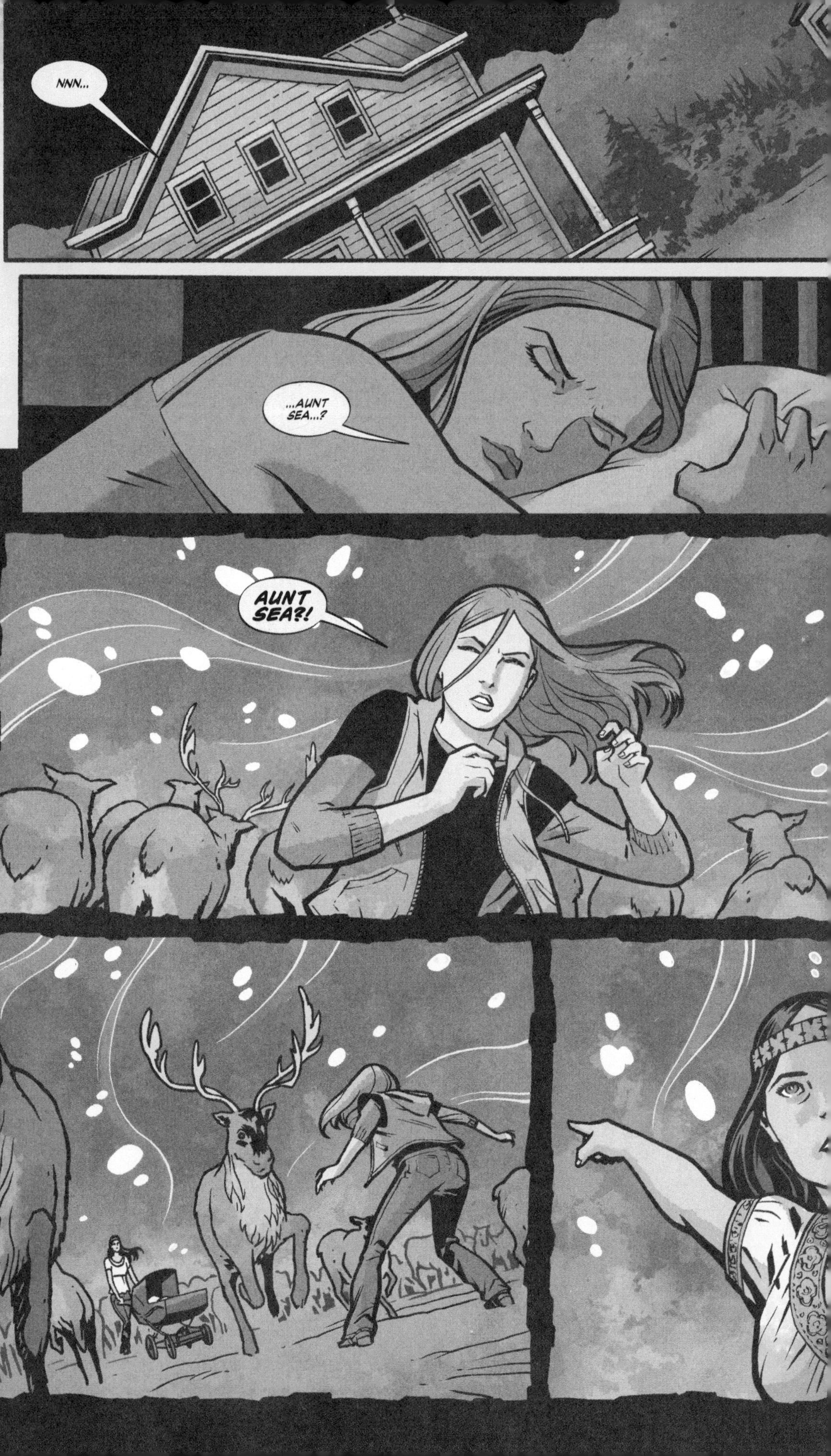
NNN...
...AUNT SEA...?
AUNT SEA?!

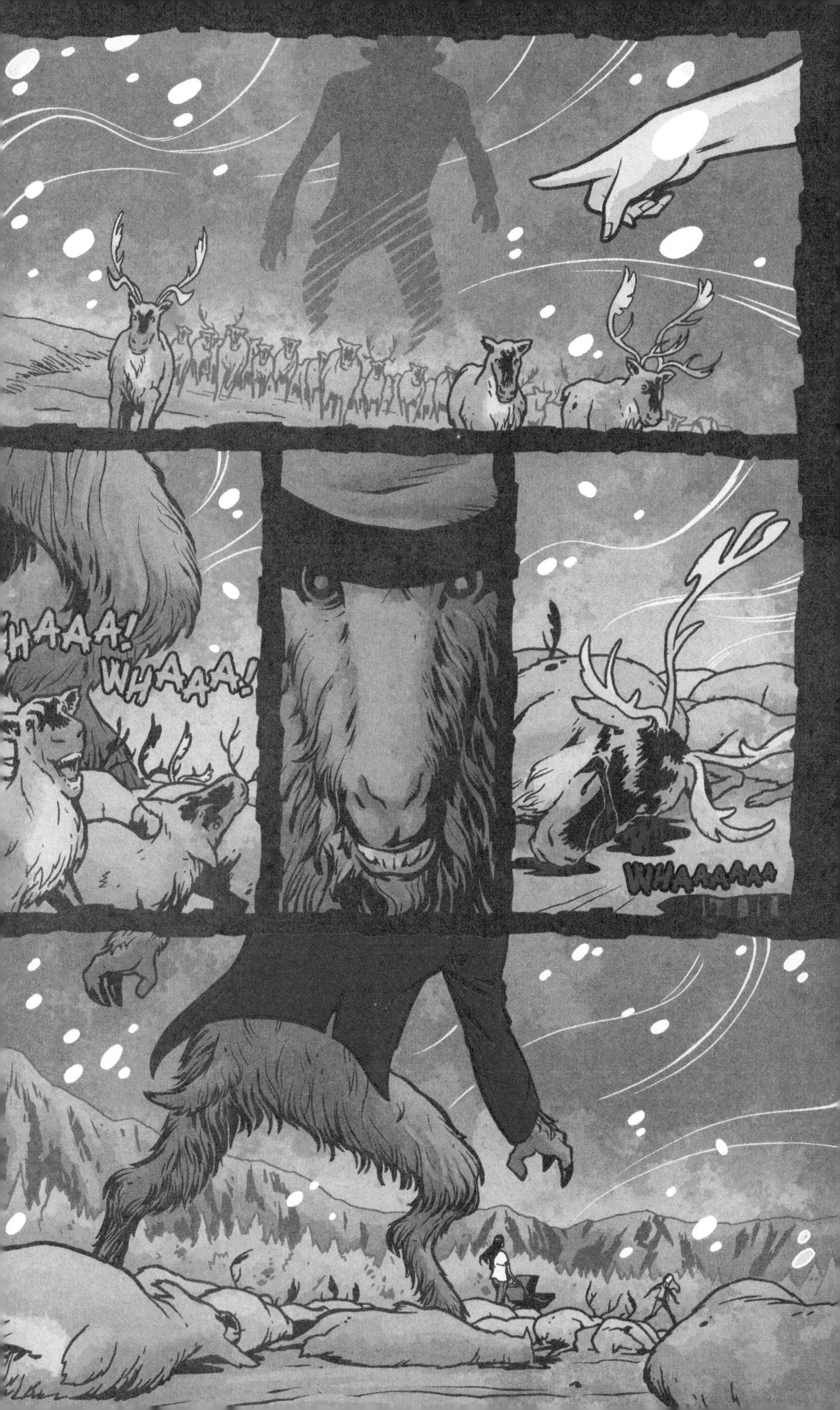

HAAA!
WHAAA!
WHAAAAAA

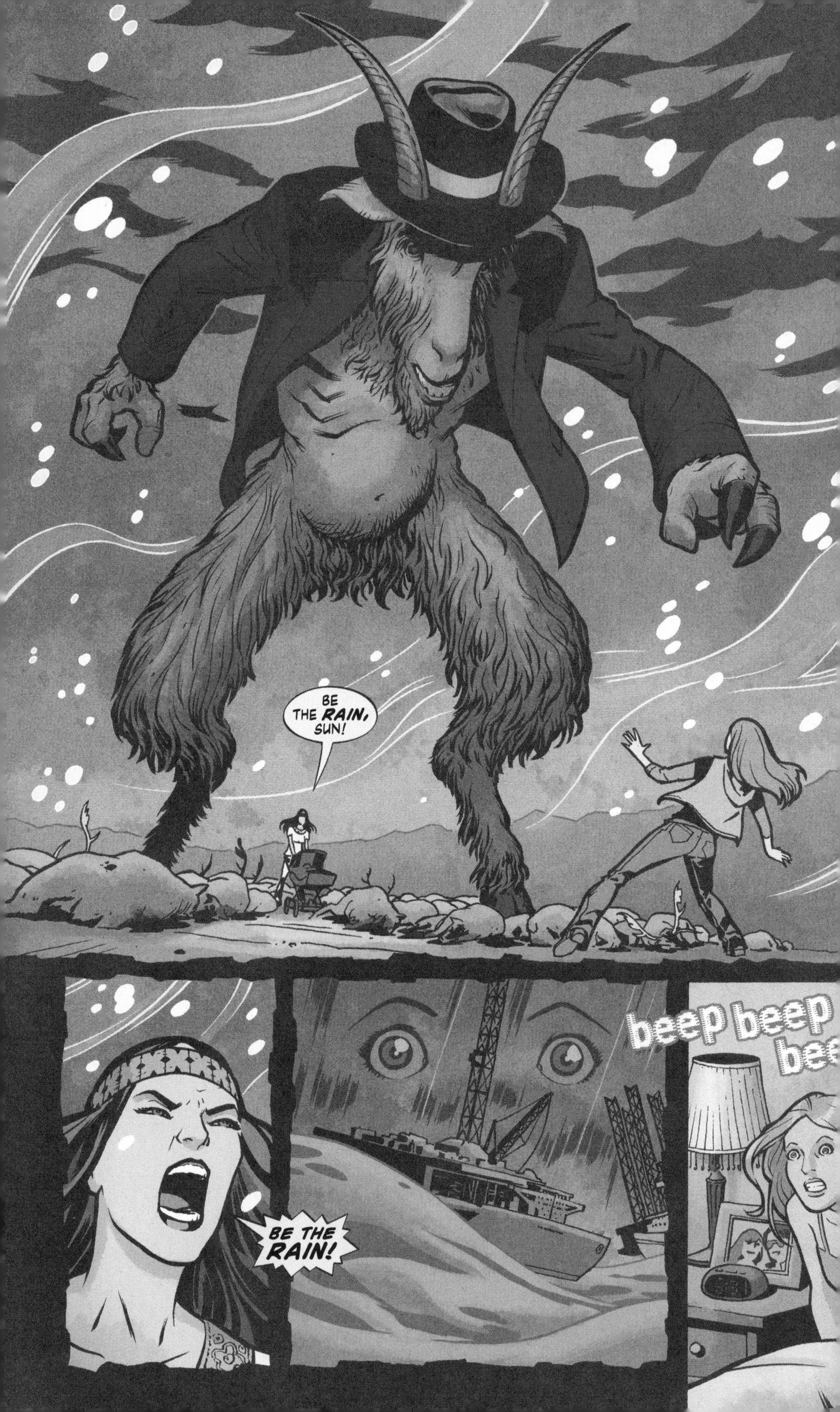
BE THE RAIN, SUN!
BE THE RAIN!
beep beep

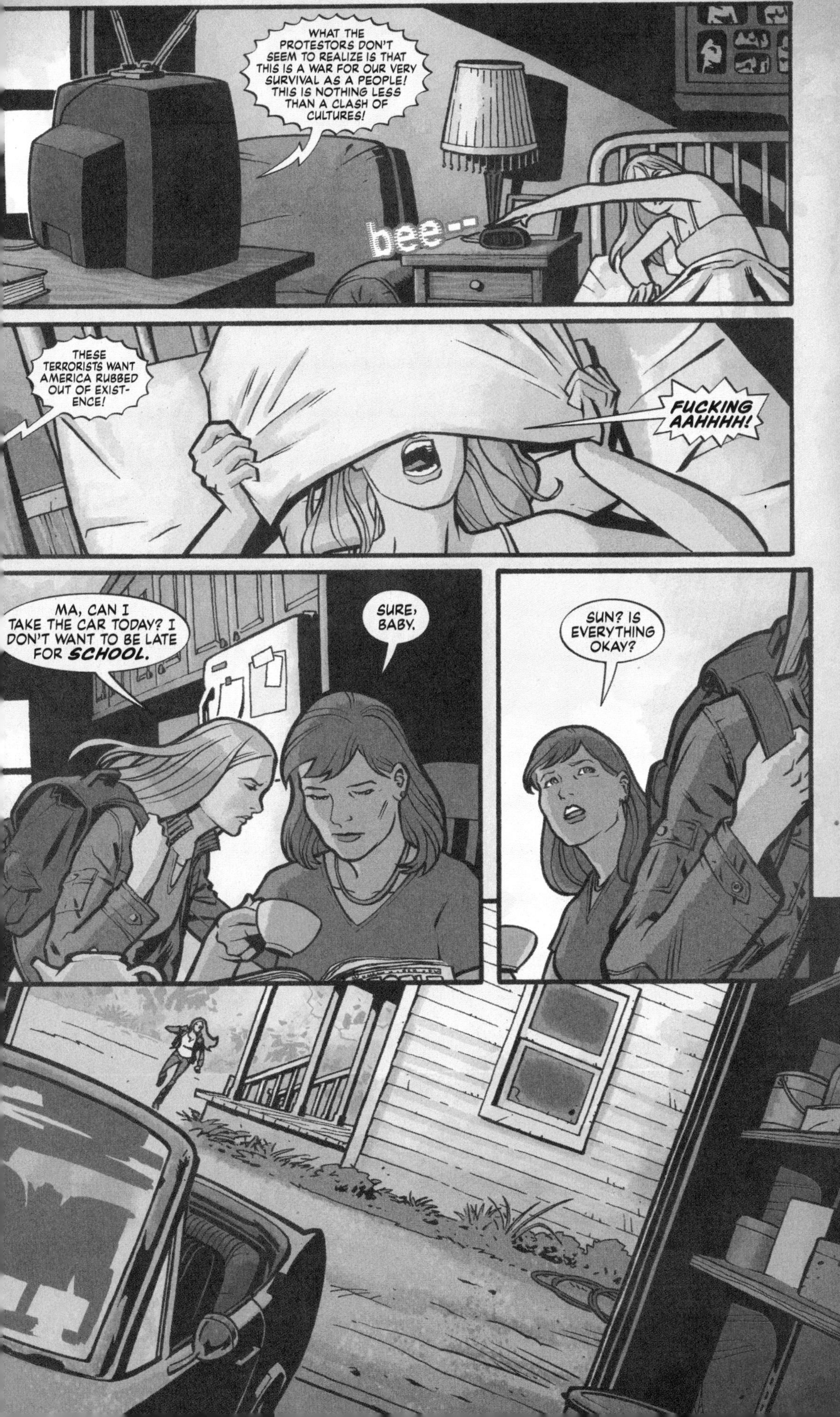

WHAT THE PROTESTORS DON'T SEEM TO REALIZE IS THAT THIS IS A WAR FOR OUR VERY SURVIVAL AS A PEOPLE! THIS IS NOTHING LESS THAN A CLASH OF CULTURES!
bee--
THESE TERRORISTS WANT AMERICA RUBBED OUT OF EXIST-ENCE!
FUCKING AAHHHH!
MA, CAN I TAKE THE CAR TODAY? I DON'T WANT TO BE LATE FOR SCHOOL.
SURE, BABY.
SUN? IS EVERYTHING OKAY?

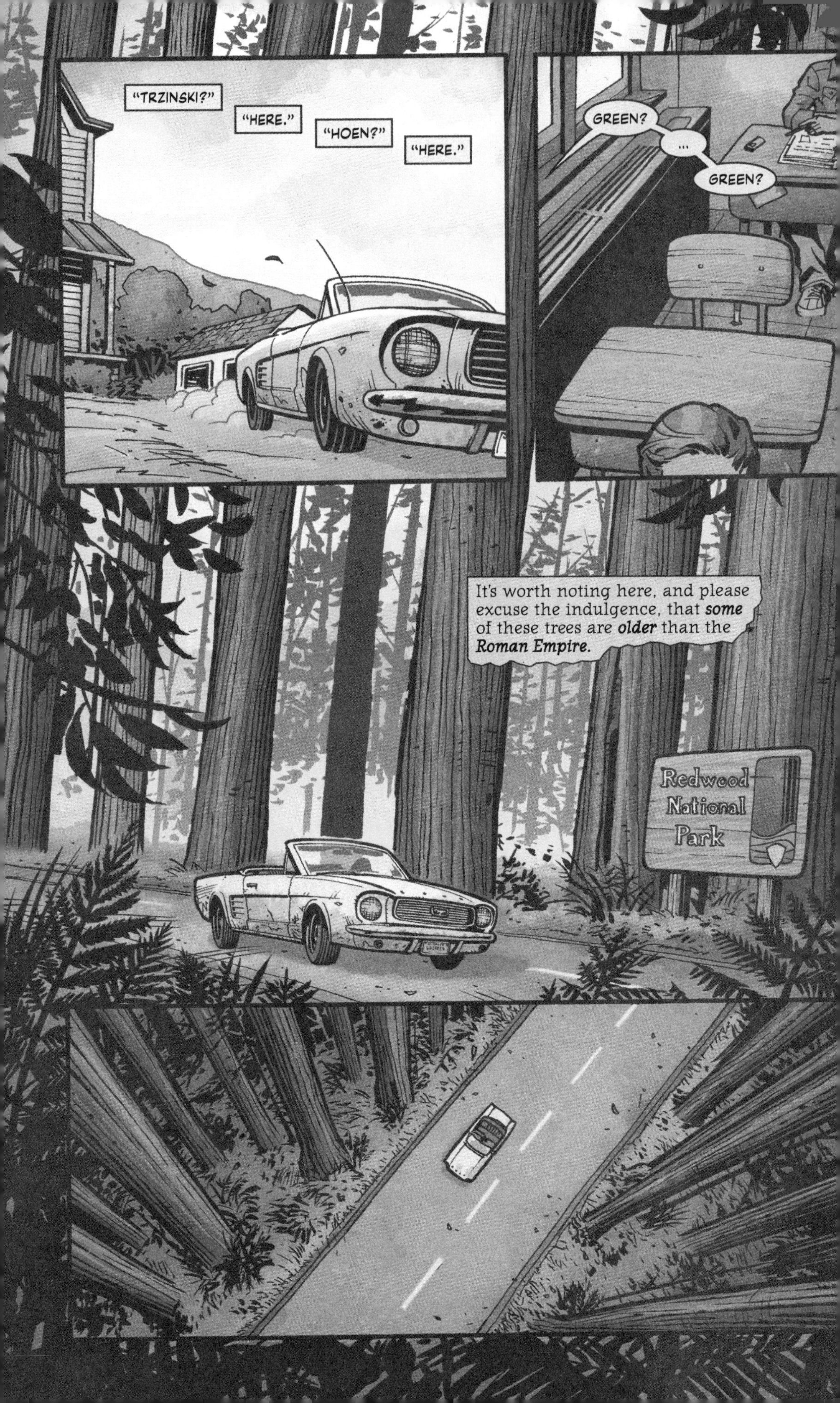
"TRZINSKI?"
"HERE."
"HOEN?"
"HERE."
GREEN?
...
GREEN?
It's worth noting here, and please excuse the indulgence, that *some* of these trees are *older* than the *Roman Empire.*
Redwood National Park

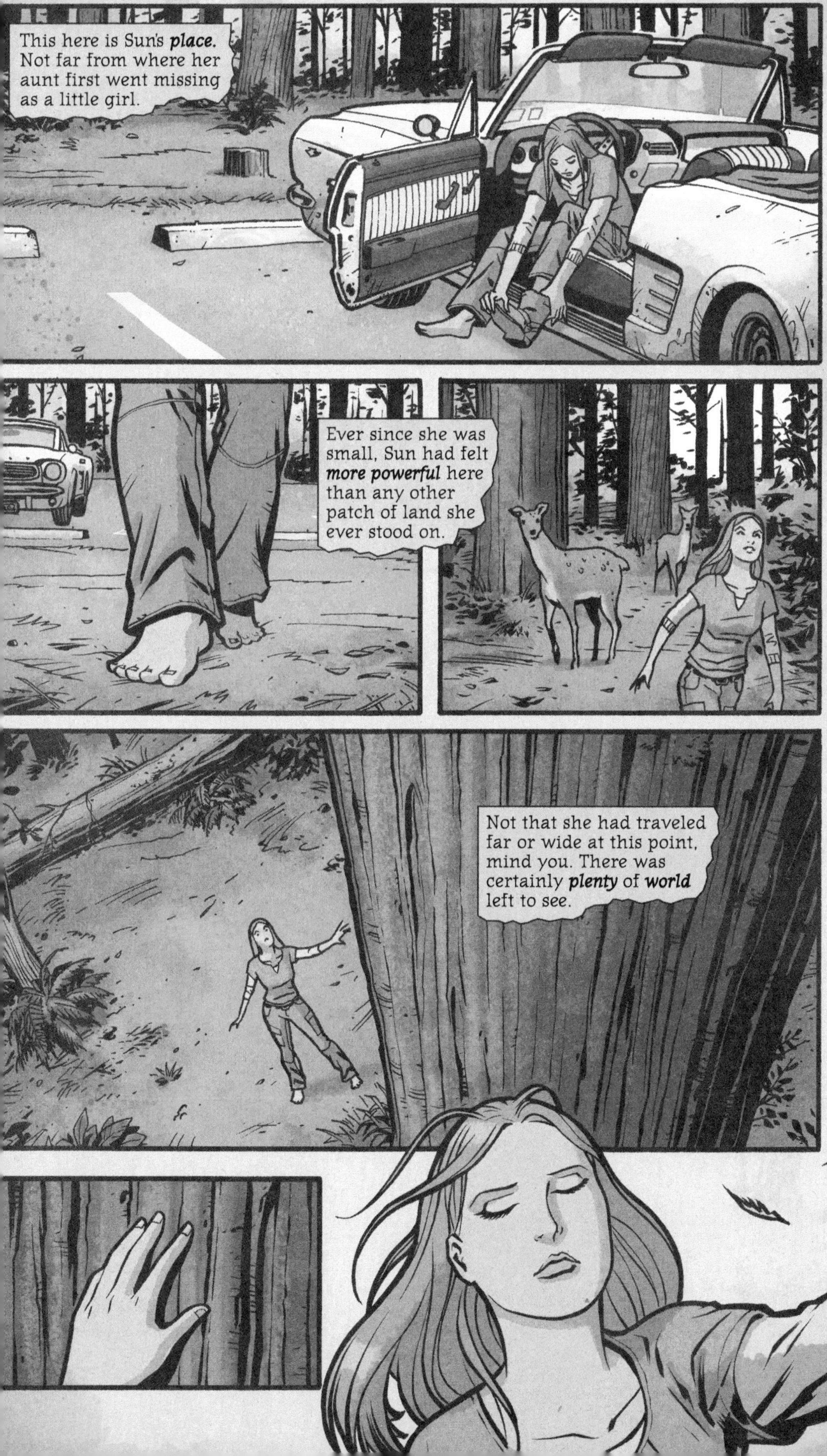
This here is Sun's *place.* Not far from where her aunt first went missing as a little girl.
Ever since she was small, Sun had felt ***more powerful*** here than any other patch of land she ever stood on.
Not that she had traveled far or wide at this point, mind you. There was certainly ***plenty*** of ***world*** left to see.

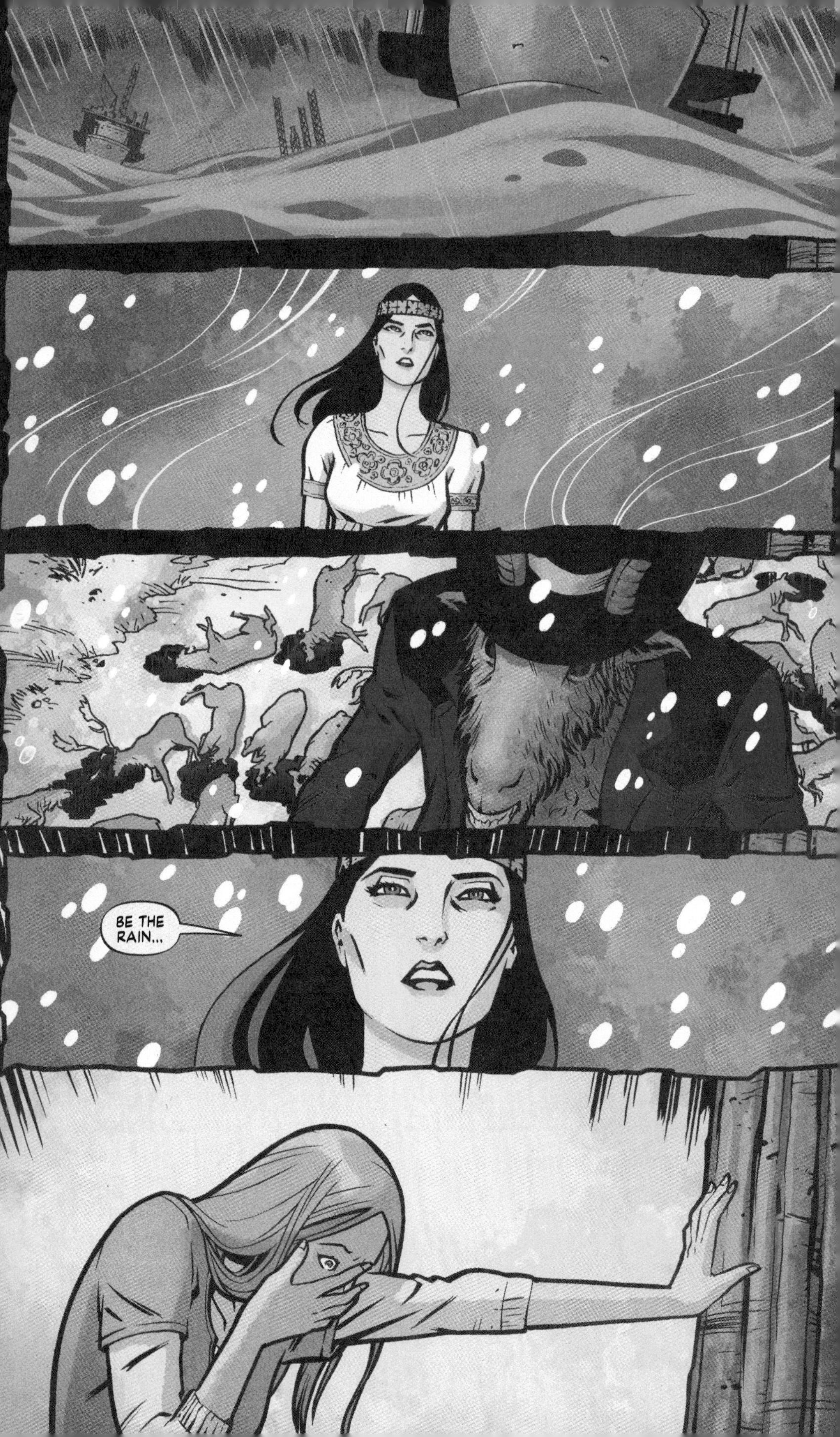
BE THE
RAIN...

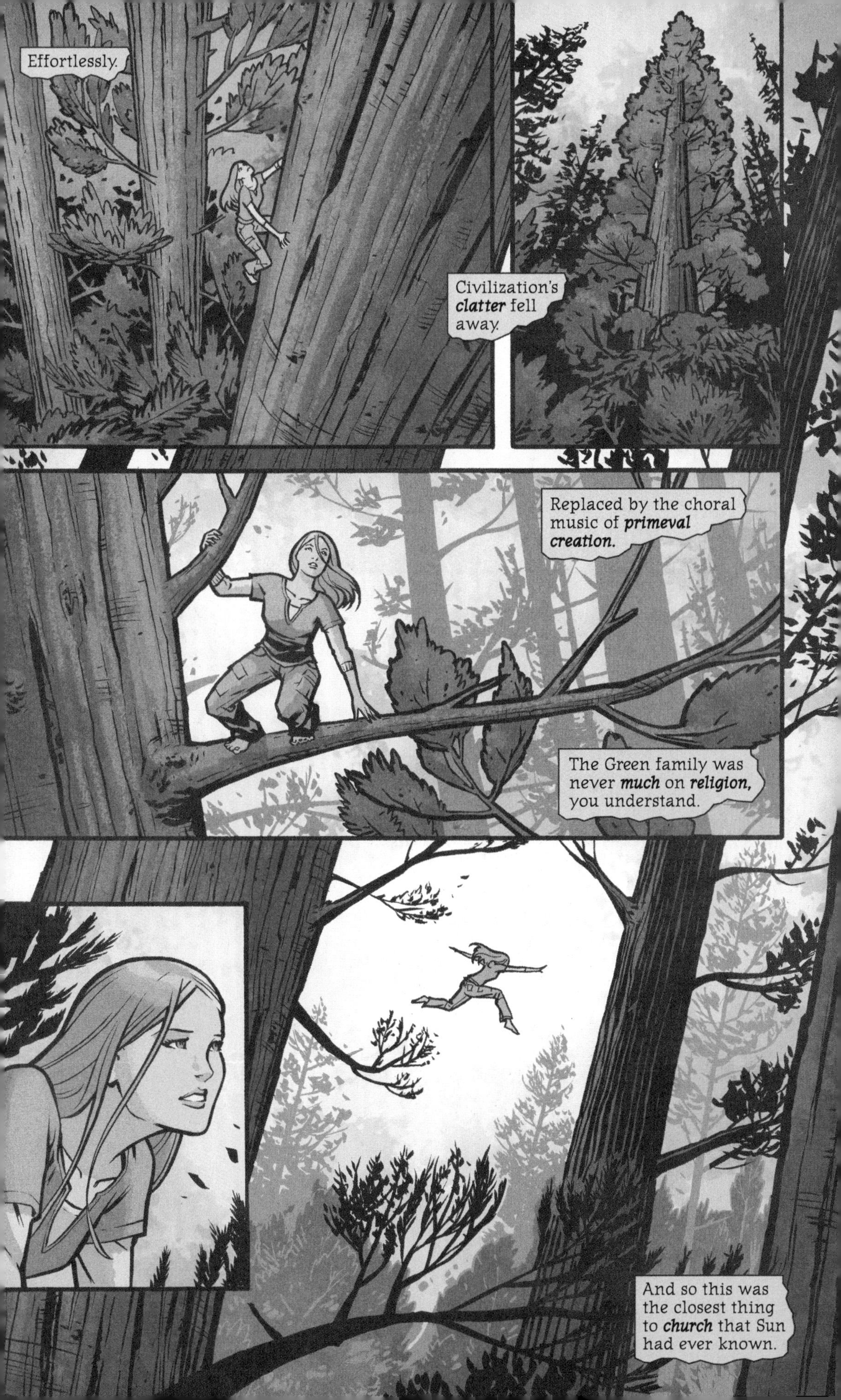
Effortlessly.
Civilization's *clatter* fell away.
Replaced by the choral music of ***primeval creation.***
The Green family was never ***much*** on ***religion,*** you understand.
And so this was the closest thing to ***church*** that Sun had ever known.

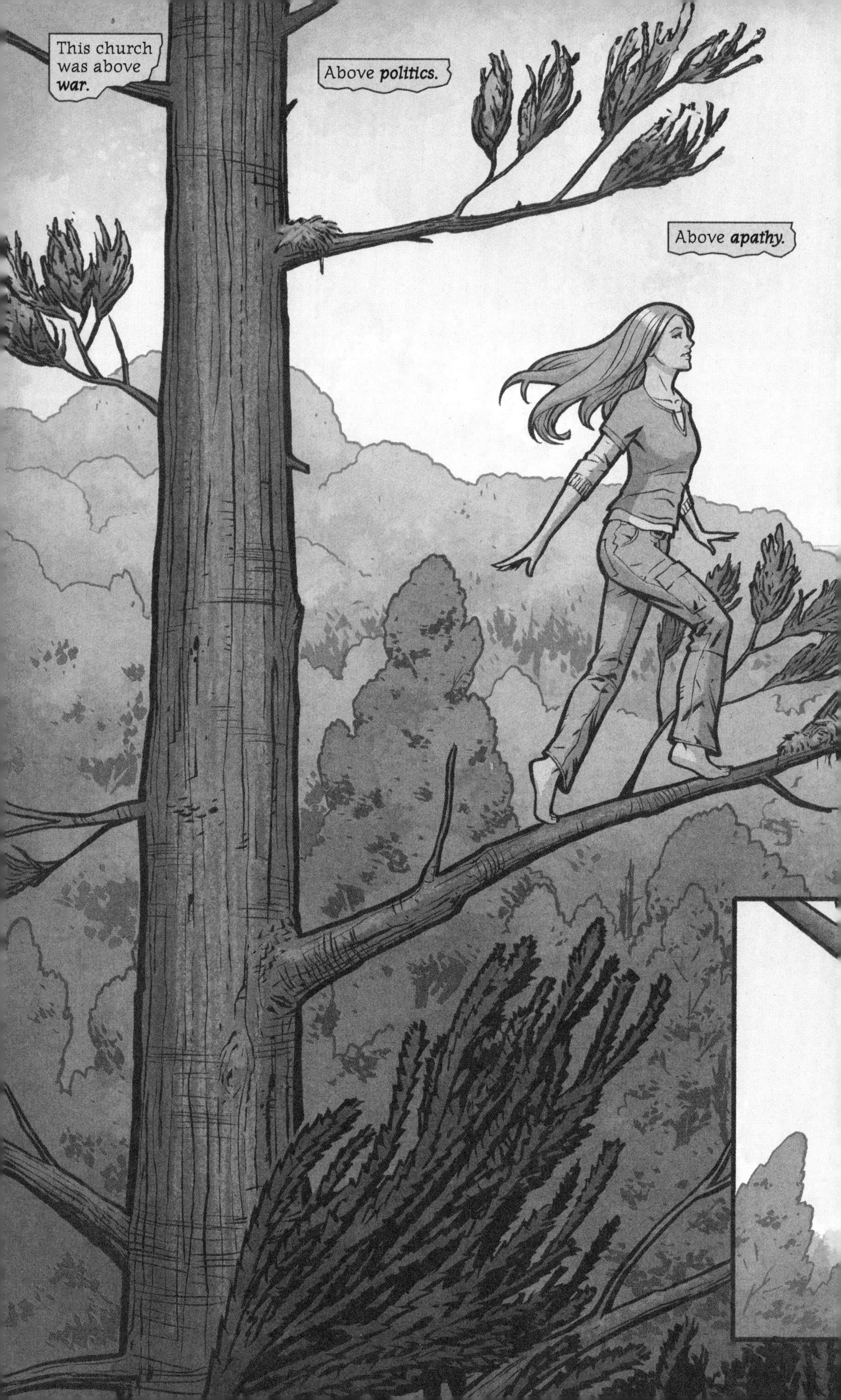
This church was above *war*.
Above *politics*.
Above *apathy*.

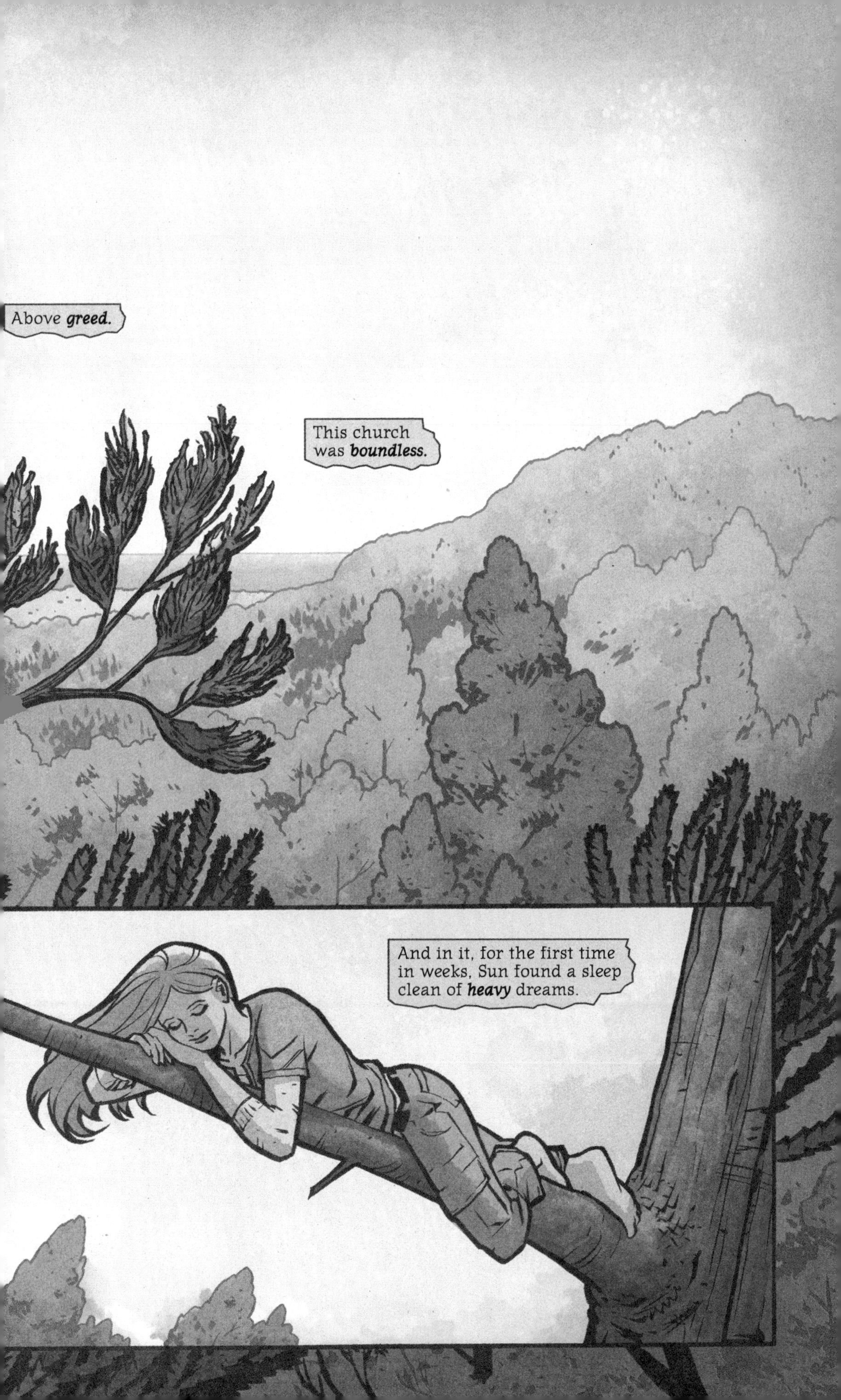
Above **greed.**
This church was **boundless.**
And in it, for the first time in weeks, Sun found a sleep clean of **heavy** dreams.

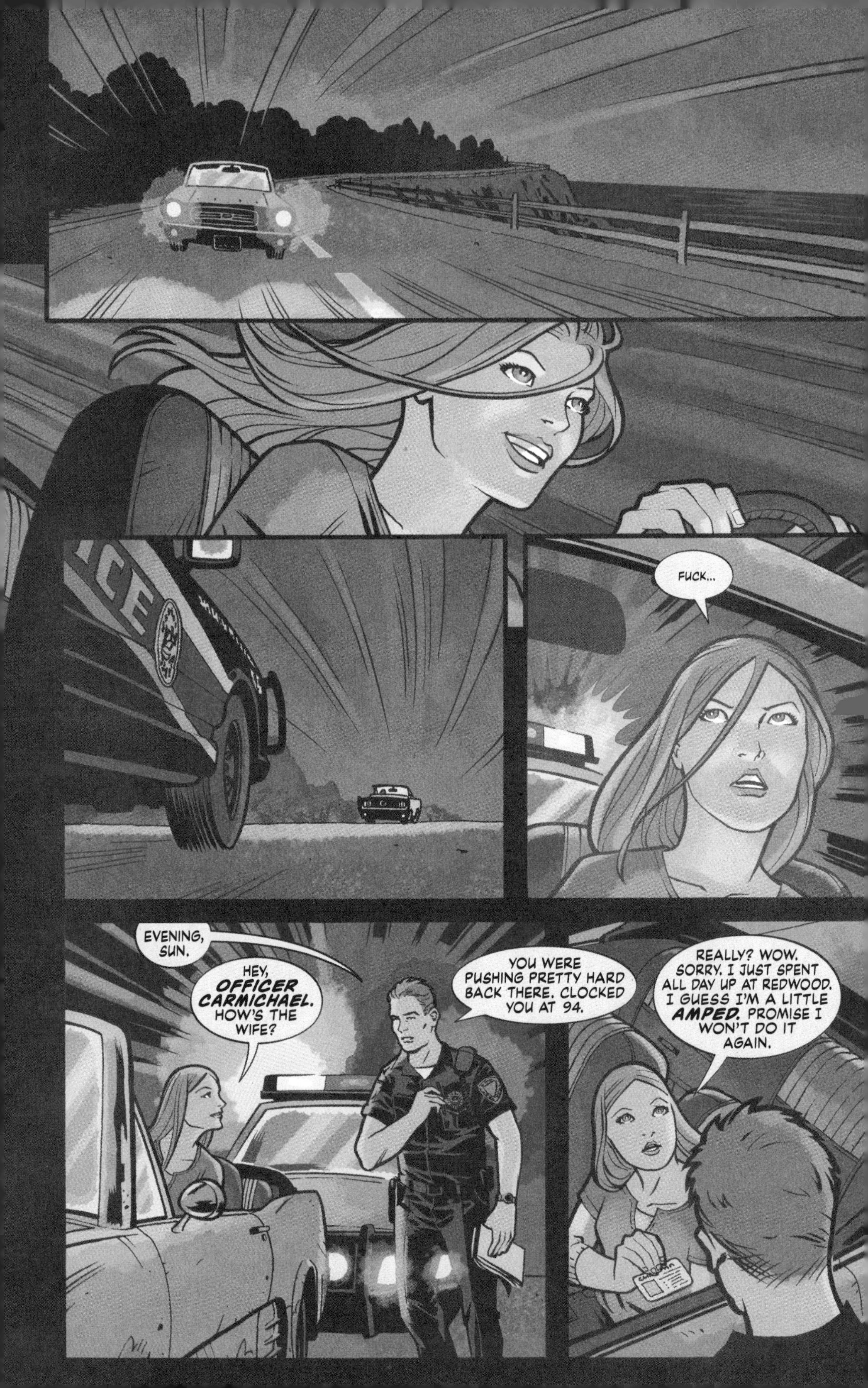

FUCK...
EVENING, SUN.
HEY, OFFICER CARMICHAEL. HOW'S THE WIFE?
YOU WERE PUSHING PRETTY HARD BACK THERE. CLOCKED YOU AT 94.
REALLY? WOW. SORRY. I JUST SPENT ALL DAY UP AT REDWOOD. I GUESS I'M A LITTLE AMPED. PROMISE I WON'T DO IT AGAIN.

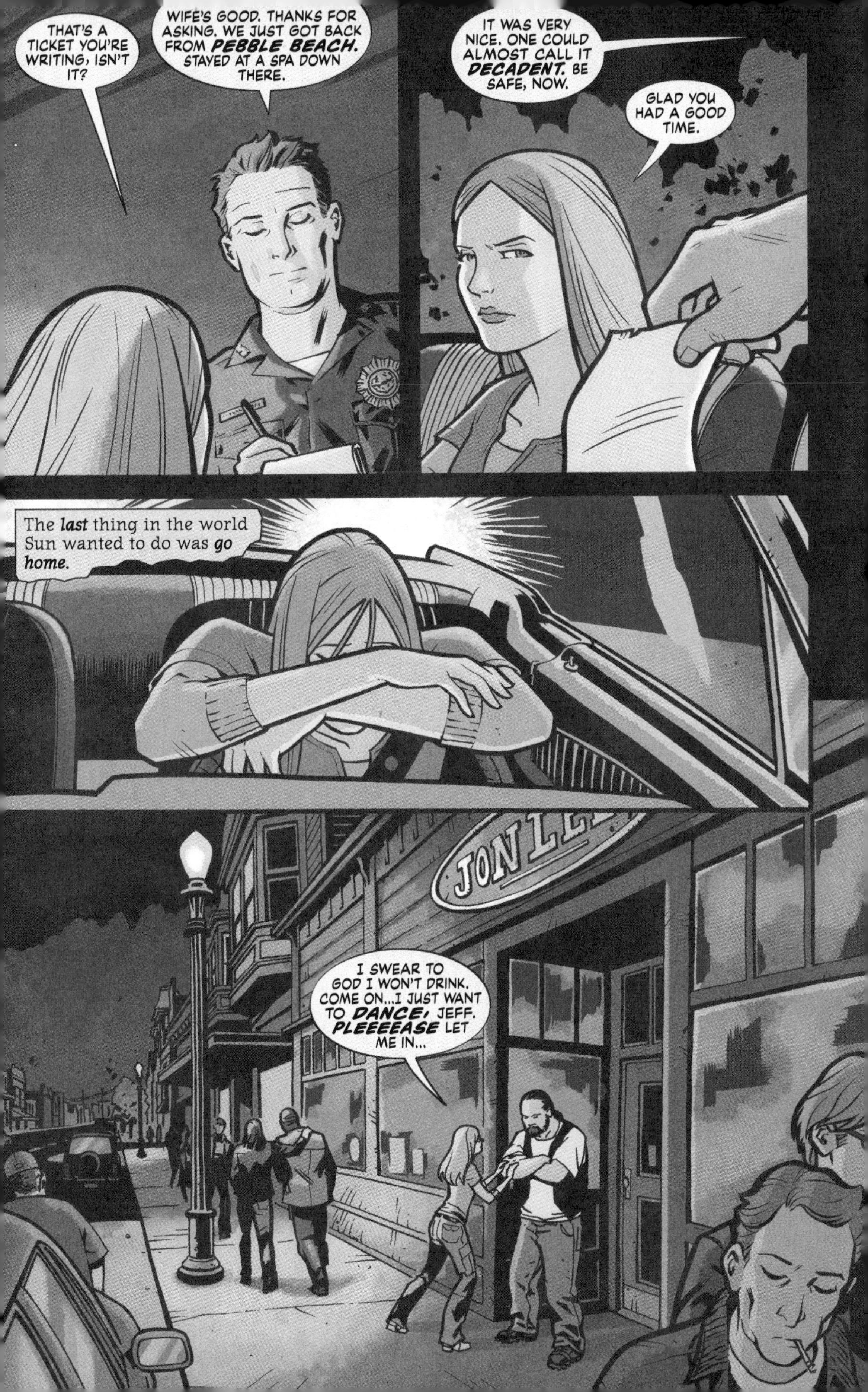
THAT'S A TICKET YOU'RE WRITING, ISN'T IT?
WIFE'S GOOD. THANKS FOR ASKING. WE JUST GOT BACK FROM PEBBLE BEACH. STAYED AT A SPA DOWN THERE.
IT WAS VERY NICE. ONE COULD ALMOST CALL IT DECADENT. BE SAFE, NOW.
GLAD YOU HAD A GOOD TIME.
The last thing in the world Sun wanted to do was go home.
JON LE
I SWEAR TO GOD I WON'T DRINK. COME ON...I JUST WANT TO DANCE, JEFF. PLEEEEASE LET ME IN...

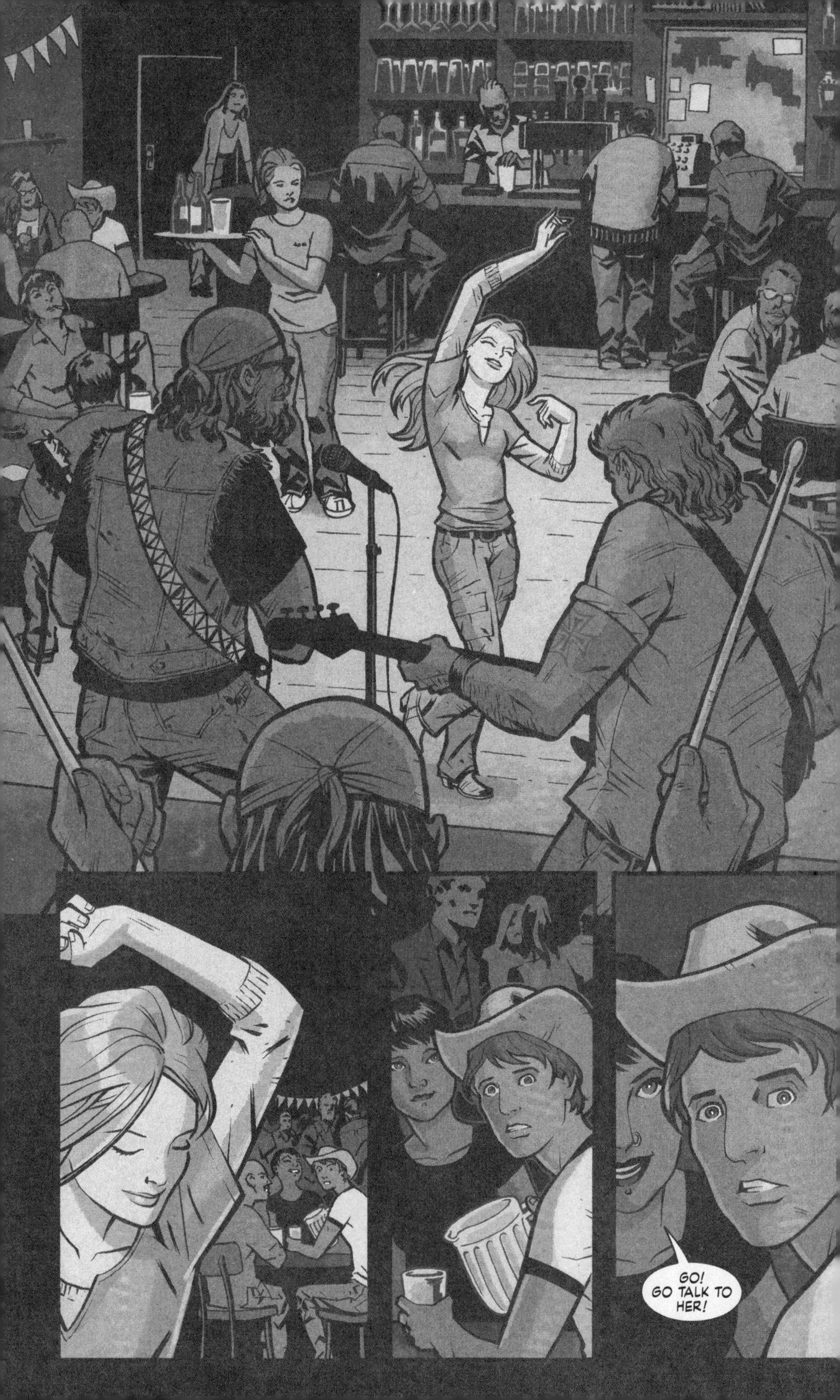
GO! GO TALK TO HER!

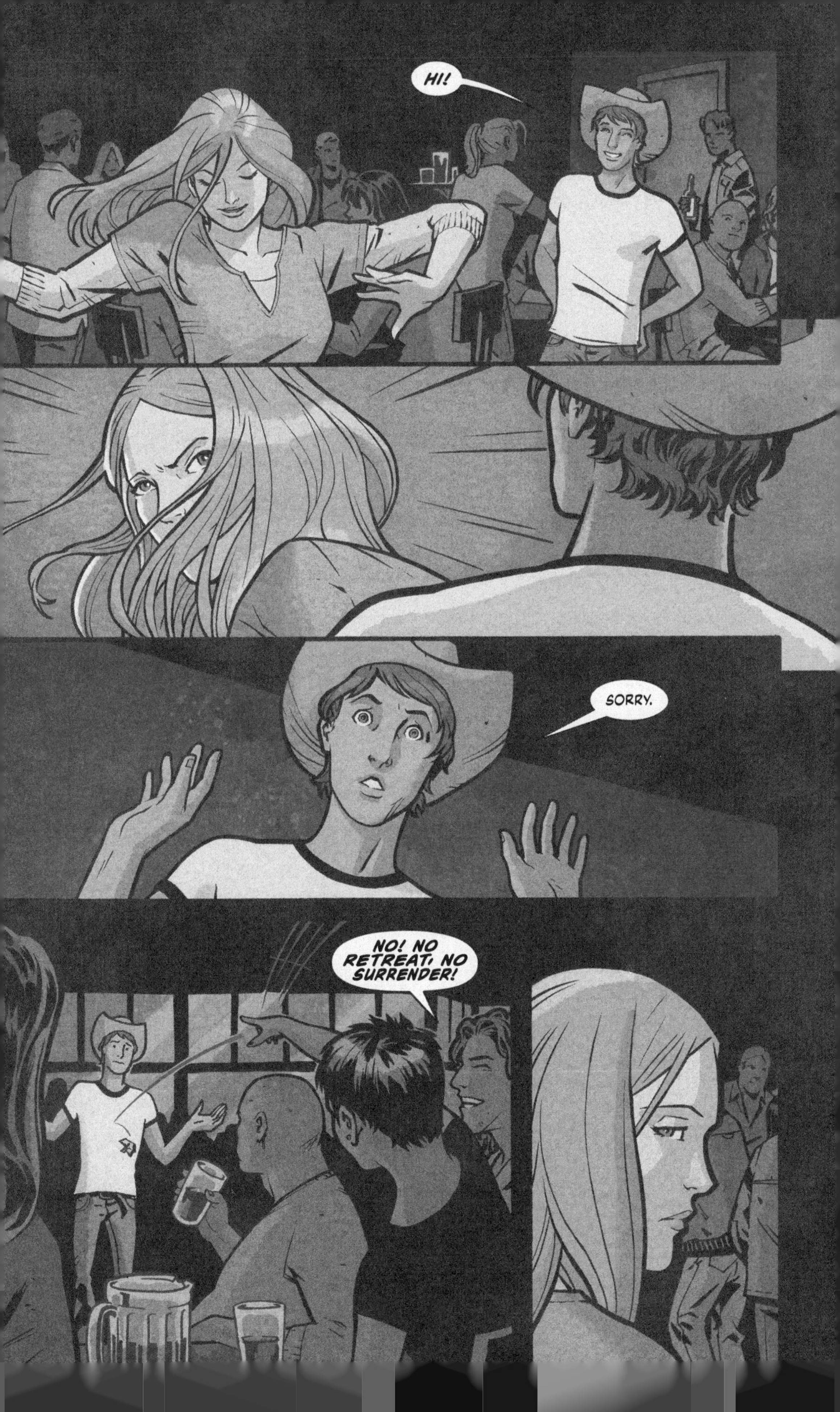
HI!
SORRY.
NO! NO RETREAT, NO SURRENDER!

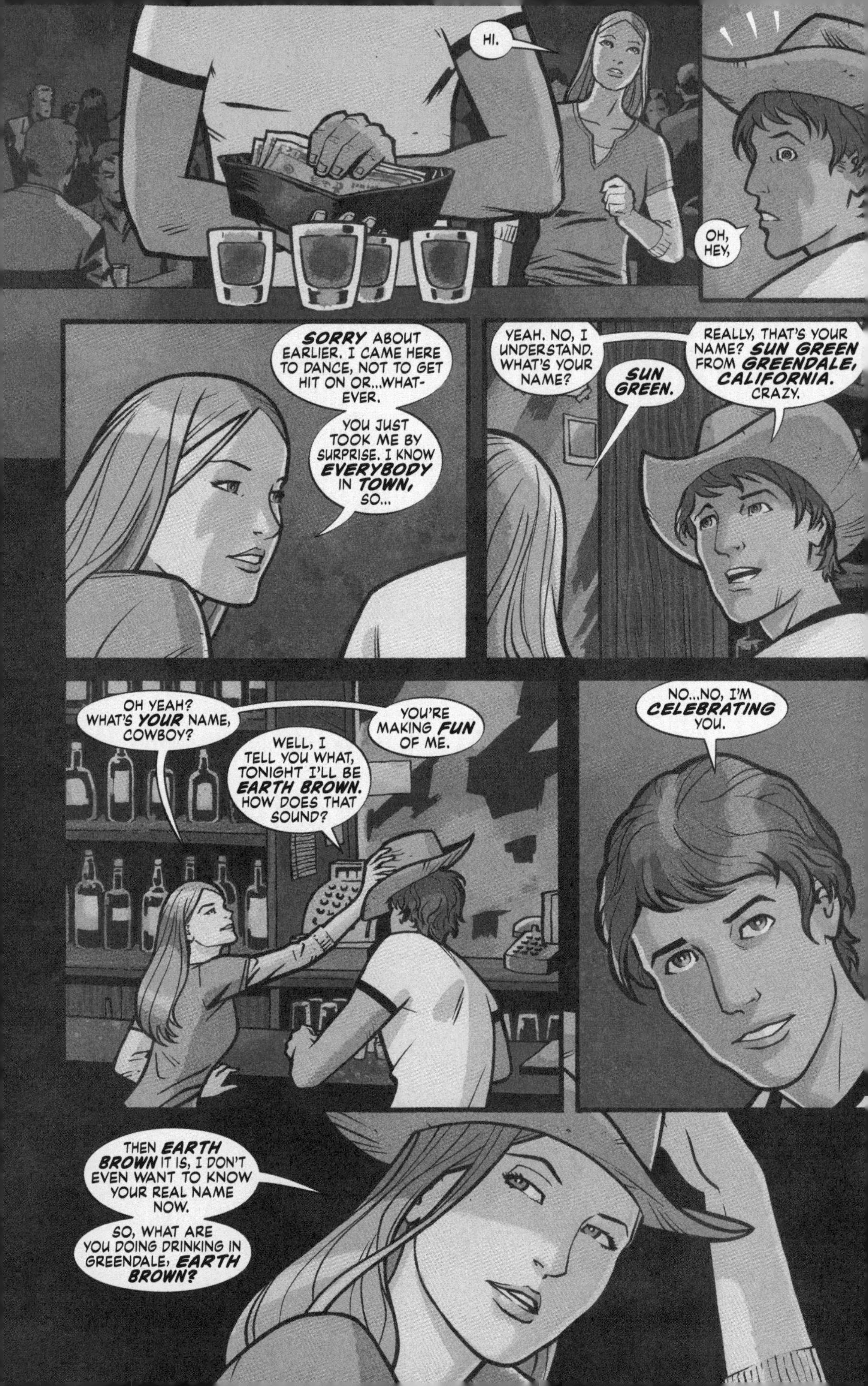
HI.
OH, HEY,
SORRY ABOUT EARLIER. I CAME HERE TO DANCE, NOT TO GET HIT ON OR...WHATEVER.
YOU JUST TOOK ME BY SURPRISE. I KNOW EVERYBODY IN TOWN, SO...
YEAH. NO, I UNDERSTAND. WHAT'S YOUR NAME?
SUN GREEN.
REALLY, THAT'S YOUR NAME? SUN GREEN FROM GREENDALE, CALIFORNIA. CRAZY.
OH YEAH? WHAT'S YOUR NAME, COWBOY?
YOU'RE MAKING FUN OF ME.
WELL, I TELL YOU WHAT, TONIGHT I'LL BE EARTH BROWN. HOW DOES THAT SOUND?
NO...NO, I'M CELEBRATING YOU.
THEN EARTH BROWN IT IS, I DON'T EVEN WANT TO KNOW YOUR REAL NAME NOW.
SO, WHAT ARE YOU DOING DRINKING IN GREENDALE, EARTH BROWN?

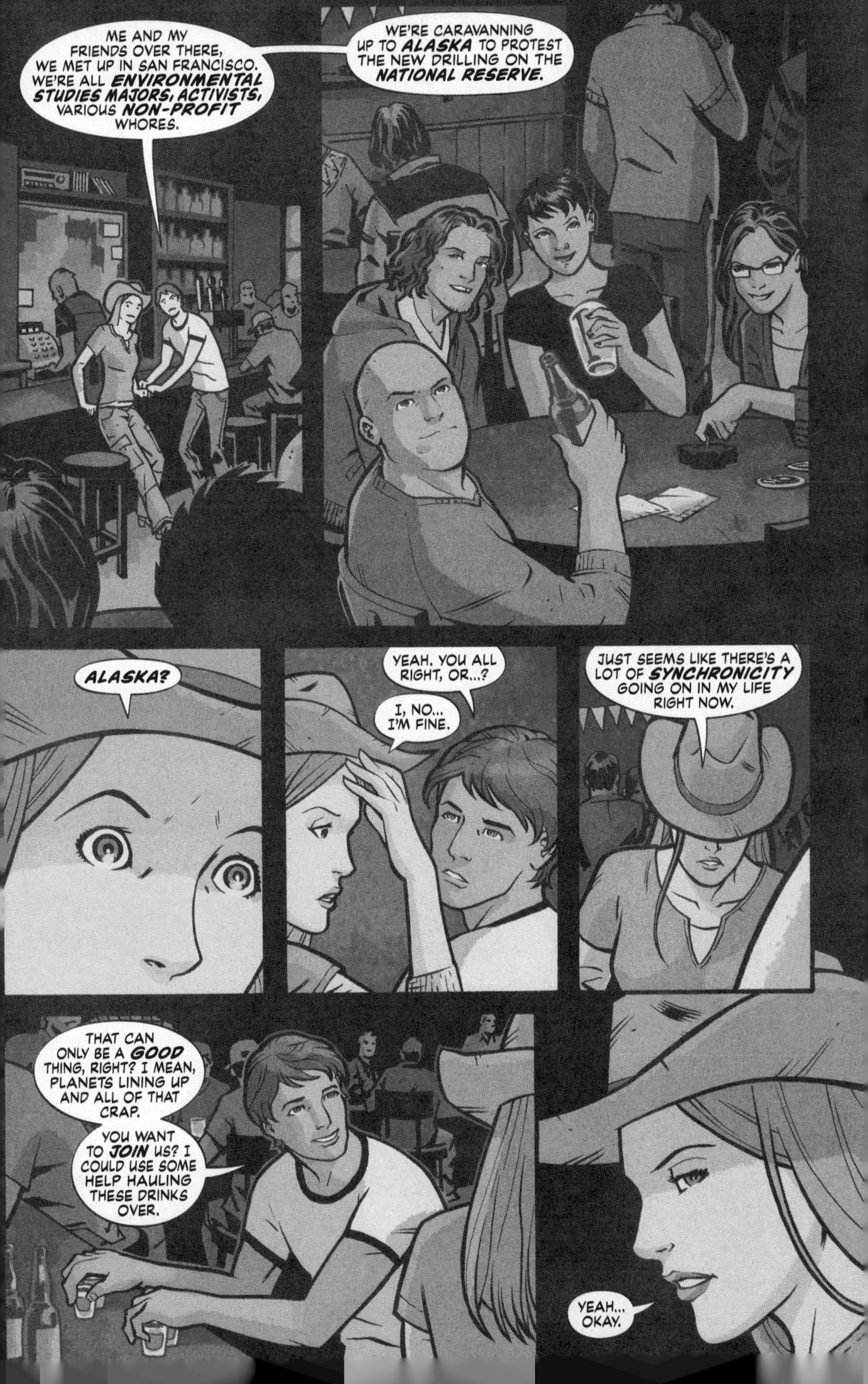

ME AND MY FRIENDS OVER THERE, WE MET UP IN SAN FRANCISCO. WE'RE ALL ENVIRONMENTAL STUDIES MAJORS, ACTIVISTS, VARIOUS NON-PROFIT WHORES.
WE'RE CARAVANNING UP TO ALASKA TO PROTEST THE NEW DRILLING ON THE NATIONAL RESERVE.
ALASKA?
YEAH. YOU ALL RIGHT, OR...?
I, NO... I'M FINE.
JUST SEEMS LIKE THERE'S A LOT OF SYNCHRONICITY GOING ON IN MY LIFE RIGHT NOW.
THAT CAN ONLY BE A GOOD THING, RIGHT? I MEAN, PLANETS LINING UP AND ALL OF THAT CRAP.
YOU WANT TO JOIN US? I COULD USE SOME HELP HAULING THESE DRINKS OVER.
YEAH... OKAY.

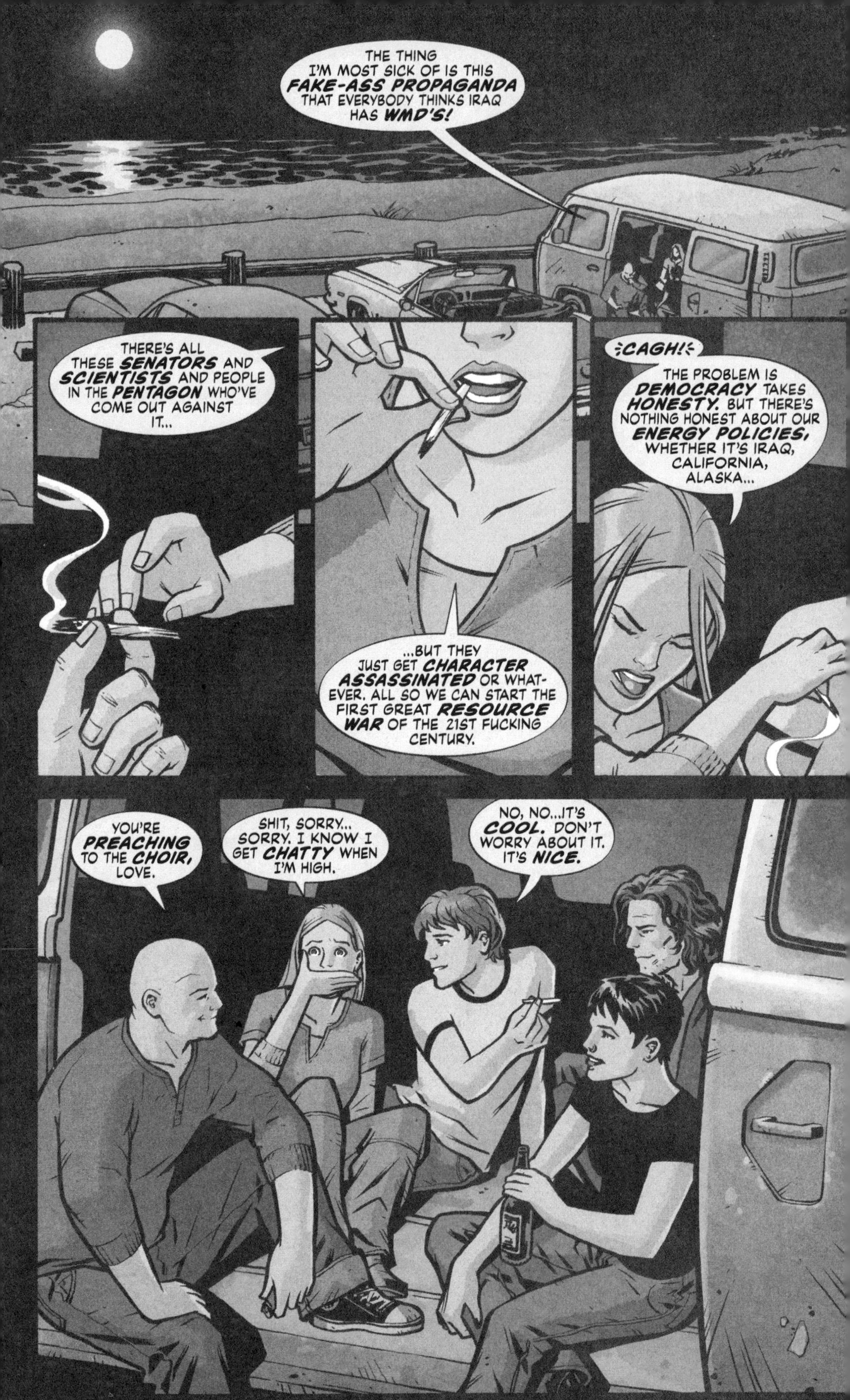
THE THING I'M MOST SICK OF IS THIS FAKE-ASS PROPAGANDA THAT EVERYBODY THINKS IRAQ HAS WMD'S!
THERE'S ALL THESE SENATORS AND SCIENTISTS AND PEOPLE IN THE PENTAGON WHO'VE COME OUT AGAINST IT...
...BUT THEY JUST GET CHARACTER ASSASSINATED OR WHAT-EVER. ALL SO WE CAN START THE FIRST GREAT RESOURCE WAR OF THE 21ST FUCKING CENTURY.
CAGH!
THE PROBLEM IS DEMOCRACY TAKES HONESTY. BUT THERE'S NOTHING HONEST ABOUT OUR ENERGY POLICIES, WHETHER IT'S IRAQ, CALIFORNIA, ALASKA...
YOU'RE PREACHING TO THE CHOIR, LOVE.
SHIT, SORRY... SORRY. I KNOW I GET CHATTY WHEN I'M HIGH.
NO, NO...IT'S COOL. DON'T WORRY ABOUT IT. IT'S NICE.

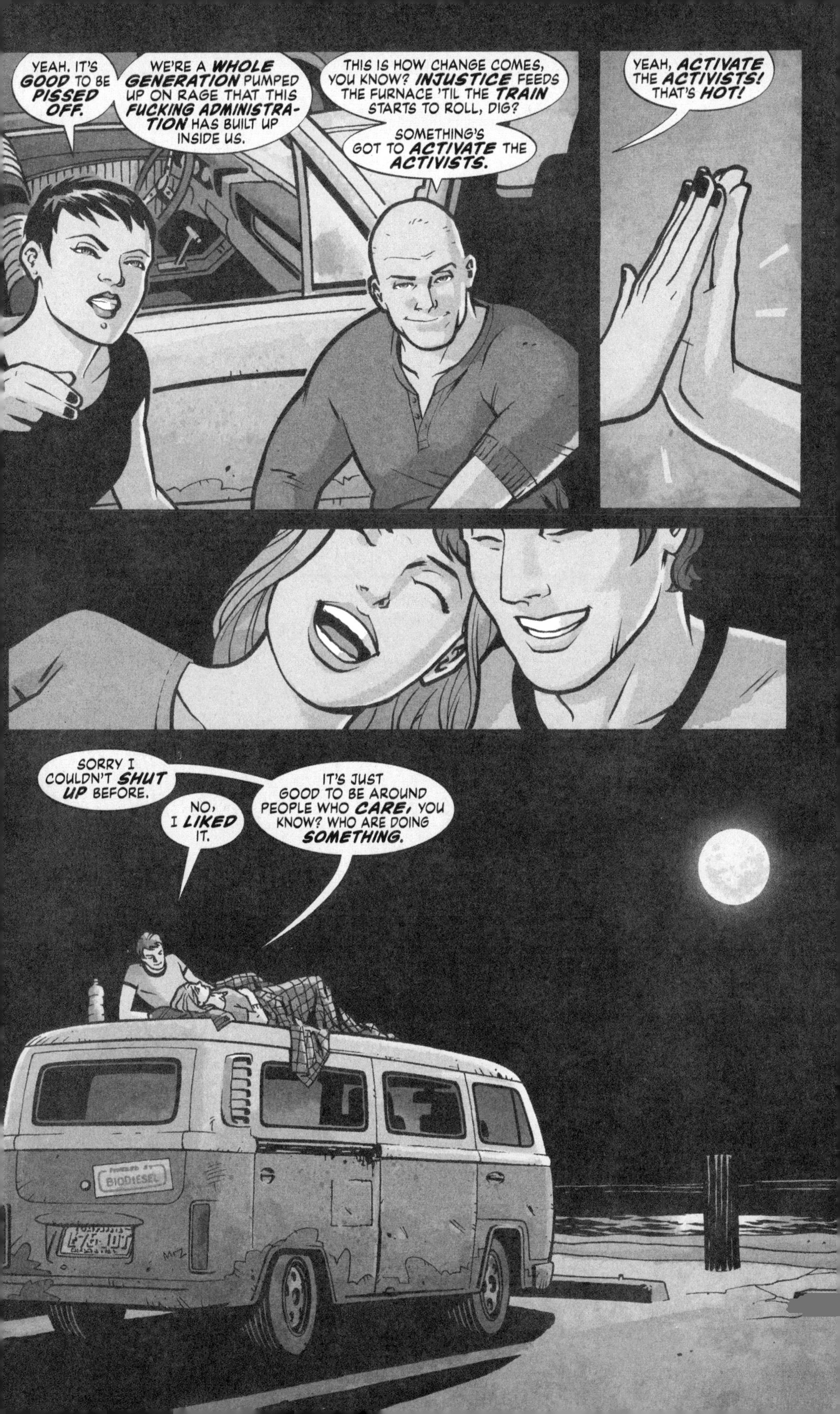
YEAH. IT'S GOOD TO BE PISSED OFF.
WE'RE A WHOLE GENERATION PUMPED UP ON RAGE THAT THIS FUCKING ADMINISTRATION HAS BUILT UP INSIDE US.
THIS IS HOW CHANGE COMES, YOU KNOW? INJUSTICE FEEDS THE FURNACE 'TIL THE TRAIN STARTS TO ROLL, DIG?
SOMETHING'S GOT TO ACTIVATE THE ACTIVISTS.
YEAH, ACTIVATE THE ACTIVISTS! THAT'S HOT!
SORRY I COULDN'T SHUT UP BEFORE.
IT'S JUST GOOD TO BE AROUND PEOPLE WHO CARE, YOU KNOW? WHO ARE DOING SOMETHING.
NO, I LIKED IT.
BIODIESEL

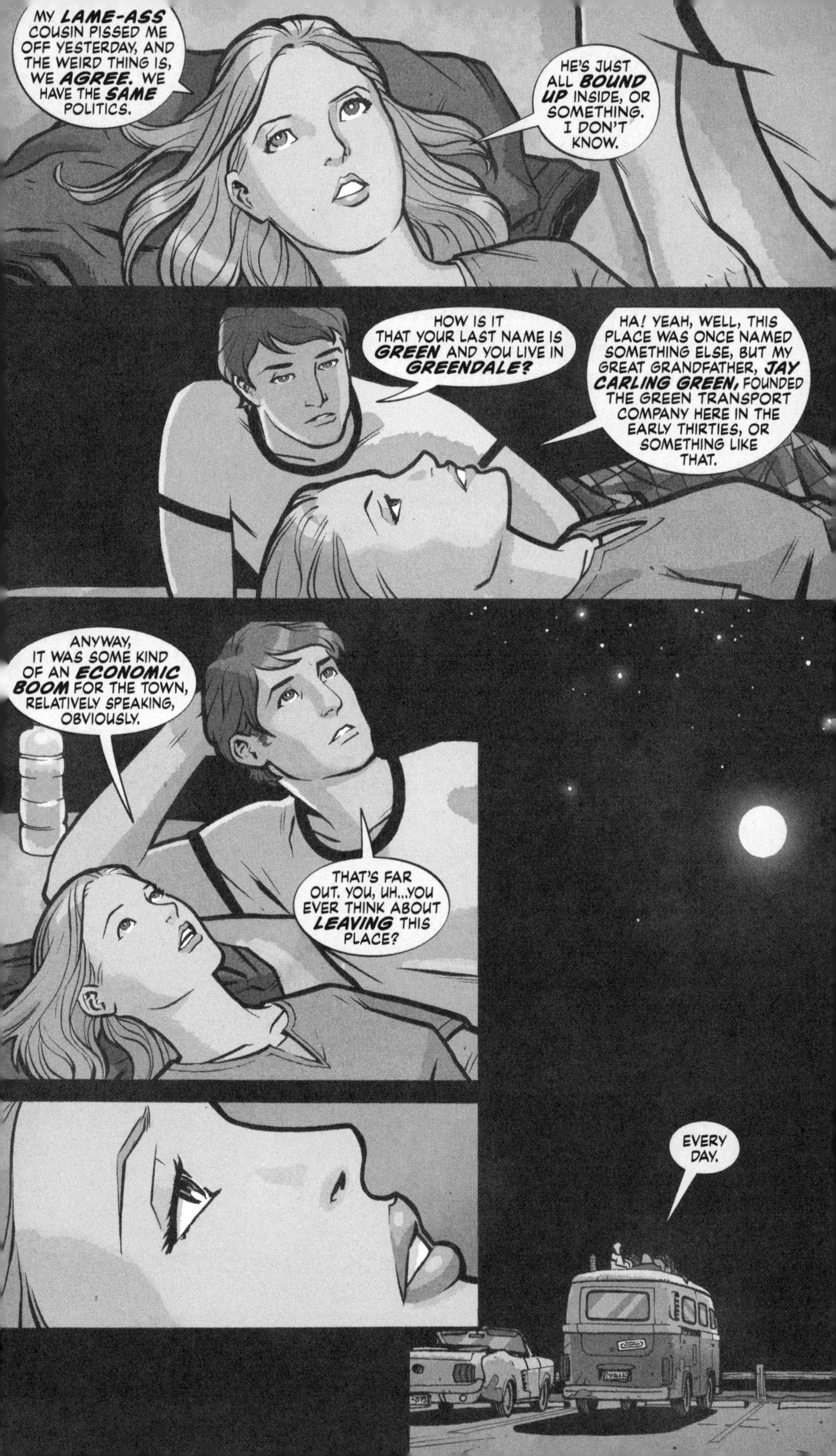
MY LAME-ASS COUSIN PISSED ME OFF YESTERDAY, AND THE WEIRD THING IS, WE AGREE. WE HAVE THE SAME POLITICS.
HE'S JUST ALL BOUND UP INSIDE, OR SOMETHING. I DON'T KNOW.
HOW IS IT THAT YOUR LAST NAME IS GREEN AND YOU LIVE IN GREENDALE?
HA! YEAH, WELL, THIS PLACE WAS ONCE NAMED SOMETHING ELSE, BUT MY GREAT GRANDFATHER, JAY CARLING GREEN, FOUNDED THE GREEN TRANSPORT COMPANY HERE IN THE EARLY THIRTIES, OR SOMETHING LIKE THAT.
ANYWAY, IT WAS SOME KIND OF AN ECONOMIC BOOM FOR THE TOWN, RELATIVELY SPEAKING, OBVIOUSLY.
THAT'S FAR OUT. YOU, UH...YOU EVER THINK ABOUT LEAVING THIS PLACE?
EVERY DAY.

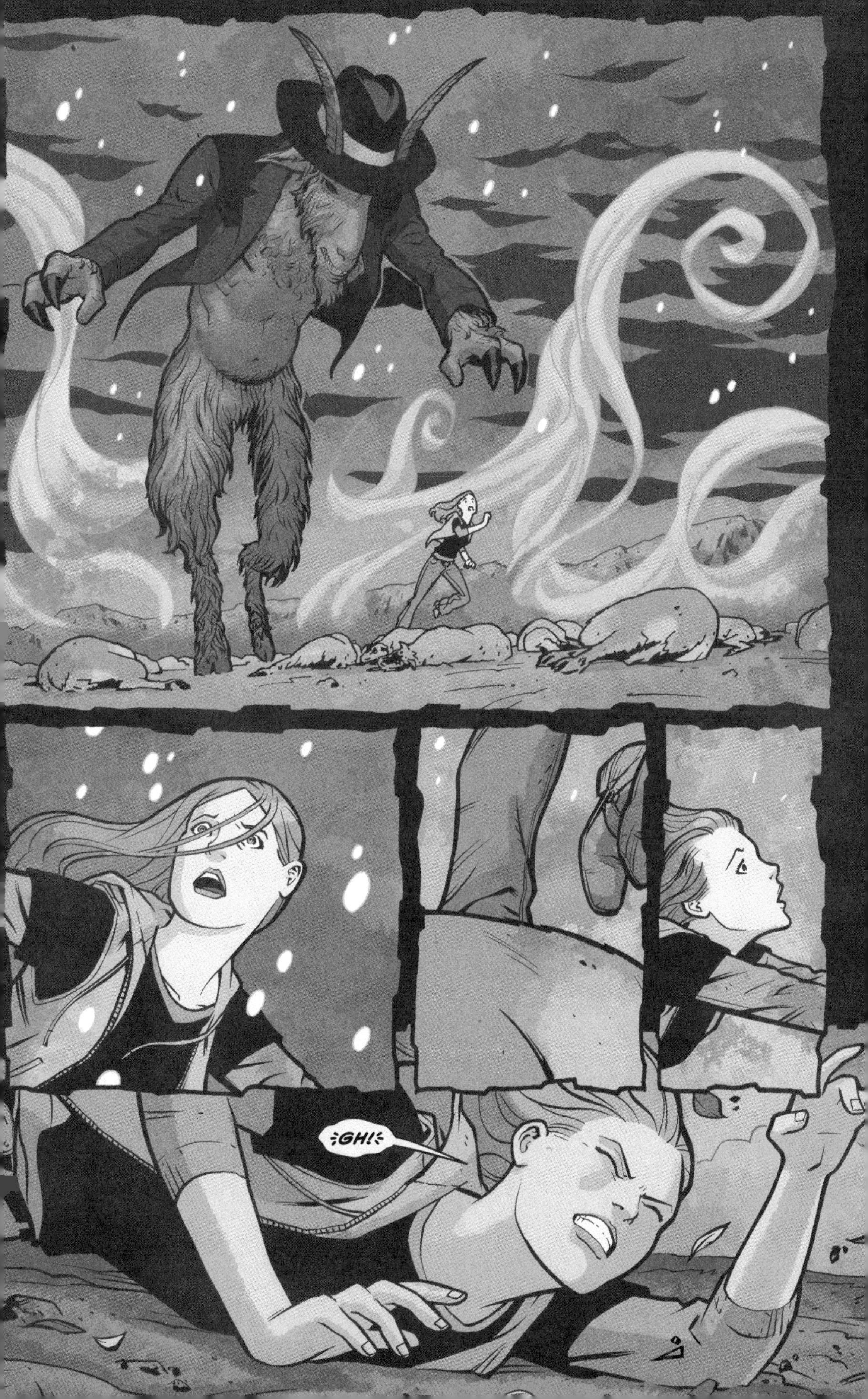
GH!

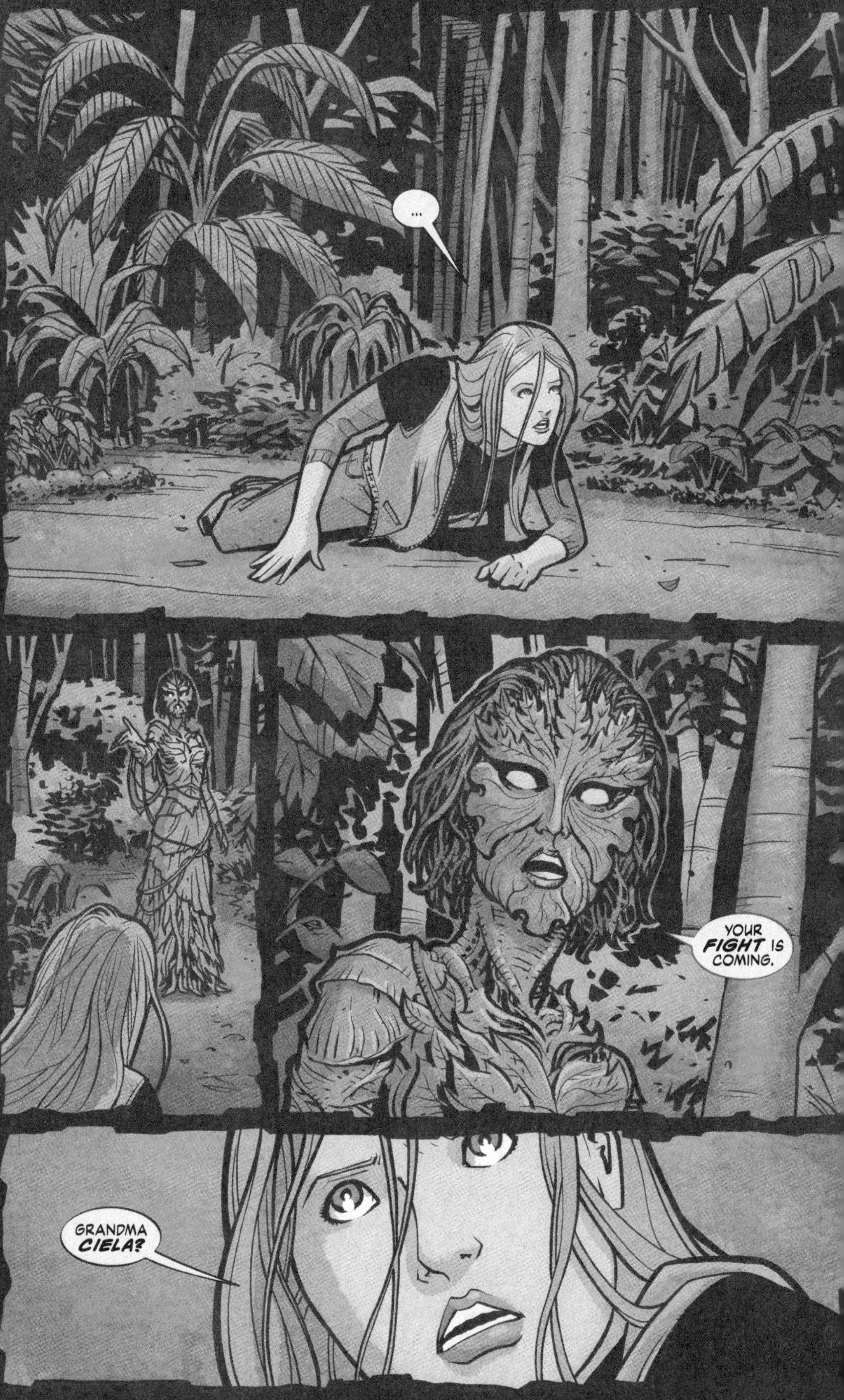
...
YOUR FIGHT IS COMING.
GRANDMA CIELA?

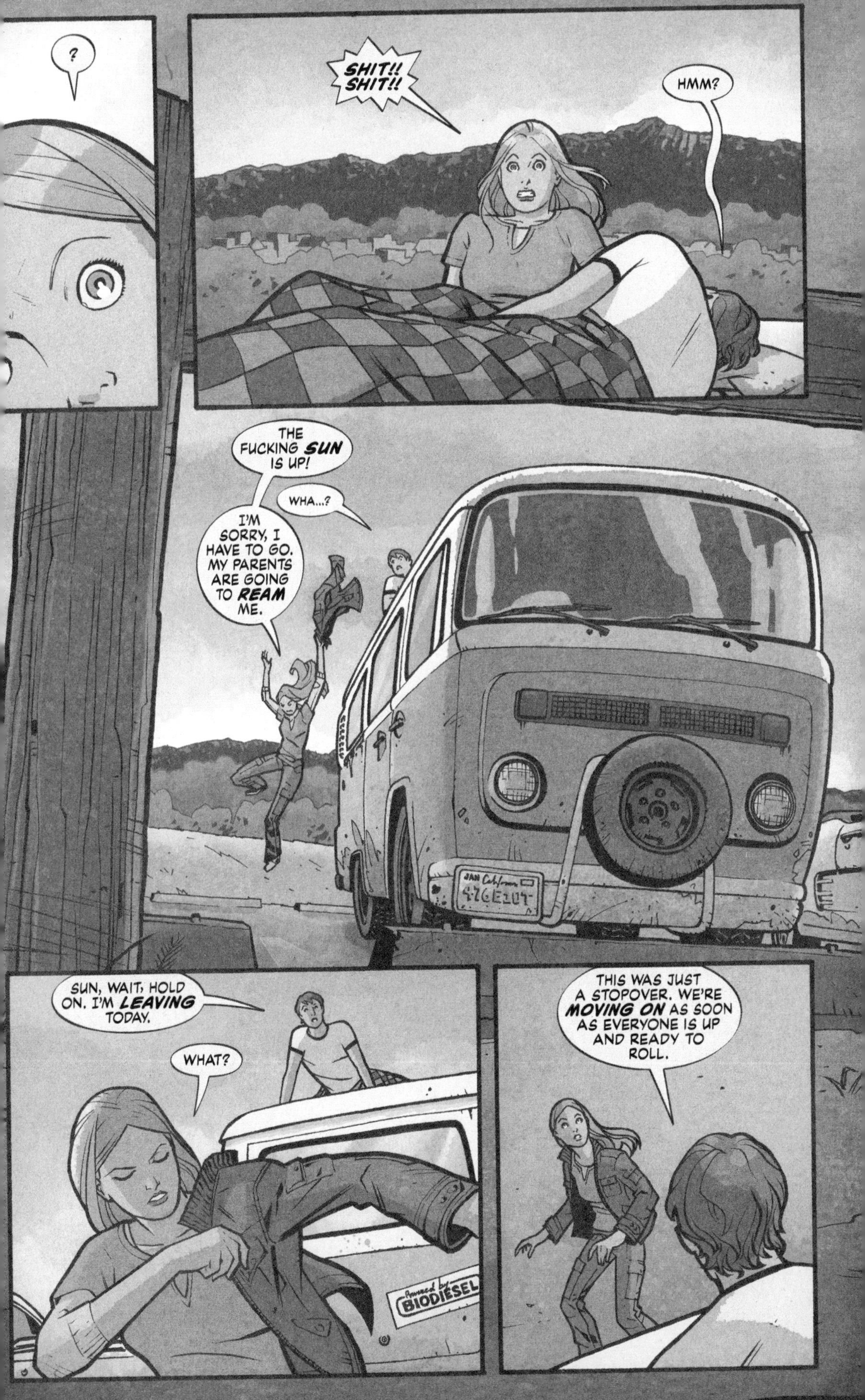
?
SHIT!! SHIT!!
HMM?
THE FUCKING SUN IS UP!
WHA...?
I'M SORRY, I HAVE TO GO. MY PARENTS ARE GOING TO REAM ME.
SUN, WAIT, HOLD ON. I'M LEAVING TODAY.
WHAT?
BIODIESEL
THIS WAS JUST A STOPOVER. WE'RE MOVING ON AS SOON AS EVERYONE IS UP AND READY TO ROLL.

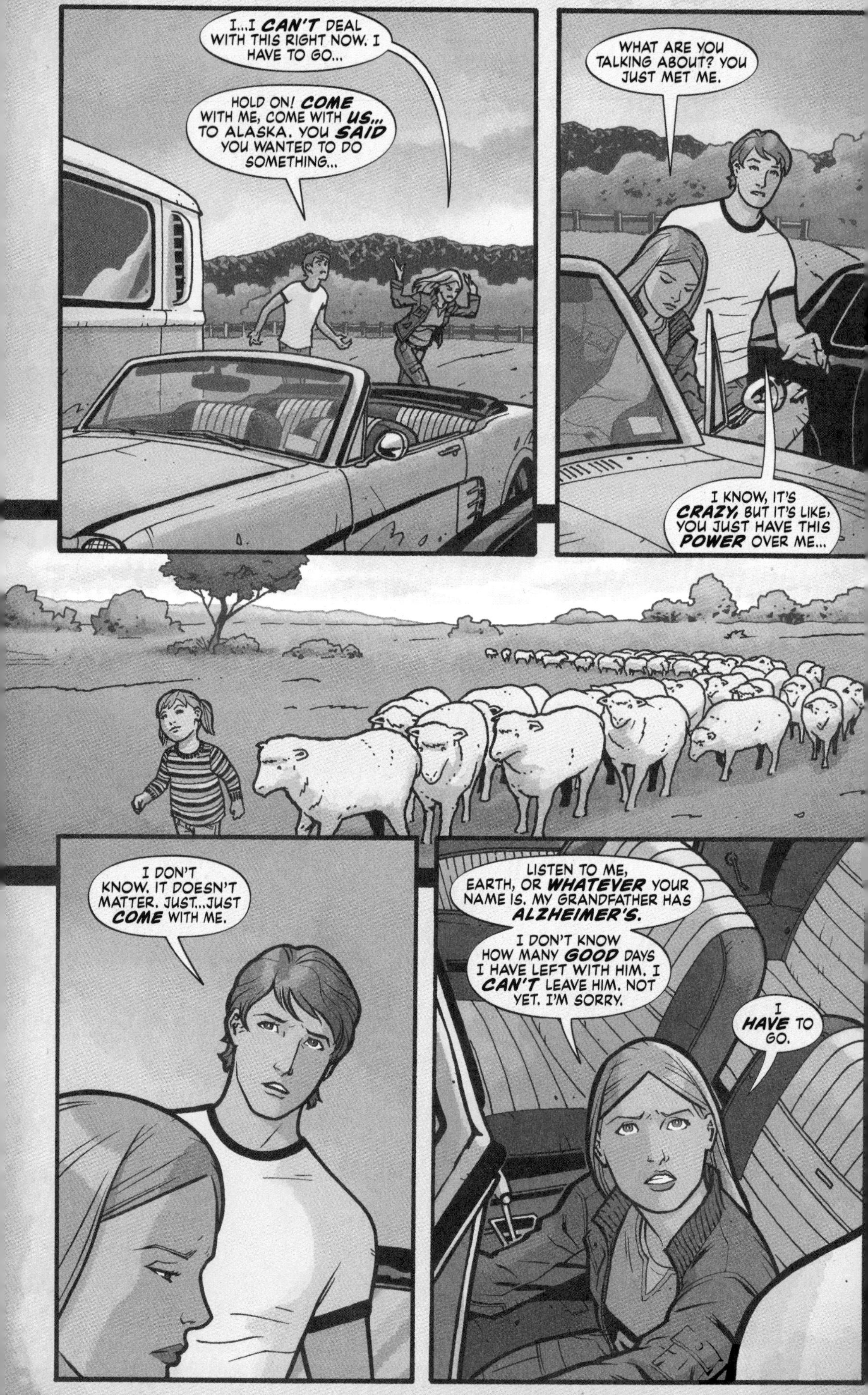

I...I CAN'T DEAL WITH THIS RIGHT NOW. I HAVE TO GO...
HOLD ON! COME WITH ME, COME WITH US... TO ALASKA. YOU SAID YOU WANTED TO DO SOMETHING...
WHAT ARE YOU TALKING ABOUT? YOU JUST MET ME.
I KNOW, IT'S CRAZY, BUT IT'S LIKE, YOU JUST HAVE THIS POWER OVER ME...
I DON'T KNOW. IT DOESN'T MATTER. JUST...JUST COME WITH ME.
LISTEN TO ME, EARTH, OR WHATEVER YOUR NAME IS. MY GRANDFATHER HAS ALZHEIMER'S.
I DON'T KNOW HOW MANY GOOD DAYS I HAVE LEFT WITH HIM. I CAN'T LEAVE HIM. NOT YET. I'M SORRY.
I HAVE TO GO.

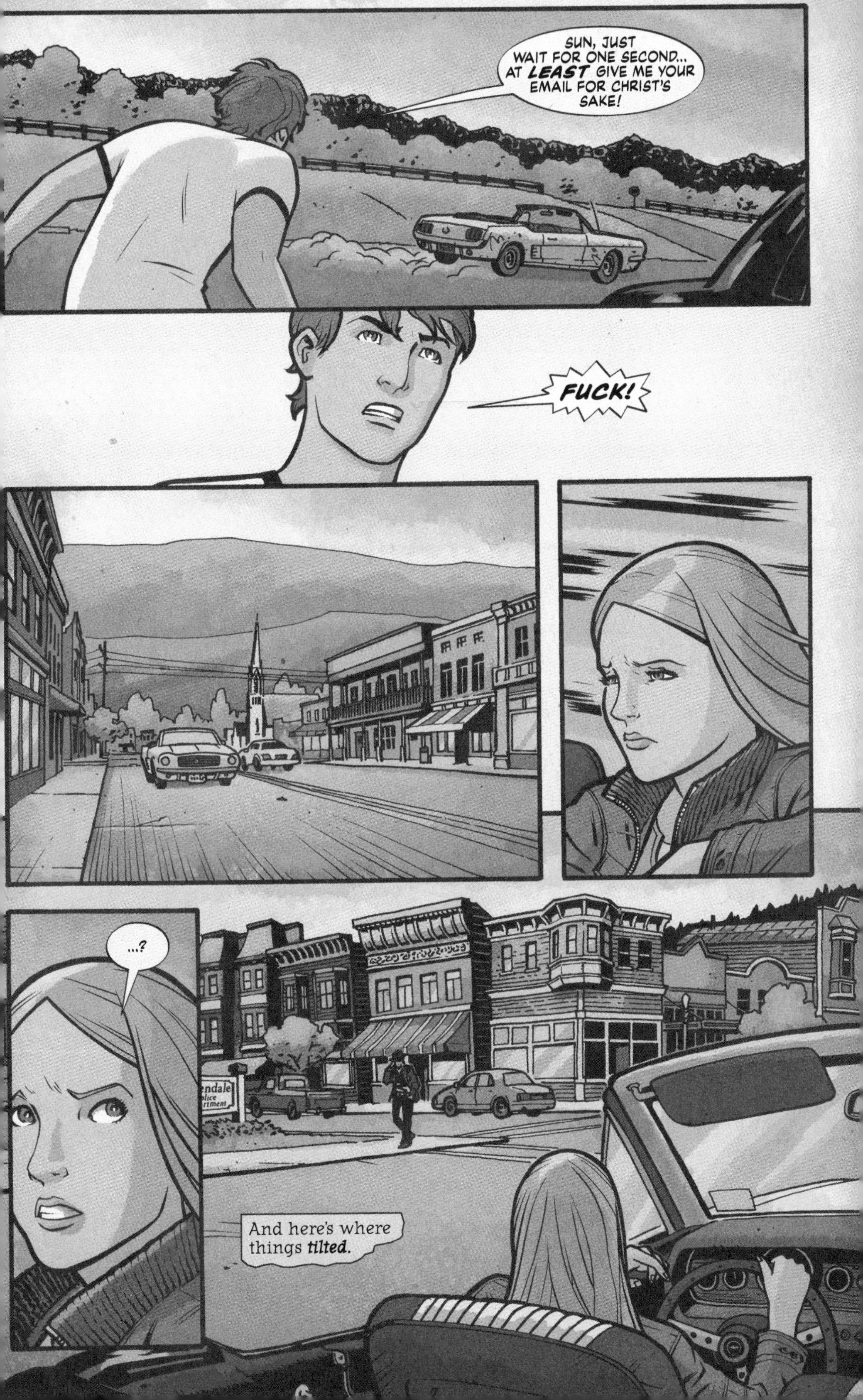
SUN, JUST WAIT FOR ONE SECOND... AT LEAST GIVE ME YOUR EMAIL FOR CHRIST'S SAKE!
FUCK!
...?
And here's where things tilted.

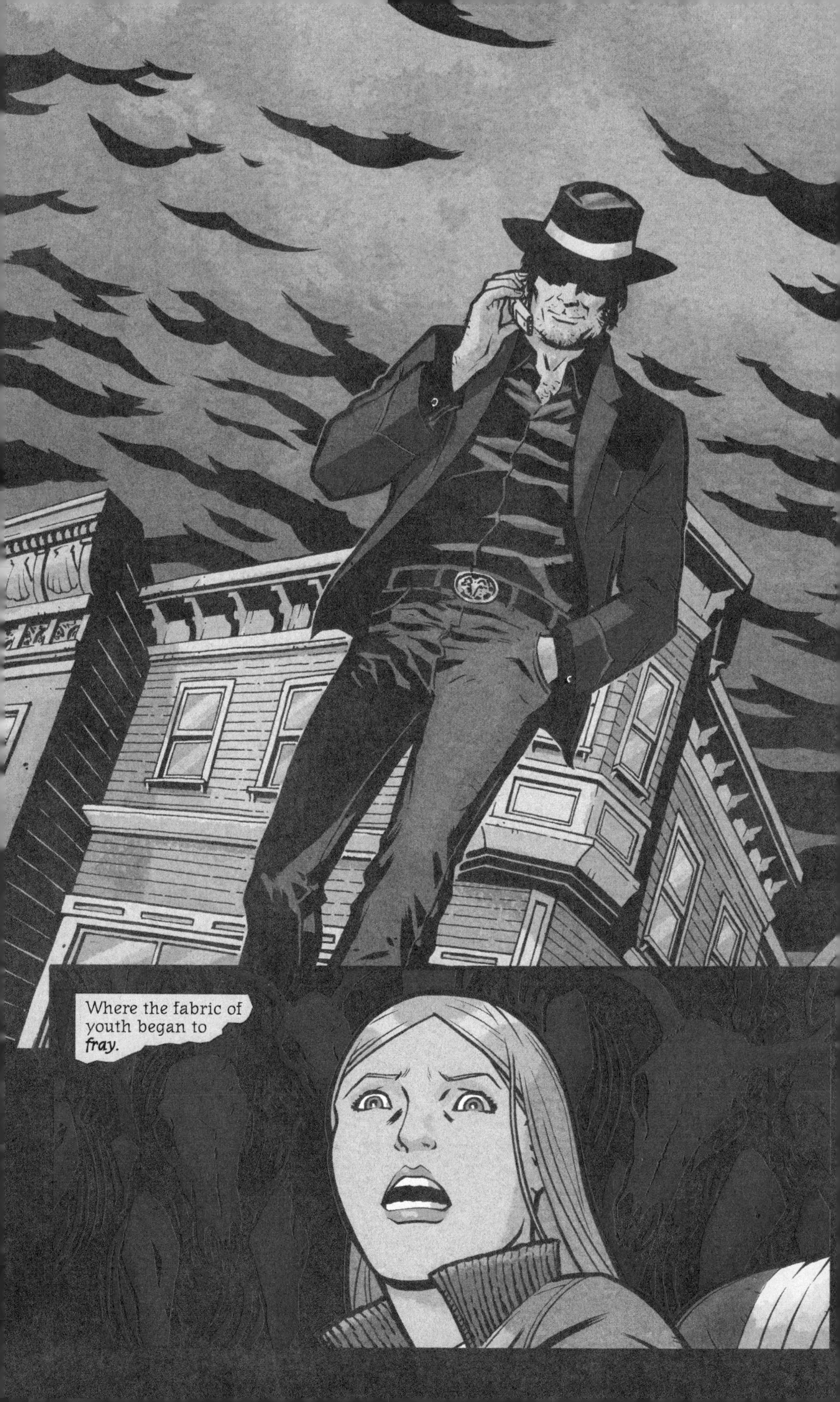
Where the fabric of youth began to *fray*.

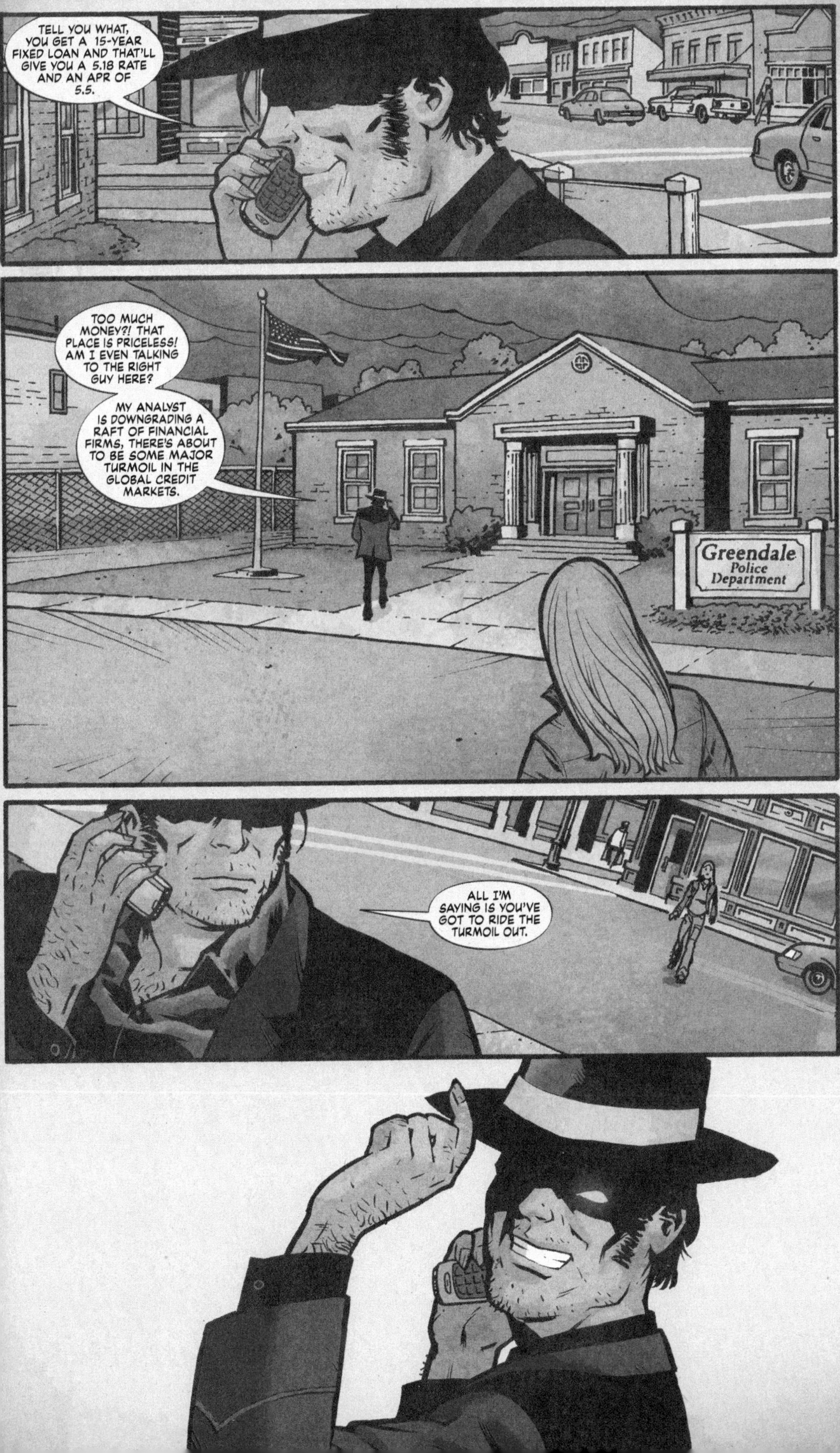
TELL YOU WHAT, YOU GET A 15-YEAR FIXED LOAN AND THAT'LL GIVE YOU A 5.18 RATE AND AN APR OF 5.5.
TOO MUCH MONEY?! THAT PLACE IS PRICELESS! AM I EVEN TALKING TO THE RIGHT GUY HERE?
MY ANALYST IS DOWNGRADING A RAFT OF FINANCIAL FIRMS, THERE'S ABOUT TO BE SOME MAJOR TURMOIL IN THE GLOBAL CREDIT MARKETS.
Greendale Police Department
ALL I'M SAYING IS YOU'VE GOT TO RIDE THE TURMOIL OUT.

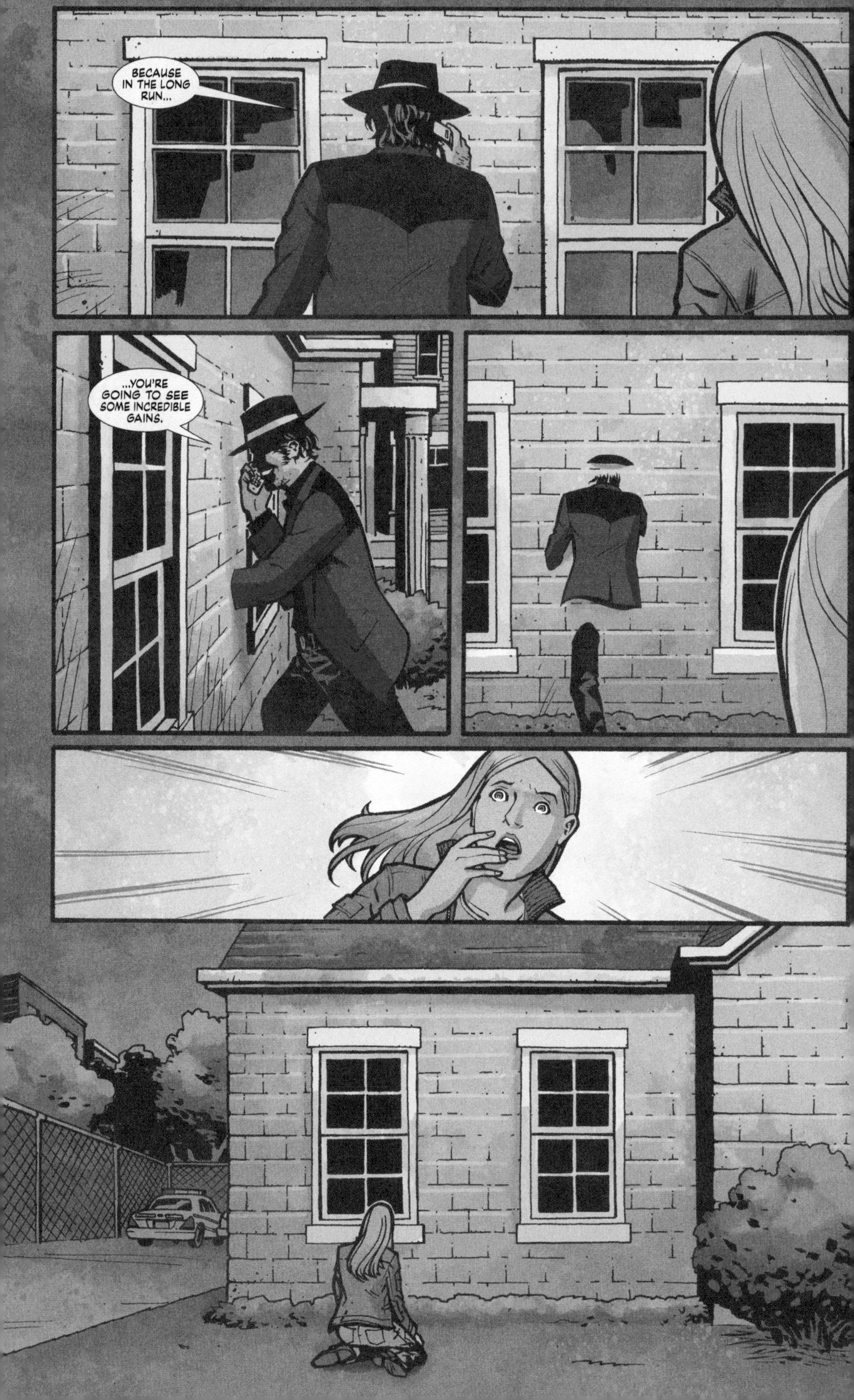
BECAUSE IN THE LONG RUN...
...YOU'RE GOING TO SEE SOME INCREDIBLE GAINS.

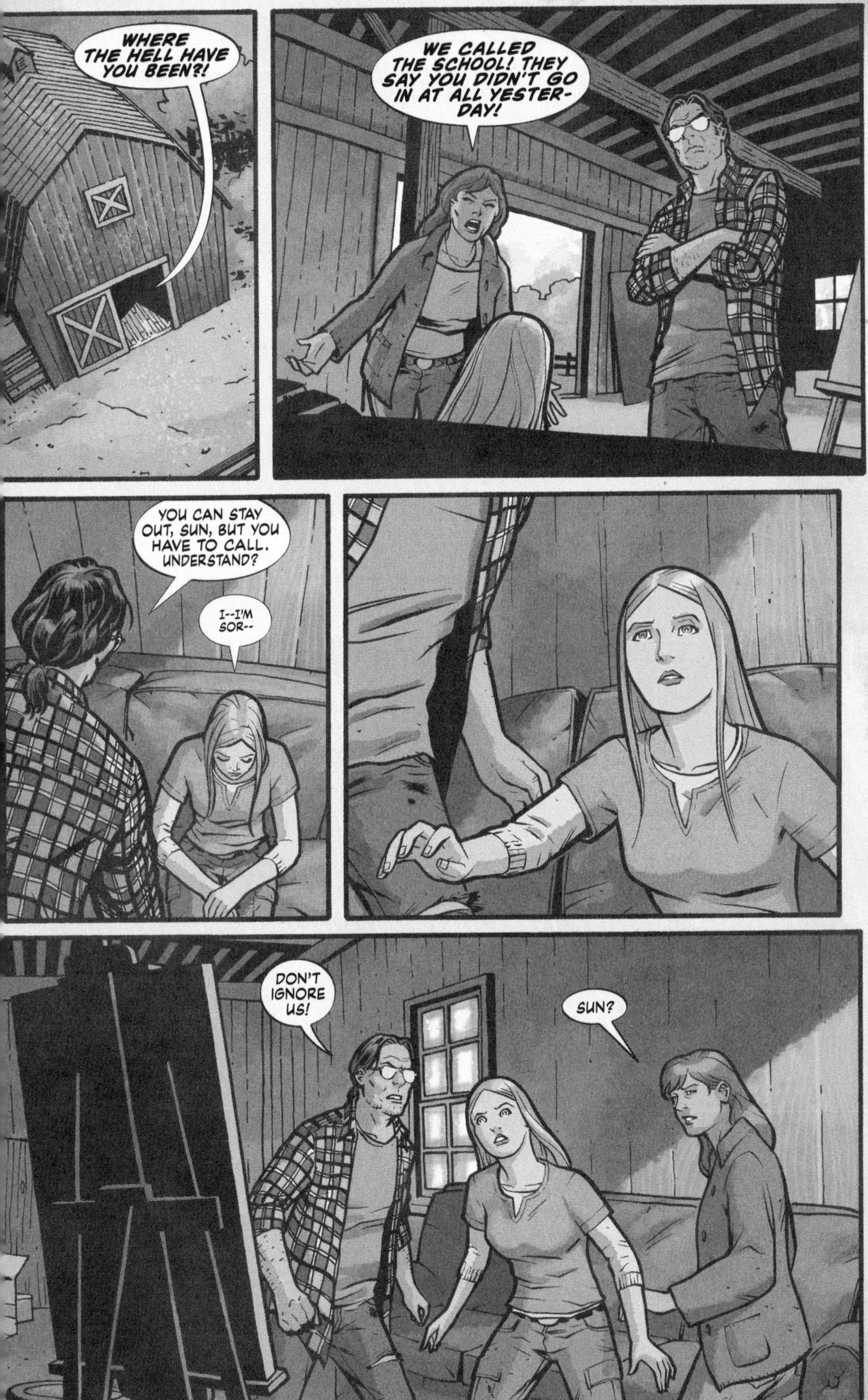
WHERE THE HELL HAVE YOU BEEN?!
WE CALLED THE SCHOOL! THEY SAY YOU DIDN'T GO IN AT ALL YESTER-DAY!
YOU CAN STAY OUT, SUN, BUT YOU HAVE TO CALL. UNDERSTAND?
I--I'M SOR--
DON'T IGNORE US!
SUN?

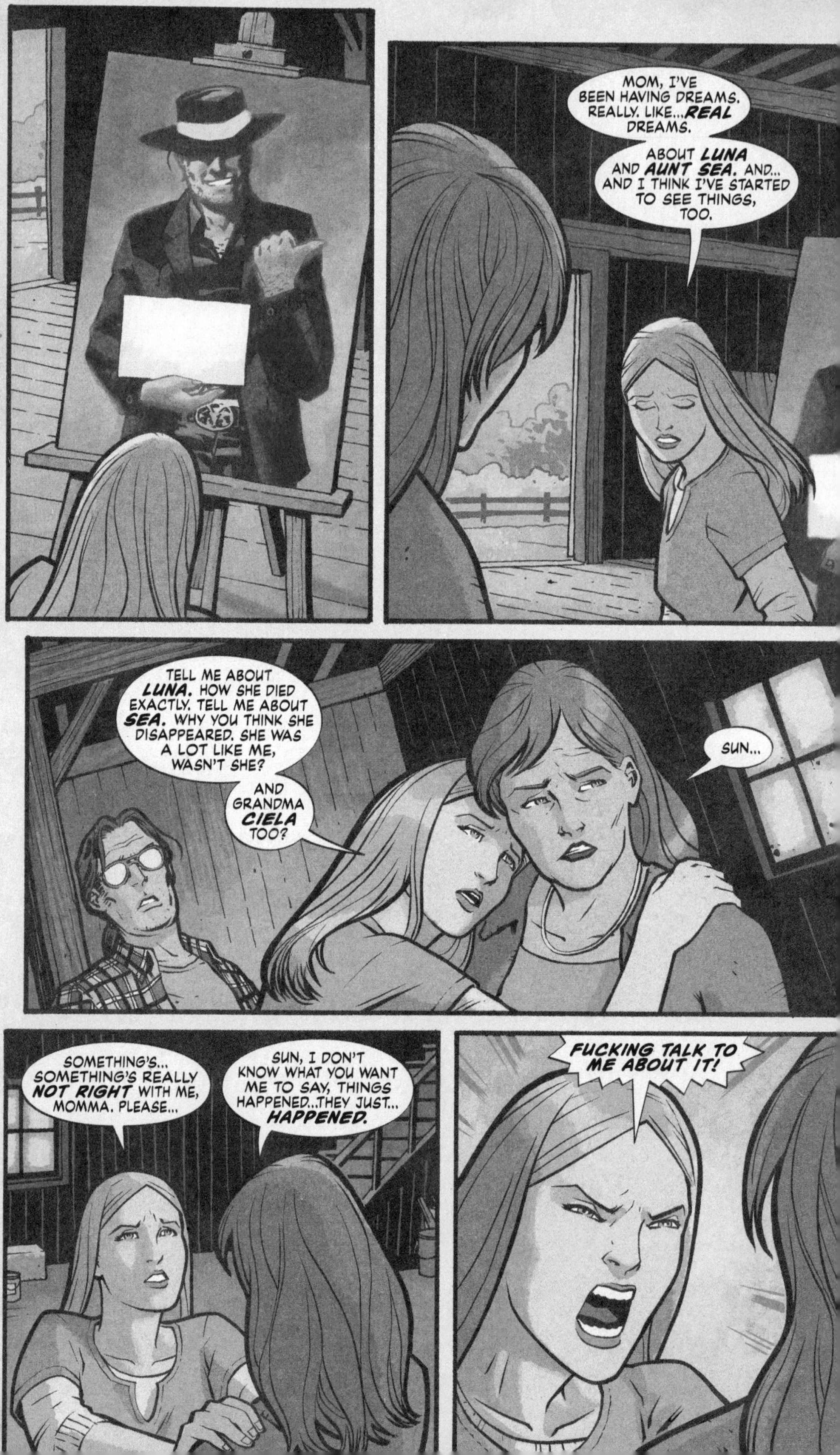

MOM, I'VE BEEN HAVING DREAMS. REALLY. LIKE... **REAL** DREAMS.
ABOUT **LUNA** AND **AUNT SEA.** AND... AND I THINK I'VE STARTED TO SEE THINGS, TOO.
TELL ME ABOUT **LUNA.** HOW SHE DIED EXACTLY. TELL ME ABOUT **SEA.** WHY YOU THINK SHE DISAPPEARED. SHE WAS A LOT LIKE ME, WASN'T SHE?
AND GRANDMA **CIELA** TOO?
SUN...
SOMETHING'S... SOMETHING'S REALLY **NOT RIGHT** WITH ME, MOMMA. PLEASE...
SUN, I DON'T KNOW WHAT YOU WANT ME TO SAY, THINGS HAPPENED... THEY JUST... **HAPPENED.**
FUCKING TALK TO ME ABOUT IT!

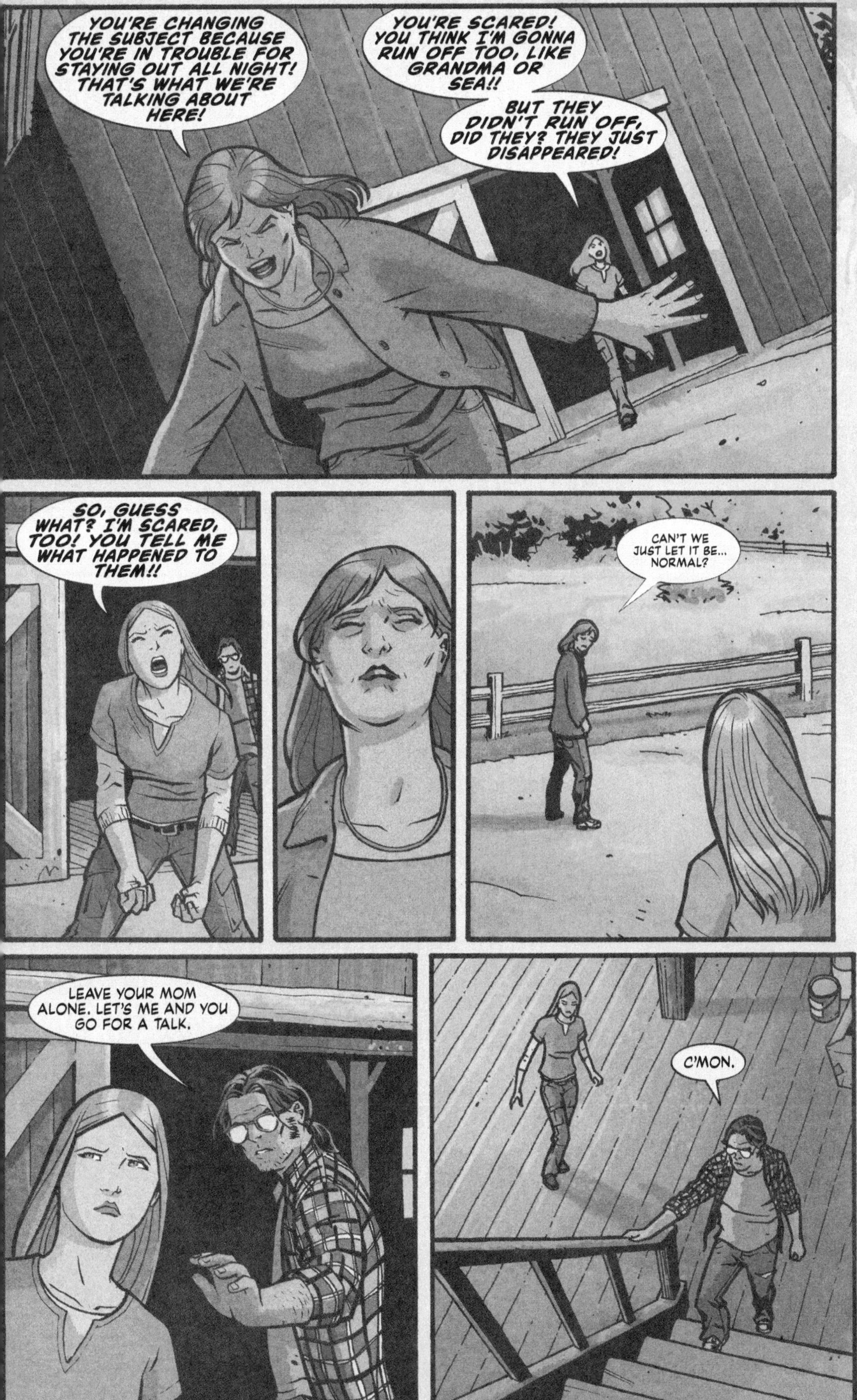
YOU'RE CHANGING THE SUBJECT BECAUSE YOU'RE IN TROUBLE FOR STAYING OUT ALL NIGHT! THAT'S WHAT WE'RE TALKING ABOUT HERE!
YOU'RE SCARED! YOU THINK I'M GONNA RUN OFF TOO, LIKE GRANDMA OR SEA!!
BUT THEY DIDN'T RUN OFF, DID THEY? THEY JUST DISAPPEARED!
SO, GUESS WHAT? I'M SCARED, TOO! YOU TELL ME WHAT HAPPENED TO THEM!!
CAN'T WE JUST LET IT BE... NORMAL?
LEAVE YOUR MOM ALONE. LET'S ME AND YOU GO FOR A TALK.
C'MON.

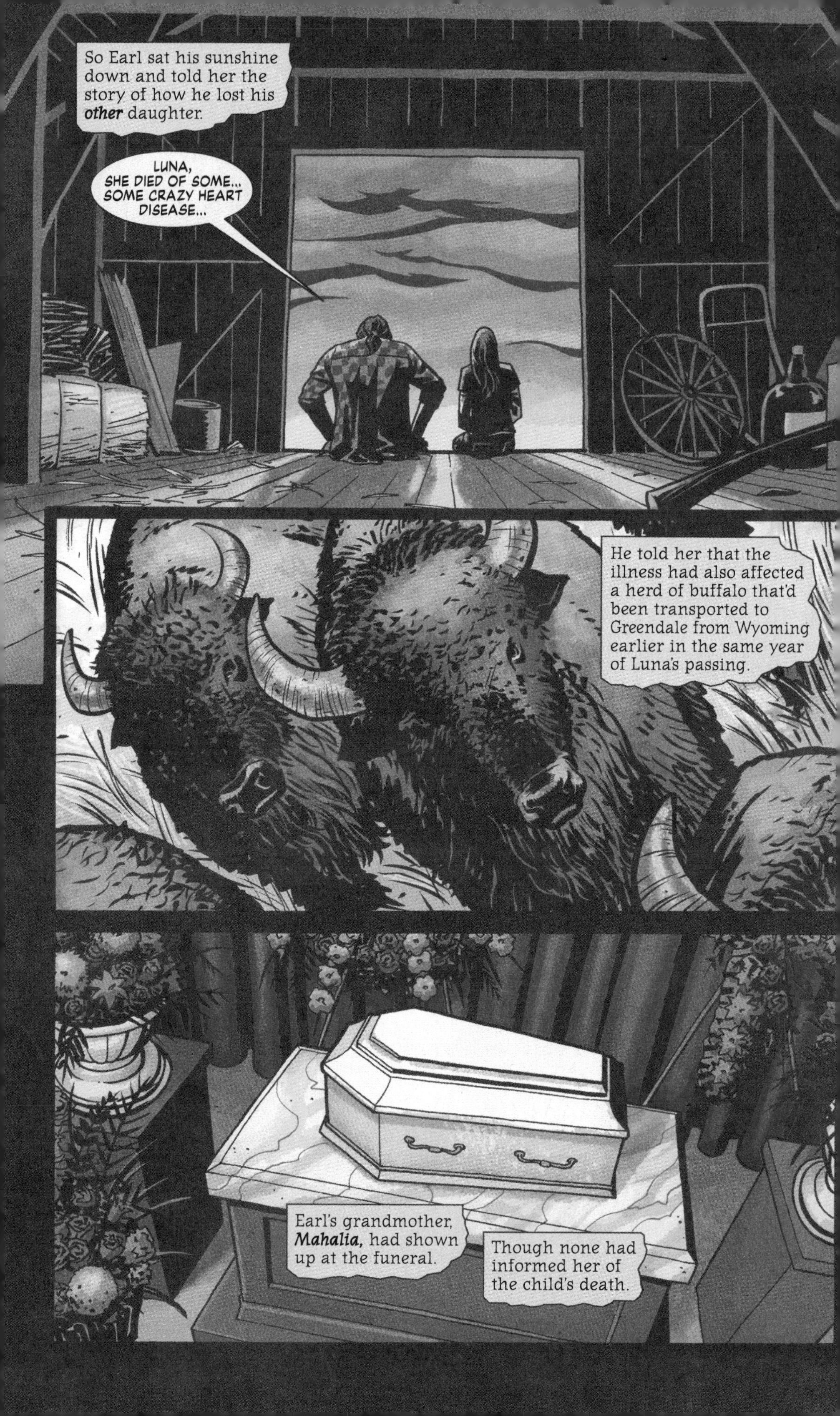
So Earl sat his sunshine down and told her the story of how he lost his *other* daughter.
LUNA, SHE DIED OF SOME... SOME CRAZY HEART DISEASE...
He told her that the illness had also affected a herd of buffalo that'd been transported to Greendale from Wyoming earlier in the same year of Luna's passing.
Earl's grandmother, *Mahalia,* had shown up at the funeral.
Though none had informed her of the child's death.

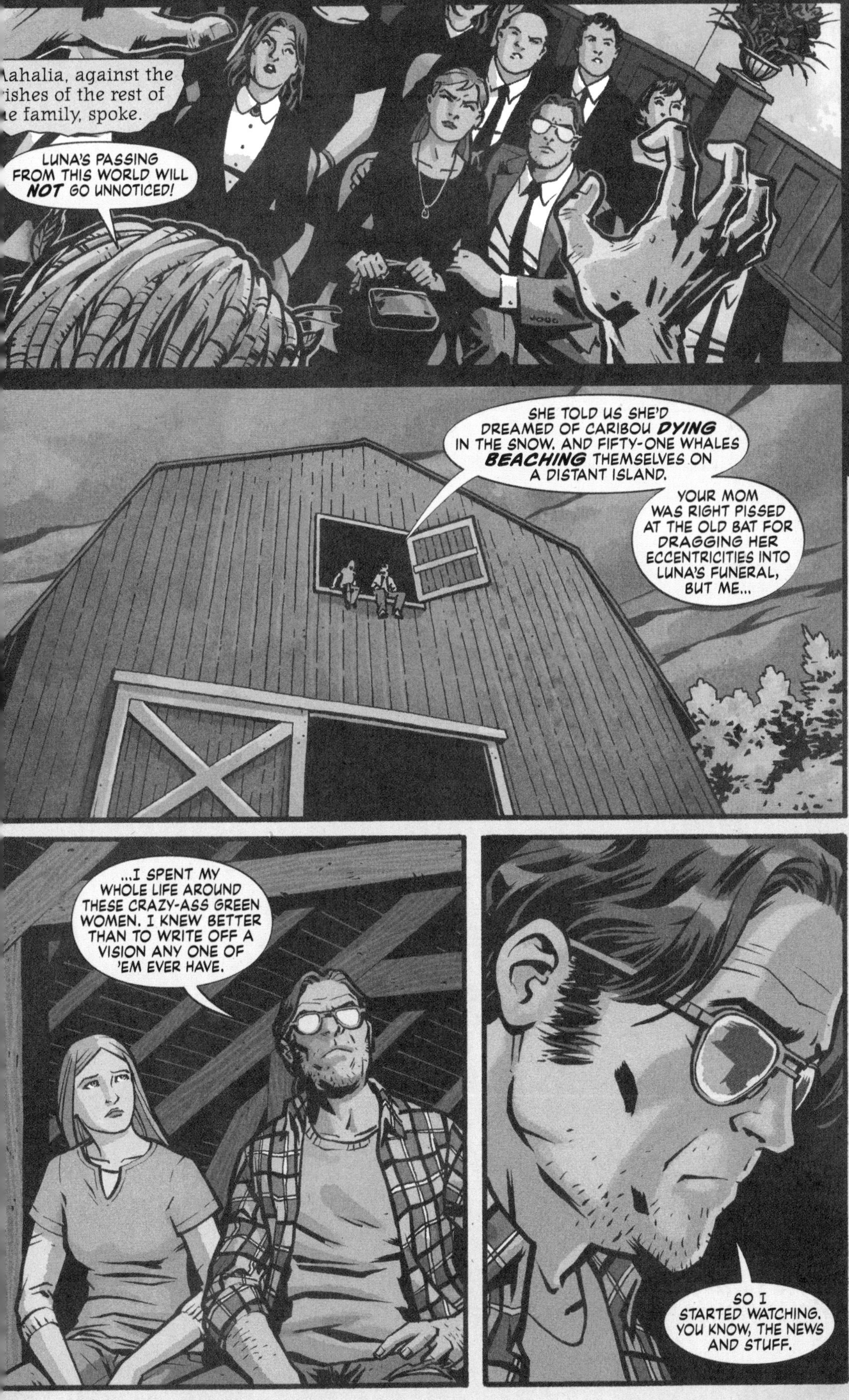
ahalia, against the ishes of the rest of e family, spoke.
LUNA'S PASSING FROM THIS WORLD WILL NOT GO UNNOTICED!
SHE TOLD US SHE'D DREAMED OF CARIBOU DYING IN THE SNOW. AND FIFTY-ONE WHALES BEACHING THEMSELVES ON A DISTANT ISLAND.
YOUR MOM WAS RIGHT PISSED AT THE OLD BAT FOR DRAGGING HER ECCENTRICITIES INTO LUNA'S FUNERAL, BUT ME...
...I SPENT MY WHOLE LIFE AROUND THESE CRAZY-ASS GREEN WOMEN. I KNEW BETTER THAN TO WRITE OFF A VISION ANY ONE OF 'EM EVER HAVE.
SO I STARTED WATCHING. YOU KNOW, THE NEWS AND STUFF.

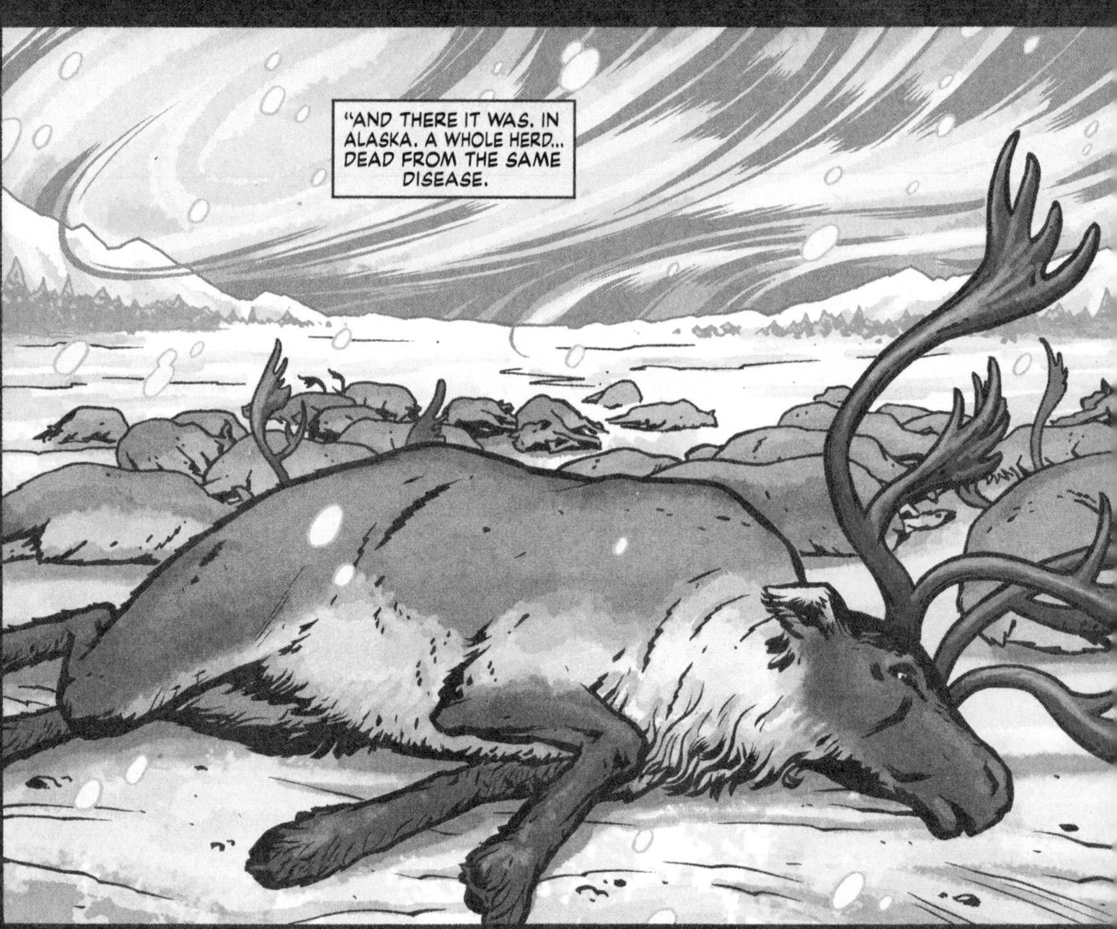
"AND THERE IT WAS. IN ALASKA. A WHOLE HERD... DEAD FROM THE SAME DISEASE.

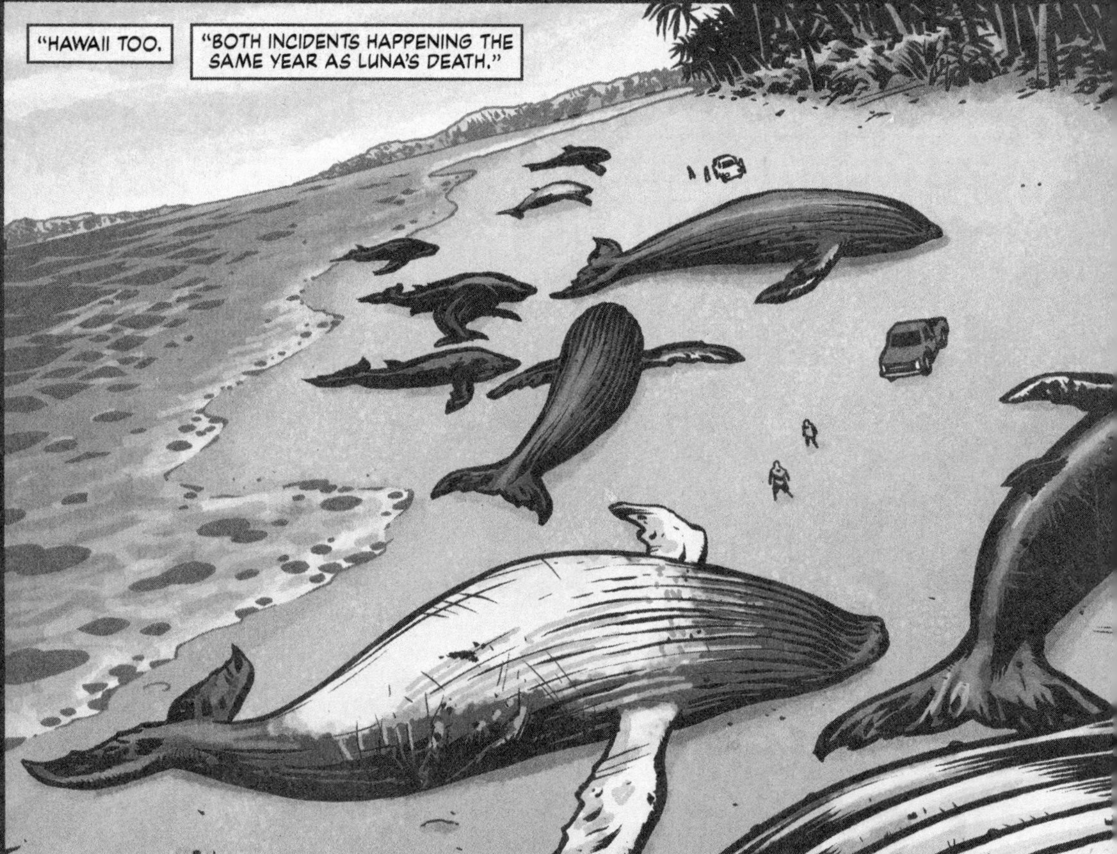
"HAWAII TOO.
"BOTH INCIDENTS HAPPENING THE SAME YEAR AS LUNA'S DEATH."

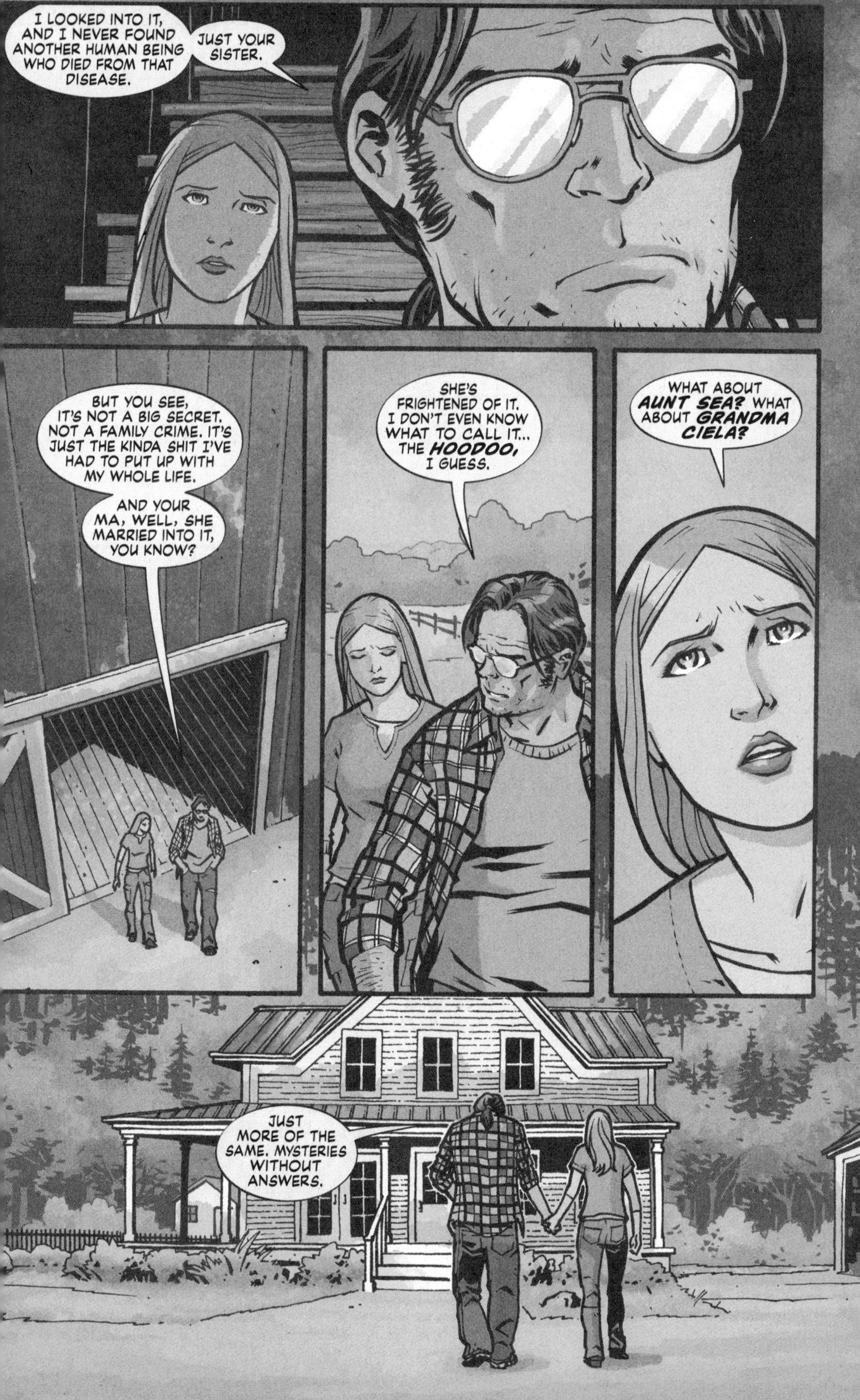

I LOOKED INTO IT, AND I NEVER FOUND ANOTHER HUMAN BEING WHO DIED FROM THAT DISEASE.
JUST YOUR SISTER.
BUT YOU SEE, IT'S NOT A BIG SECRET. NOT A FAMILY CRIME. IT'S JUST THE KINDA SHIT I'VE HAD TO PUT UP WITH MY WHOLE LIFE.
AND YOUR MA, WELL, SHE MARRIED INTO IT, YOU KNOW?
SHE'S FRIGHTENED OF IT. I DON'T EVEN KNOW WHAT TO CALL IT... THE HOODOO, I GUESS.
WHAT ABOUT AUNT SEA? WHAT ABOUT GRANDMA CIELA?
JUST MORE OF THE SAME. MYSTERIES WITHOUT ANSWERS.

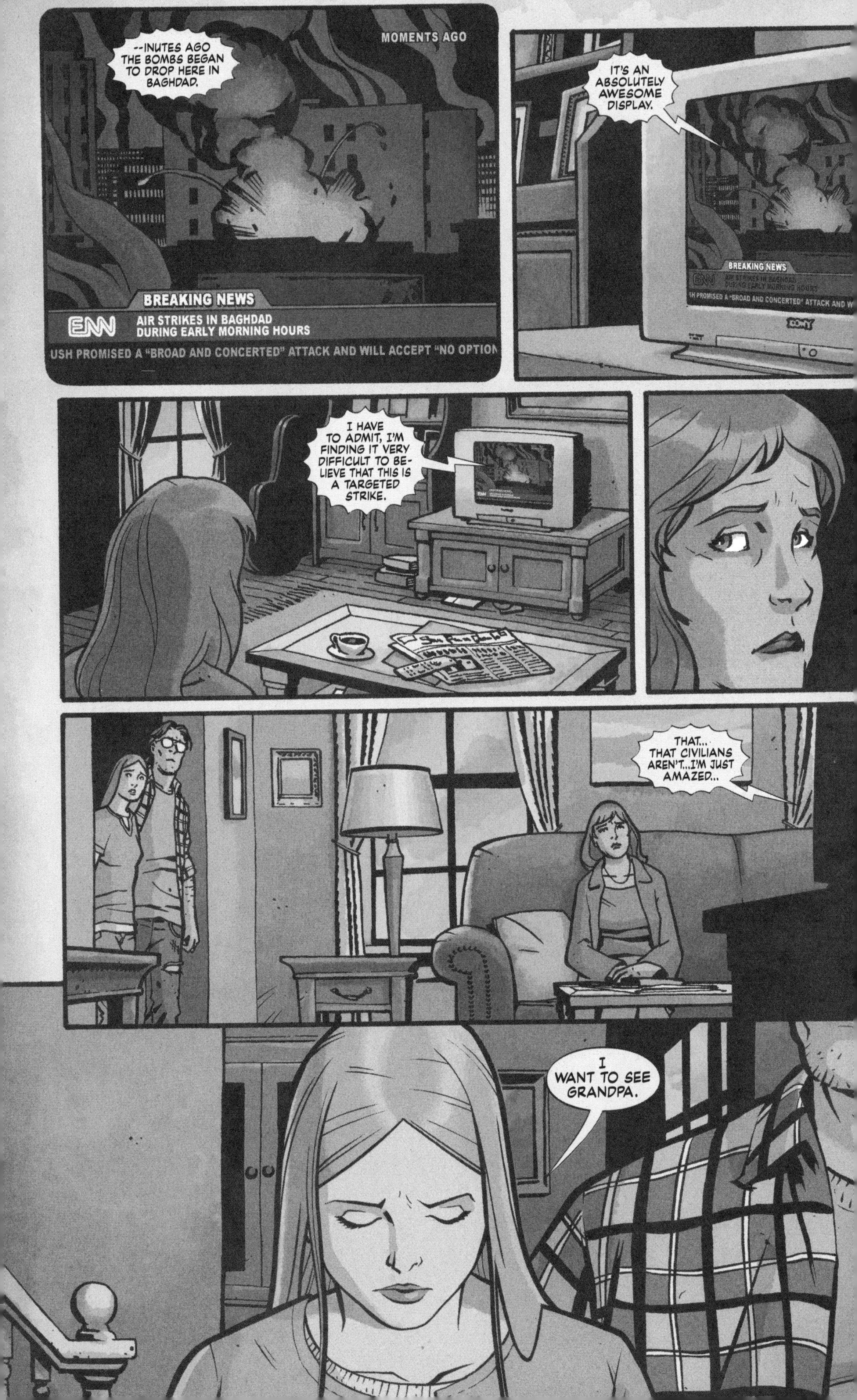
MOMENTS AGO
--INUTES AGO THE BOMBS BEGAN TO DROP HERE IN BAGHDAD.
BREAKING NEWS
ENN
AIR STRIKES IN BAGHDAD
DURING EARLY MORNING HOURS
USH PROMISED A "BROAD AND CONCERTED" ATTACK AND WILL ACCEPT "NO OPTION
IT'S AN ABSOLUTELY AWESOME DISPLAY.
BREAKING NEWS
I HAVE TO ADMIT, I'M FINDING IT VERY DIFFICULT TO BE-LIEVE THAT THIS IS A TARGETED STRIKE.
THAT... THAT CIVILIANS AREN'T...I'M JUST AMAZED...
I WANT TO SEE GRANDPA.

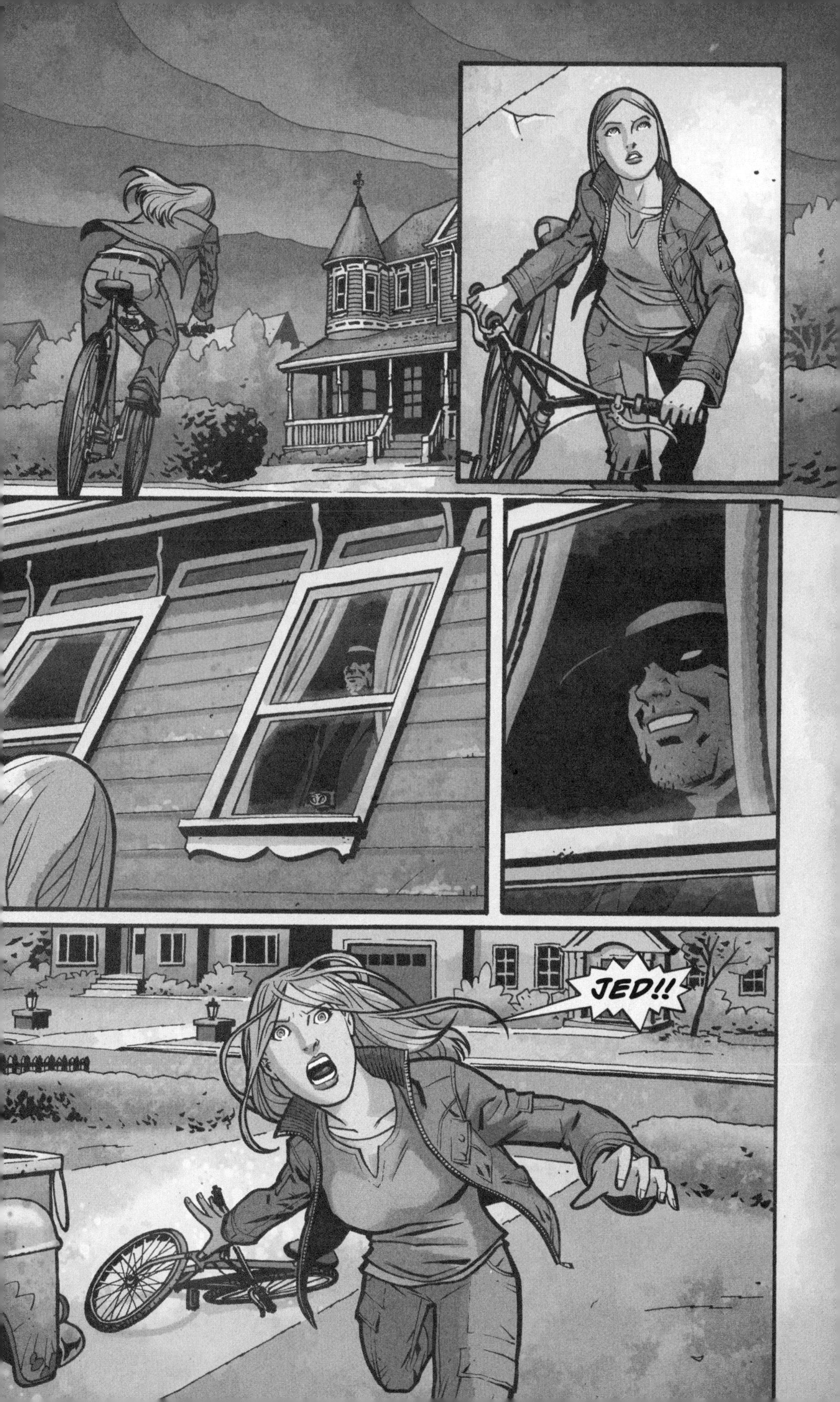
JED!!

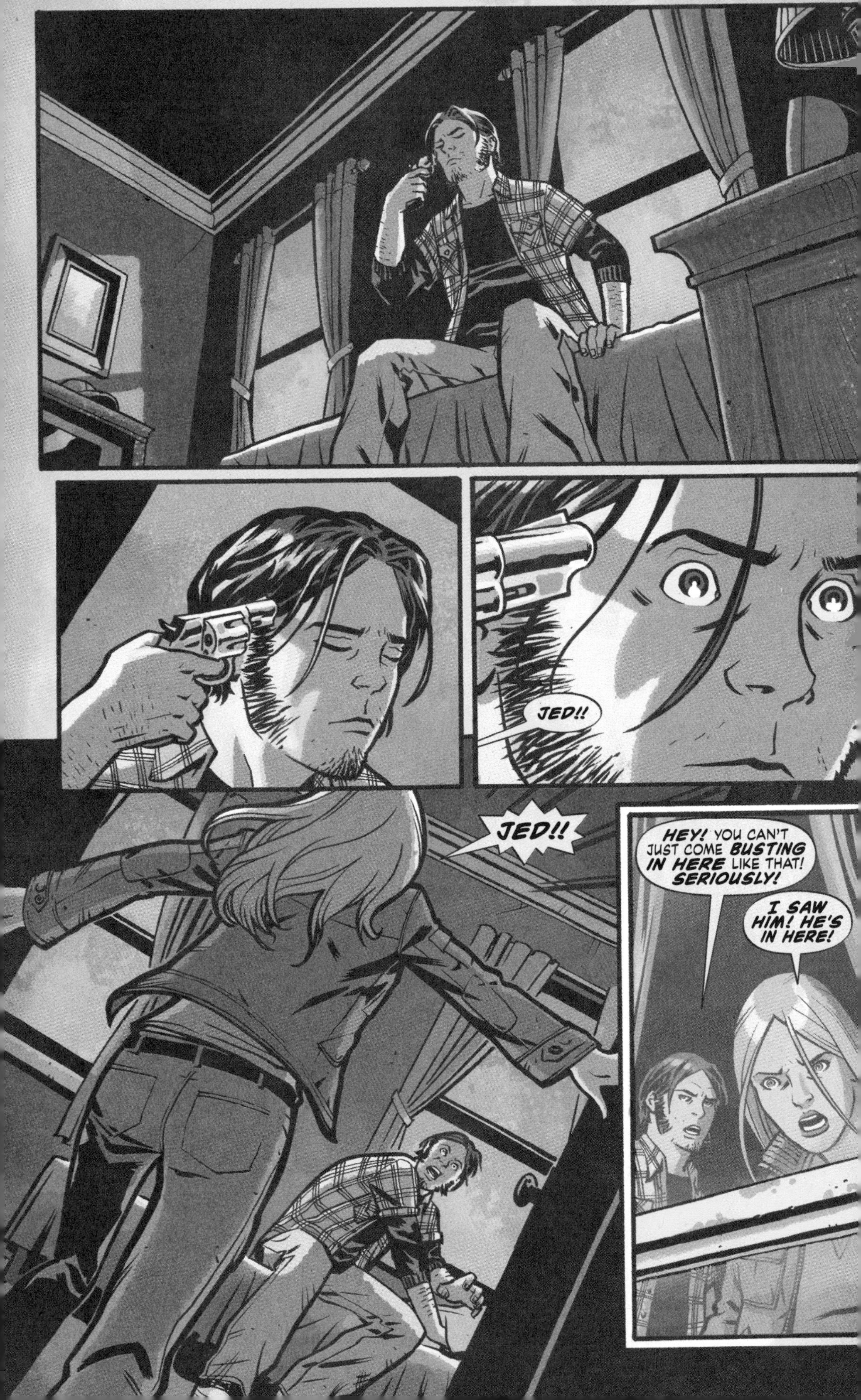
JED!!
JED!!
HEY! YOU CAN'T JUST COME BUSTING IN HERE LIKE THAT! SERIOUSLY!
I SAW HIM! HE'S IN HERE!

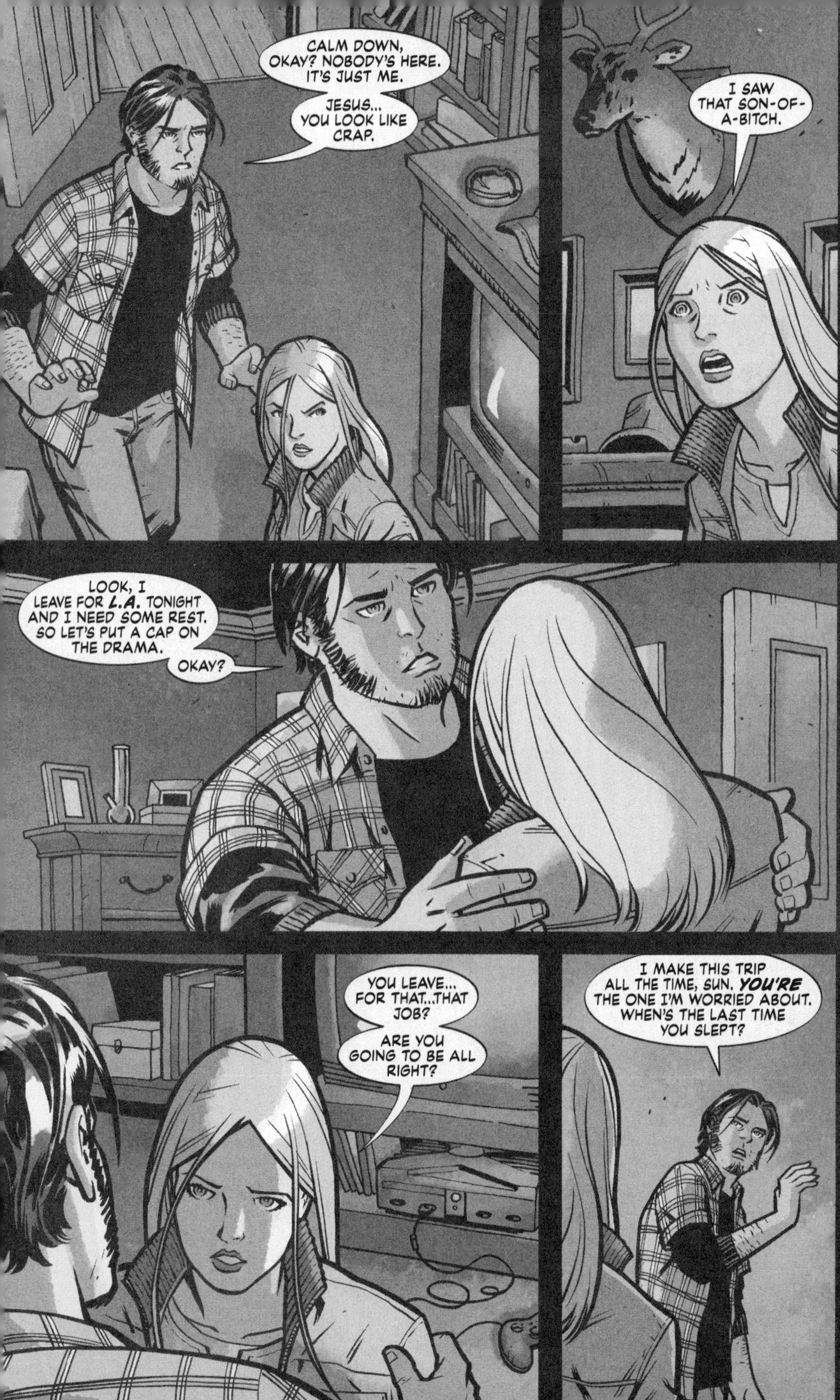

CALM DOWN, OKAY? NOBODY'S HERE. IT'S JUST ME.
JESUS... YOU LOOK LIKE CRAP.
I SAW THAT SON-OF-A-BITCH.
LOOK, I LEAVE FOR *L.A.* TONIGHT AND I NEED SOME REST. SO LET'S PUT A CAP ON THE DRAMA.
OKAY?
YOU LEAVE... FOR THAT...THAT JOB?
ARE YOU GOING TO BE ALL RIGHT?
I MAKE THIS TRIP ALL THE TIME, SUN. ***YOU'RE*** THE ONE I'M WORRIED ABOUT. WHEN'S THE LAST TIME YOU SLEPT?

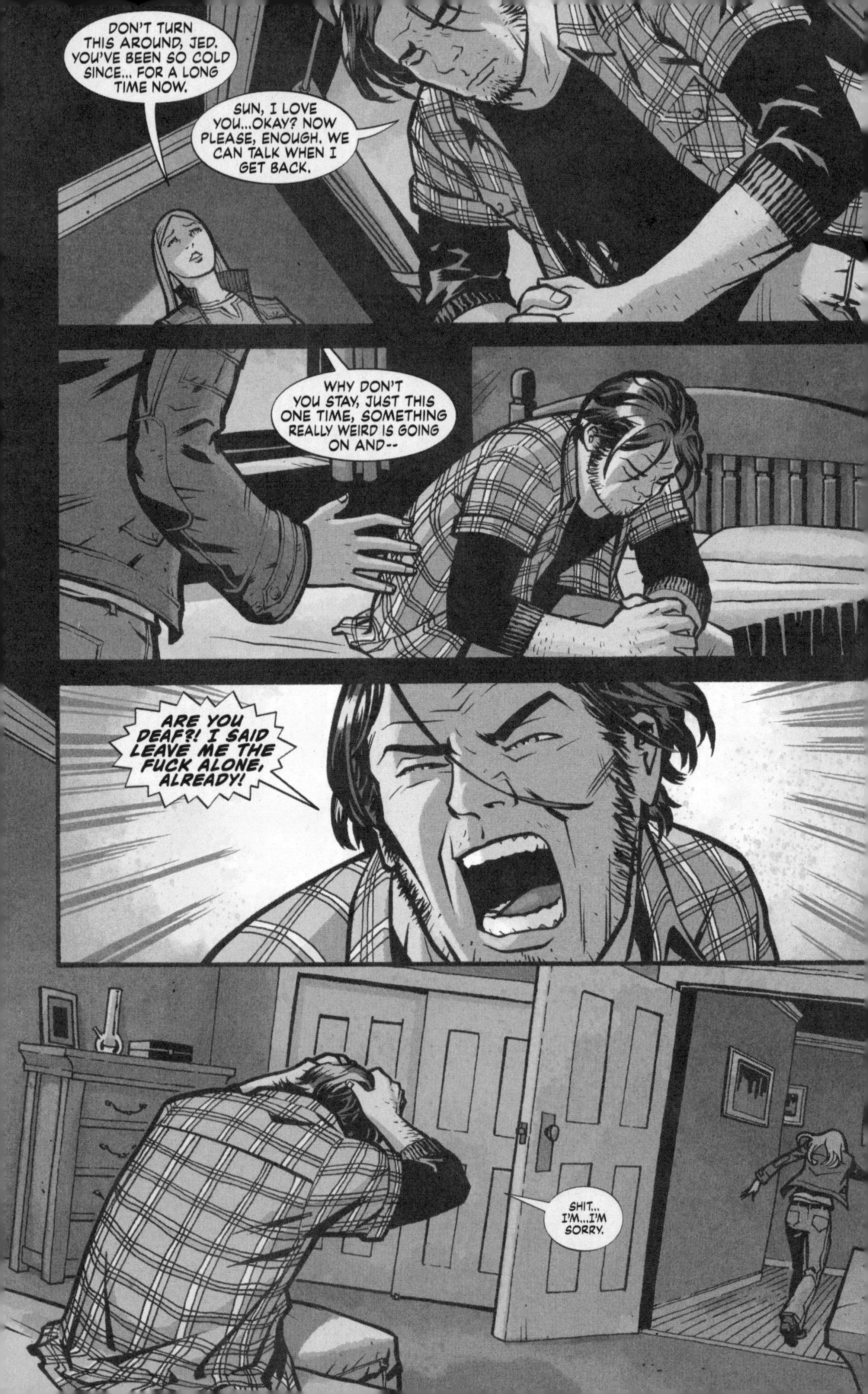
DON'T TURN THIS AROUND, JED. YOU'VE BEEN SO COLD SINCE... FOR A LONG TIME NOW.
SUN, I LOVE YOU...OKAY? NOW PLEASE, ENOUGH. WE CAN TALK WHEN I GET BACK.
WHY DON'T YOU STAY, JUST THIS ONE TIME, SOMETHING REALLY WEIRD IS GOING ON AND--
ARE YOU DEAF?! I SAID LEAVE ME THE FUCK ALONE, ALREADY!
SHIT... I'M...I'M SORRY.

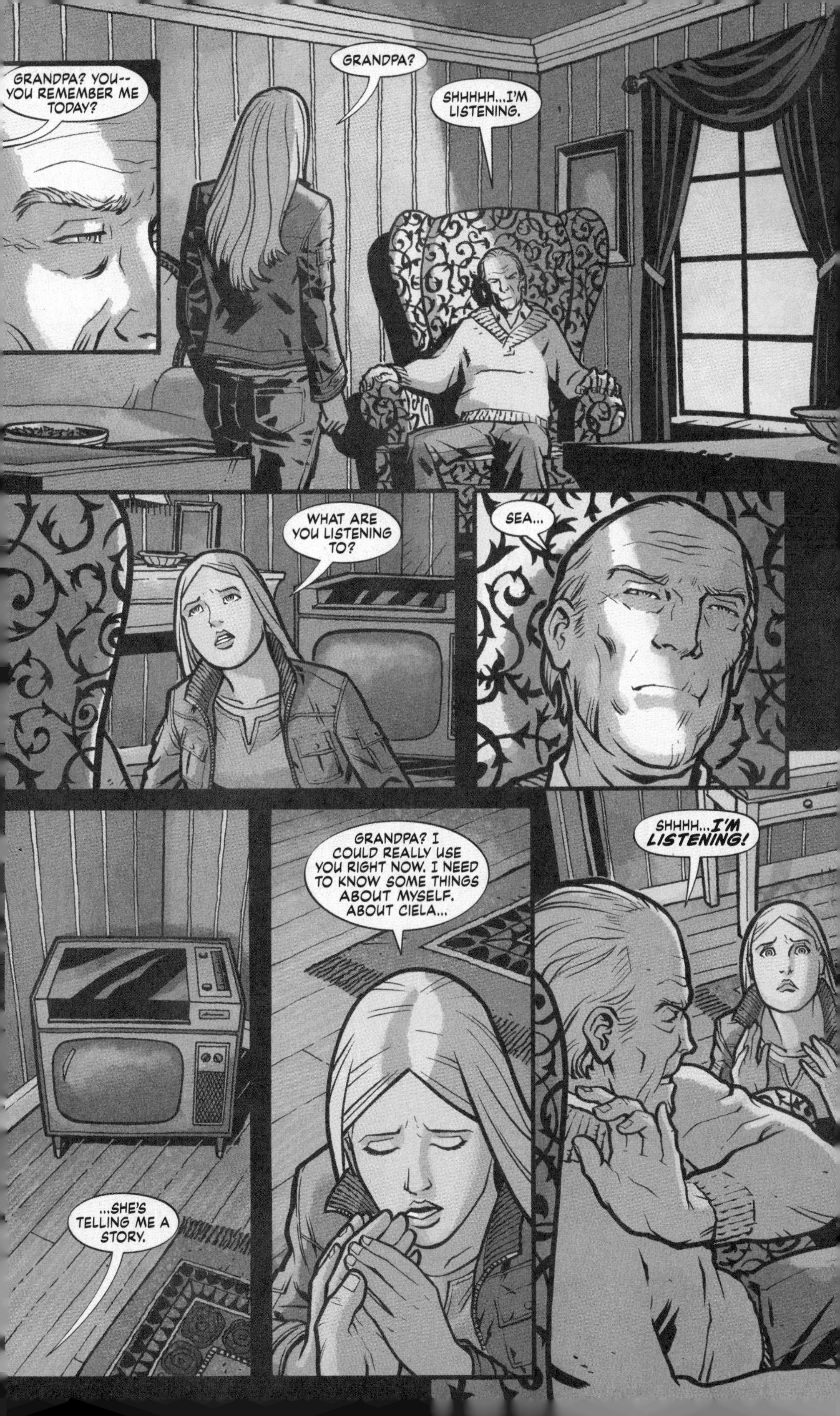
GRANDPA?
GRANDPA? YOU-- YOU REMEMBER ME TODAY?
SHHHHH...I'M LISTENING.
WHAT ARE YOU LISTENING TO?
SEA...
...SHE'S TELLING ME A STORY.
GRANDPA? I COULD REALLY USE YOU RIGHT NOW. I NEED TO KNOW SOME THINGS ABOUT MYSELF. ABOUT CIELA...
SHHHH...I'M LISTENING!

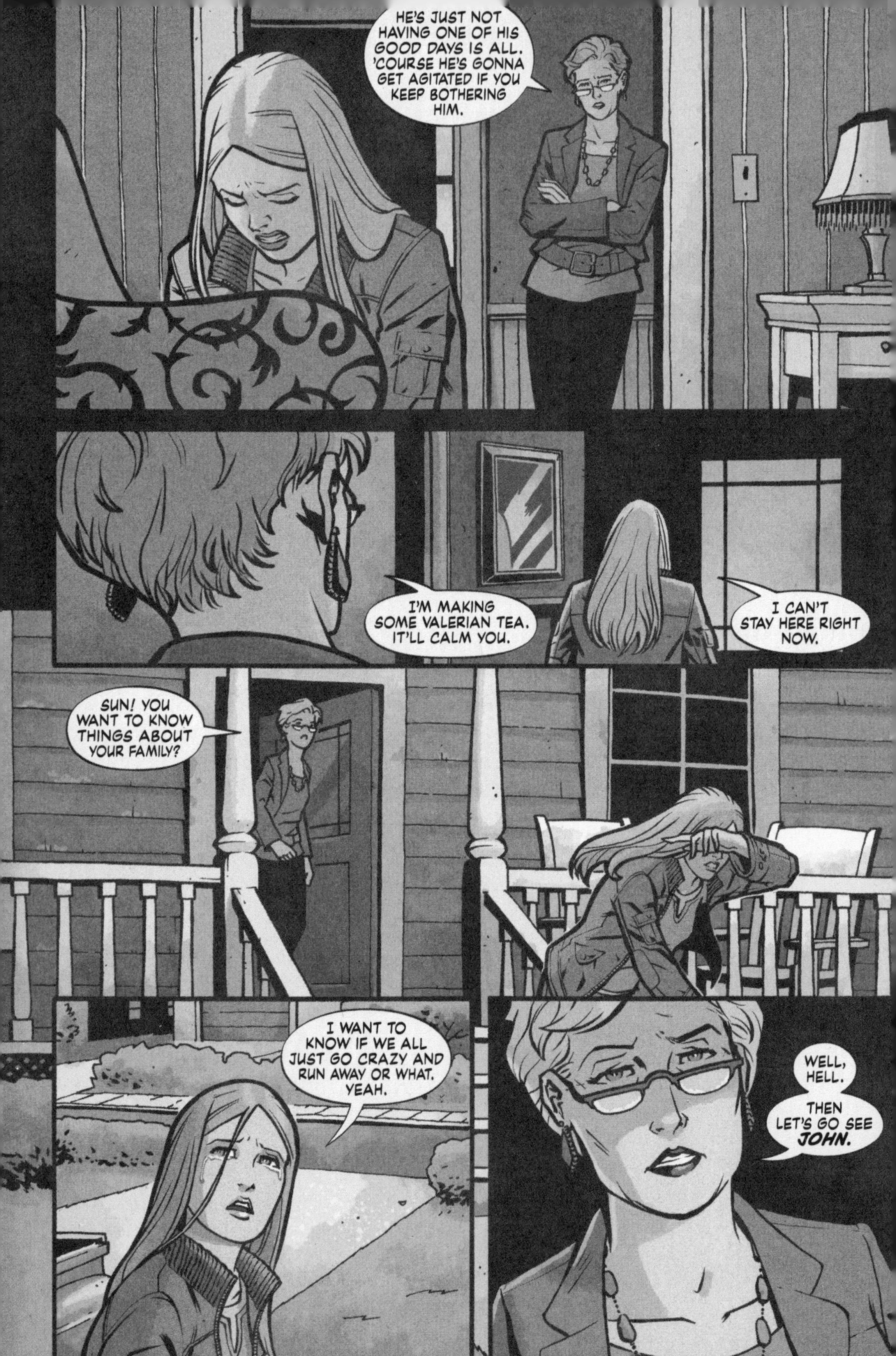
HE'S JUST NOT HAVING ONE OF HIS GOOD DAYS IS ALL. 'COURSE HE'S GONNA GET AGITATED IF YOU KEEP BOTHERING HIM.
I'M MAKING SOME VALERIAN TEA. IT'LL CALM YOU.
I CAN'T STAY HERE RIGHT NOW.
SUN! YOU WANT TO KNOW THINGS ABOUT YOUR FAMILY?
I WANT TO KNOW IF WE ALL JUST GO CRAZY AND RUN AWAY OR WHAT. YEAH.
WELL, HELL.
THEN LET'S GO SEE JOHN.

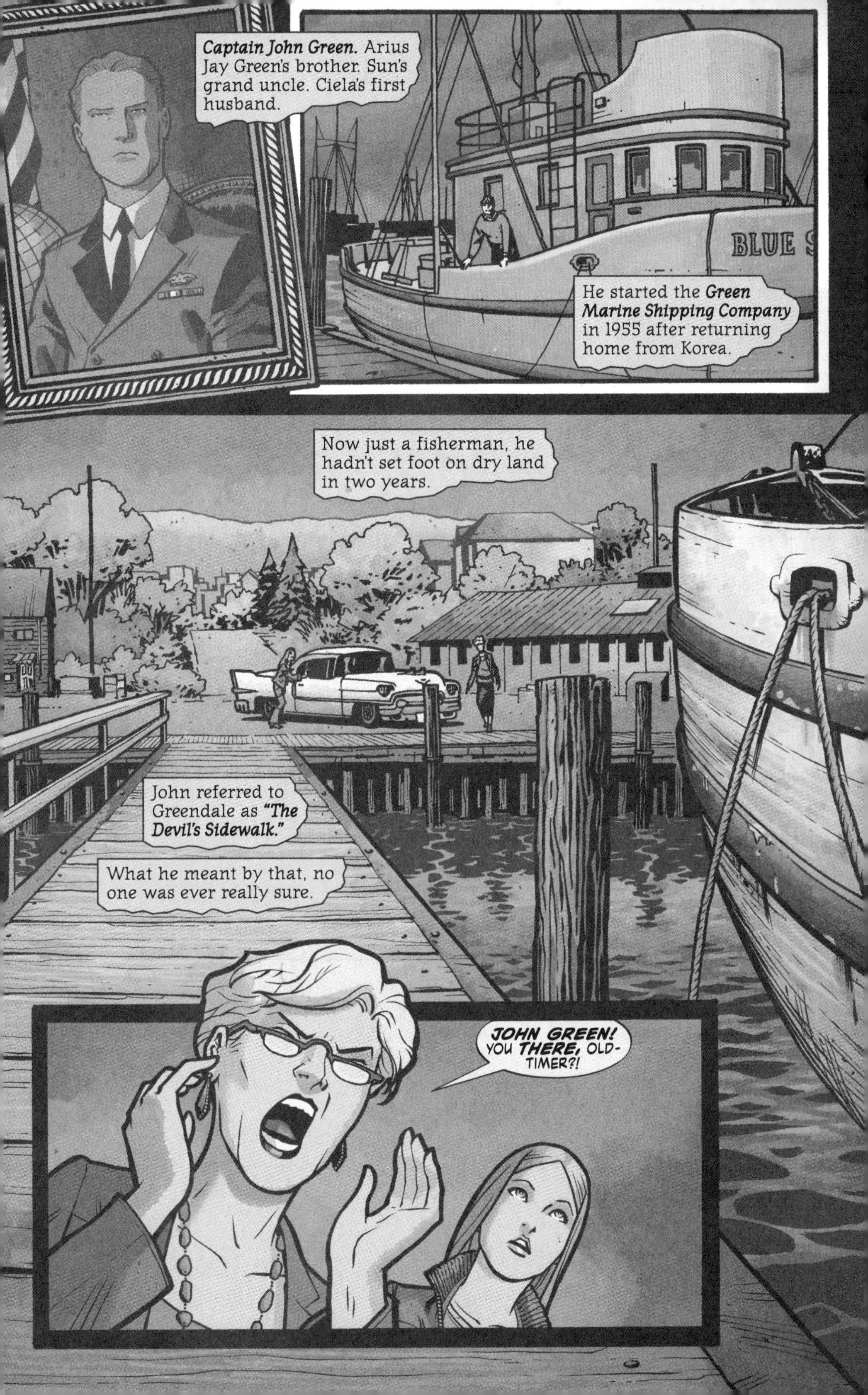

Captain John Green. Arius Jay Green's brother. Sun's grand uncle. Ciela's first husband.
BLUE S
He started the Green Marine Shipping Company in 1955 after returning home from Korea.
Now just a fisherman, he hadn't set foot on dry land in two years.
John referred to Greendale as "The Devil's Sidewalk."
What he meant by that, no one was ever really sure.
JOHN GREEN! YOU THERE, OLD-TIMER?!

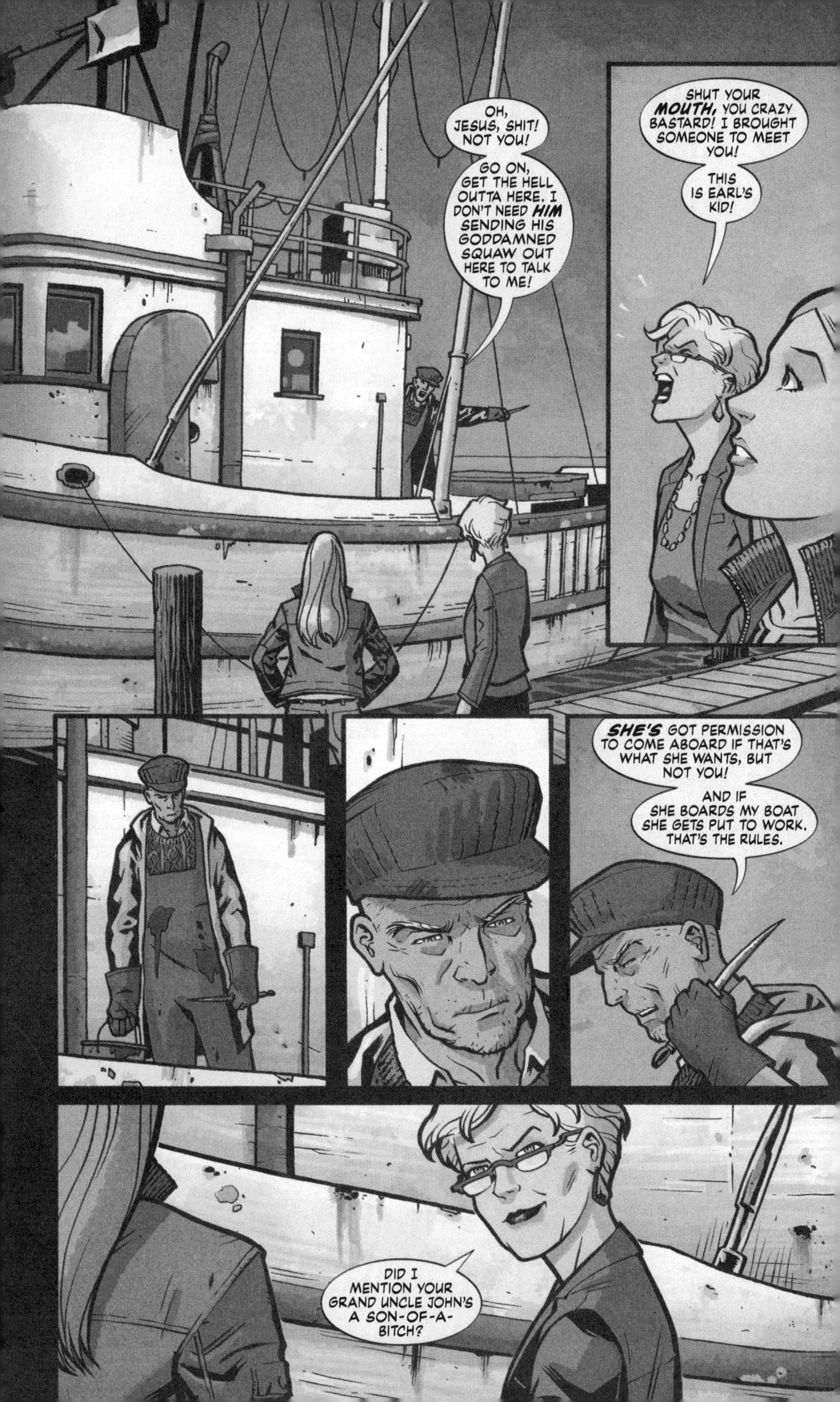
OH, JESUS, SHIT! NOT YOU!
GO ON, GET THE HELL OUTTA HERE. I DON'T NEED HIM SENDING HIS GODDAMNED SQUAW OUT HERE TO TALK TO ME!
SHUT YOUR MOUTH, YOU CRAZY BASTARD! I BROUGHT SOMEONE TO MEET YOU!
THIS IS EARL'S KID!
SHE'S GOT PERMISSION TO COME ABOARD IF THAT'S WHAT SHE WANTS, BUT NOT YOU!
AND IF SHE BOARDS MY BOAT SHE GETS PUT TO WORK. THAT'S THE RULES.
DID I MENTION YOUR GRAND UNCLE JOHN'S A SON-OF-A-BITCH?

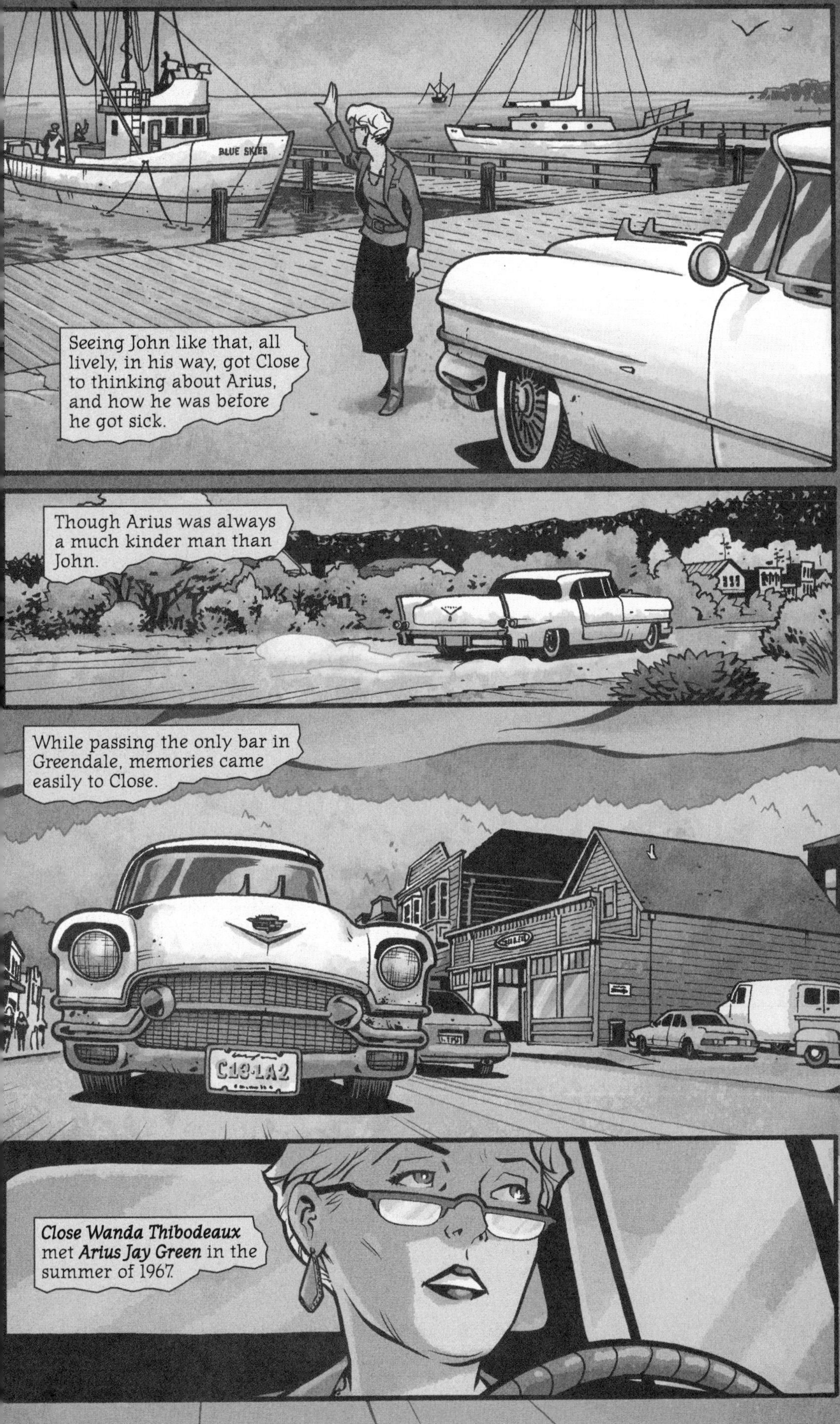
BLUE SKIES
Seeing John like that, all lively, in his way, got Close to thinking about Arius, and how he was before he got sick.
Though Arius was always a much kinder man than John.
While passing the only bar in Greendale, memories came easily to Close.
C13-LA2
Close Wanda Thibodeaux met *Arius Jay Green* in the summer of 1967.

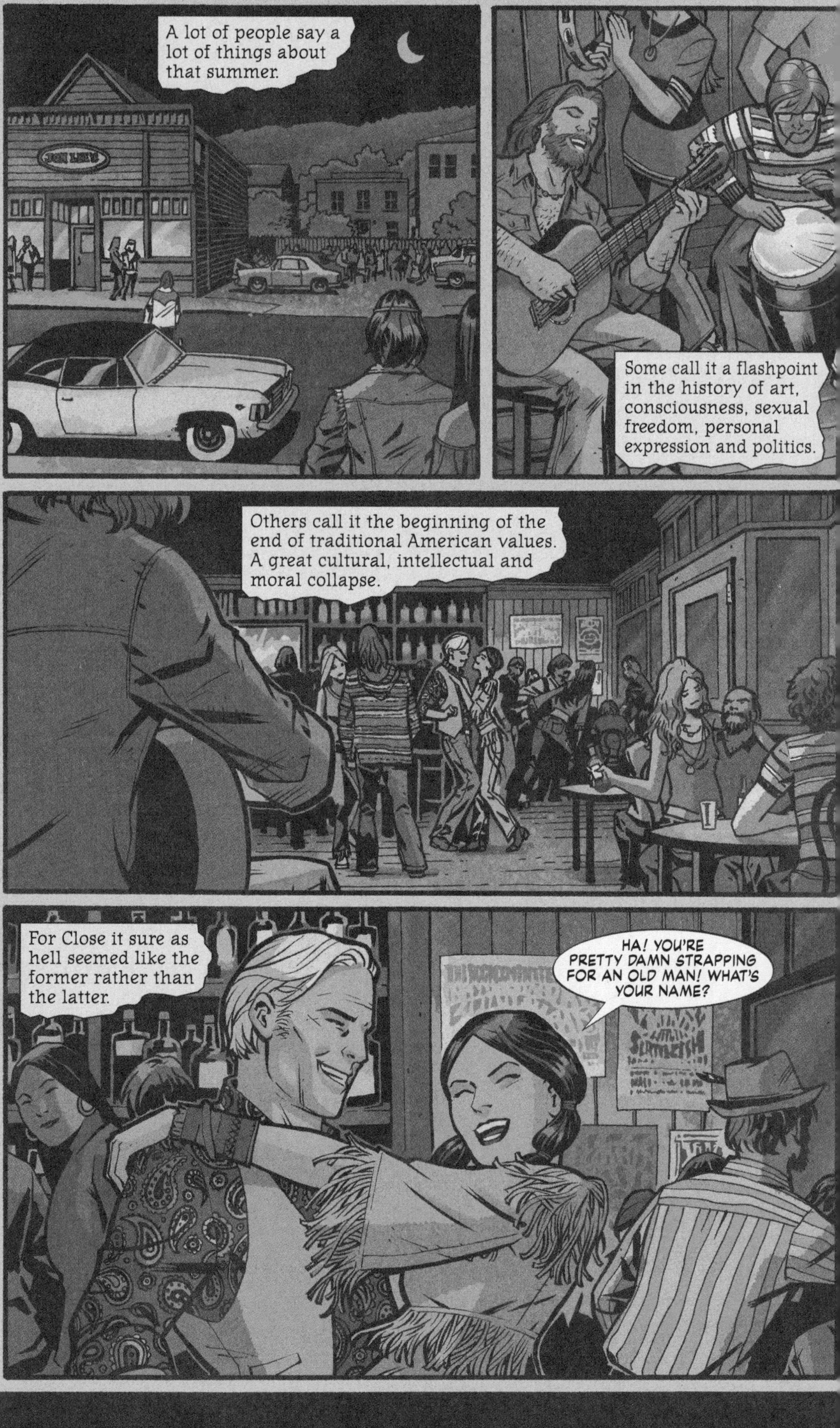
A lot of people say a lot of things about that summer.
Some call it a flashpoint in the history of art, consciousness, sexual freedom, personal expression and politics.
Others call it the beginning of the end of traditional American values. A great cultural, intellectual and moral collapse.
For Close it sure as hell seemed like the former rather than the latter.
HA! YOU'RE PRETTY DAMN STRAPPING FOR AN OLD MAN! WHAT'S YOUR NAME?

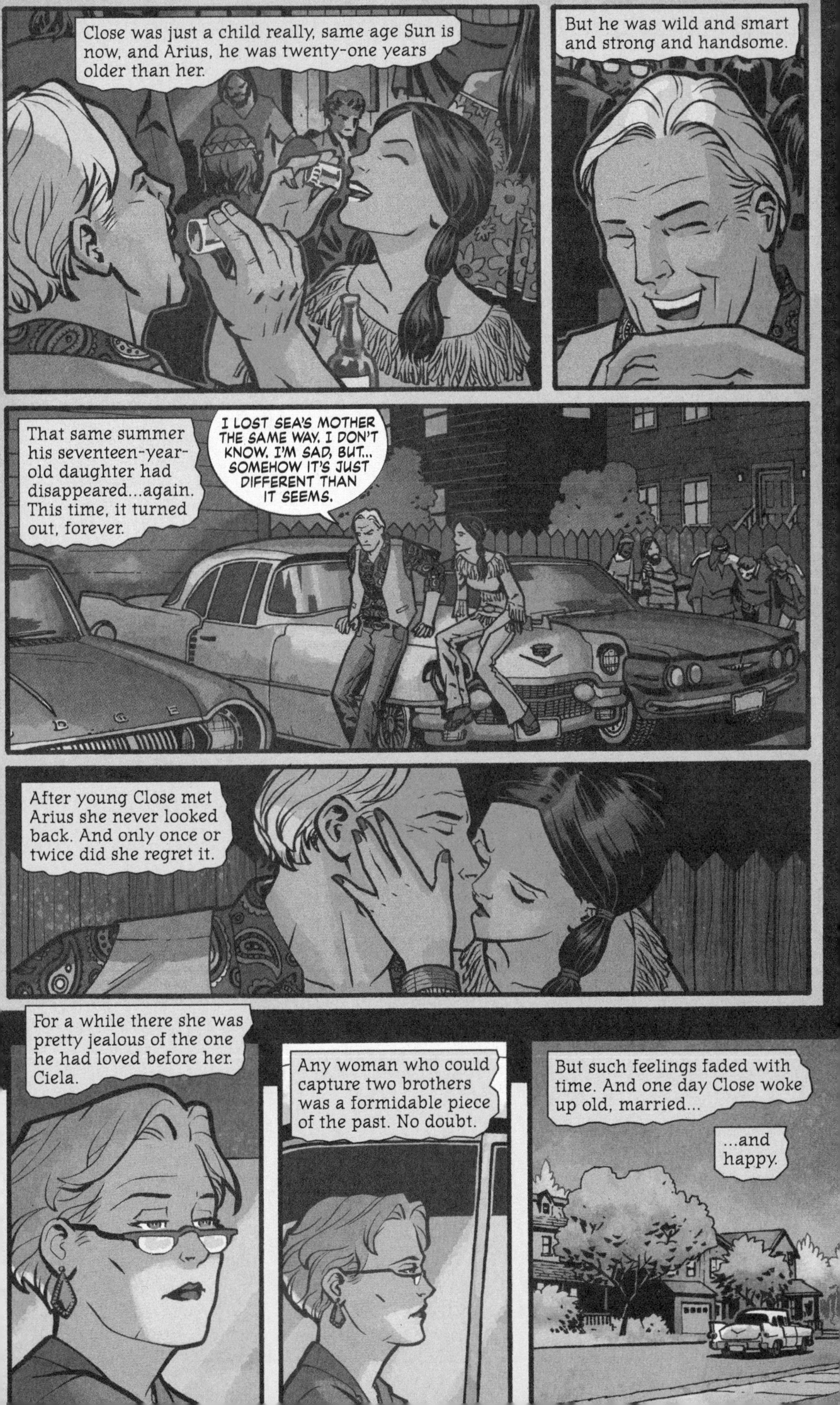
Close was just a child really, same age Sun is now, and Arius, he was twenty-one years older than her.
But he was wild and smart and strong and handsome.
That same summer his seventeen-year-old daughter had disappeared...again. This time, it turned out, forever.
I LOST SEA'S MOTHER THE SAME WAY. I DON'T KNOW. I'M SAD, BUT... SOMEHOW IT'S JUST DIFFERENT THAN IT SEEMS.
After young Close met Arius she never looked back. And only once or twice did she regret it.
For a while there she was pretty jealous of the one he had loved before her. Ciela.
Any woman who could capture two brothers was a formidable piece of the past. No doubt.
But such feelings faded with time. And one day Close woke up old, married...
...and happy.

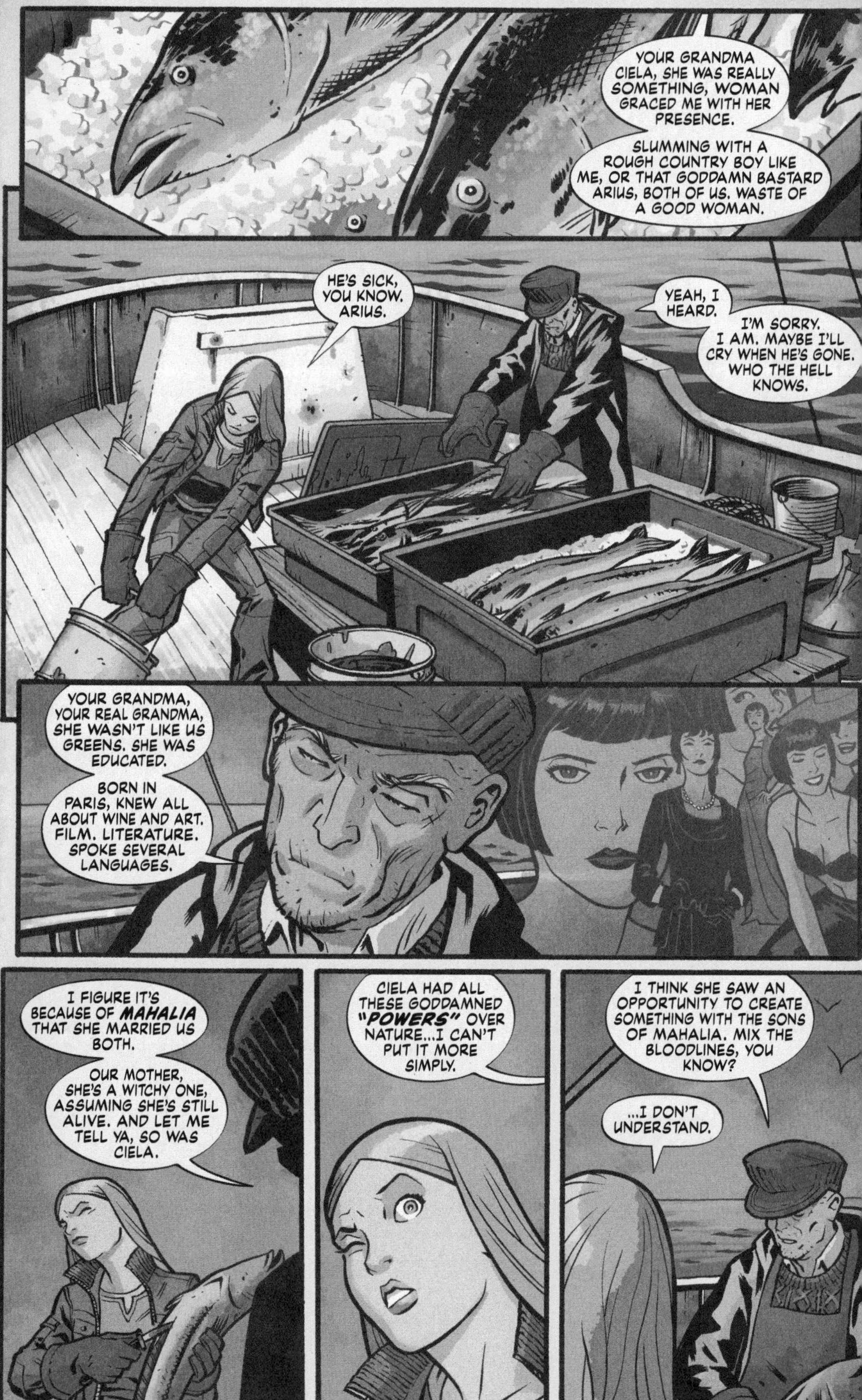
YOUR GRANDMA CIELA, SHE WAS REALLY SOMETHING, WOMAN GRACED ME WITH HER PRESENCE.
SLUMMING WITH A ROUGH COUNTRY BOY LIKE ME, OR THAT GODDAMN BASTARD ARIUS, BOTH OF US. WASTE OF A GOOD WOMAN.
HE'S SICK, YOU KNOW. ARIUS.
YEAH, I HEARD.
I'M SORRY. I AM. MAYBE I'LL CRY WHEN HE'S GONE. WHO THE HELL KNOWS.
YOUR GRANDMA, YOUR REAL GRANDMA, SHE WASN'T LIKE US GREENS. SHE WAS EDUCATED.
BORN IN PARIS, KNEW ALL ABOUT WINE AND ART. FILM. LITERATURE. SPOKE SEVERAL LANGUAGES.
I FIGURE IT'S BECAUSE OF MAHALIA THAT SHE MARRIED US BOTH.
OUR MOTHER, SHE'S A WITCHY ONE, ASSUMING SHE'S STILL ALIVE. AND LET ME TELL YA, SO WAS CIELA.
CIELA HAD ALL THESE GODDAMNED "POWERS" OVER NATURE...I CAN'T PUT IT MORE SIMPLY.
I THINK SHE SAW AN OPPORTUNITY TO CREATE SOMETHING WITH THE SONS OF MAHALIA. MIX THE BLOODLINES, YOU KNOW?
...I DON'T UNDERSTAND.

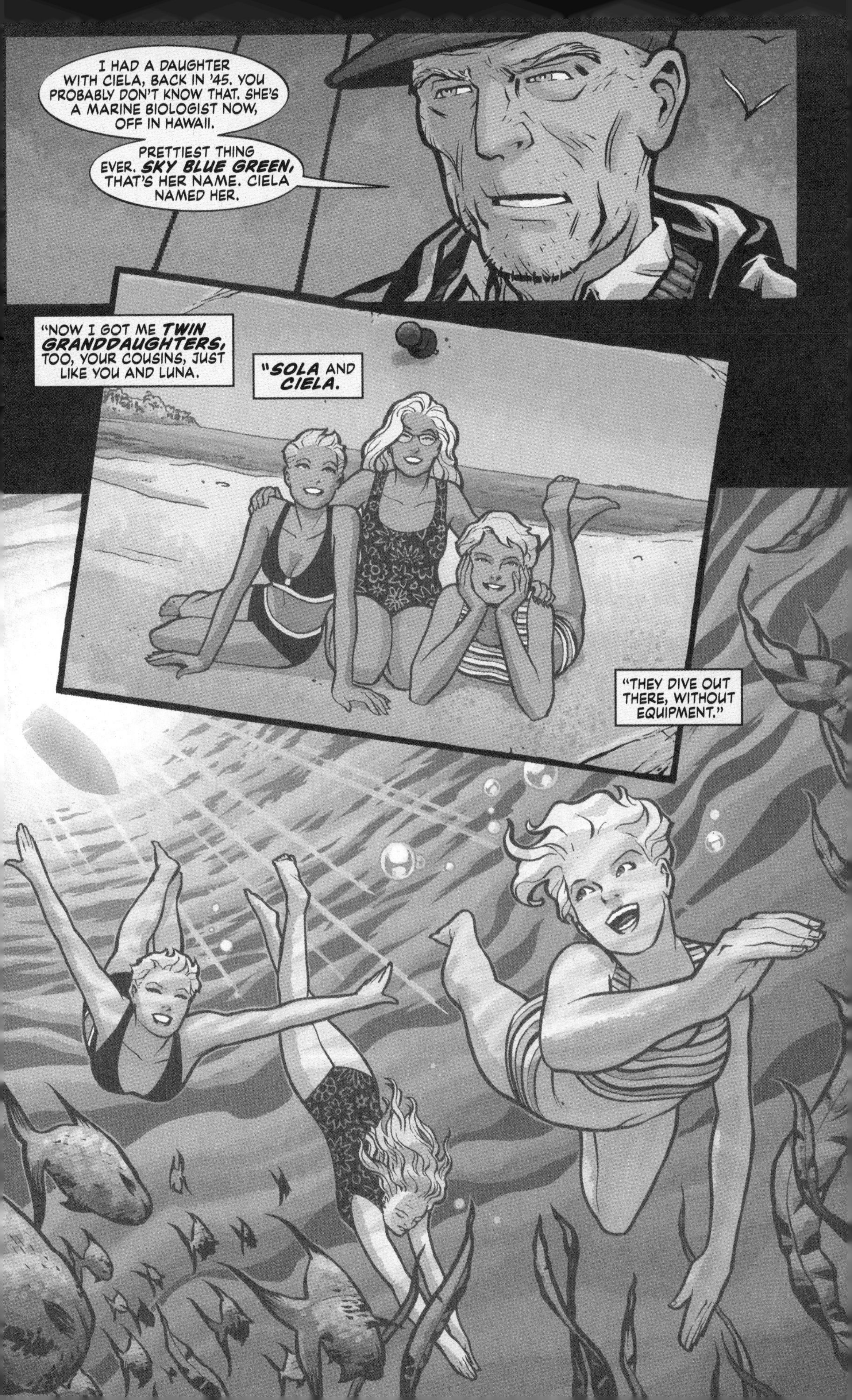
I HAD A DAUGHTER WITH CIELA, BACK IN '45. YOU PROBABLY DON'T KNOW THAT. SHE'S A MARINE BIOLOGIST NOW, OFF IN HAWAII.
PRETTIEST THING EVER. SKY BLUE GREEN, THAT'S HER NAME. CIELA NAMED HER.
"NOW I GOT ME TWIN GRANDDAUGHTERS, TOO, YOUR COUSINS, JUST LIKE YOU AND LUNA.
"SOLA AND CIELA.
"THEY DIVE OUT THERE, WITHOUT EQUIPMENT."

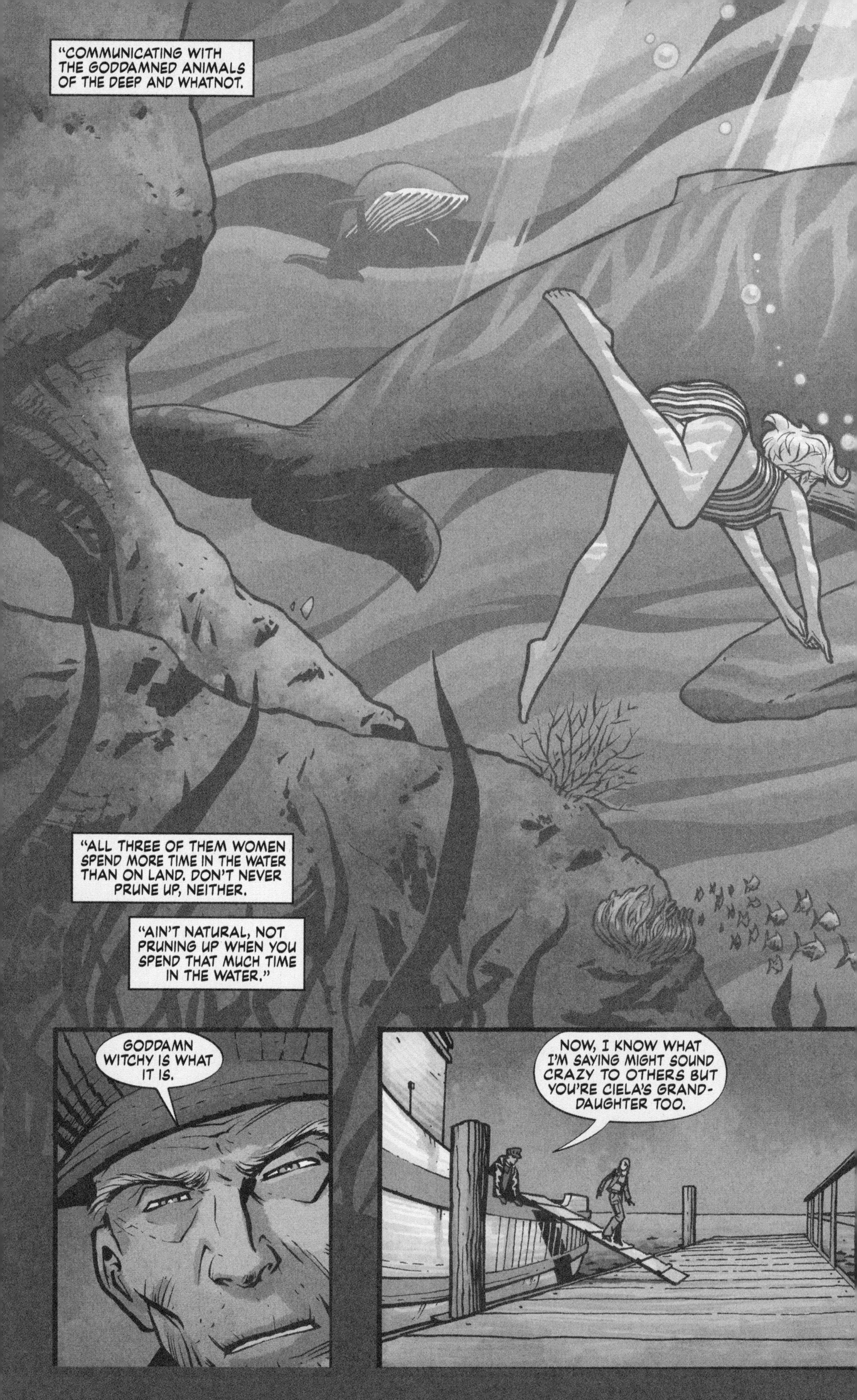
"COMMUNICATING WITH THE GODDAMNED ANIMALS OF THE DEEP AND WHATNOT.
"ALL THREE OF THEM WOMEN SPEND MORE TIME IN THE WATER THAN ON LAND. DON'T NEVER PRUNE UP, NEITHER.
"AIN'T NATURAL, NOT PRUNING UP WHEN YOU SPEND THAT MUCH TIME IN THE WATER."
GODDAMN WITCHY IS WHAT IT IS.
NOW, I KNOW WHAT I'M SAYING MIGHT SOUND CRAZY TO OTHERS BUT YOU'RE CIELA'S GRAND-DAUGHTER TOO.

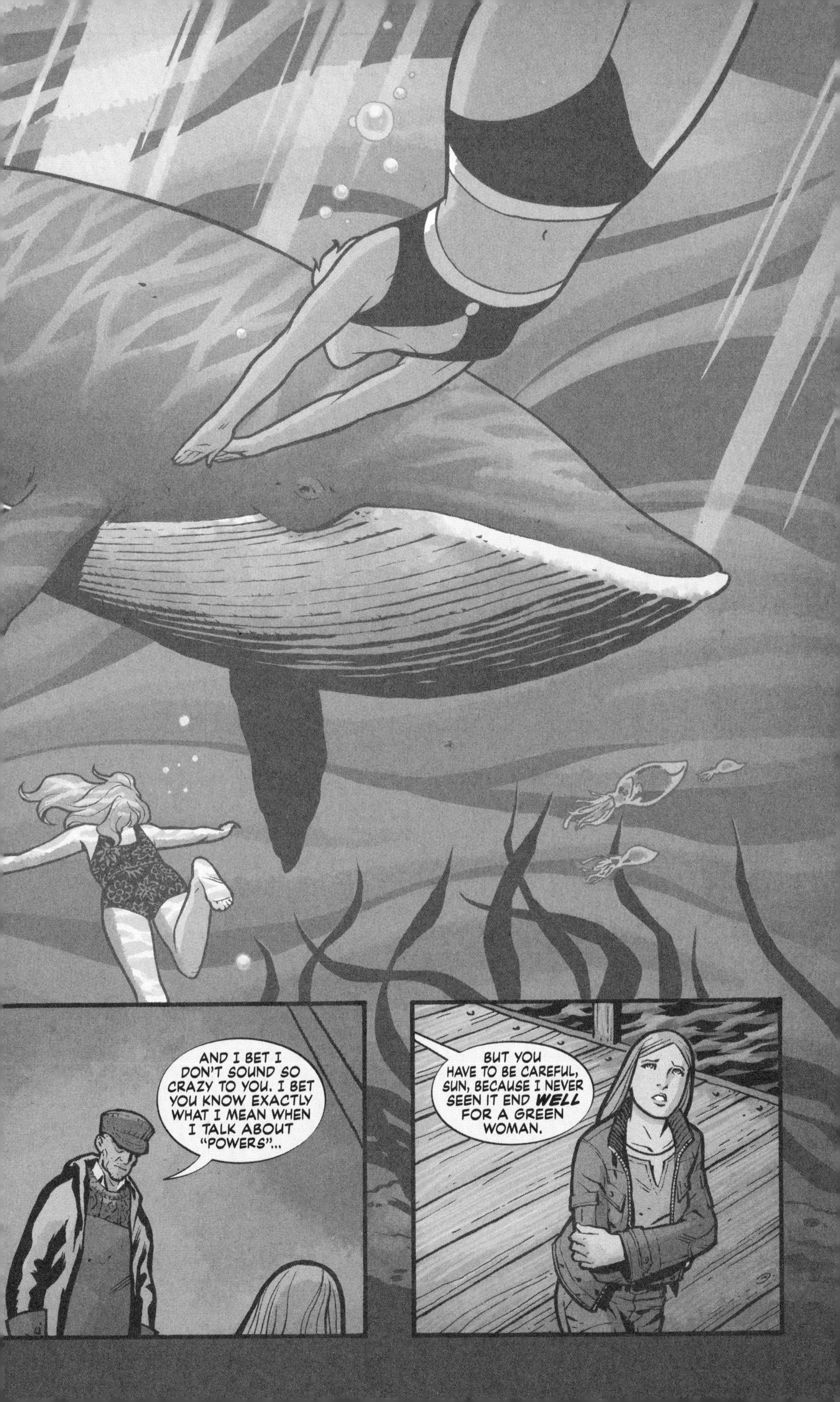
AND I BET I DON'T SOUND SO CRAZY TO YOU. I BET YOU KNOW EXACTLY WHAT I MEAN WHEN I TALK ABOUT "POWERS"...
BUT YOU HAVE TO BE CAREFUL, SUN, BECAUSE I NEVER SEEN IT END WELL FOR A GREEN WOMAN.

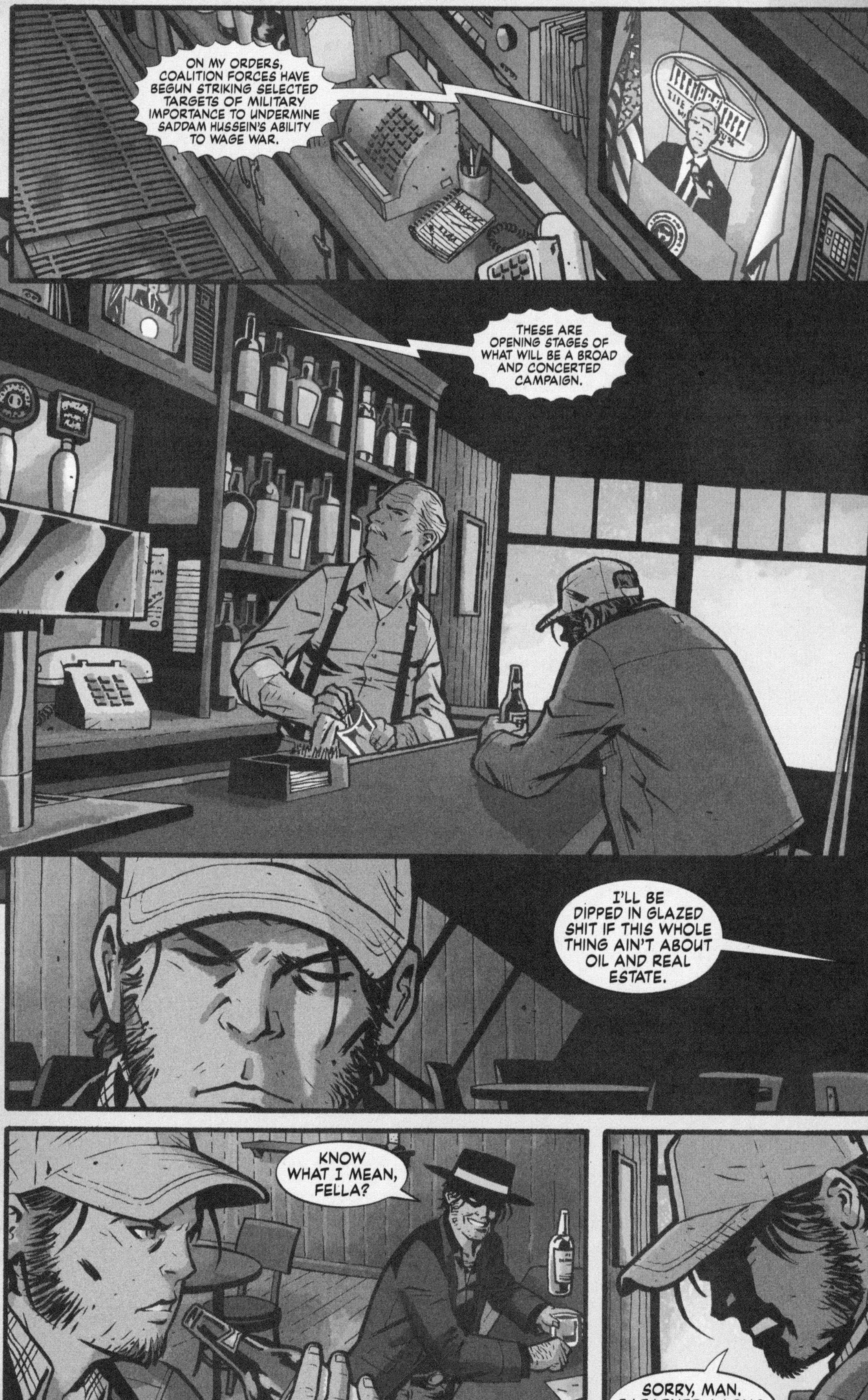
ON MY ORDERS, COALITION FORCES HAVE BEGUN STRIKING SELECTED TARGETS OF MILITARY IMPORTANCE TO UNDERMINE SADDAM HUSSEIN'S ABILITY TO WAGE WAR.
THESE ARE OPENING STAGES OF WHAT WILL BE A BROAD AND CONCERTED CAMPAIGN.
I'LL BE DIPPED IN GLAZED SHIT IF THIS WHOLE THING AIN'T ABOUT OIL AND REAL ESTATE.
KNOW WHAT I MEAN, FELLA?
SORRY, MAN. I LEARNED A LONG TIME AGO NOT TO TALK POLITICS IN BARS WITH STRANGERS.

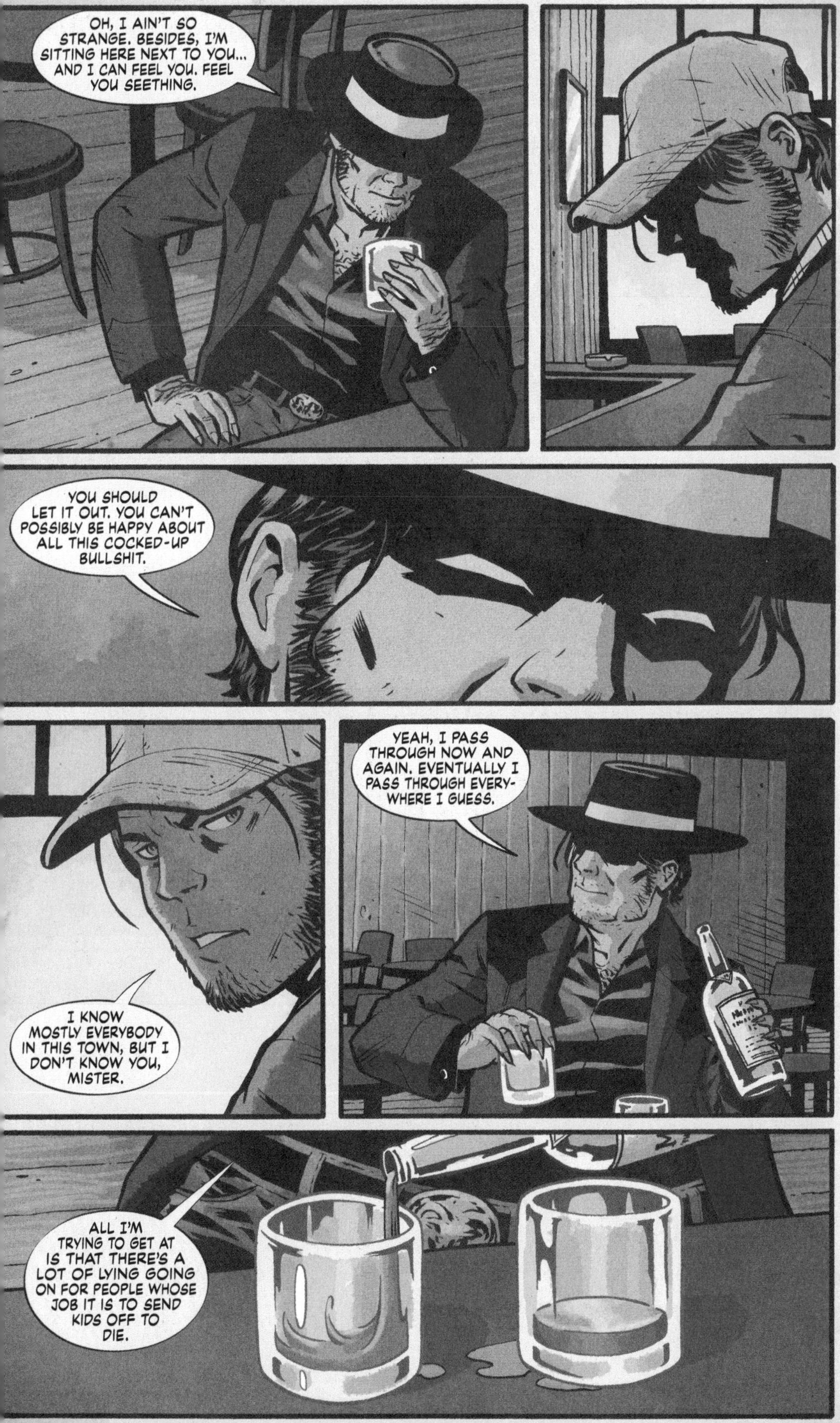
OH, I AIN'T SO STRANGE. BESIDES, I'M SITTING HERE NEXT TO YOU... AND I CAN FEEL YOU. FEEL YOU SEETHING.
YOU SHOULD LET IT OUT. YOU CAN'T POSSIBLY BE HAPPY ABOUT ALL THIS COCKED-UP BULLSHIT.
I KNOW MOSTLY EVERYBODY IN THIS TOWN, BUT I DON'T KNOW YOU, MISTER.
YEAH, I PASS THROUGH NOW AND AGAIN. EVENTUALLY I PASS THROUGH EVERY-WHERE I GUESS.
ALL I'M TRYING TO GET AT IS THAT THERE'S A LOT OF LYING GOING ON FOR PEOPLE WHOSE JOB IT IS TO SEND KIDS OFF TO DIE.

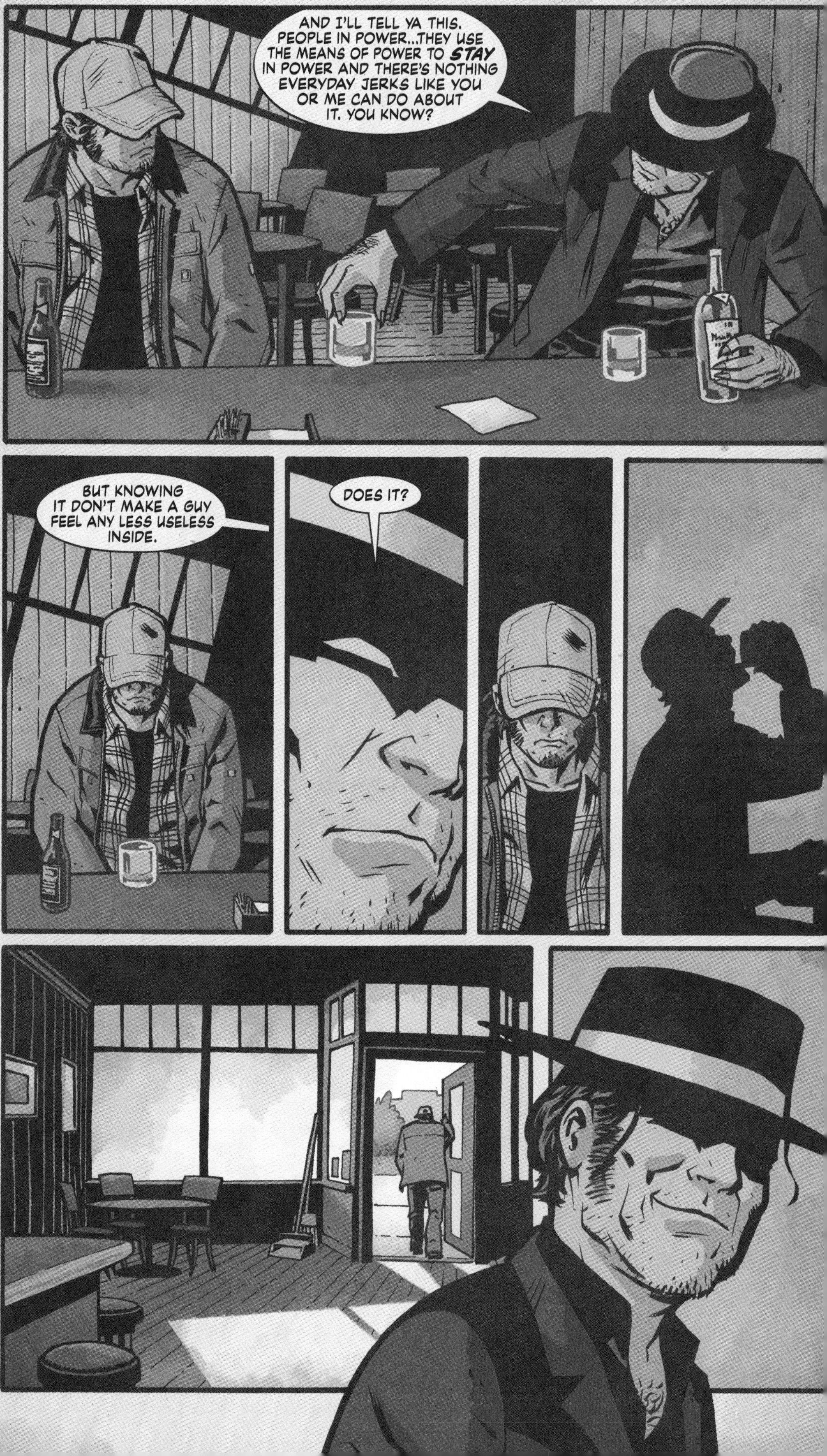
AND I'LL TELL YA THIS. PEOPLE IN POWER...THEY USE THE MEANS OF POWER TO STAY IN POWER AND THERE'S NOTHING EVERYDAY JERKS LIKE YOU OR ME CAN DO ABOUT IT. YOU KNOW?
BUT KNOWING IT DON'T MAKE A GUY FEEL ANY LESS USELESS INSIDE.
DOES IT?

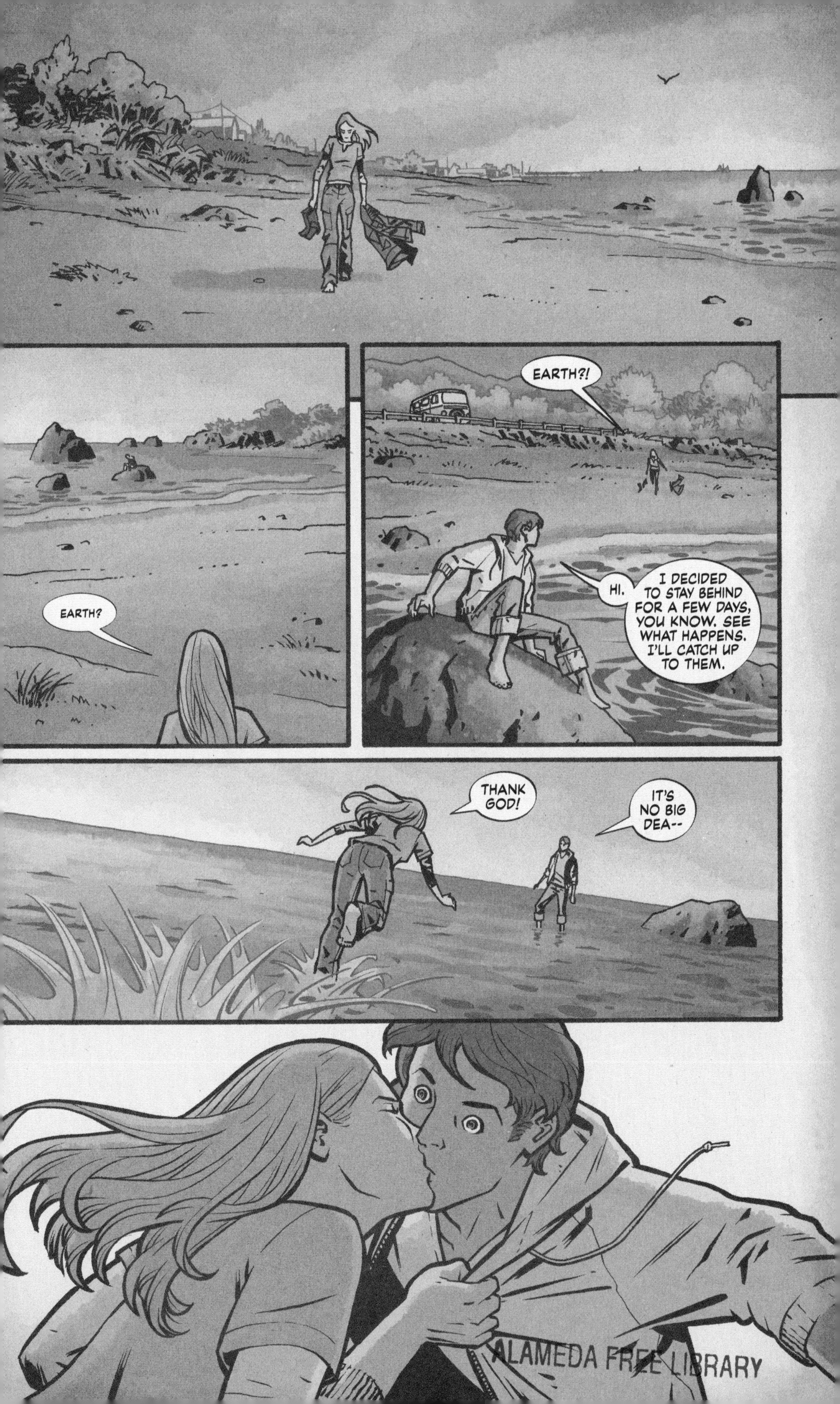
EARTH?
EARTH?!
HI.
I DECIDED TO STAY BEHIND FOR A FEW DAYS, YOU KNOW. SEE WHAT HAPPENS. I'LL CATCH UP TO THEM.
THANK GOD!
IT'S NO BIG DEA--

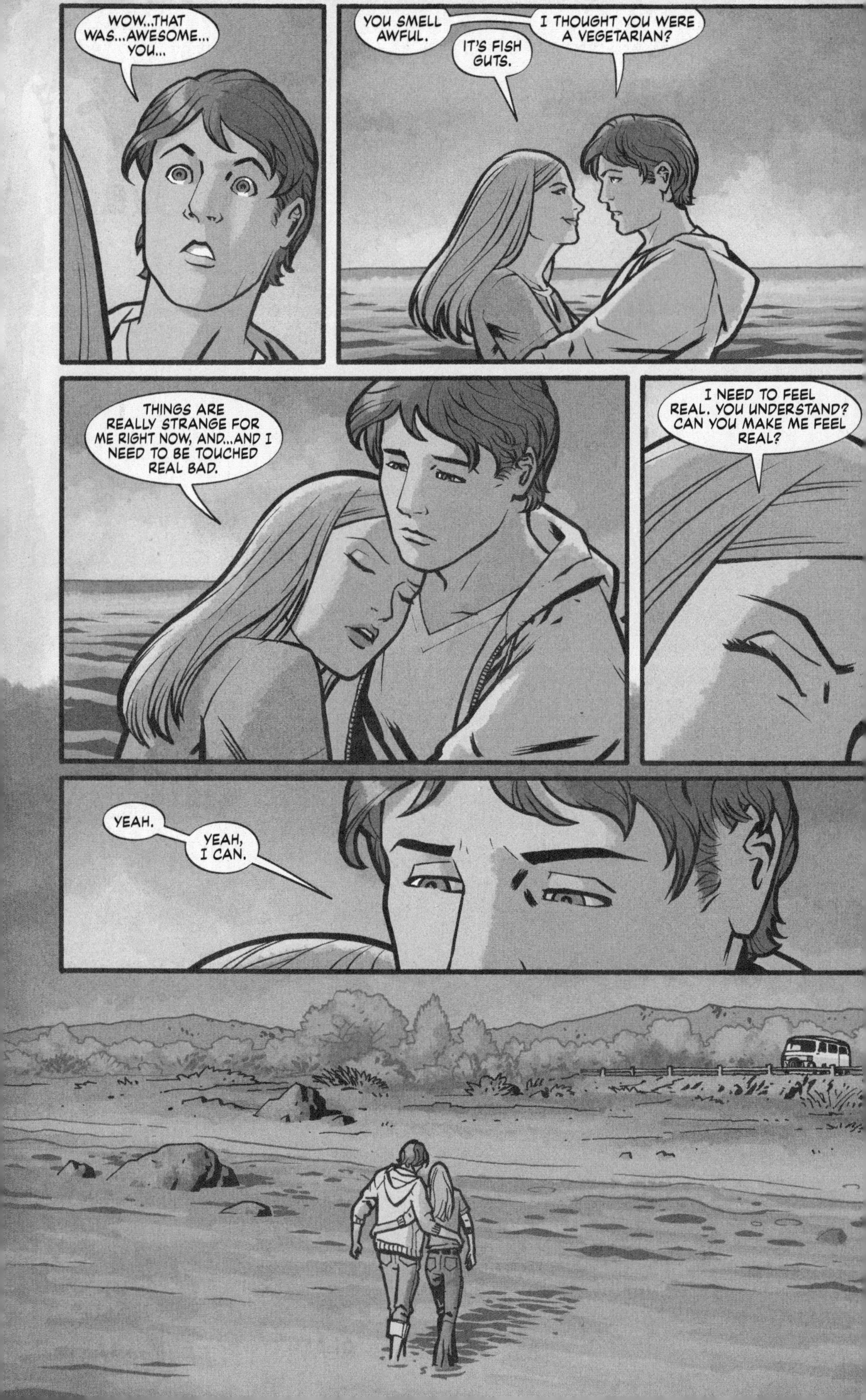
WOW...THAT WAS...AWESOME... YOU...
YOU SMELL AWFUL.
IT'S FISH GUTS.
I THOUGHT YOU WERE A VEGETARIAN?
THINGS ARE REALLY STRANGE FOR ME RIGHT NOW, AND...AND I NEED TO BE TOUCHED REAL BAD.
I NEED TO FEEL REAL. YOU UNDERSTAND? CAN YOU MAKE ME FEEL REAL?
YEAH.
YEAH, I CAN.

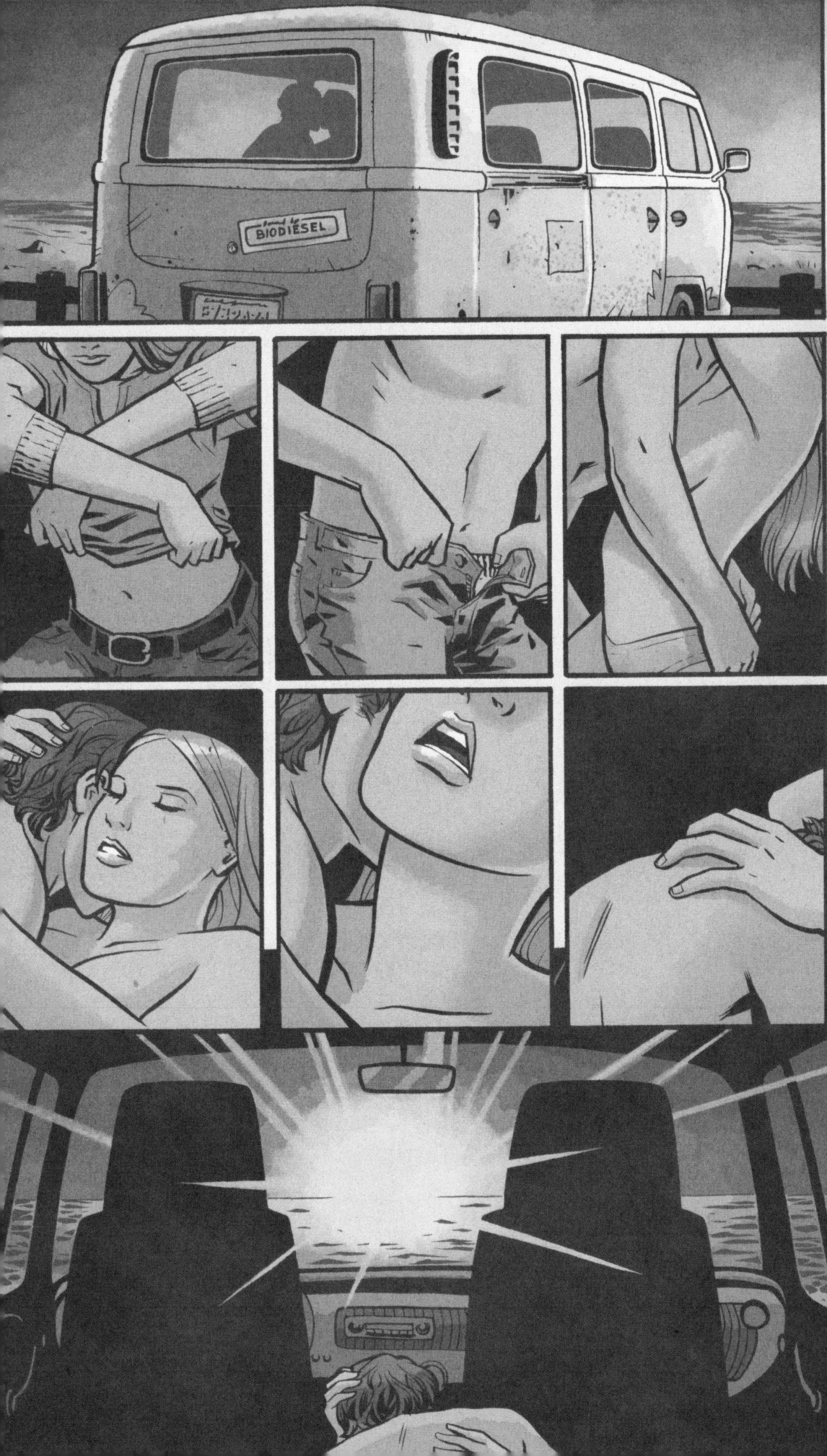
BIODIESEL

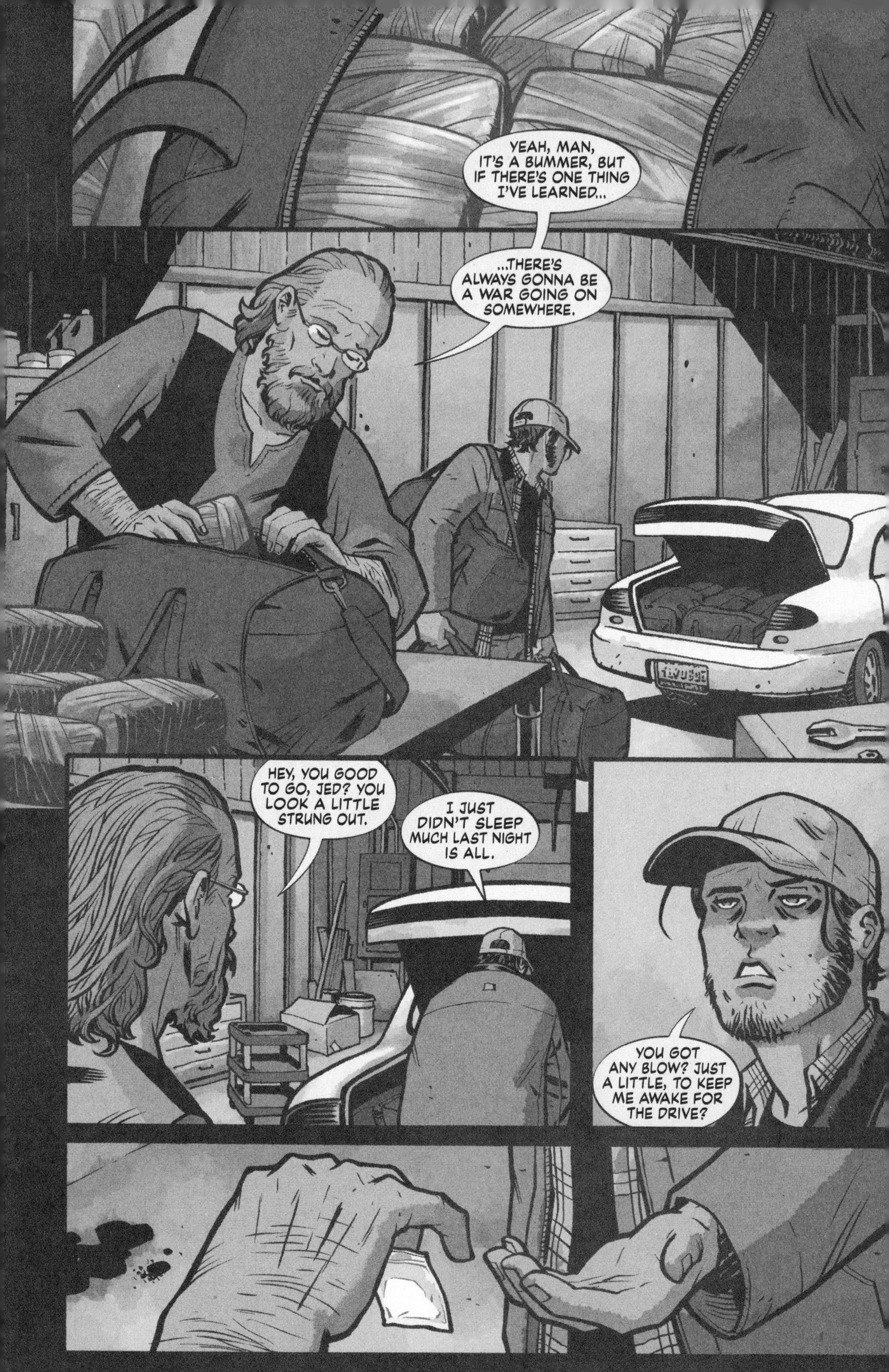
YEAH, MAN, IT'S A BUMMER, BUT IF THERE'S ONE THING I'VE LEARNED...
...THERE'S ALWAYS GONNA BE A WAR GOING ON SOMEWHERE.
HEY, YOU GOOD TO GO, JED? YOU LOOK A LITTLE STRUNG OUT.
I JUST DIDN'T SLEEP MUCH LAST NIGHT IS ALL.
YOU GOT ANY BLOW? JUST A LITTLE, TO KEEP ME AWAKE FOR THE DRIVE?

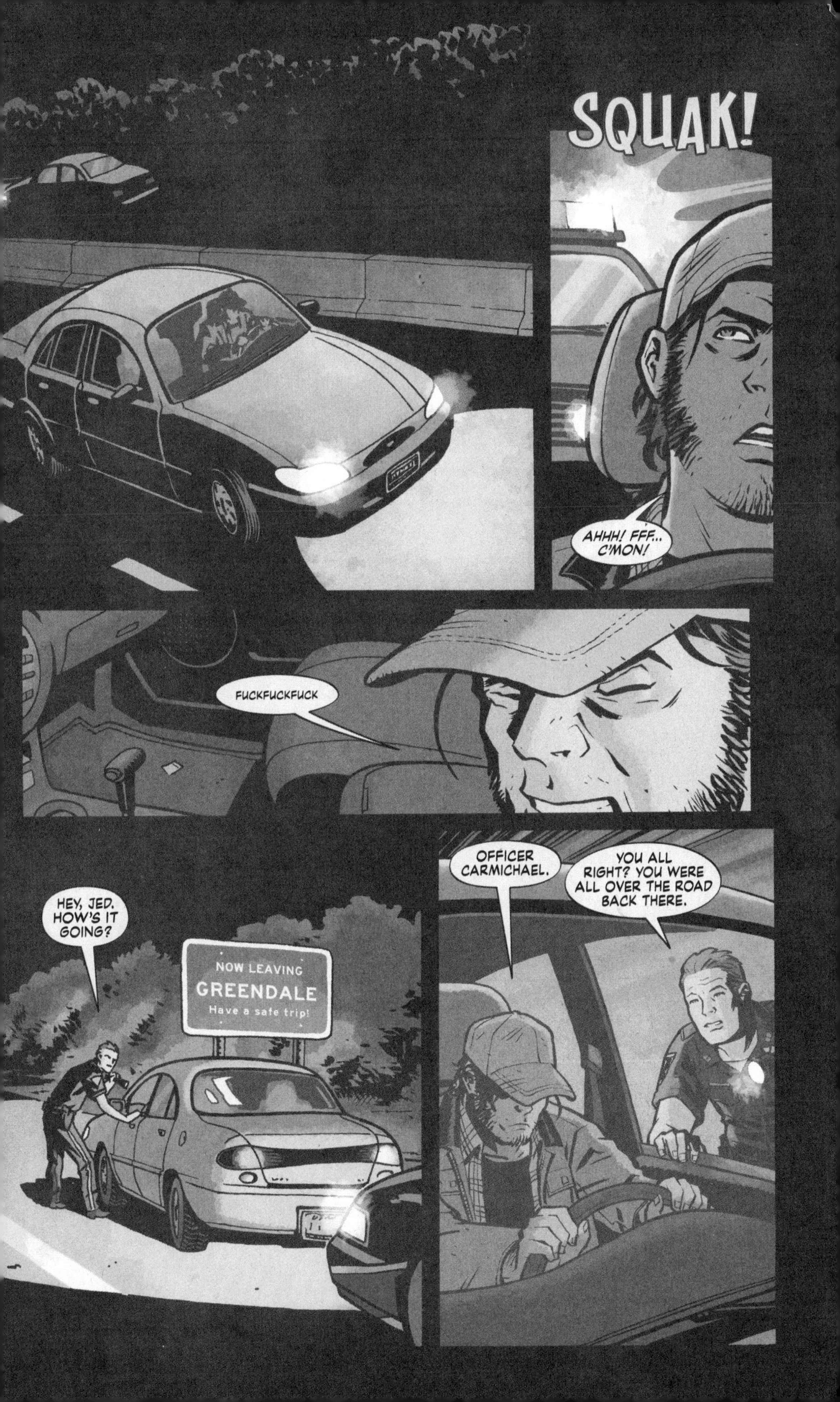
SQUAK!
AHHH! FFF.. C'MON!
FUCKFUCKFUCK
HEY, JED. HOW'S IT GOING?
NOW LEAVING
GREENDALE
Have a safe trip!
OFFICER CARMICHAEL.
YOU ALL RIGHT? YOU WERE ALL OVER THE ROAD BACK THERE.

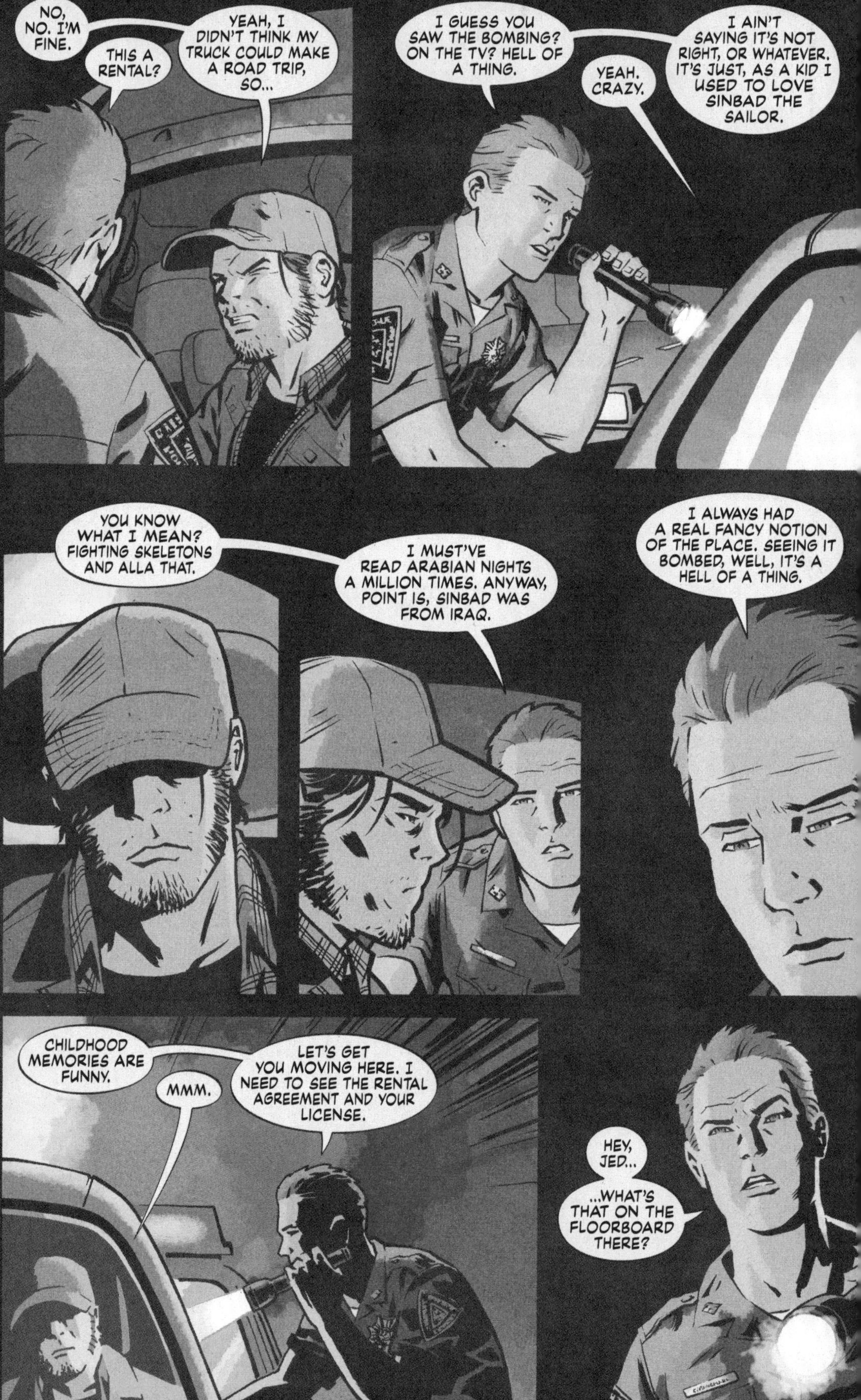

NO, NO. I'M FINE.
THIS A RENTAL?
YEAH, I DIDN'T THINK MY TRUCK COULD MAKE A ROAD TRIP, SO...
I GUESS YOU SAW THE BOMBING? ON THE TV? HELL OF A THING.
YEAH. CRAZY.
I AIN'T SAYING IT'S NOT RIGHT, OR WHATEVER. IT'S JUST, AS A KID I USED TO LOVE SINBAD THE SAILOR.
YOU KNOW WHAT I MEAN? FIGHTING SKELETONS AND ALLA THAT.
I MUST'VE READ ARABIAN NIGHTS A MILLION TIMES. ANYWAY, POINT IS, SINBAD WAS FROM IRAQ.
I ALWAYS HAD A REAL FANCY NOTION OF THE PLACE. SEEING IT BOMBED, WELL, IT'S A HELL OF A THING.
CHILDHOOD MEMORIES ARE FUNNY.
MMM.
LET'S GET YOU MOVING HERE. I NEED TO SEE THE RENTAL AGREEMENT AND YOUR LICENSE.
HEY, JED...
...WHAT'S THAT ON THE FLOORBOARD THERE?

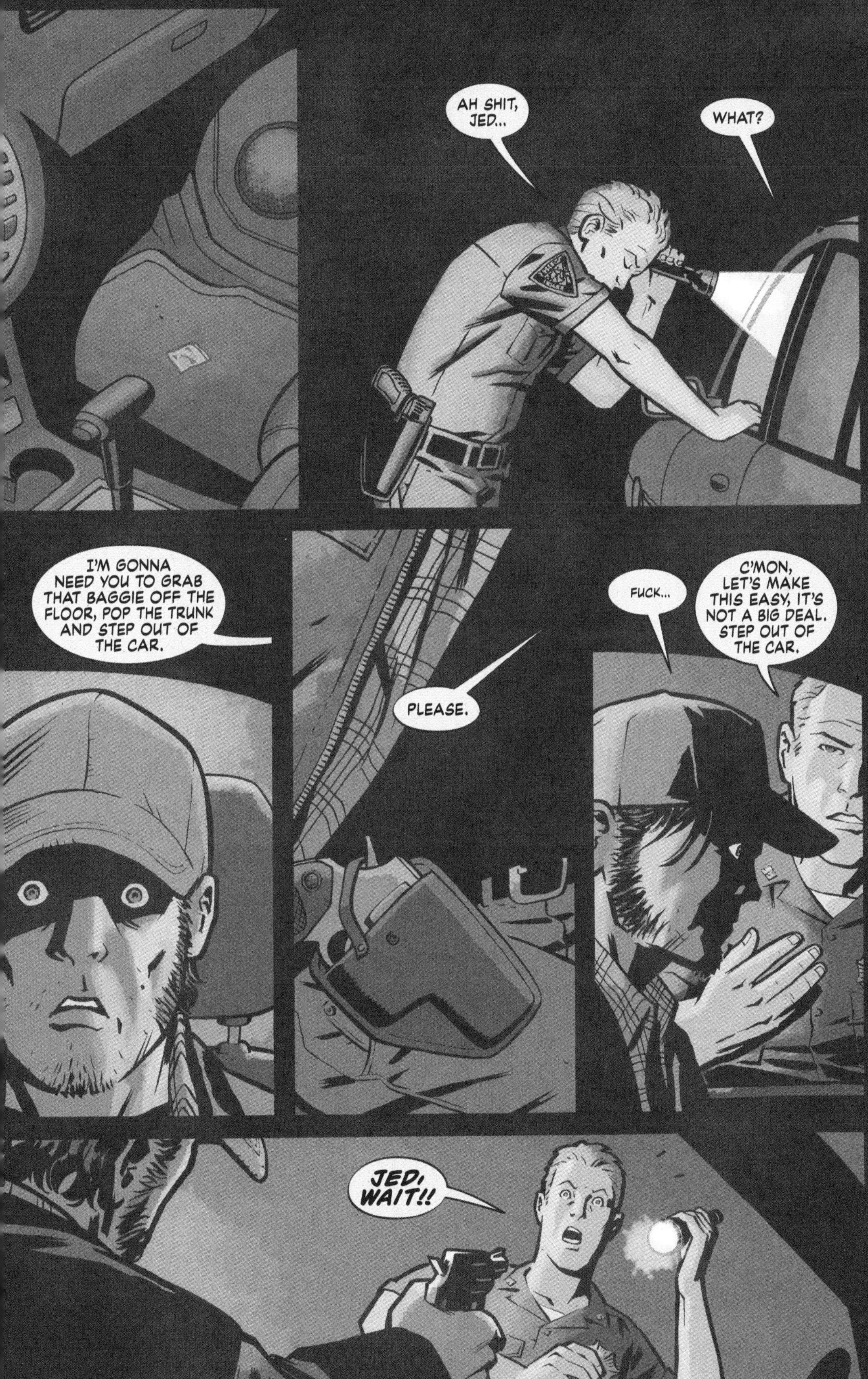
AH SHIT, JED...
WHAT?
I'M GONNA NEED YOU TO GRAB THAT BAGGIE OFF THE FLOOR, POP THE TRUNK AND STEP OUT OF THE CAR.
PLEASE.
FUCK...
C'MON, LET'S MAKE THIS EASY, IT'S NOT A BIG DEAL. STEP OUT OF THE CAR.
JED, WAIT!!

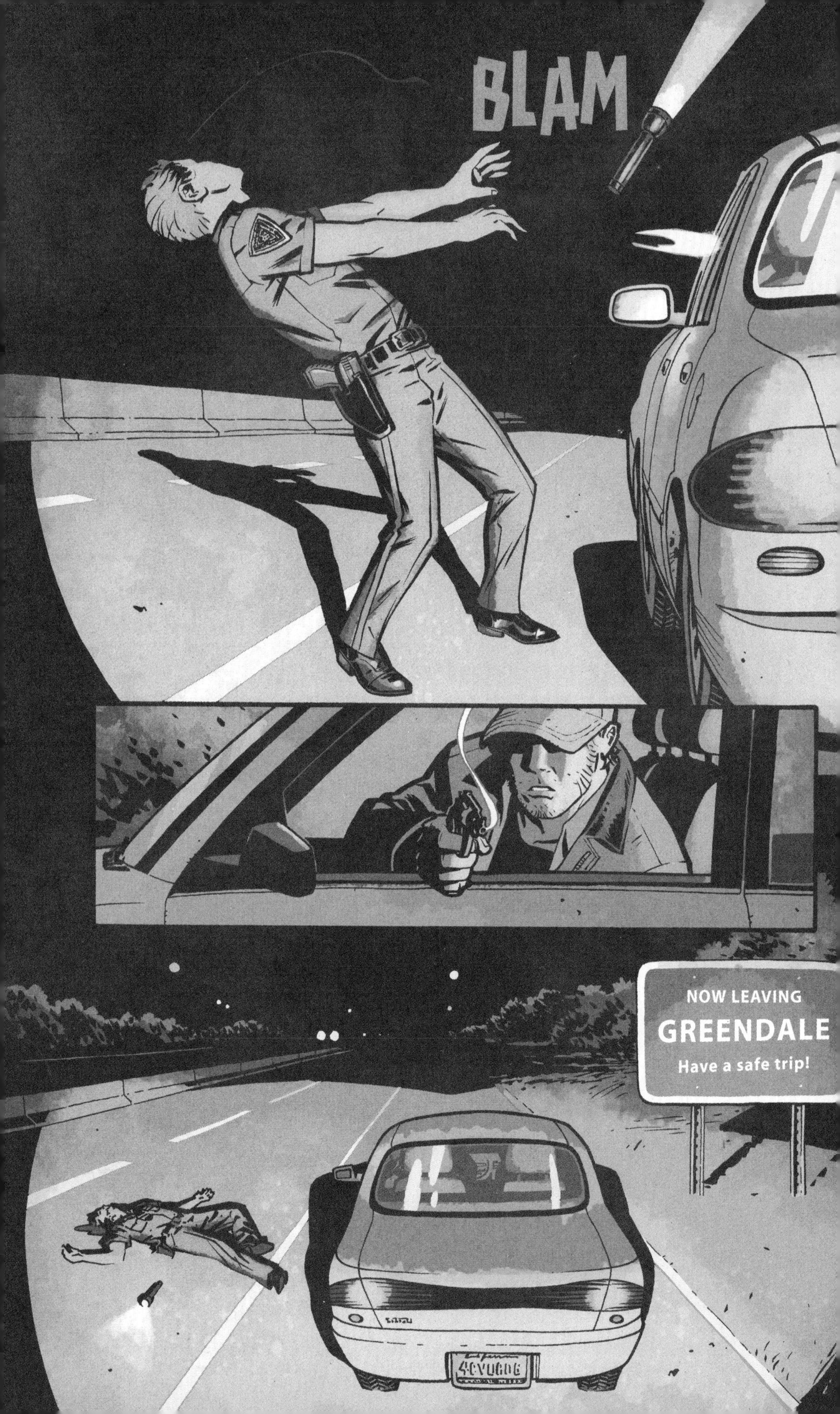
BLAM
NOW LEAVING
GREENDALE
Have a safe trip!

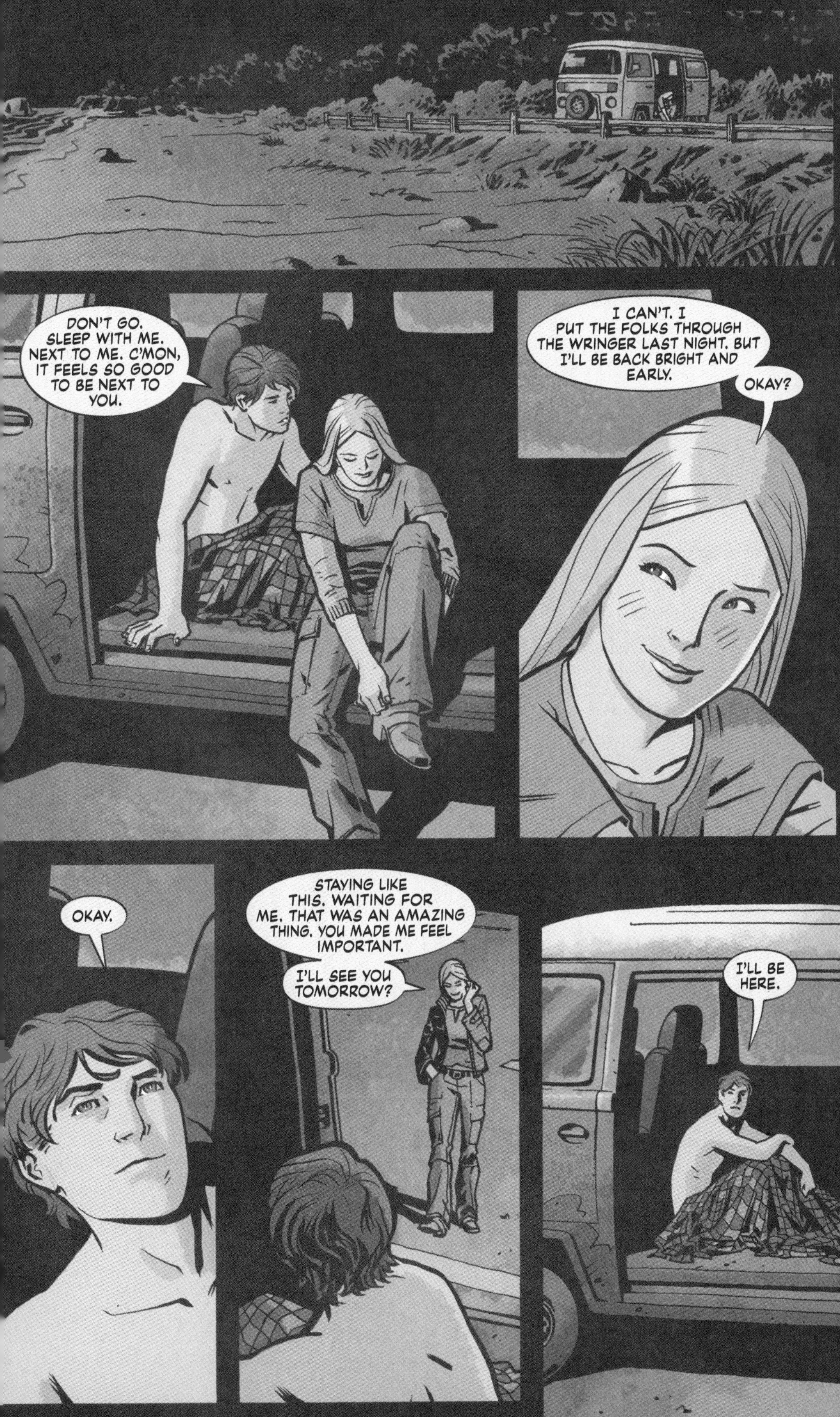
DON'T GO. SLEEP WITH ME. NEXT TO ME. C'MON, IT FEELS SO GOOD TO BE NEXT TO YOU.
I CAN'T. I PUT THE FOLKS THROUGH THE WRINGER LAST NIGHT. BUT I'LL BE BACK BRIGHT AND EARLY.
OKAY?
OKAY.
STAYING LIKE THIS. WAITING FOR ME. THAT WAS AN AMAZING THING. YOU MADE ME FEEL IMPORTANT.
I'LL SEE YOU TOMORROW?
I'LL BE HERE.

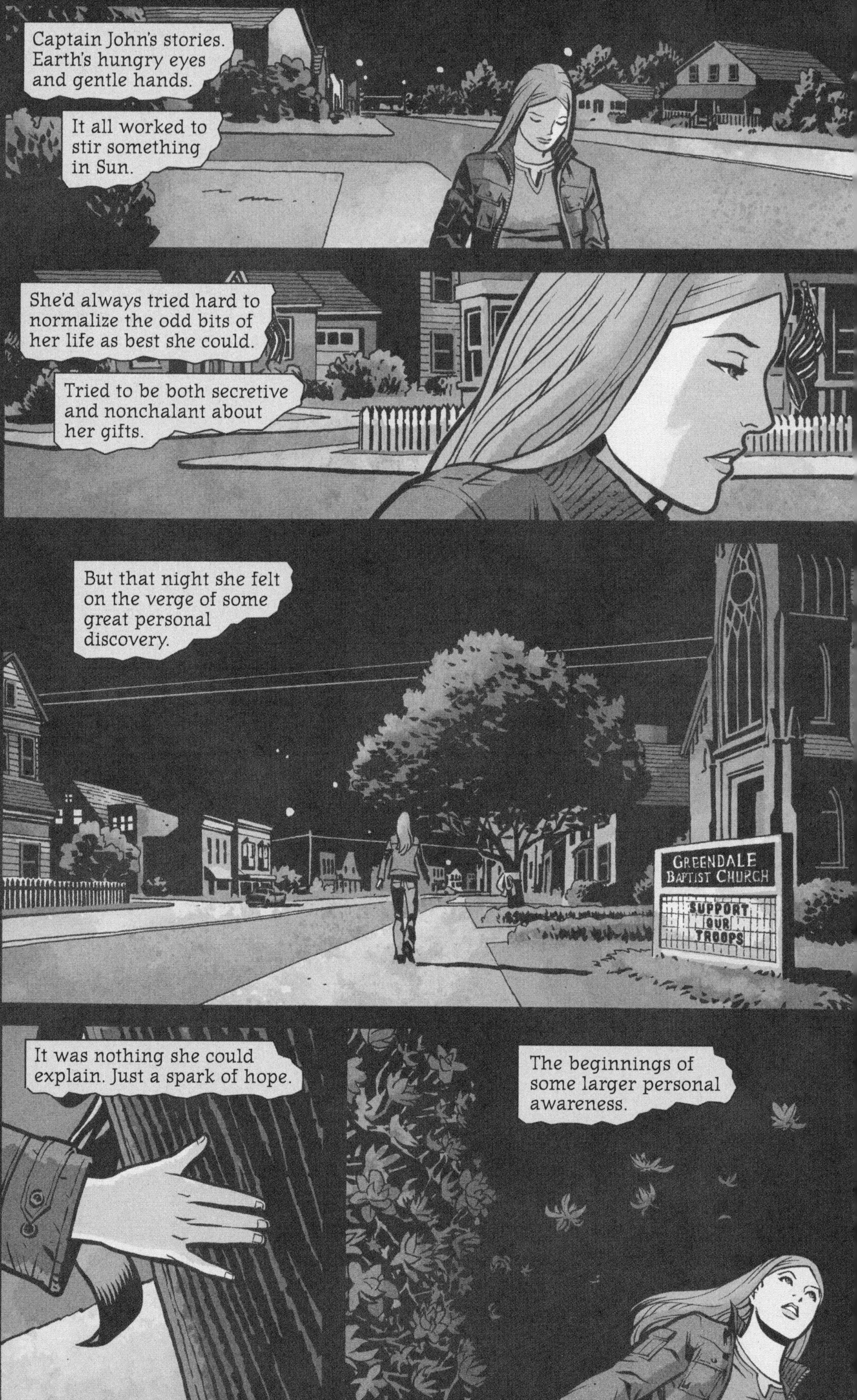
Captain John's stories. Earth's hungry eyes and gentle hands.
It all worked to stir something in Sun.
She'd always tried hard to normalize the odd bits of her life as best she could.
Tried to be both secretive and nonchalant about her gifts.
But that night she felt on the verge of some great personal discovery.
GREENDALE BAPTIST CHURCH
SUPPORT OUR TROOPS
It was nothing she could explain. Just a spark of hope.
The beginnings of some larger personal awareness.

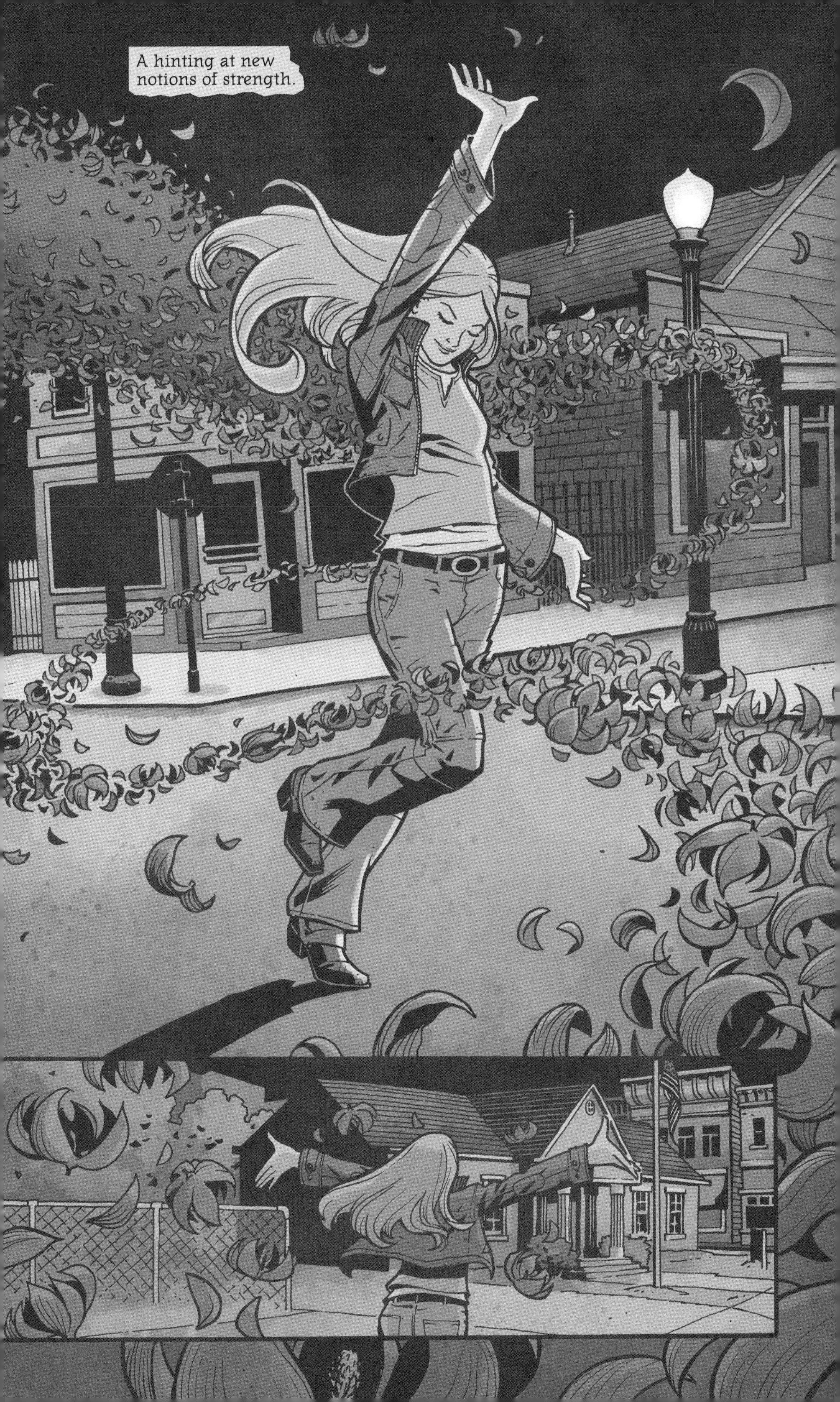
A hinting at new notions of strength.

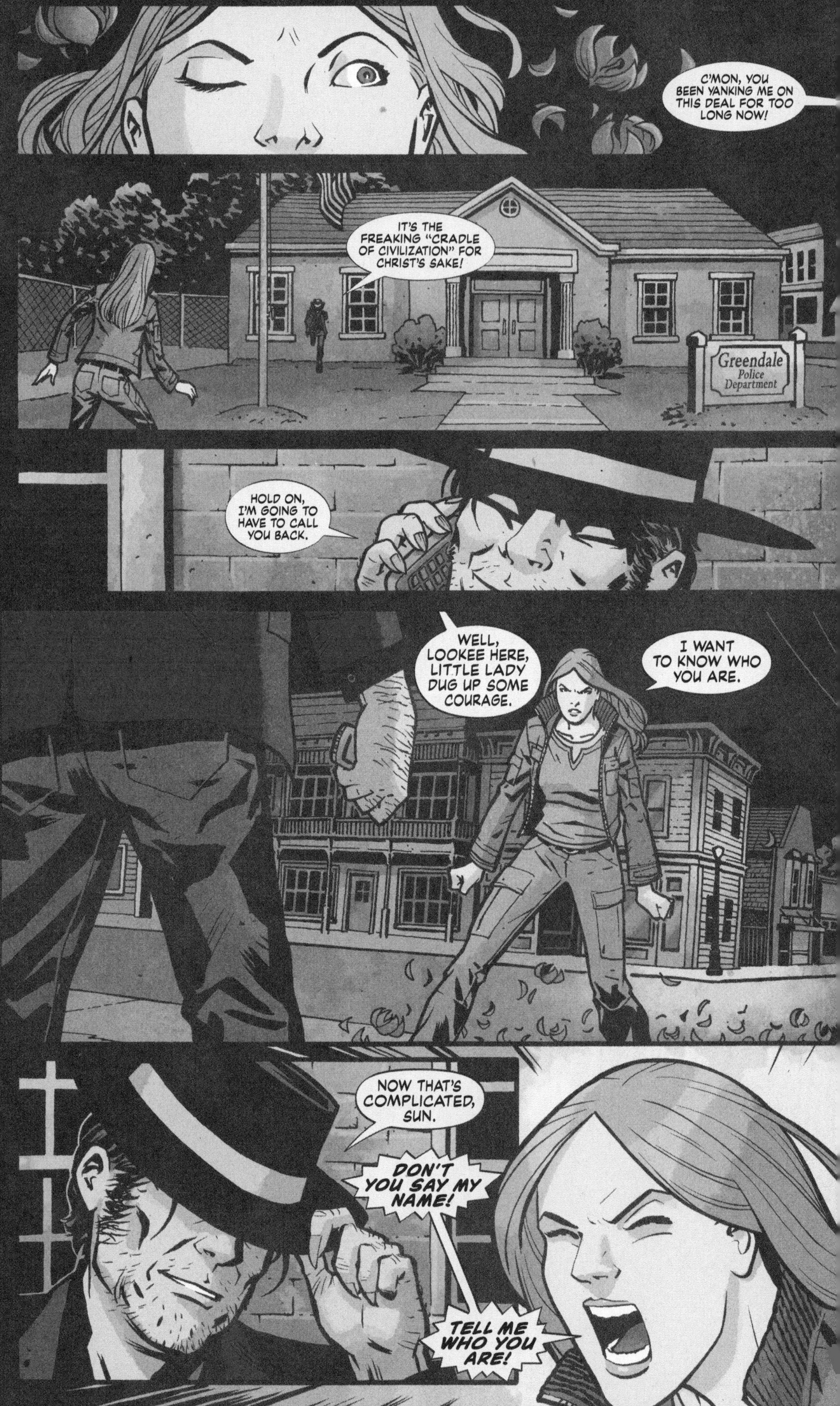

C'MON, YOU BEEN YANKING ME ON THIS DEAL FOR TOO LONG NOW!
IT'S THE FREAKING "CRADLE OF CIVILIZATION" FOR CHRIST'S SAKE!
Greendale Police Department
HOLD ON, I'M GOING TO HAVE TO CALL YOU BACK.
WELL, LOOKEE HERE, LITTLE LADY DUG UP SOME COURAGE.
I WANT TO KNOW WHO YOU ARE.
NOW THAT'S COMPLICATED, SUN.
DON'T YOU SAY MY NAME!
TELL ME WHO YOU ARE!

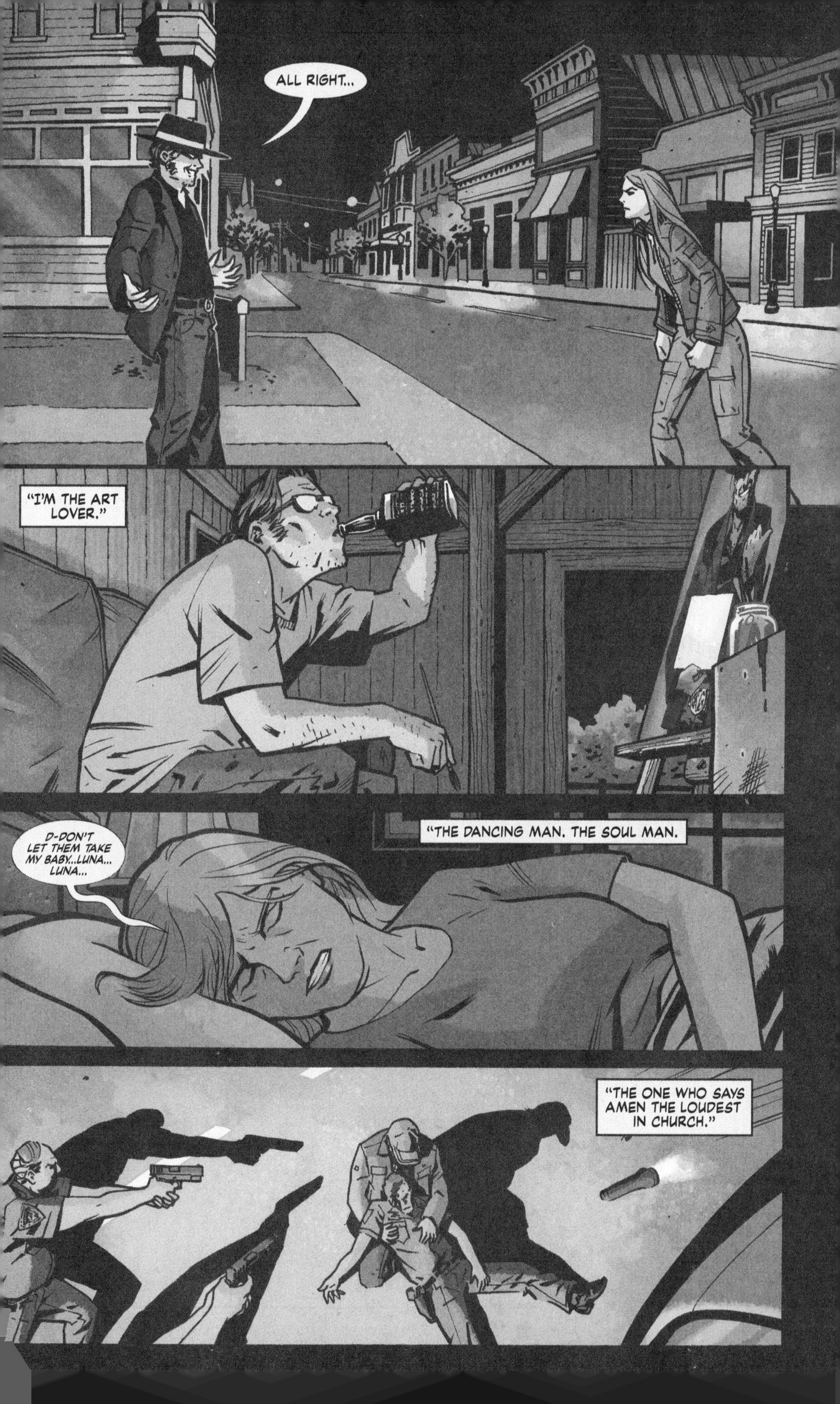
ALL RIGHT...
"I'M THE ART LOVER."
"THE DANCING MAN. THE SOUL MAN.
D-DON'T LET THEM TAKE MY BABY...LUNA... LUNA...
"THE ONE WHO SAYS AMEN THE LOUDEST IN CHURCH."

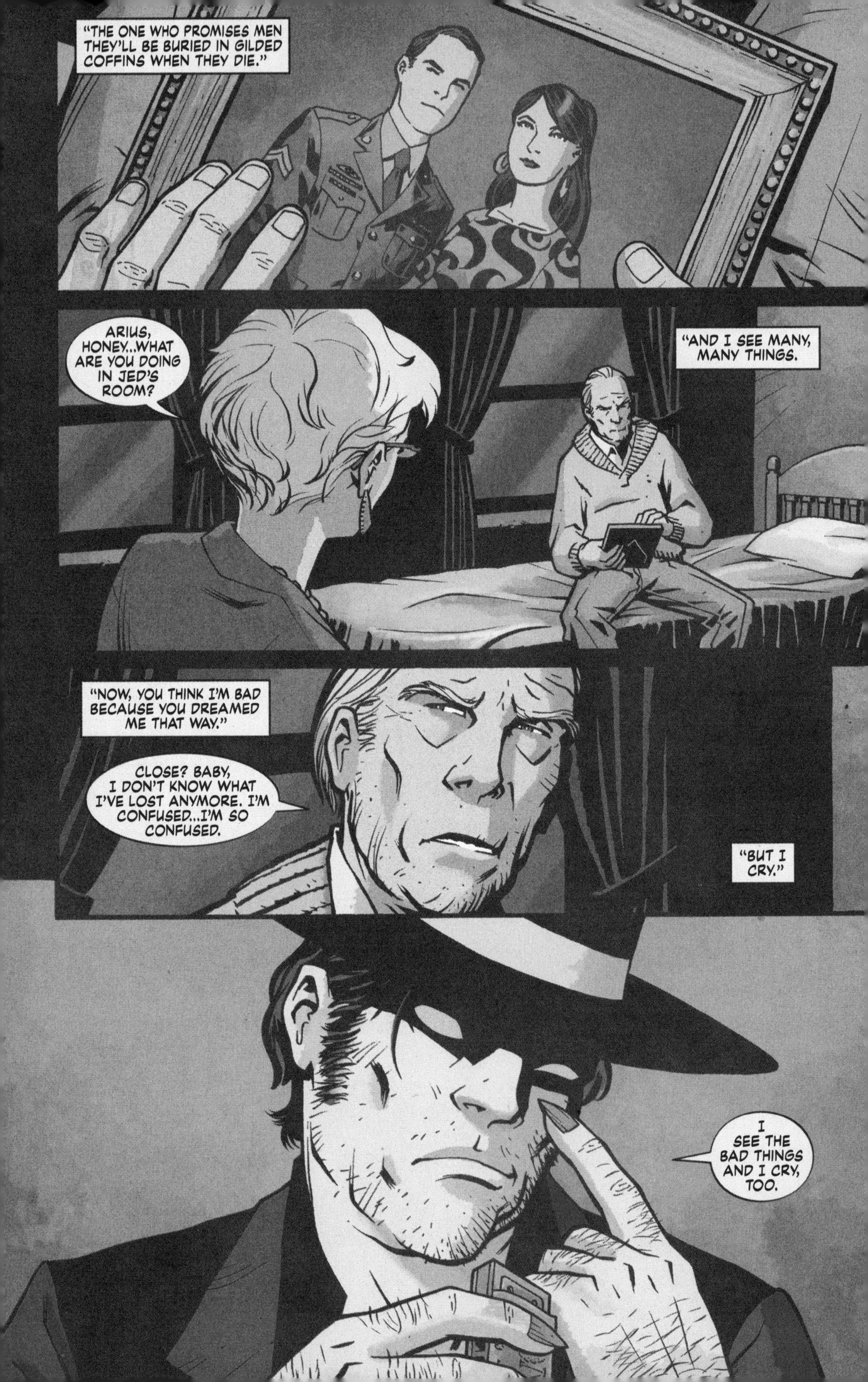
"THE ONE WHO PROMISES MEN THEY'LL BE BURIED IN GILDED COFFINS WHEN THEY DIE."
ARIUS, HONEY...WHAT ARE YOU DOING IN JED'S ROOM?
"AND I SEE MANY, MANY THINGS.
"NOW, YOU THINK I'M BAD BECAUSE YOU DREAMED ME THAT WAY."
CLOSE? BABY, I DON'T KNOW WHAT I'VE LOST ANYMORE. I'M CONFUSED...I'M SO CONFUSED.
"BUT I CRY."
I SEE THE BAD THINGS AND I CRY, TOO.

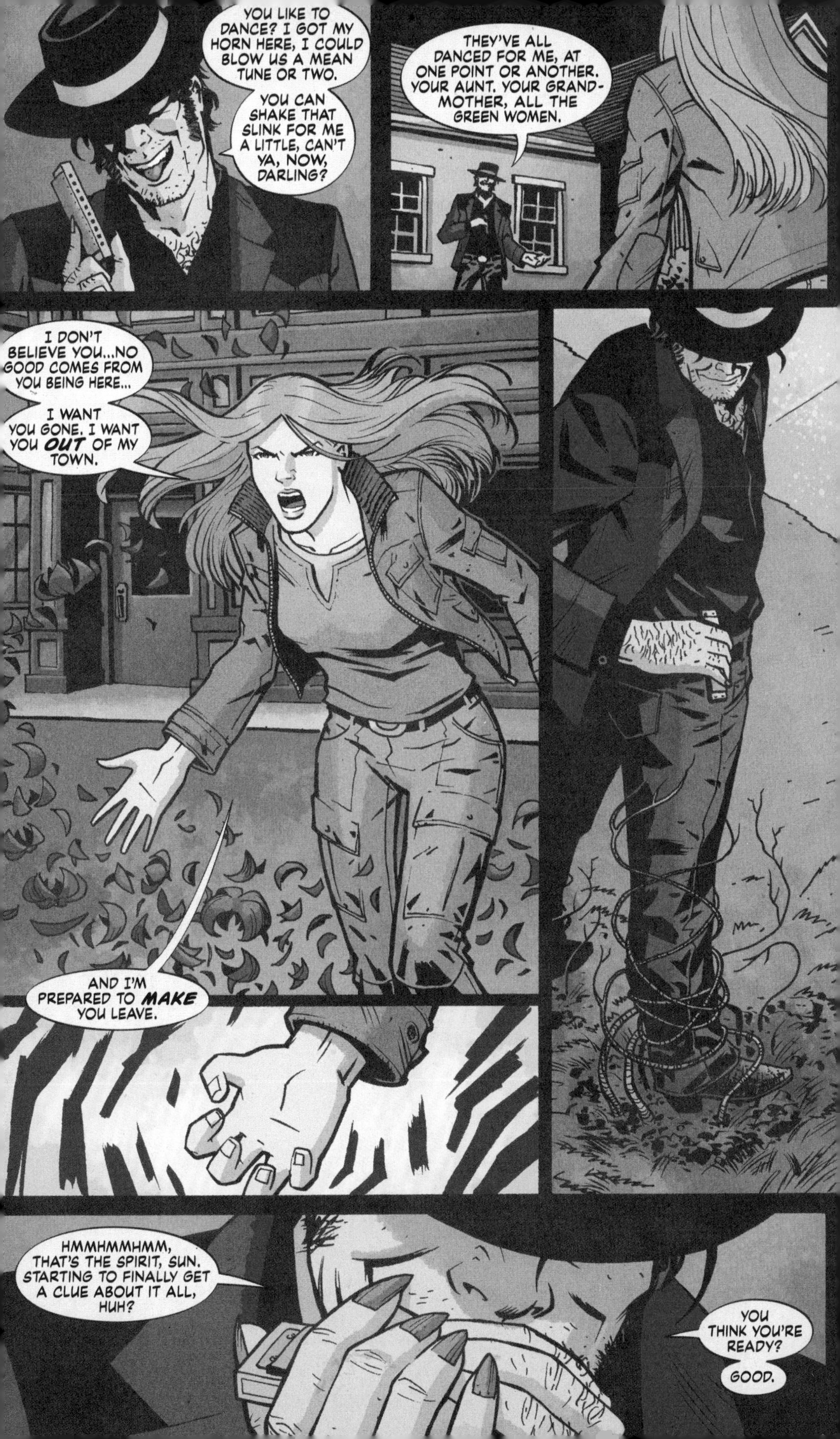

YOU LIKE TO DANCE? I GOT MY HORN HERE, I COULD BLOW US A MEAN TUNE OR TWO.
YOU CAN SHAKE THAT SLINK FOR ME A LITTLE, CAN'T YA, NOW, DARLING?
THEY'VE ALL DANCED FOR ME, AT ONE POINT OR ANOTHER. YOUR AUNT. YOUR GRAND-MOTHER, ALL THE GREEN WOMEN.
I DON'T BELIEVE YOU...NO GOOD COMES FROM YOU BEING HERE...
I WANT YOU GONE. I WANT YOU OUT OF MY TOWN.
AND I'M PREPARED TO MAKE YOU LEAVE.
HMMHMMHMM, THAT'S THE SPIRIT, SUN. STARTING TO FINALLY GET A CLUE ABOUT IT ALL, HUH?
YOU THINK YOU'RE READY?
GOOD.

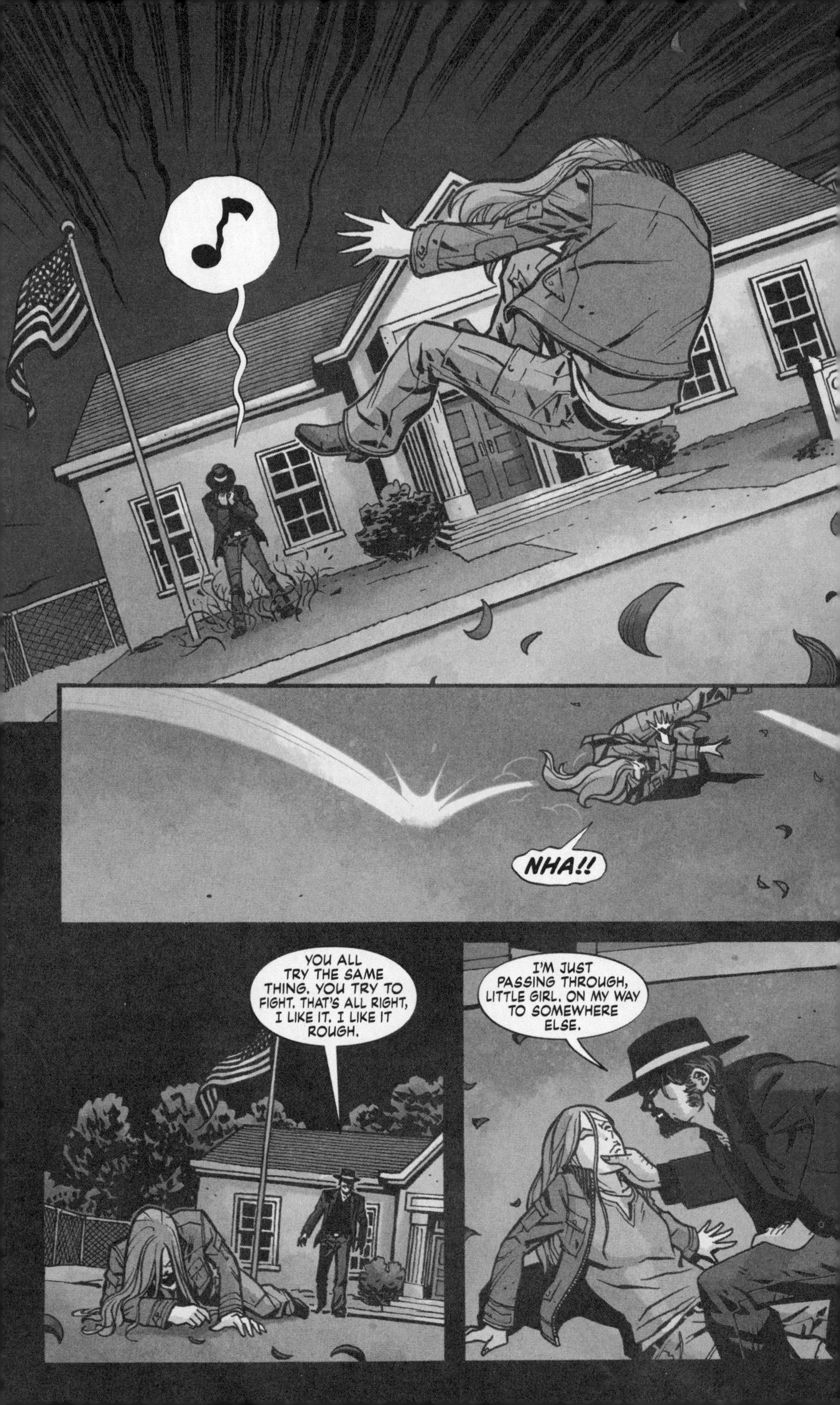
NHA!!
YOU ALL TRY THE SAME THING. YOU TRY TO FIGHT. THAT'S ALL RIGHT, I LIKE IT. I LIKE IT ROUGH.
I'M JUST PASSING THROUGH, LITTLE GIRL. ON MY WAY TO SOMEWHERE ELSE.

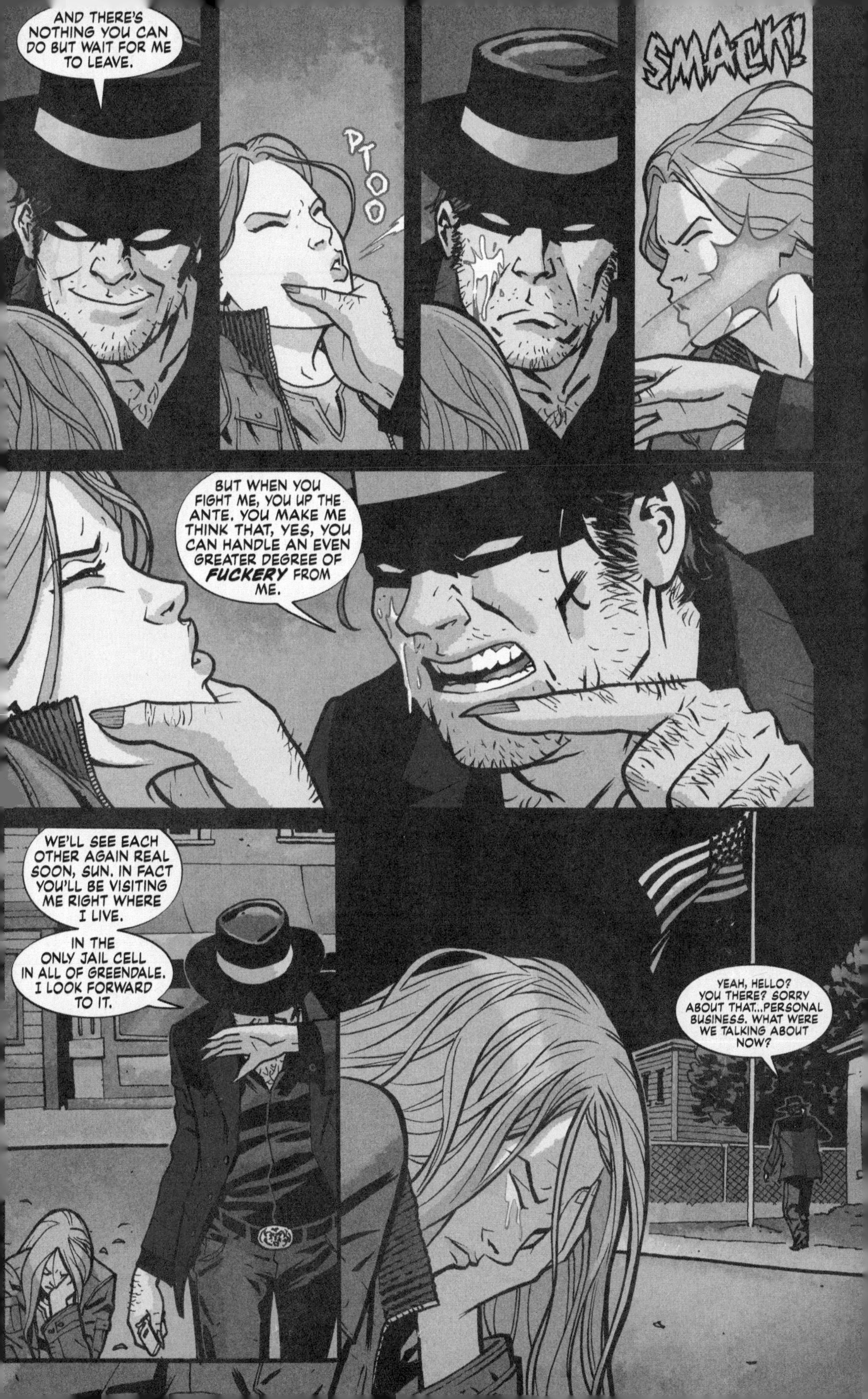
AND THERE'S NOTHING YOU CAN DO BUT WAIT FOR ME TO LEAVE.
PTOO
SMACK!
BUT WHEN YOU FIGHT ME, YOU UP THE ANTE. YOU MAKE ME THINK THAT, YES, YOU CAN HANDLE AN EVEN GREATER DEGREE OF FUCKERY FROM ME.
WE'LL SEE EACH OTHER AGAIN REAL SOON, SUN. IN FACT YOU'LL BE VISITING ME RIGHT WHERE I LIVE.
IN THE ONLY JAIL CELL IN ALL OF GREENDALE. I LOOK FORWARD TO IT.
YEAH, HELLO? YOU THERE? SORRY ABOUT THAT...PERSONAL BUSINESS. WHAT WERE WE TALKING ABOUT NOW?

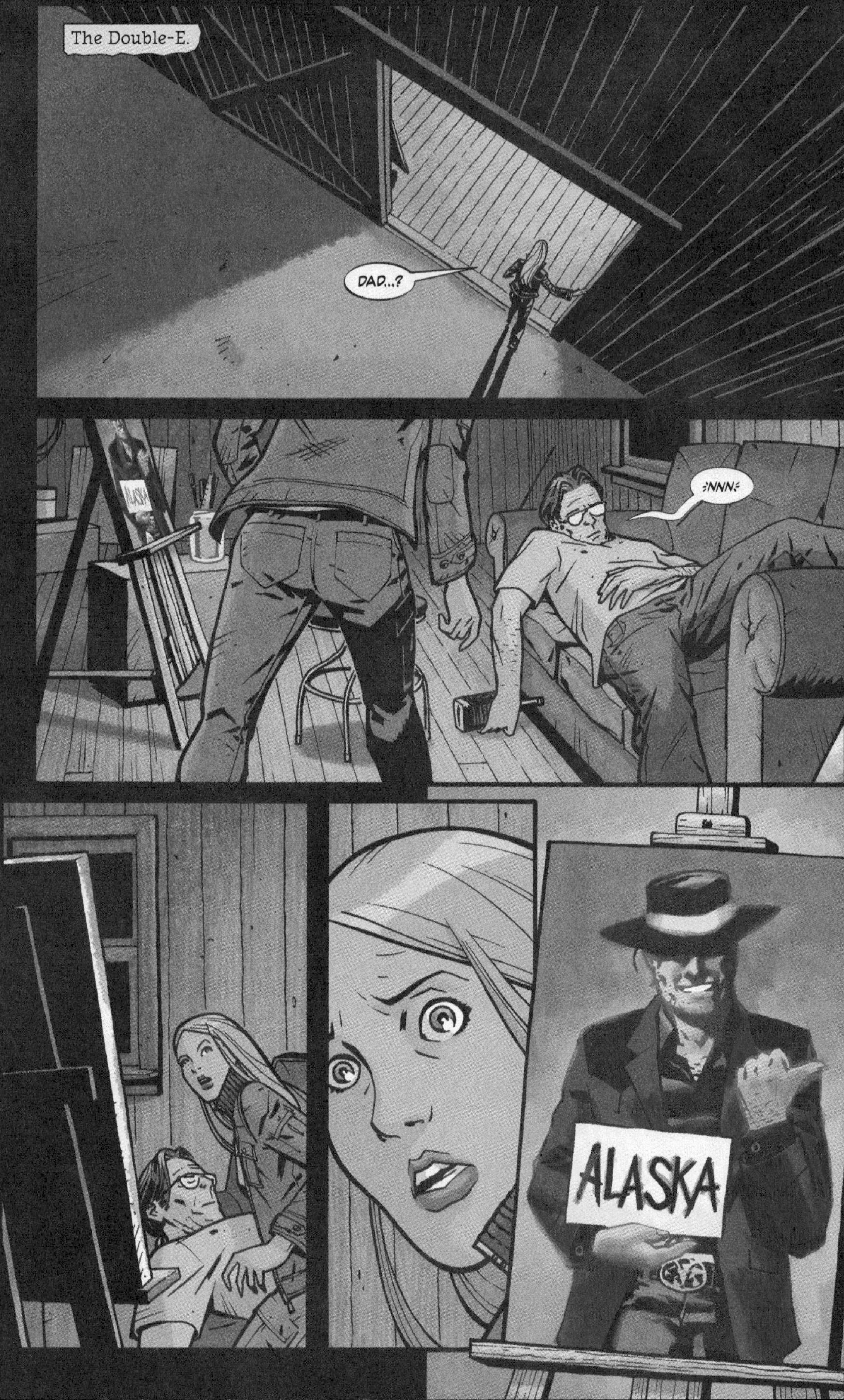
The Double-E.
DAD...?
:NNN:
ALASKA

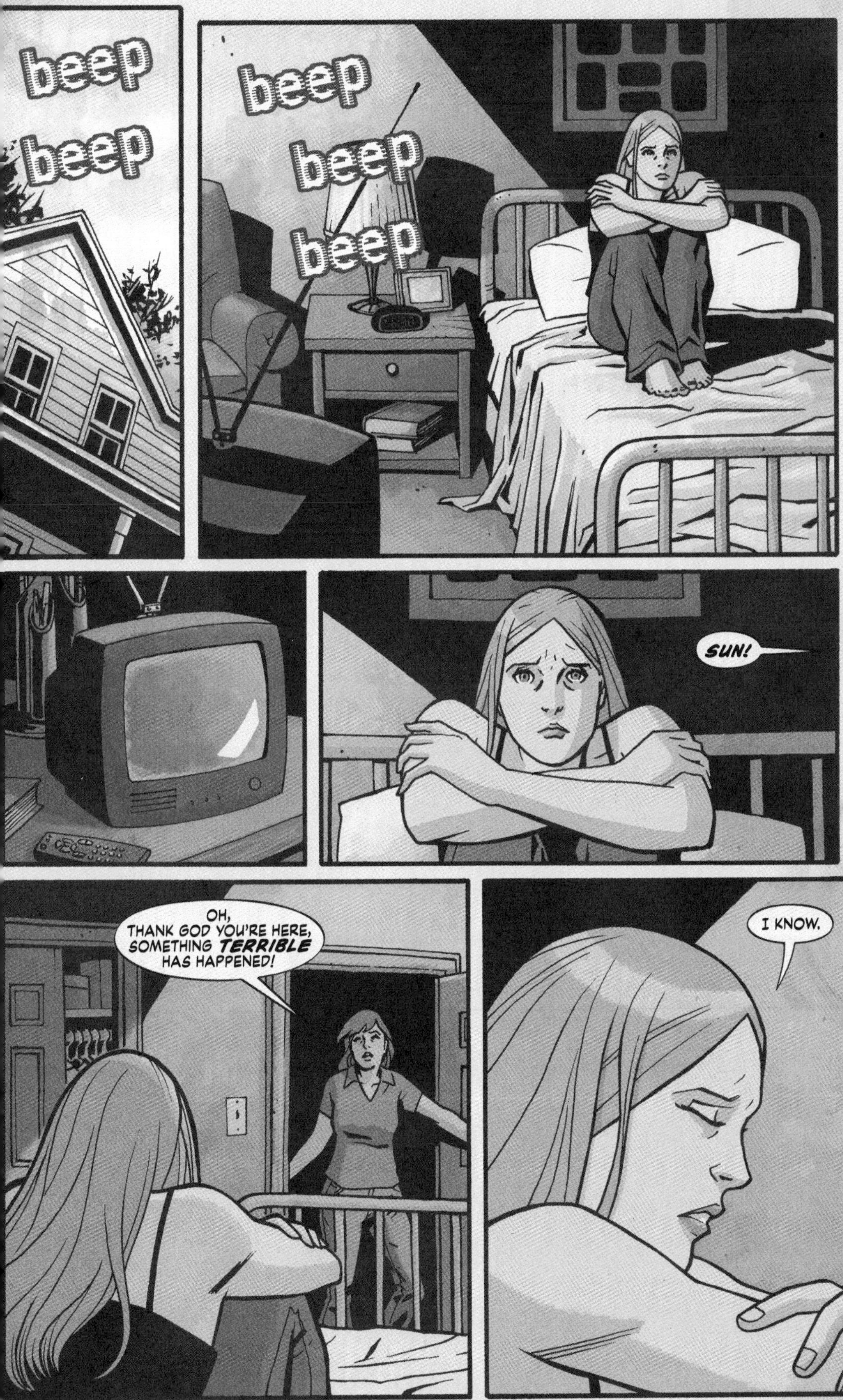
beep
beep
beep
beep
beep
SUN!
OH, THANK GOD YOU'RE HERE, SOMETHING TERRIBLE HAS HAPPENED!
I KNOW.

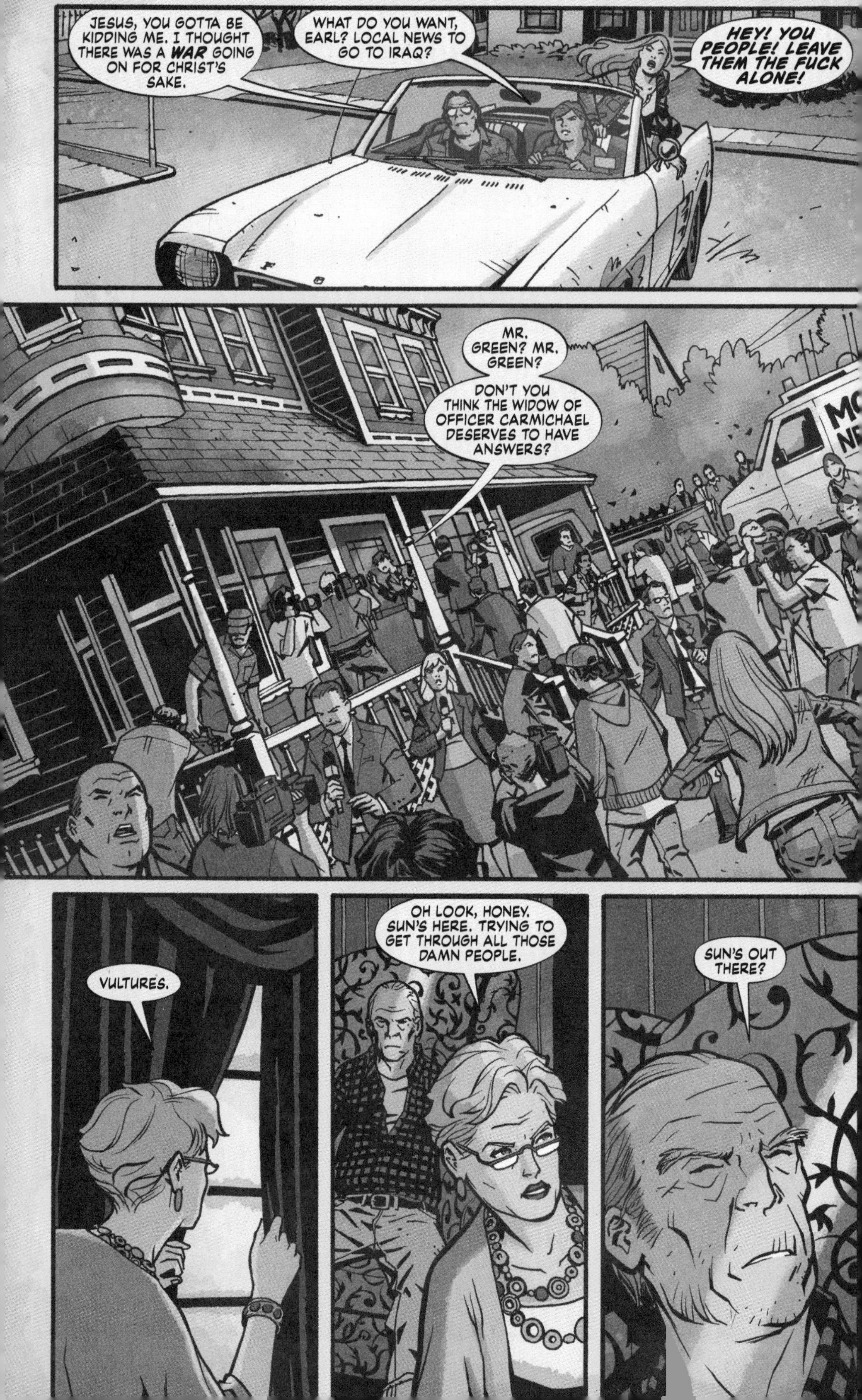
JESUS, YOU GOTTA BE KIDDING ME. I THOUGHT THERE WAS A WAR GOING ON FOR CHRIST'S SAKE.
WHAT DO YOU WANT, EARL? LOCAL NEWS TO GO TO IRAQ?
HEY! YOU PEOPLE! LEAVE THEM THE FUCK ALONE!
MR. GREEN? MR. GREEN?
DON'T YOU THINK THE WIDOW OF OFFICER CARMICHAEL DESERVES TO HAVE ANSWERS?
VULTURES.
OH LOOK, HONEY. SUN'S HERE. TRYING TO GET THROUGH ALL THOSE DAMN PEOPLE.
SUN'S OUT THERE?

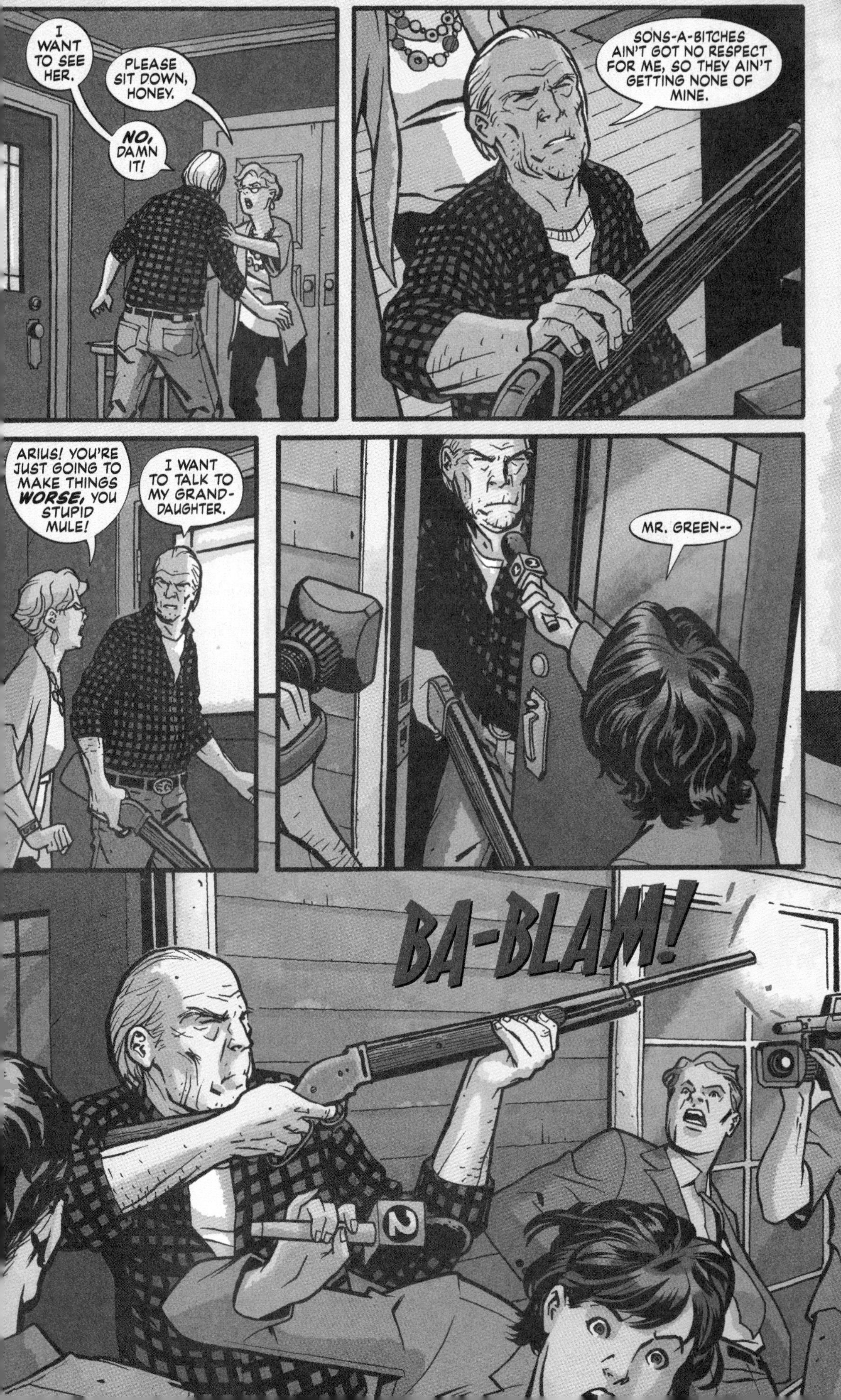

I WANT TO SEE HER.
PLEASE SIT DOWN, HONEY.
NO, DAMN IT!
SONS-A-BITCHES AIN'T GOT NO RESPECT FOR ME, SO THEY AIN'T GETTING NONE OF MINE.
ARIUS! YOU'RE JUST GOING TO MAKE THINGS WORSE, YOU STUPID MULE!
I WANT TO TALK TO MY GRAND-DAUGHTER.
MR. GREEN--
BA-BLAM!
2

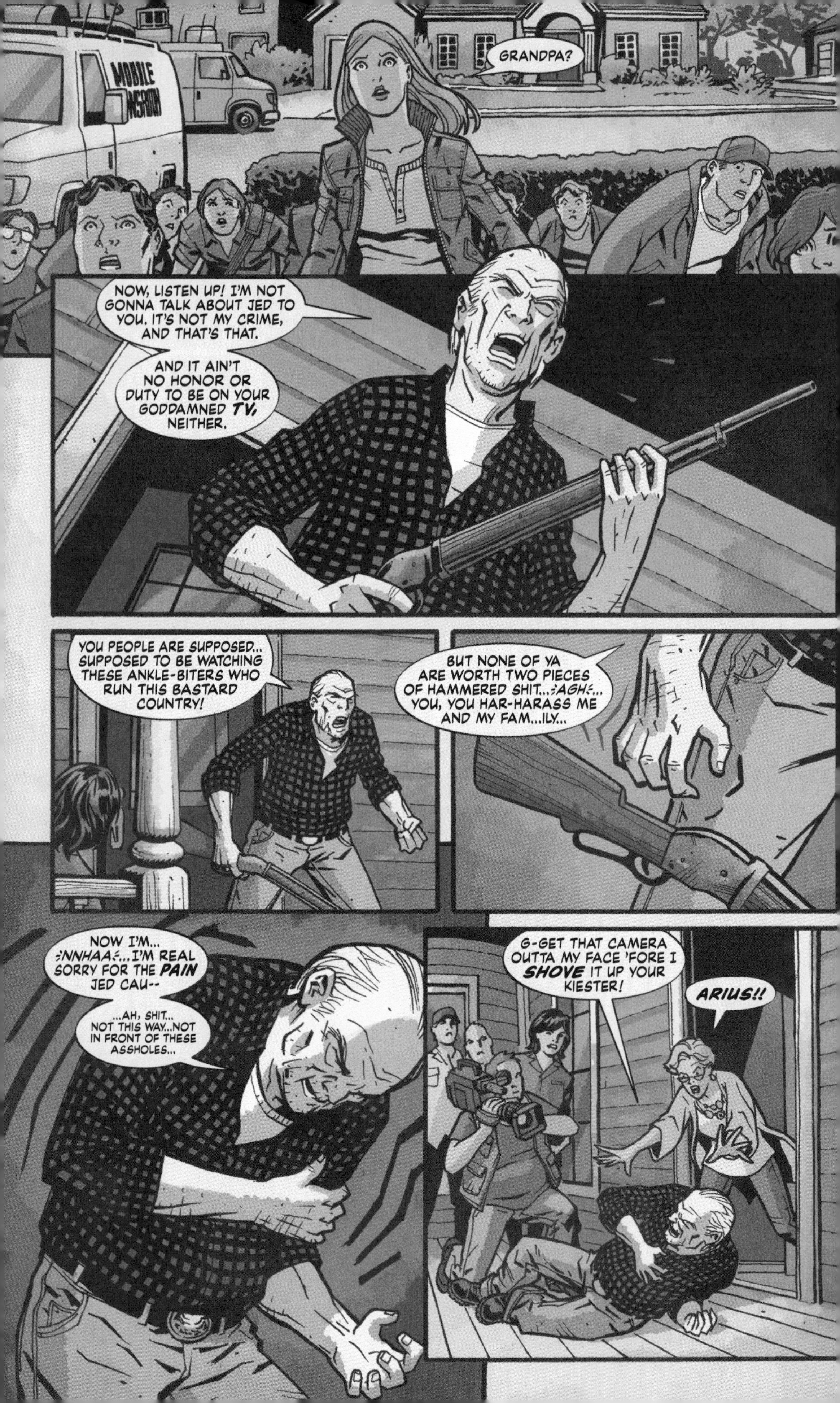
MOBILE NEWSROOM
GRANDPA?
NOW, LISTEN UP! I'M NOT GONNA TALK ABOUT JED TO YOU. IT'S NOT MY CRIME, AND THAT'S THAT.
AND IT AIN'T NO HONOR OR DUTY TO BE ON YOUR GODDAMNED TV, NEITHER.
YOU PEOPLE ARE SUPPOSED... SUPPOSED TO BE WATCHING THESE ANKLE-BITERS WHO RUN THIS BASTARD COUNTRY!
BUT NONE OF YA ARE WORTH TWO PIECES OF HAMMERED SHIT... AGH... YOU, YOU HAR-HARASS ME AND MY FAM...ILY...
NOW I'M... NNHAA... I'M REAL SORRY FOR THE PAIN JED CAU--
...AH, SHIT... NOT THIS WAY...NOT IN FRONT OF THESE ASSHOLES...
G-GET THAT CAMERA OUTTA MY FACE 'FORE I SHOVE IT UP YOUR KIESTER!
ARIUS!!

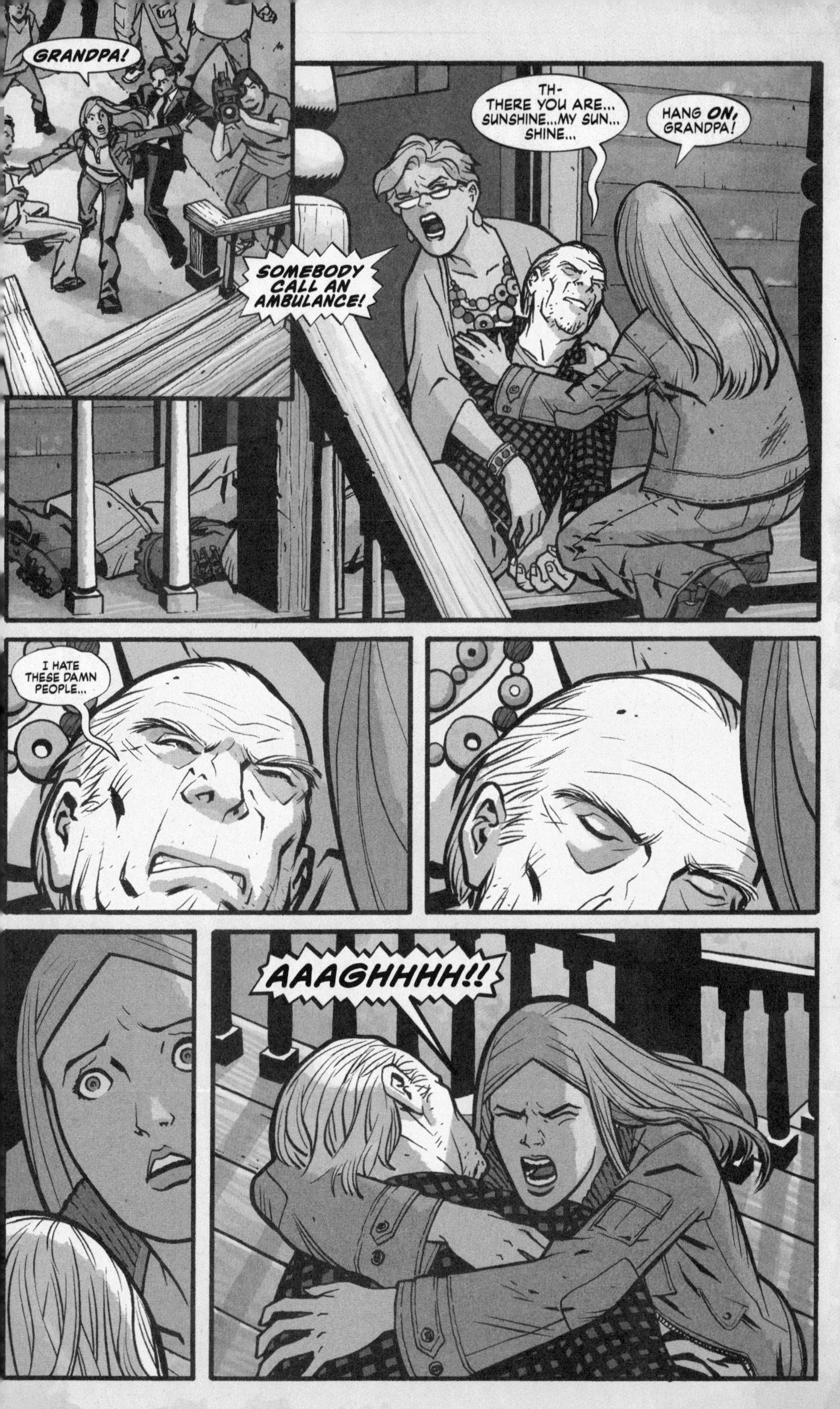

GRANDPA!
TH- THERE YOU ARE... SUNSHINE...MY SUN... SHINE...
HANG ON, GRANDPA!
SOMEBODY CALL AN AMBULANCE!
I HATE THESE DAMN PEOPLE...
AAAGHHHH!!

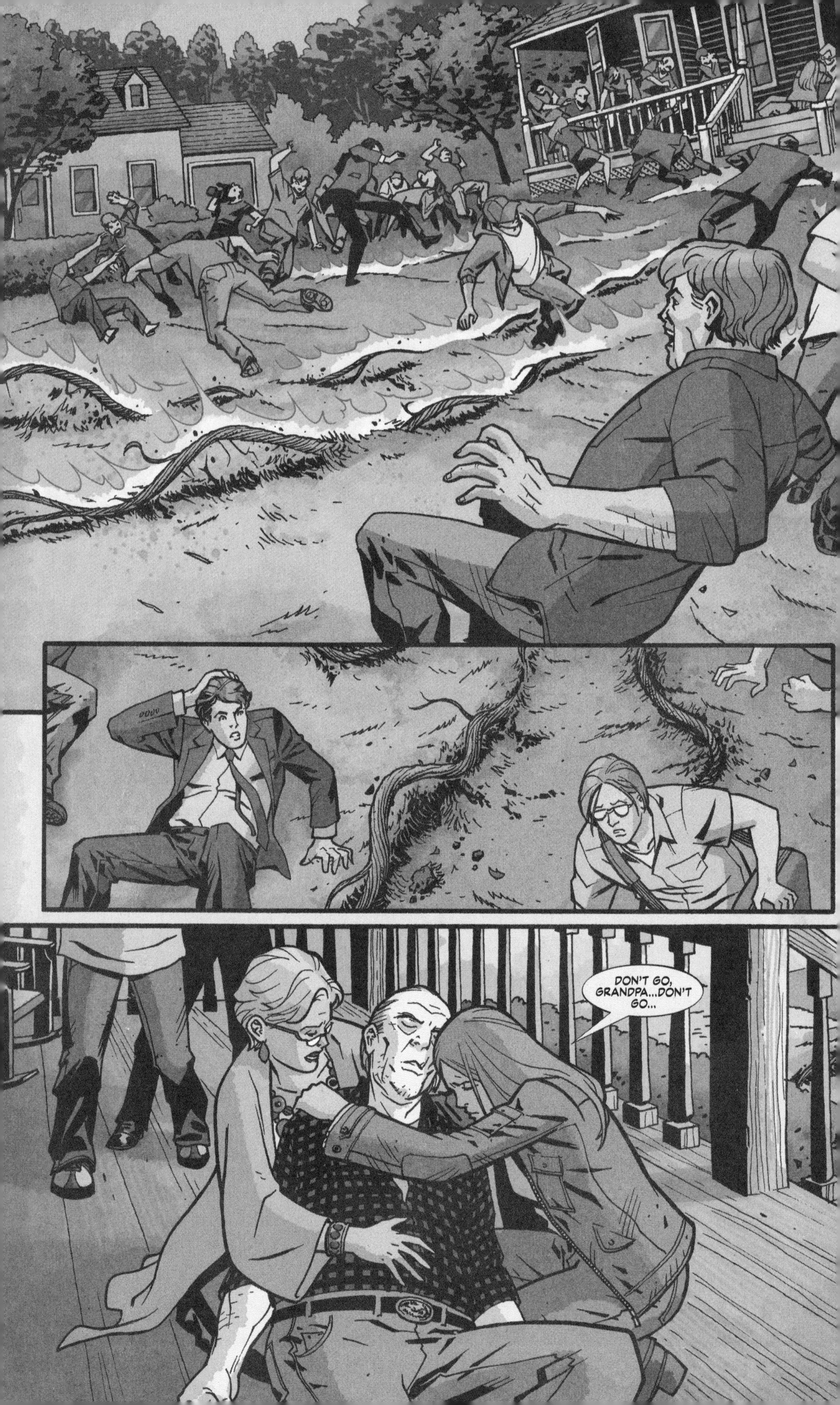
DON'T GO, GRANDPA...DON'T GO...

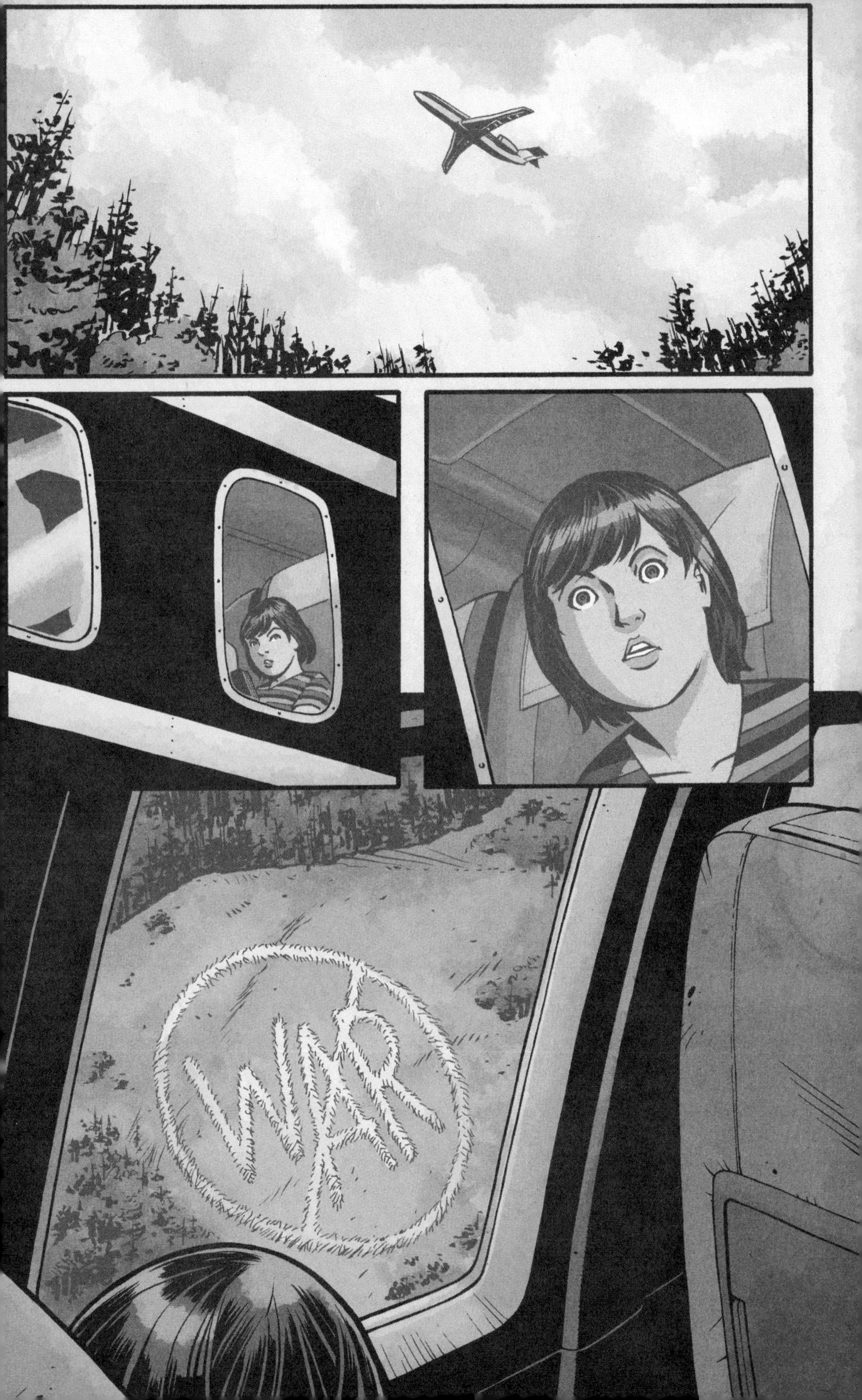
WAR

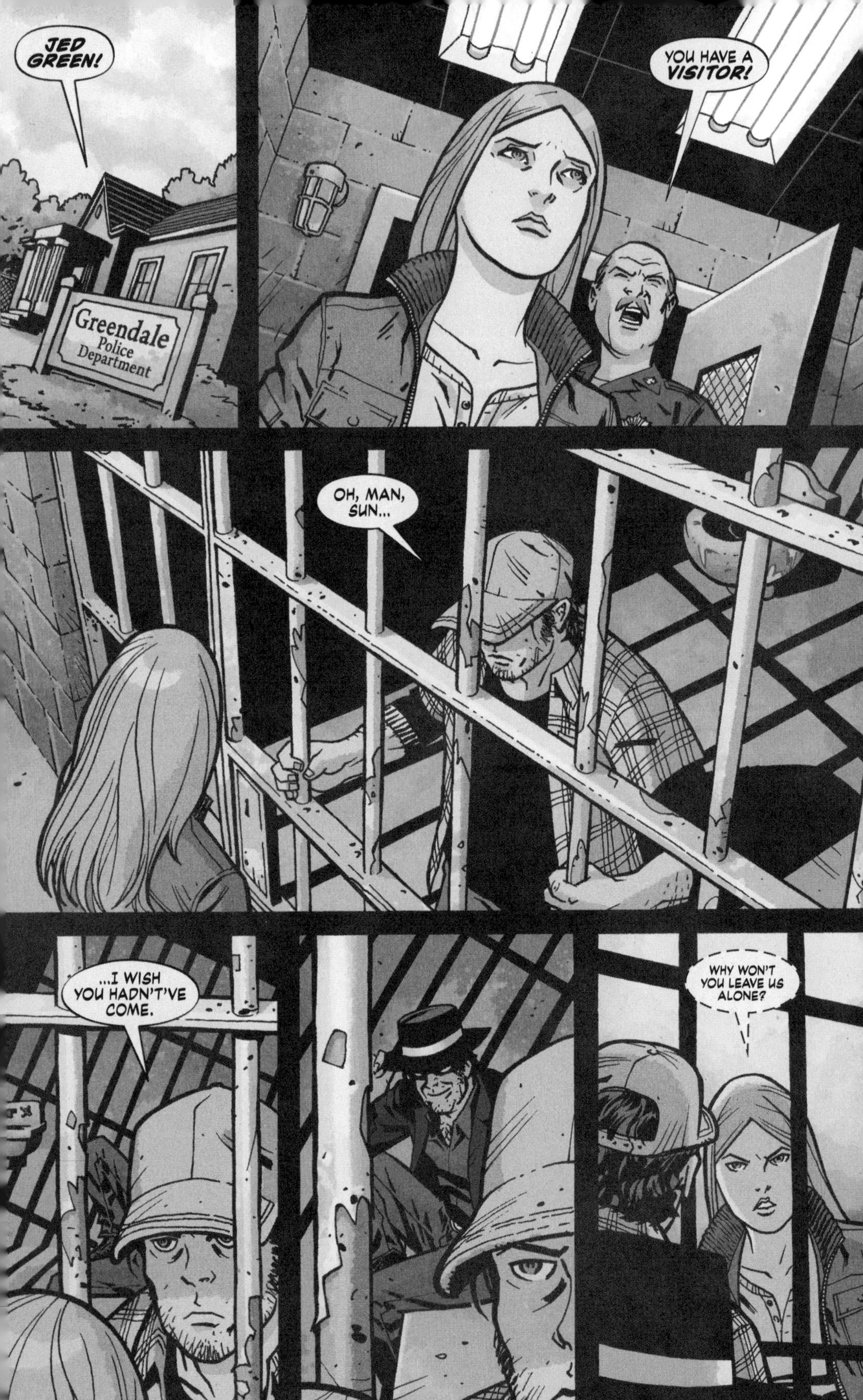
JED GREEN!
Greendale Police Department
YOU HAVE A VISITOR!
OH, MAN, SUN...
...I WISH YOU HADN'T'VE COME.
WHY WON'T YOU LEAVE US ALONE?

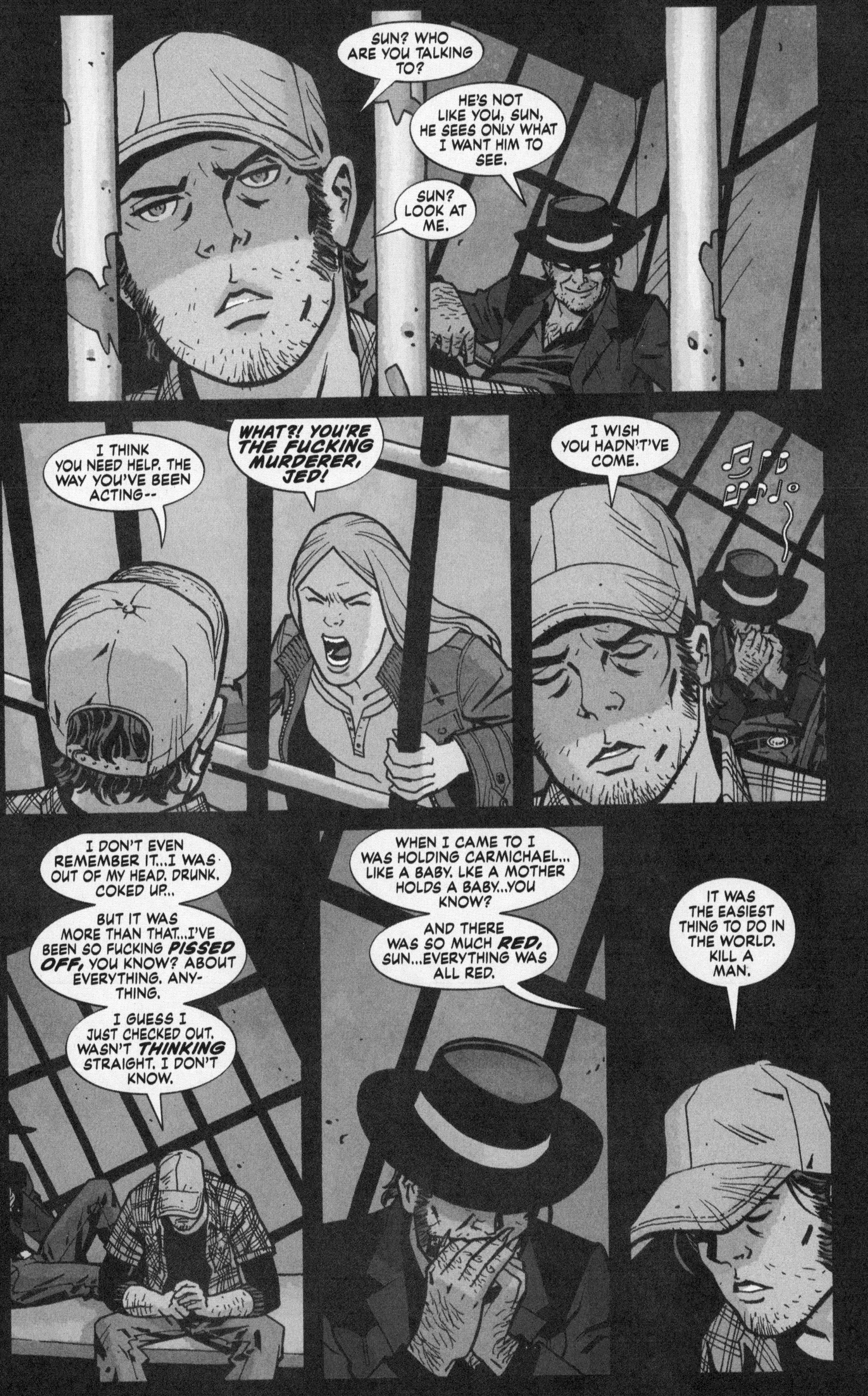
SUN? WHO ARE YOU TALKING TO?
HE'S NOT LIKE YOU, SUN, HE SEES ONLY WHAT I WANT HIM TO SEE.
SUN? LOOK AT ME.
I THINK YOU NEED HELP. THE WAY YOU'VE BEEN ACTING--
WHAT?! YOU'RE THE FUCKING MURDERER, JED!
I WISH YOU HADN'T'VE COME.
I DON'T EVEN REMEMBER IT...I WAS OUT OF MY HEAD. DRUNK. COKED UP...
BUT IT WAS MORE THAN THAT...I'VE BEEN SO FUCKING PISSED OFF, YOU KNOW? ABOUT EVERYTHING. ANY-THING.
I GUESS I JUST CHECKED OUT. WASN'T THINKING STRAIGHT. I DON'T KNOW.
WHEN I CAME TO I WAS HOLDING CARMICHAEL... LIKE A BABY. LKE A MOTHER HOLDS A BABY...YOU KNOW?
AND THERE WAS SO MUCH RED, SUN...EVERYTHING WAS ALL RED.
IT WAS THE EASIEST THING TO DO IN THE WORLD. KILL A MAN.

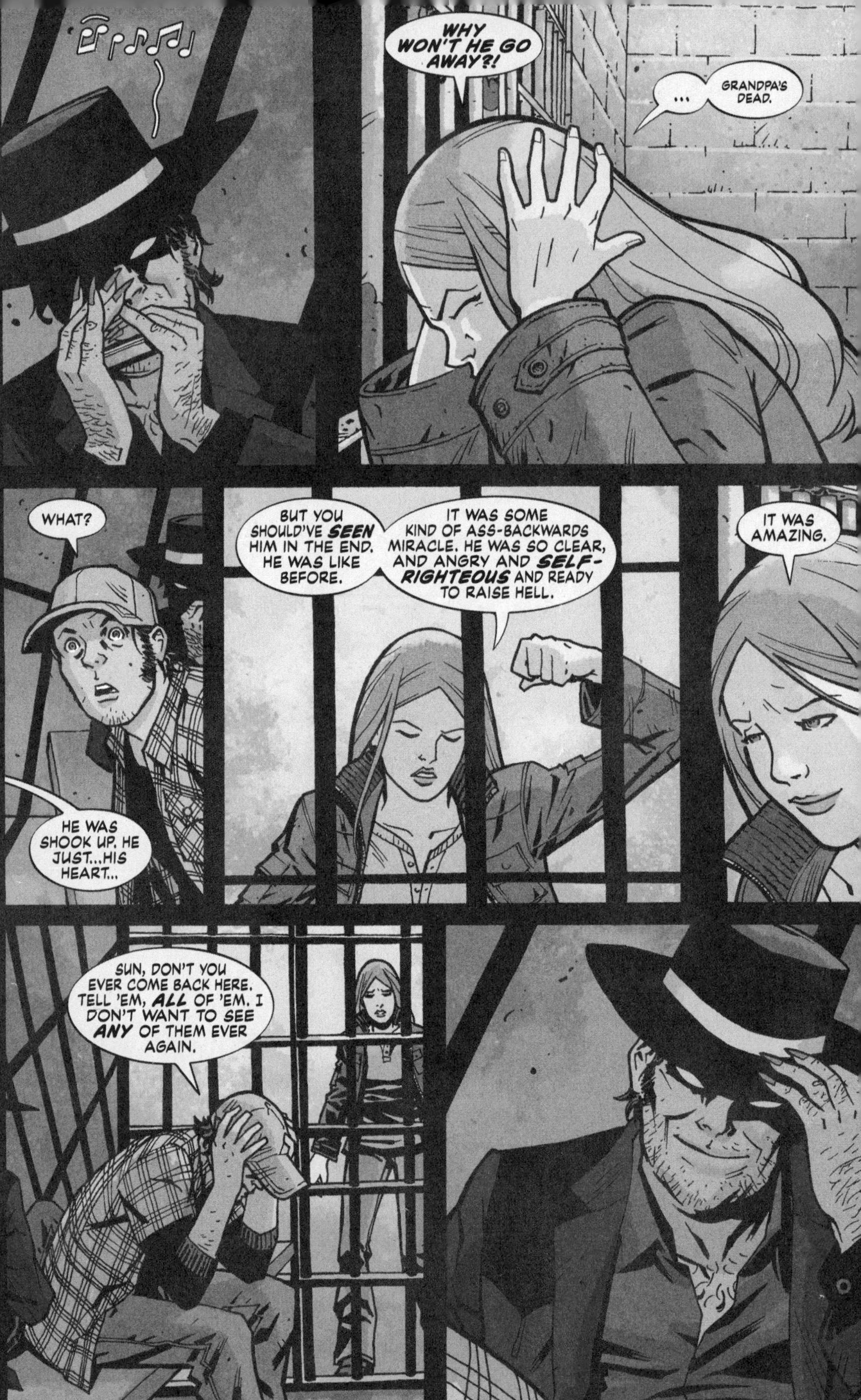
WHY WON'T HE GO AWAY?!
...
GRANDPA'S DEAD.
WHAT?
HE WAS SHOOK UP. HE JUST...HIS HEART...
BUT YOU SHOULD'VE SEEN HIM IN THE END. HE WAS LIKE BEFORE.
IT WAS SOME KIND OF ASS-BACKWARDS MIRACLE. HE WAS SO CLEAR, AND ANGRY AND SELF-RIGHTEOUS AND READY TO RAISE HELL.
IT WAS AMAZING.
SUN, DON'T YOU EVER COME BACK HERE. TELL 'EM, ALL OF 'EM. I DON'T WANT TO SEE ANY OF THEM EVER AGAIN.

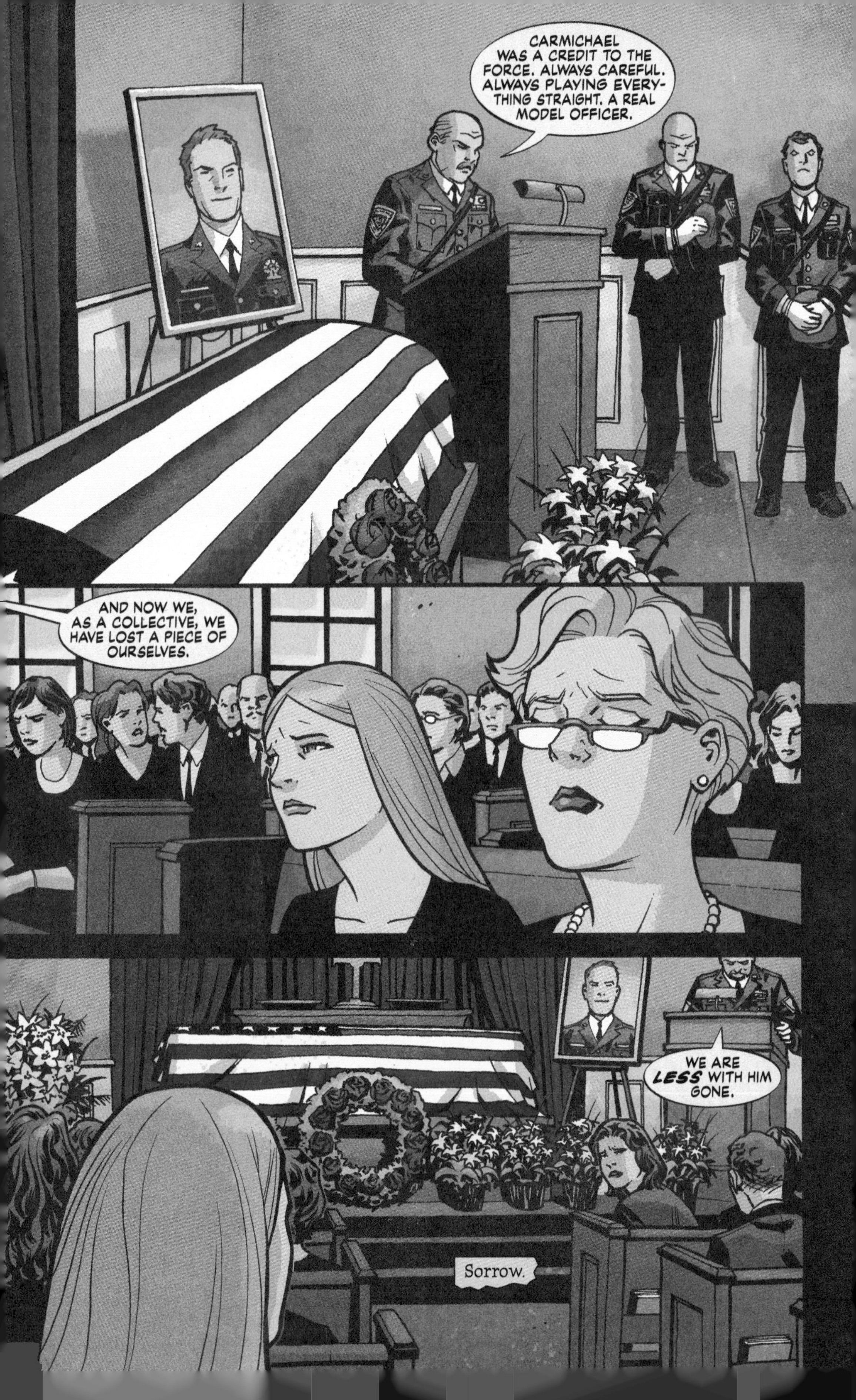
CARMICHAEL WAS A CREDIT TO THE FORCE. ALWAYS CAREFUL. ALWAYS PLAYING EVERY-THING STRAIGHT. A REAL MODEL OFFICER.
AND NOW WE, AS A COLLECTIVE, WE HAVE LOST A PIECE OF OURSELVES.
WE ARE LESS WITH HIM GONE.
Sorrow.

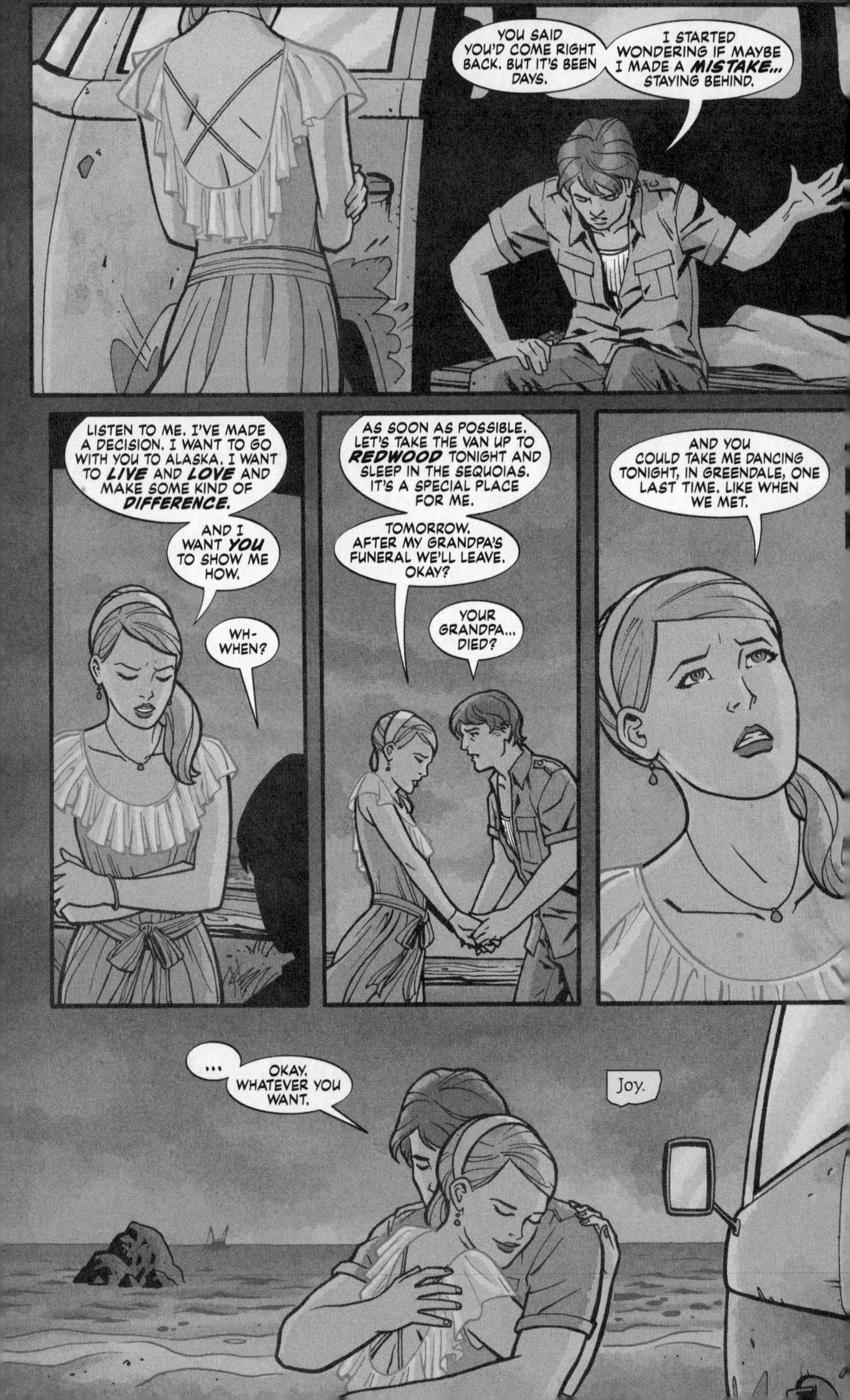
YOU SAID YOU'D COME RIGHT BACK. BUT IT'S BEEN DAYS.
I STARTED WONDERING IF MAYBE I MADE A MISTAKE... STAYING BEHIND.
LISTEN TO ME. I'VE MADE A DECISION. I WANT TO GO WITH YOU TO ALASKA. I WANT TO LIVE AND LOVE AND MAKE SOME KIND OF DIFFERENCE.
AND I WANT YOU TO SHOW ME HOW.
WH- WHEN?
AS SOON AS POSSIBLE. LET'S TAKE THE VAN UP TO REDWOOD TONIGHT AND SLEEP IN THE SEQUOIAS. IT'S A SPECIAL PLACE FOR ME.
TOMORROW. AFTER MY GRANDPA'S FUNERAL WE'LL LEAVE. OKAY?
YOUR GRANDPA... DIED?
AND YOU COULD TAKE ME DANCING TONIGHT, IN GREENDALE, ONE LAST TIME. LIKE WHEN WE MET.
...
OKAY. WHATEVER YOU WANT.
Joy.

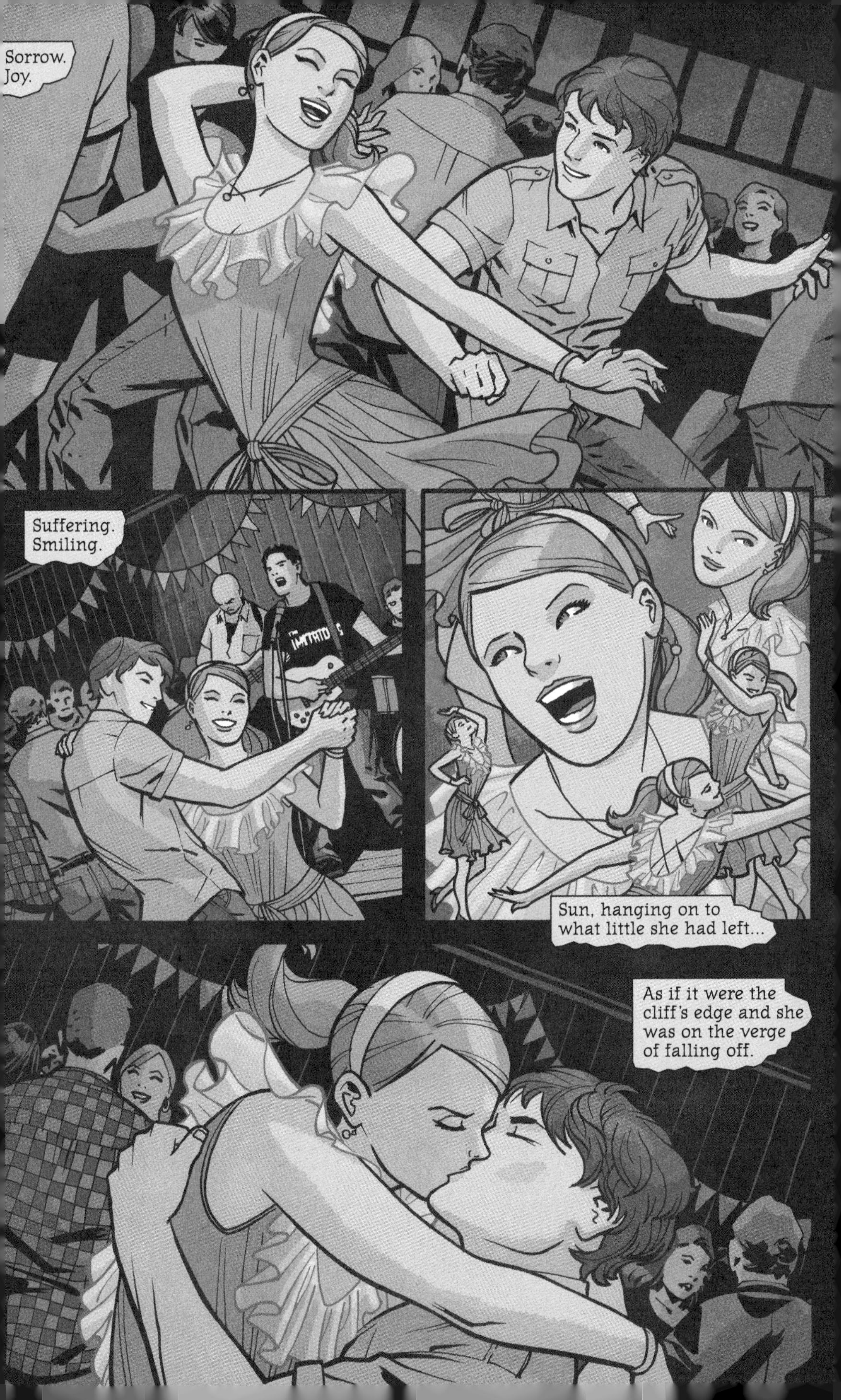
Sorrow. Joy.
Suffering. Smiling.
Sun, hanging on to what little she had left...
As if it were the cliff's edge and she was on the verge of falling off.

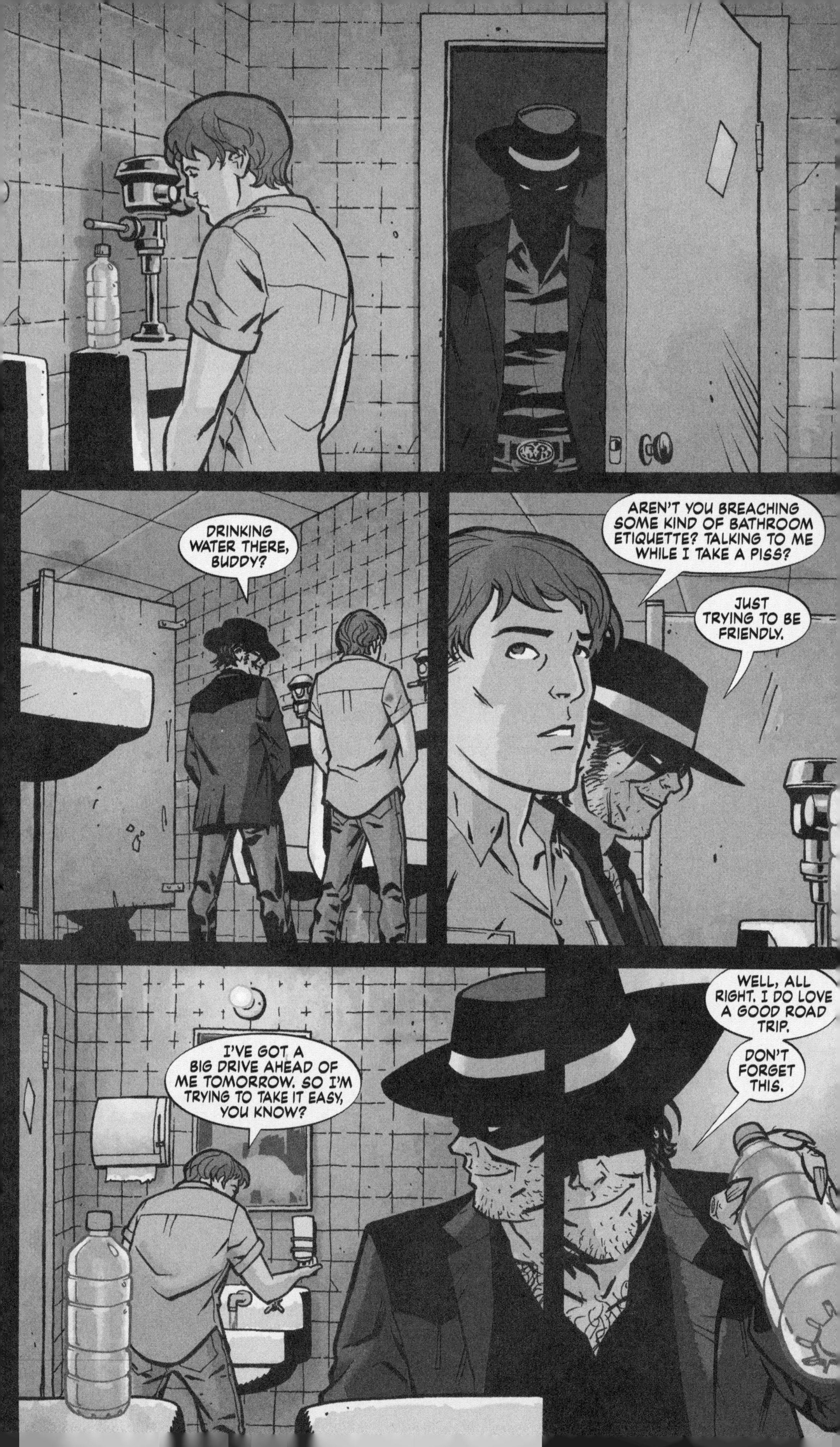
DRINKING WATER THERE, BUDDY?
AREN'T YOU BREACHING SOME KIND OF BATHROOM ETIQUETTE? TALKING TO ME WHILE I TAKE A PISS?
JUST TRYING TO BE FRIENDLY.
I'VE GOT A BIG DRIVE AHEAD OF ME TOMORROW. SO I'M TRYING TO TAKE IT EASY, YOU KNOW?
WELL, ALL RIGHT. I DO LOVE A GOOD ROAD TRIP.
DON'T FORGET THIS.

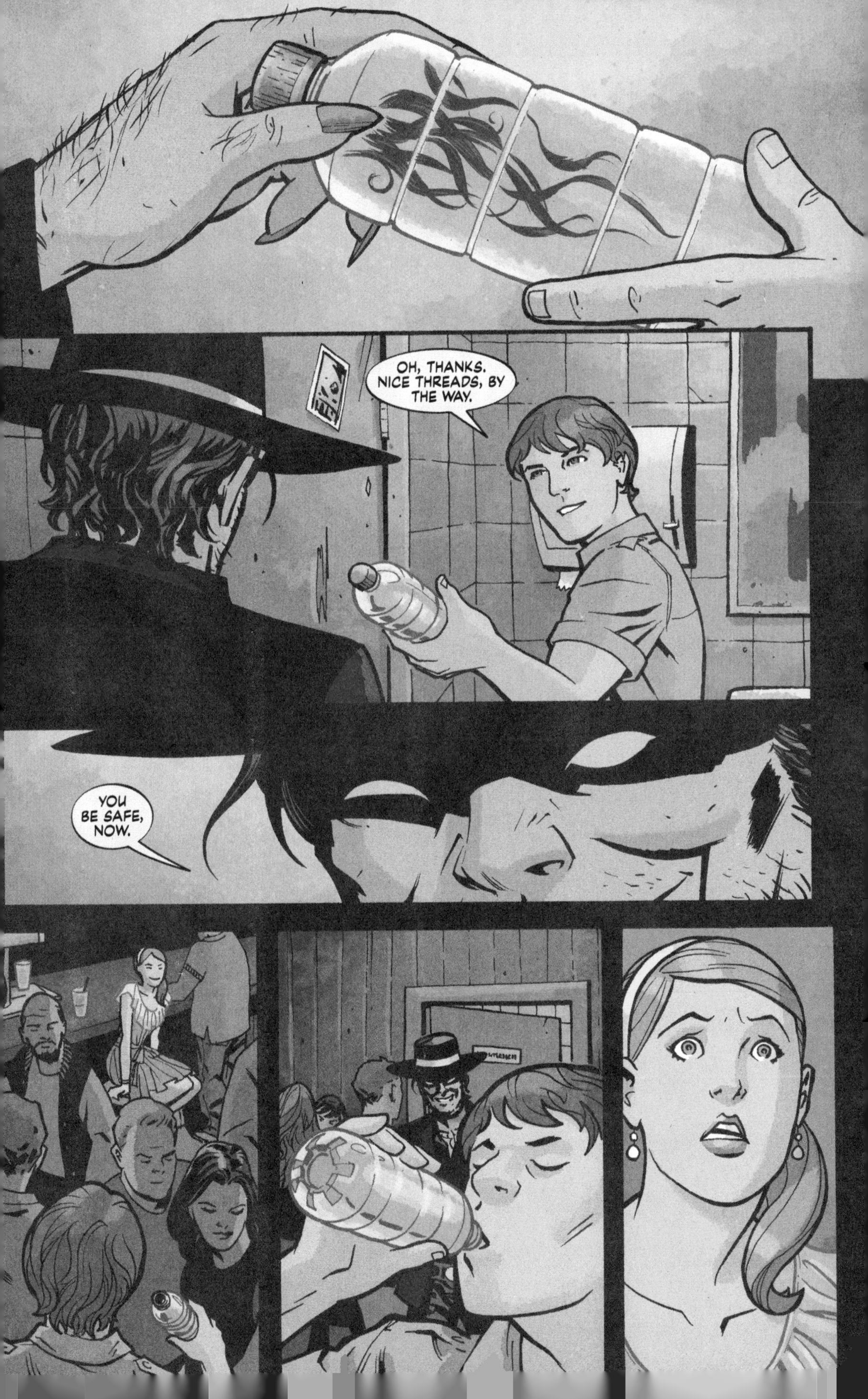
OH, THANKS. NICE THREADS, BY THE WAY.
YOU BE SAFE, NOW.

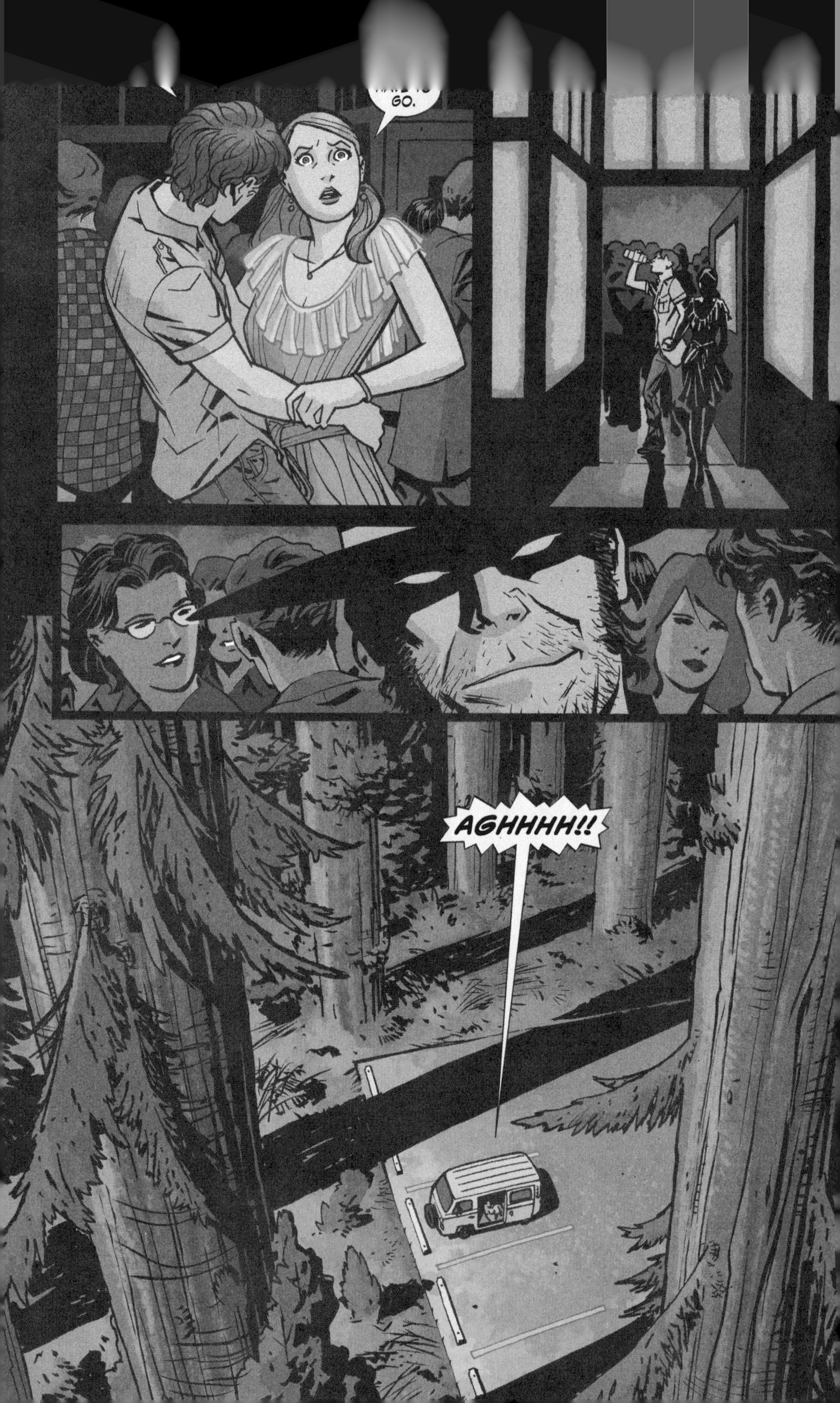
GO.
AGHHHH!!

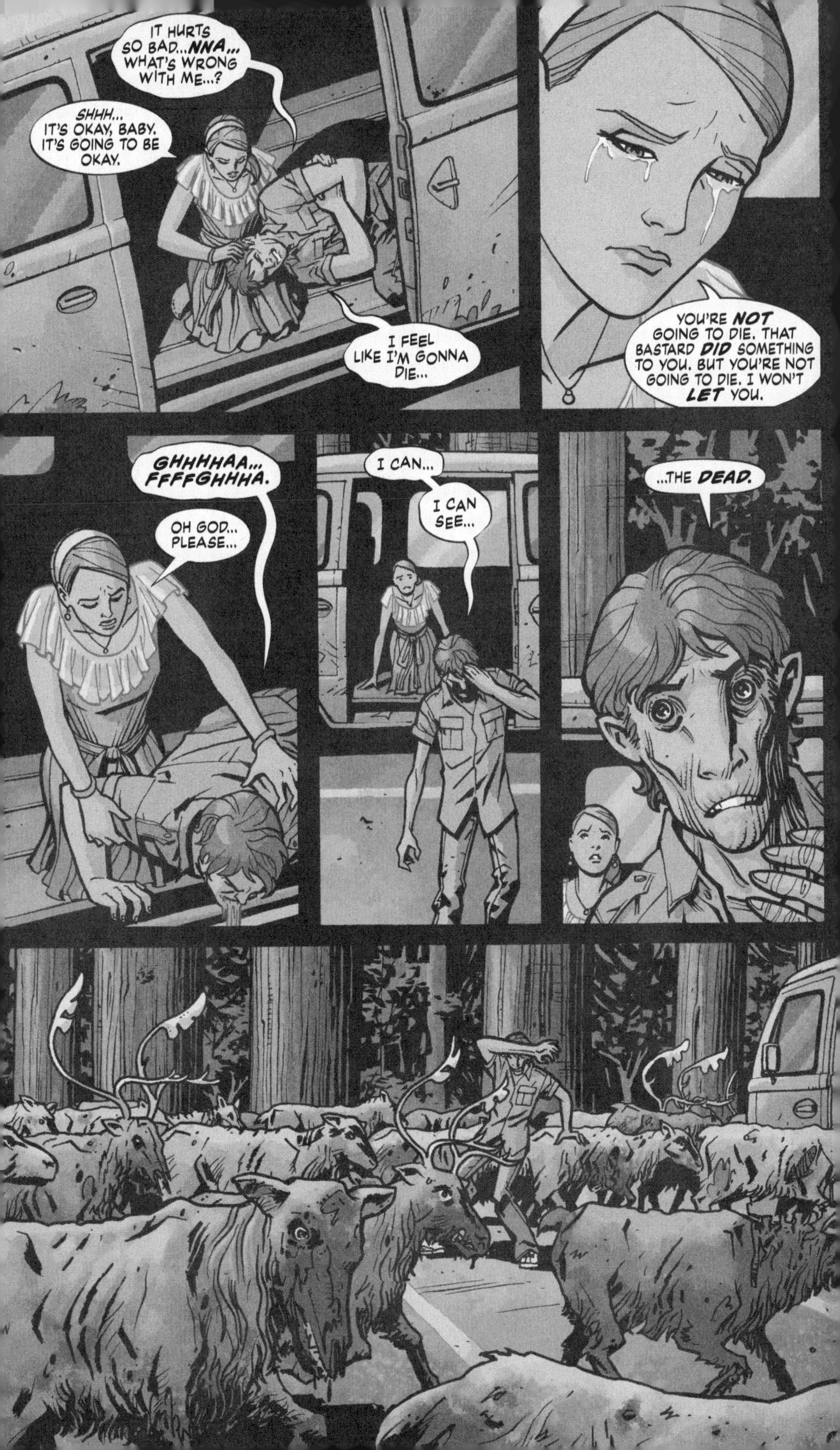
IT HURTS SO BAD...NNA... WHAT'S WRONG WITH ME...?
SHHH... IT'S OKAY, BABY. IT'S GOING TO BE OKAY.
I FEEL LIKE I'M GONNA DIE...
YOU'RE NOT GOING TO DIE. THAT BASTARD DID SOMETHING TO YOU. BUT YOU'RE NOT GOING TO DIE. I WON'T LET YOU.
GHHHHAA... FFFFGHHHA.
OH GOD... PLEASE...
I CAN...
I CAN SEE...
...THE DEAD.

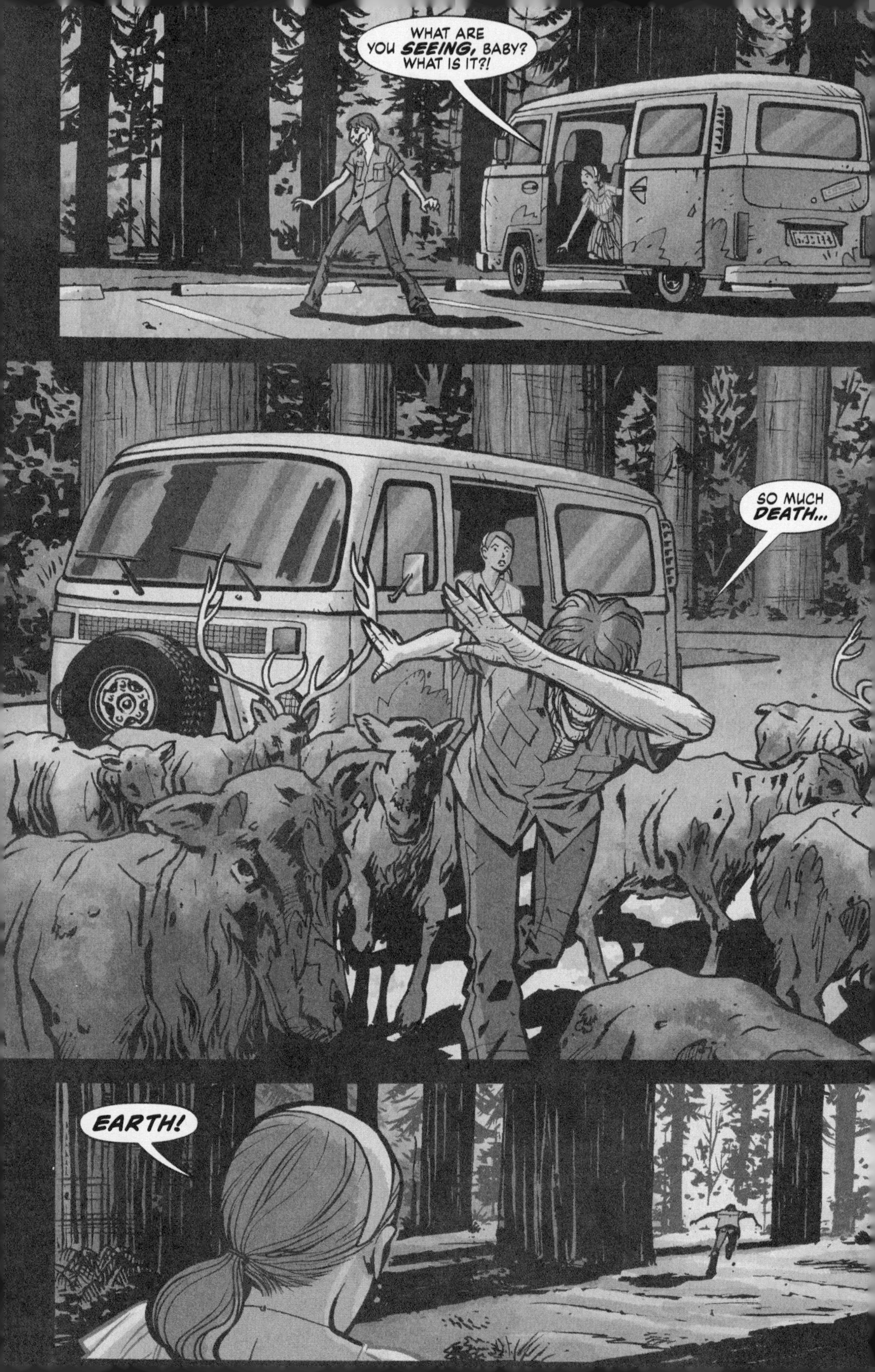
WHAT ARE YOU SEEING, BABY? WHAT IS IT?!
SO MUCH DEATH...
EARTH!

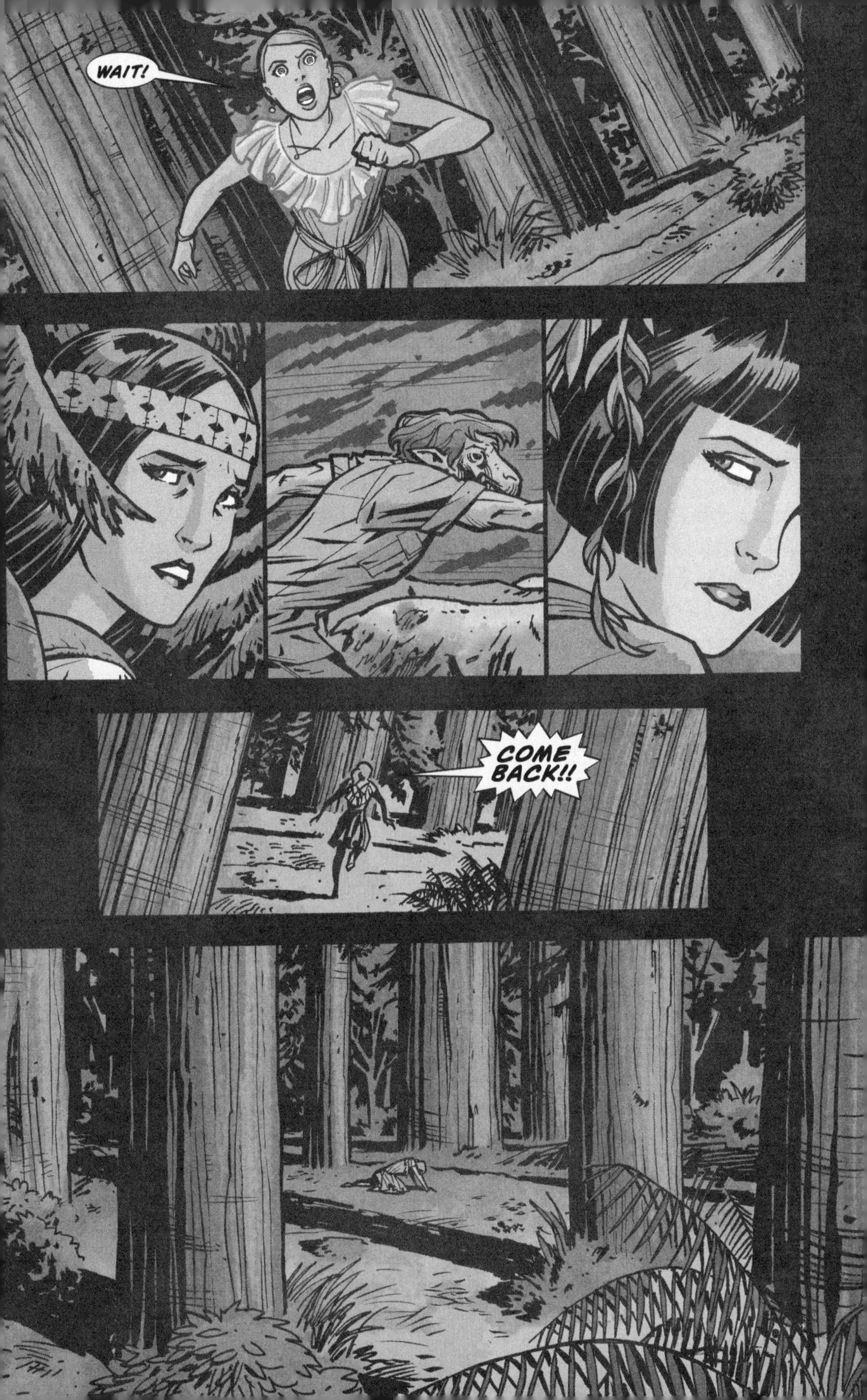
WAIT!
COME BACK!!

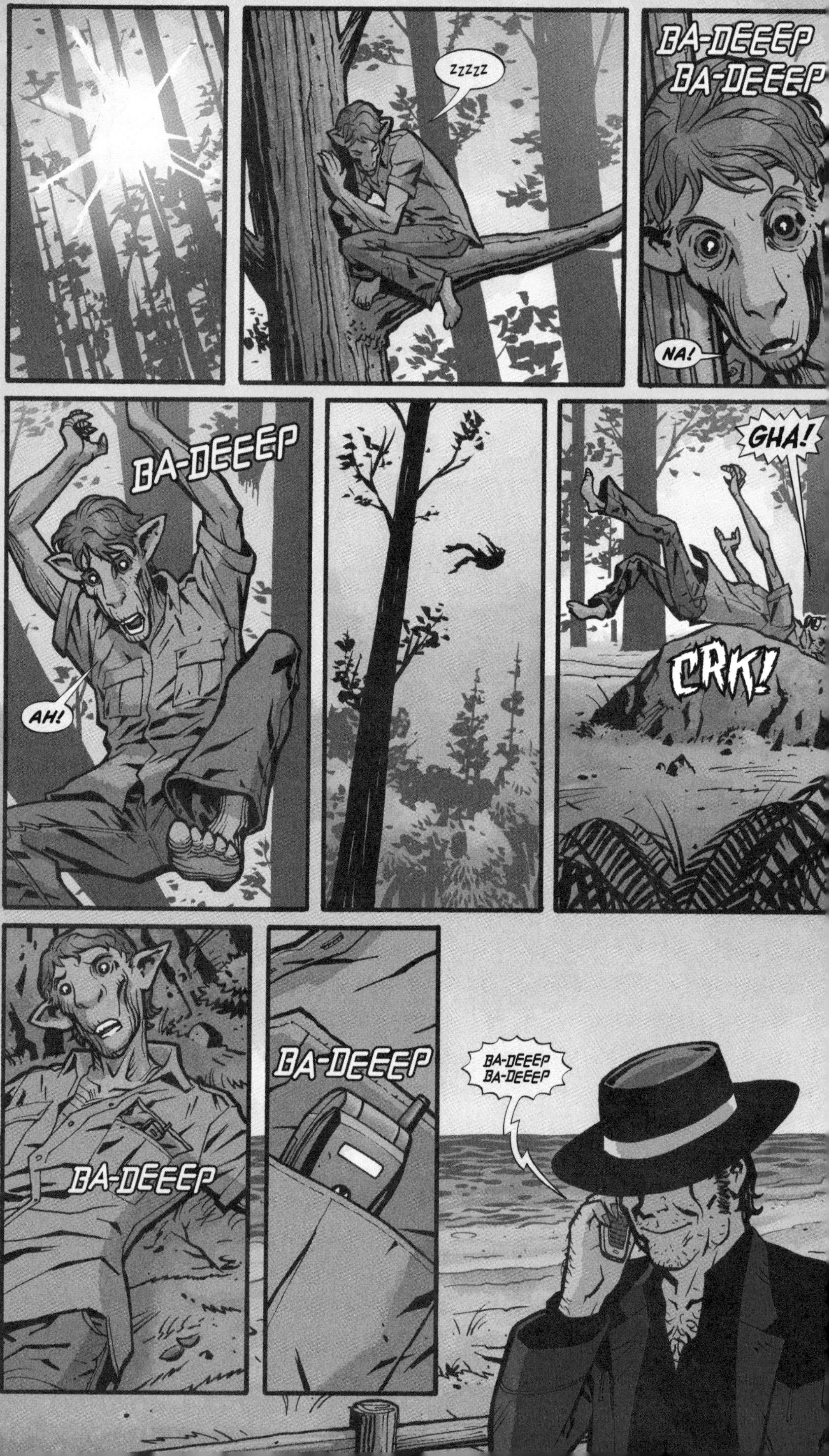
ZZZZZ
BA-DEEEP
BA-DEEEP
NA!
BA-DEEEP
AH!
GHA!
CRK!
BA-DEEEP
BA-DEEEP
BA-DEEEP
BA-DEEEP

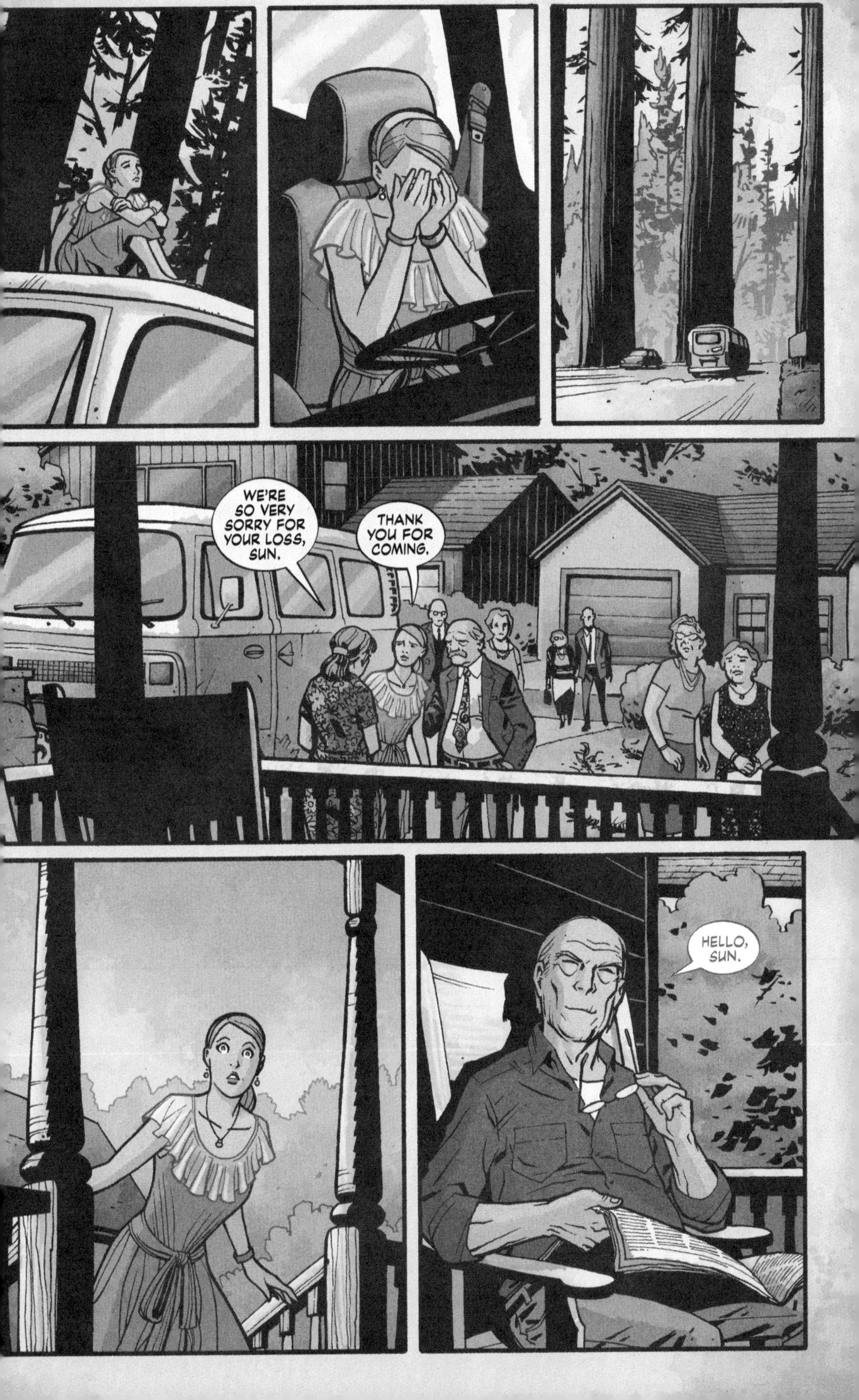
WE'RE SO VERY SORRY FOR YOUR LOSS, SUN.
THANK YOU FOR COMING.
HELLO, SUN.

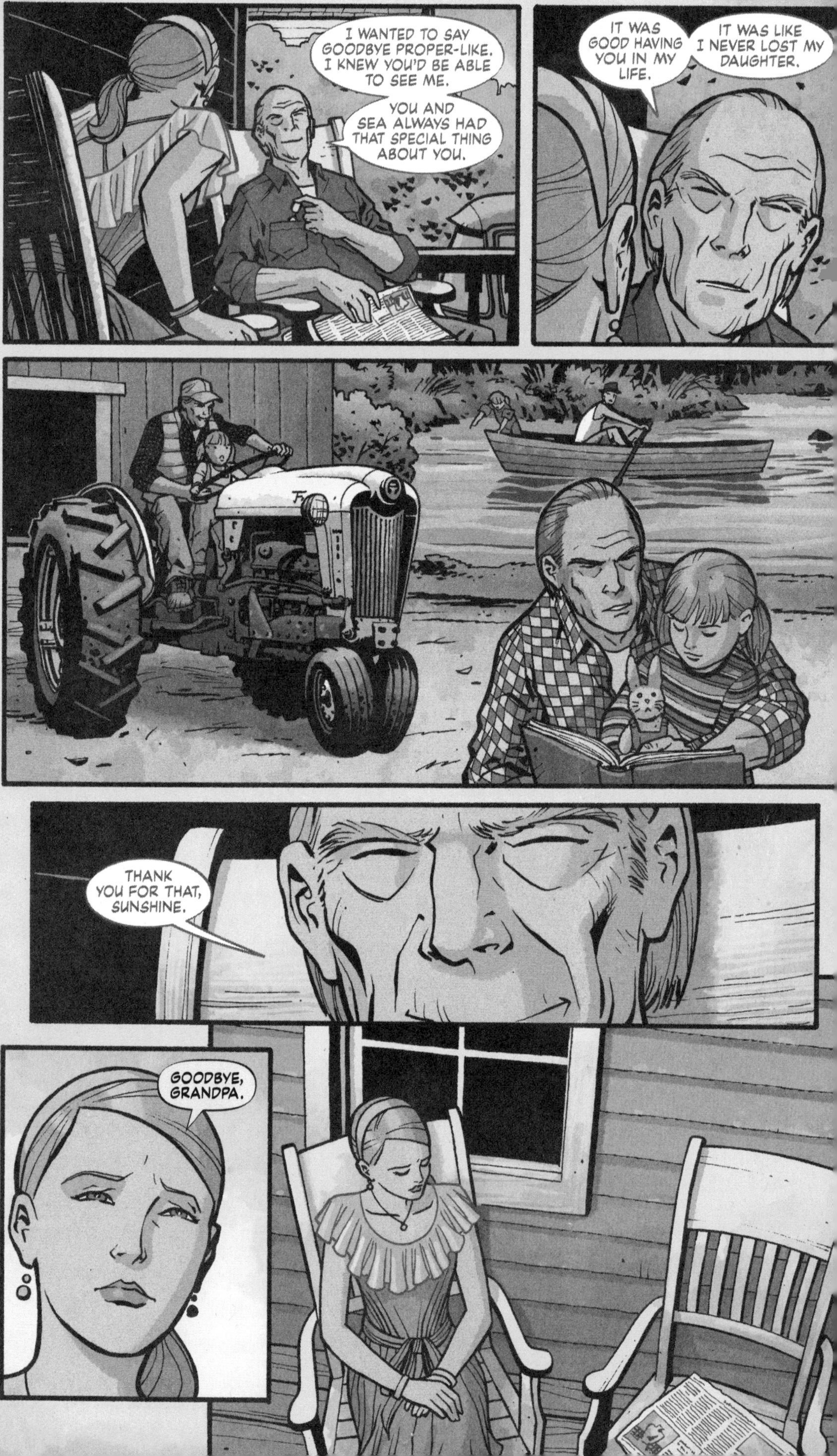
I WANTED TO SAY GOODBYE PROPER-LIKE. I KNEW YOU'D BE ABLE TO SEE ME.
YOU AND SEA ALWAYS HAD THAT SPECIAL THING ABOUT YOU.
IT WAS GOOD HAVING YOU IN MY LIFE.
IT WAS LIKE I NEVER LOST MY DAUGHTER.
THANK YOU FOR THAT, SUNSHINE.
GOODBYE, GRANDPA.

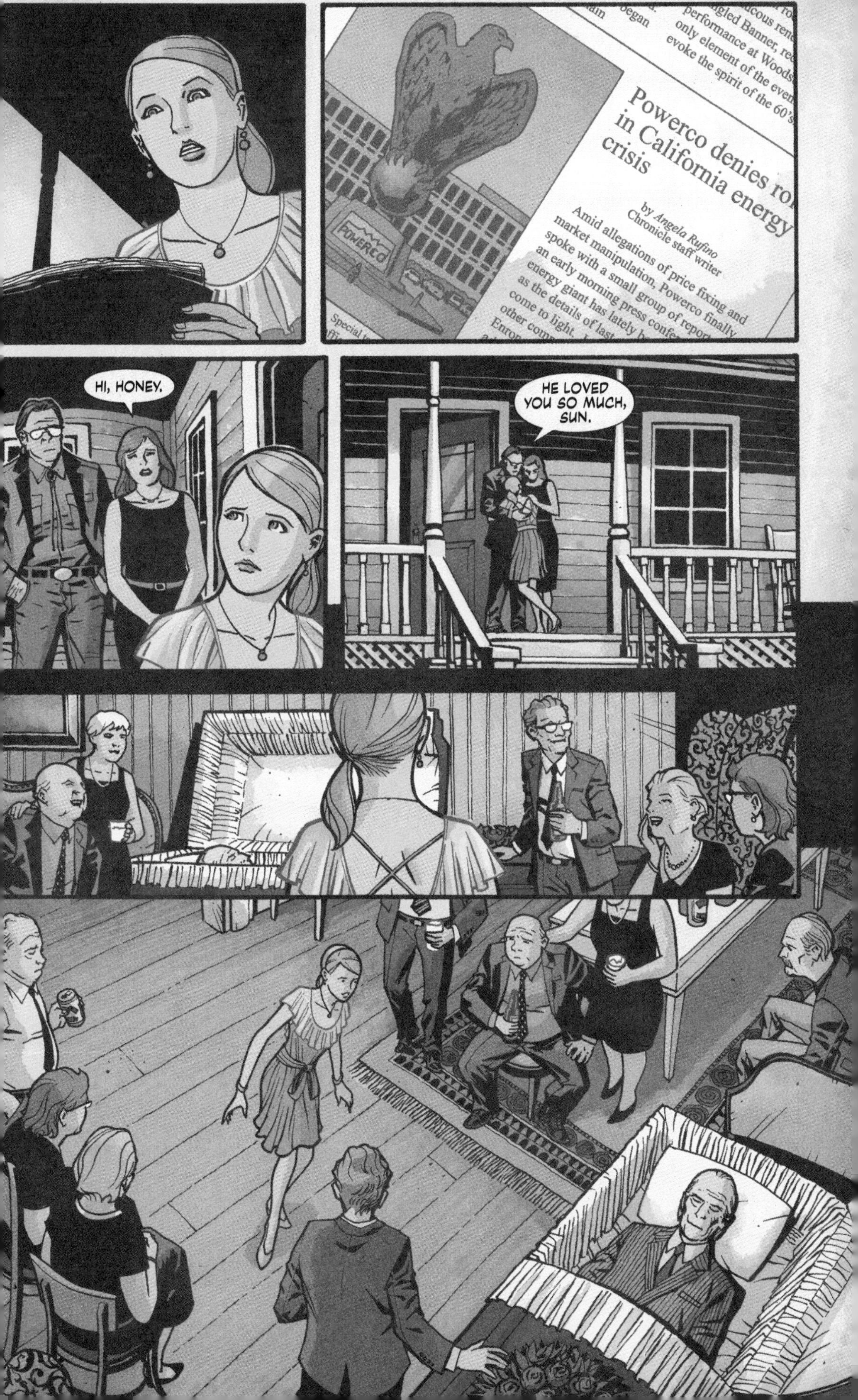
ngled Banner, re
performance at Woods
only element of the even
evoke the spirit of the 60's
Powerco denies ro
in California energy
crisis
by Angela Rufino
Chronicle staff writer
Amid allegations of price fixing and
market manipulation, Powerco finally
spoke with a small group of report
an early morning press confe
energy giant has lately
as the details of last
come to light.
other comp
Enron
POWERCO
HI, HONEY.
HE LOVED YOU SO MUCH, SUN.

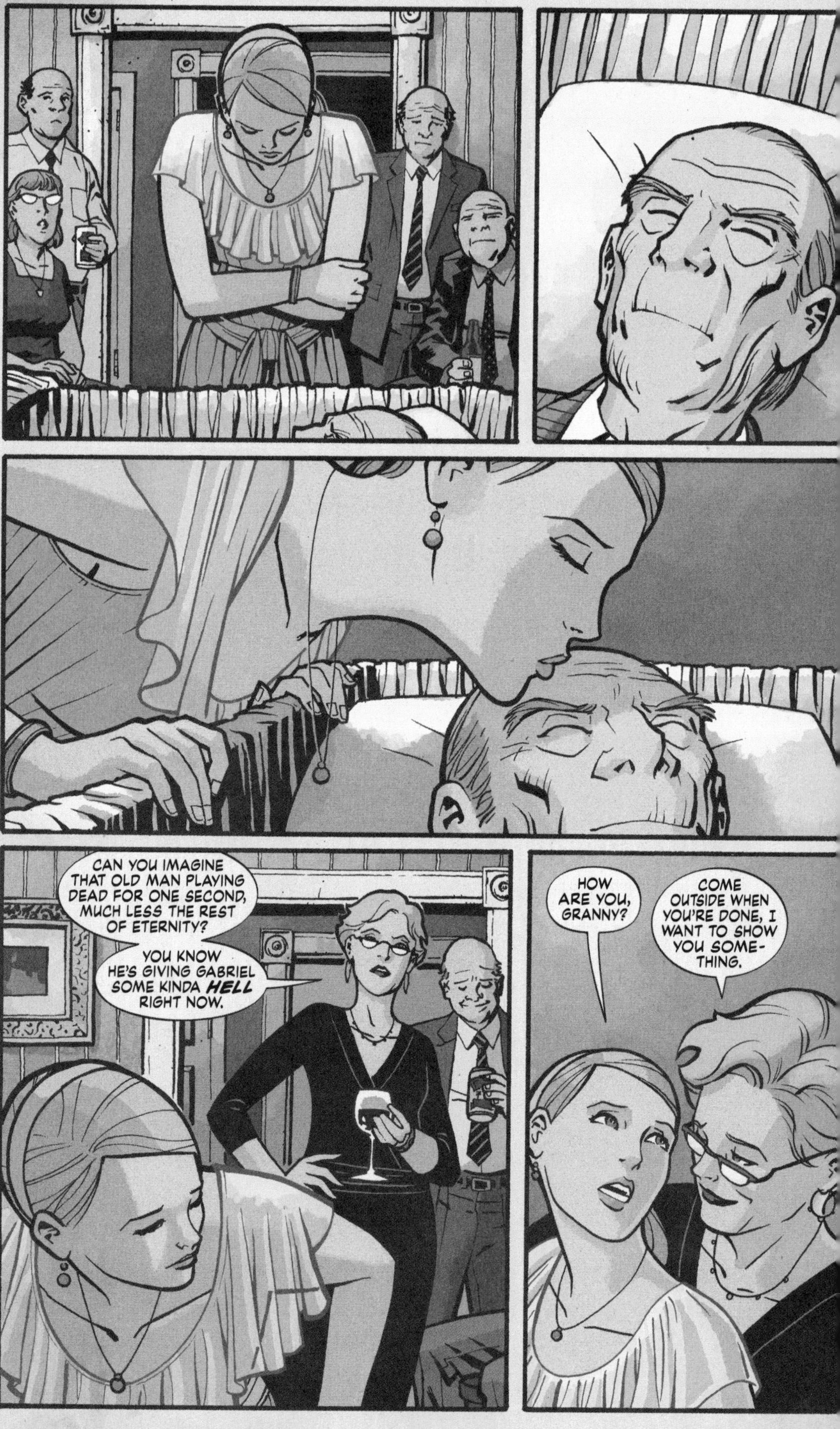
CAN YOU IMAGINE THAT OLD MAN PLAYING DEAD FOR ONE SECOND, MUCH LESS THE REST OF ETERNITY?
YOU KNOW HE'S GIVING GABRIEL SOME KINDA **HELL** RIGHT NOW.
HOW ARE YOU, GRANNY?
COME OUTSIDE WHEN YOU'RE DONE, I WANT TO SHOW YOU SOME-THING.

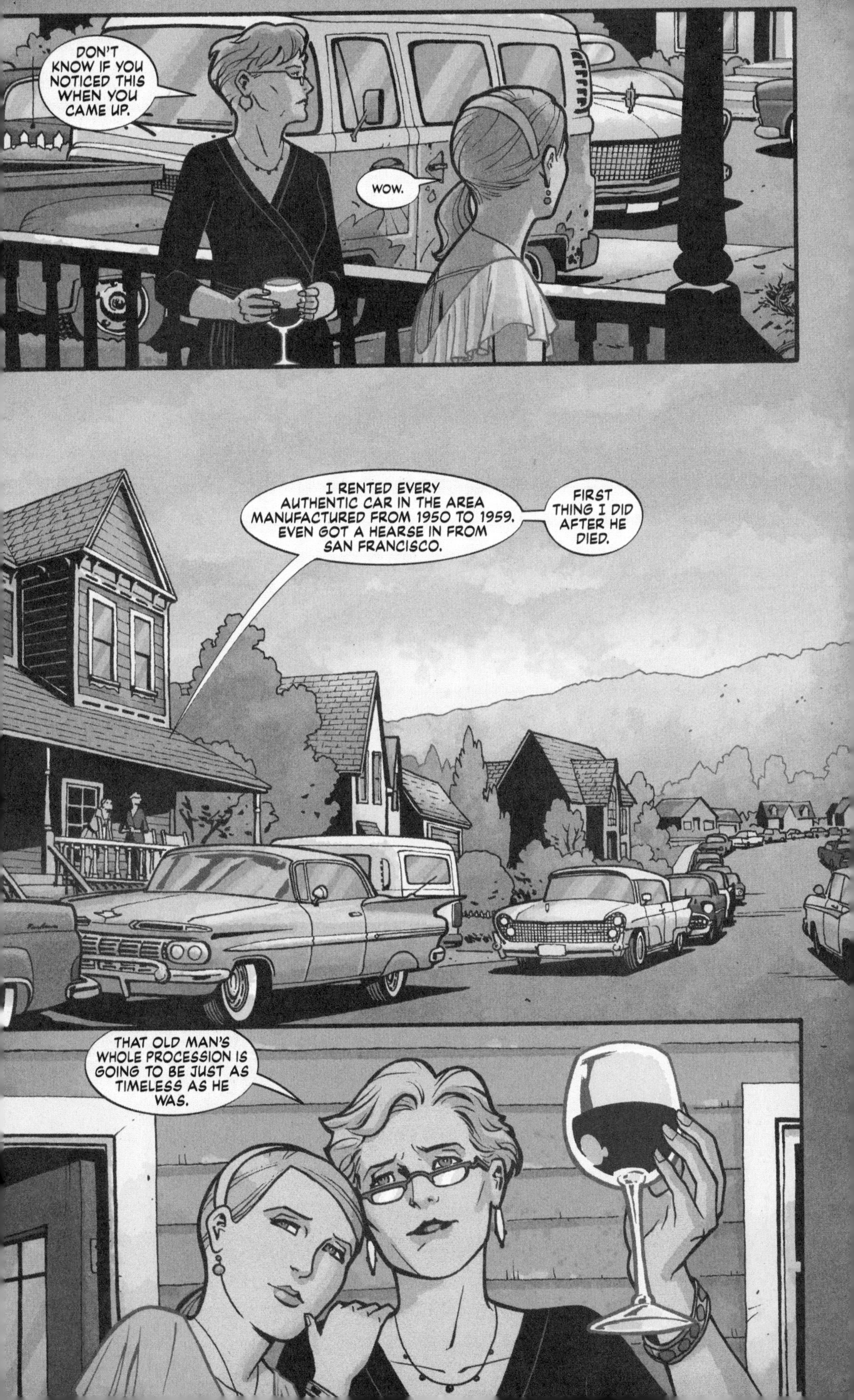
DON'T KNOW IF YOU NOTICED THIS WHEN YOU CAME UP.
WOW.
I RENTED EVERY AUTHENTIC CAR IN THE AREA MANUFACTURED FROM 1950 TO 1959. EVEN GOT A HEARSE IN FROM SAN FRANCISCO.
FIRST THING I DID AFTER HE DIED.
THAT OLD MAN'S WHOLE PROCESSION IS GOING TO BE JUST AS TIMELESS AS HE WAS.

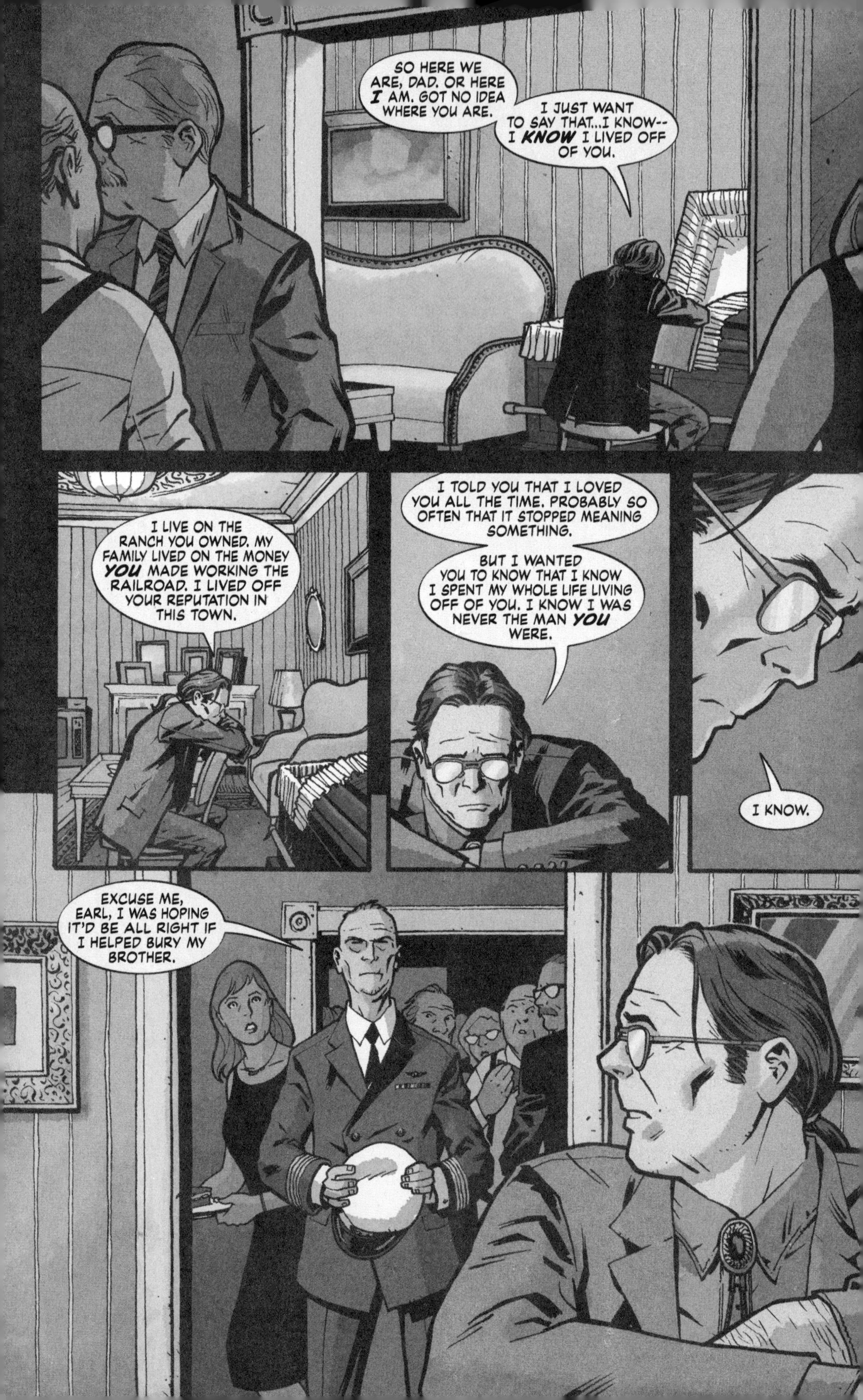
SO HERE WE ARE, DAD. OR HERE *I* AM. GOT NO IDEA WHERE YOU ARE.
I JUST WANT TO SAY THAT...I KNOW-- I **KNOW** I LIVED OFF OF YOU.
I LIVE ON THE RANCH YOU OWNED. MY FAMILY LIVED ON THE MONEY **YOU** MADE WORKING THE RAILROAD. I LIVED OFF YOUR REPUTATION IN THIS TOWN.
I TOLD YOU THAT I LOVED YOU ALL THE TIME. PROBABLY SO OFTEN THAT IT STOPPED MEANING SOMETHING.
BUT I WANTED YOU TO KNOW THAT I KNOW I SPENT MY WHOLE LIFE LIVING OFF OF YOU. I KNOW I WAS NEVER THE MAN **YOU** WERE.
I KNOW.
EXCUSE ME, EARL, I WAS HOPING IT'D BE ALL RIGHT IF I HELPED BURY MY BROTHER.

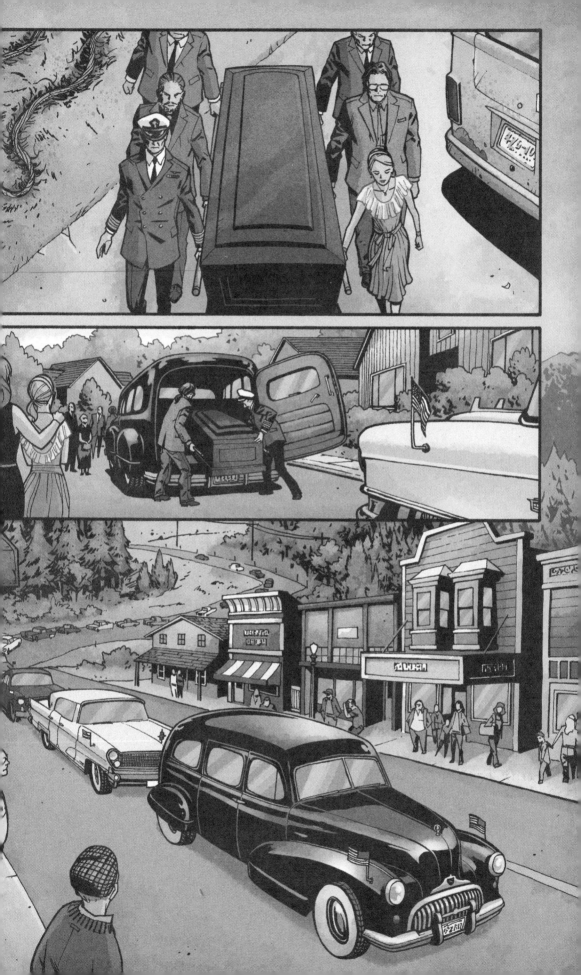

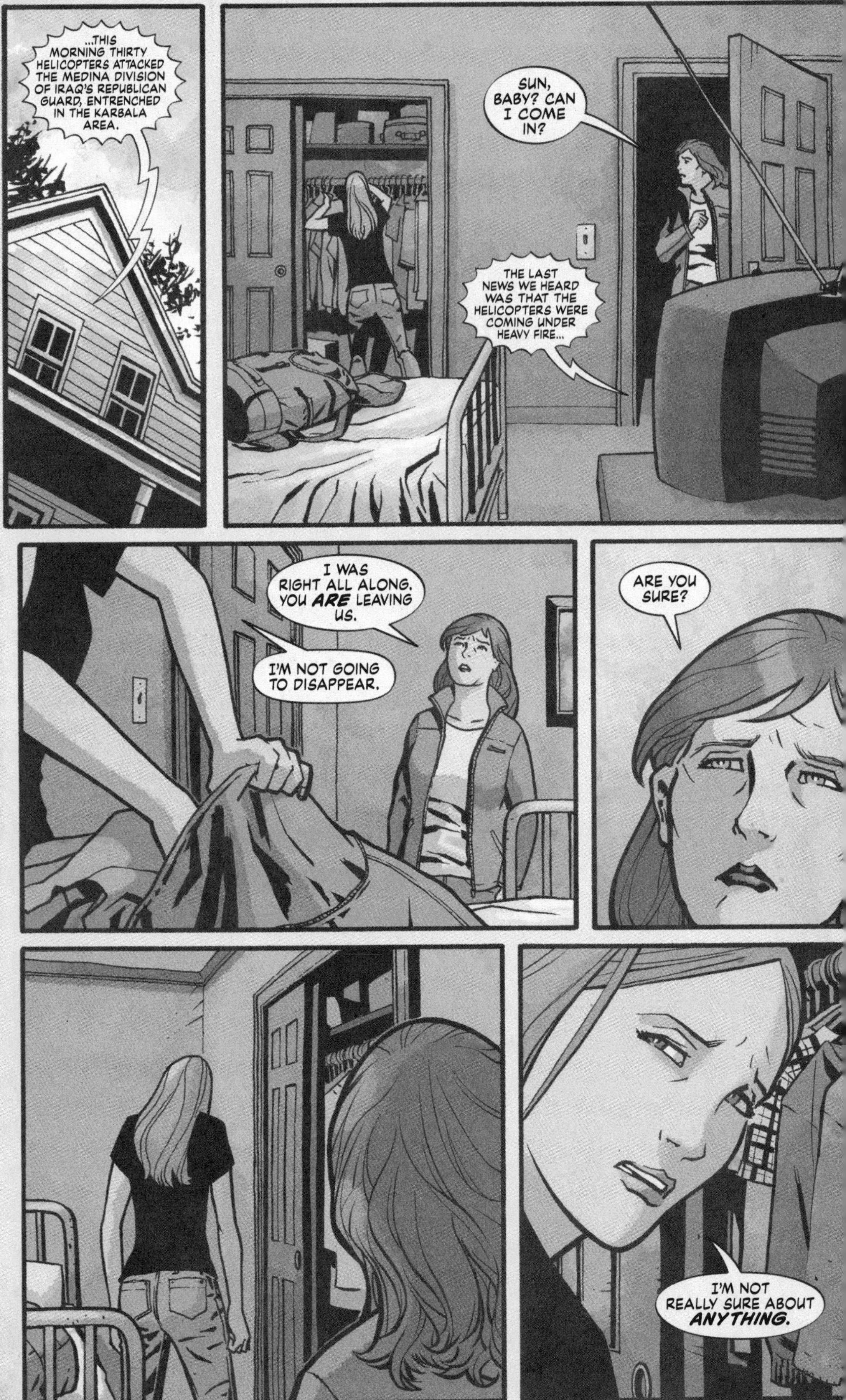

...THIS MORNING THIRTY HELICOPTERS ATTACKED THE MEDINA DIVISION OF IRAQ'S REPUBLICAN GUARD, ENTRENCHED IN THE KARBALA AREA.
SUN, BABY? CAN I COME IN?
THE LAST NEWS WE HEARD WAS THAT THE HELICOPTERS WERE COMING UNDER HEAVY FIRE...
I WAS RIGHT ALL ALONG. YOU ARE LEAVING US.
I'M NOT GOING TO DISAPPEAR.
ARE YOU SURE?
I'M NOT REALLY SURE ABOUT ANYTHING.

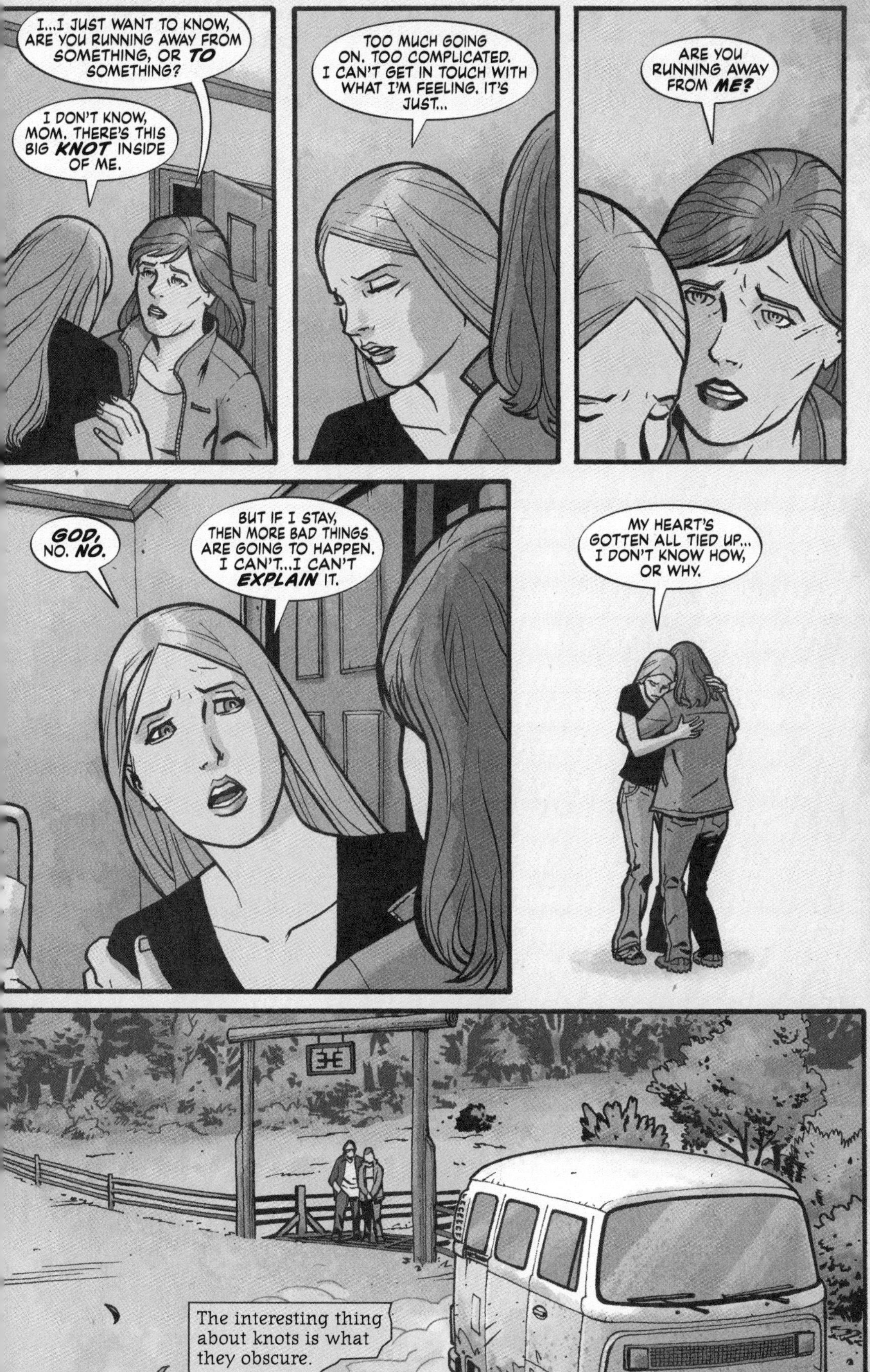

I...I JUST WANT TO KNOW, ARE YOU RUNNING AWAY FROM SOMETHING, OR *TO* SOMETHING?
I DON'T KNOW, MOM. THERE'S THIS BIG *KNOT* INSIDE OF ME.
TOO MUCH GOING ON. TOO COMPLICATED. I CAN'T GET IN TOUCH WITH WHAT I'M FEELING. IT'S JUST...
ARE YOU RUNNING AWAY FROM *ME?*
GOD, NO. *NO.*
BUT IF I STAY, THEN MORE BAD THINGS ARE GOING TO HAPPEN. I CAN'T...I CAN'T *EXPLAIN* IT.
MY HEART'S GOTTEN ALL TIED UP... I DON'T KNOW HOW, OR WHY.
The interesting thing about knots is what they obscure.

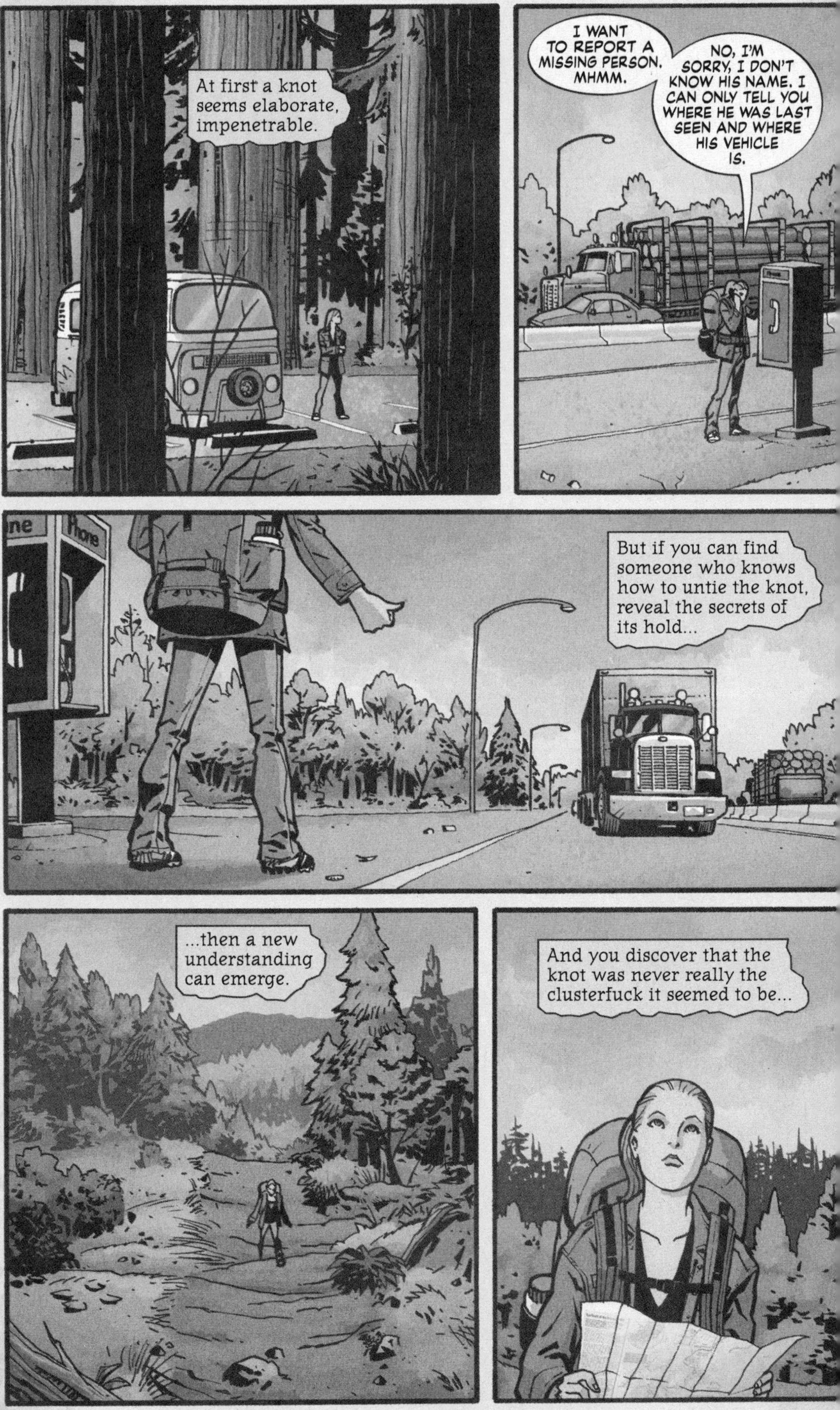
At first a knot seems elaborate, impenetrable.
I WANT TO REPORT A MISSING PERSON. MHMM.
NO, I'M SORRY, I DON'T KNOW HIS NAME. I CAN ONLY TELL YOU WHERE HE WAS LAST SEEN AND WHERE HIS VEHICLE IS.
But if you can find someone who knows how to untie the knot, reveal the secrets of its hold...
...then a new understanding can emerge.
And you discover that the knot was never really the clusterfuck it seemed to be...

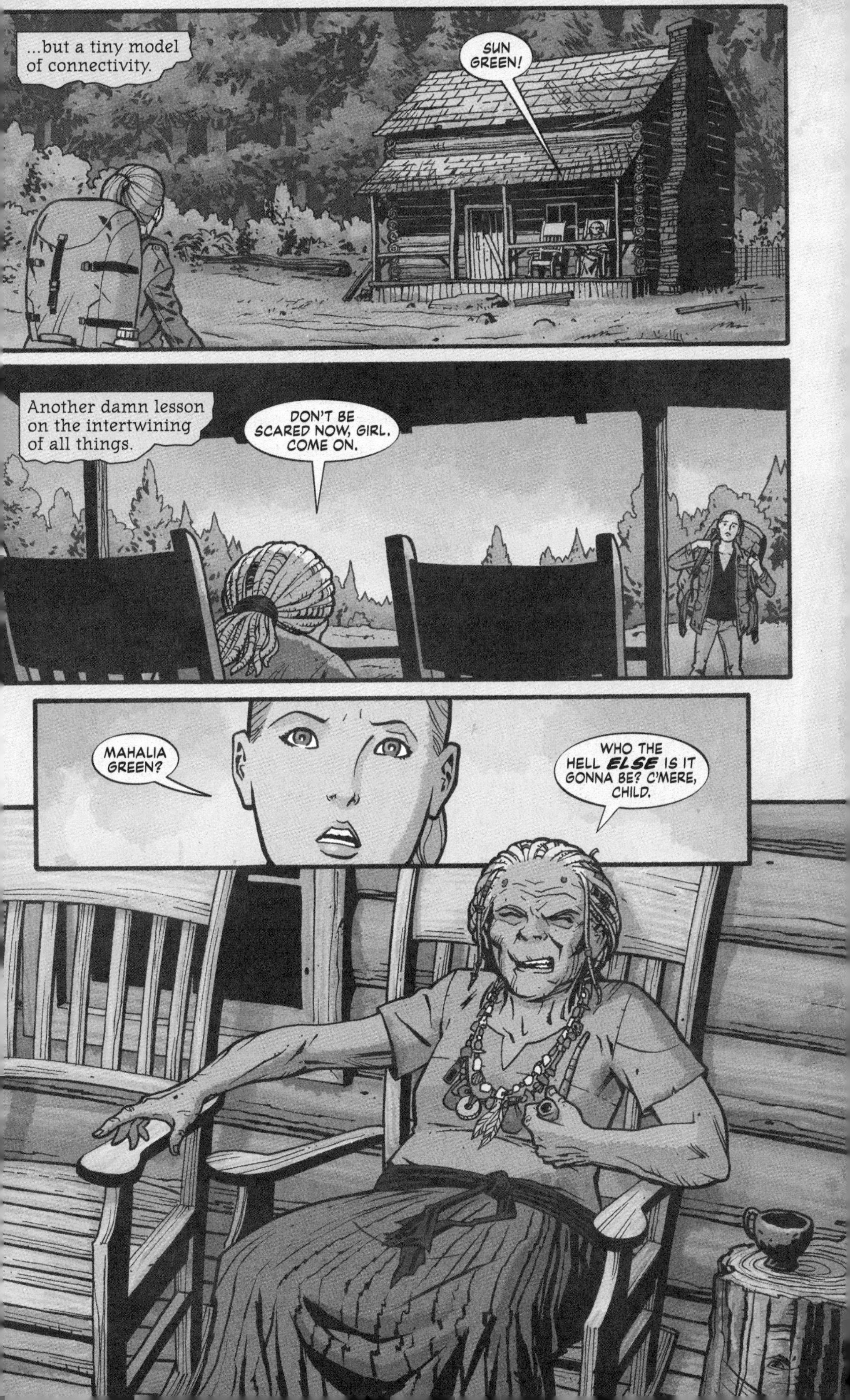
...but a tiny model of connectivity.
SUN GREEN!
Another damn lesson on the intertwining of all things.
DON'T BE SCARED NOW, GIRL. COME ON.
MAHALIA GREEN?
WHO THE HELL ELSE IS IT GONNA BE? C'MERE, CHILD.

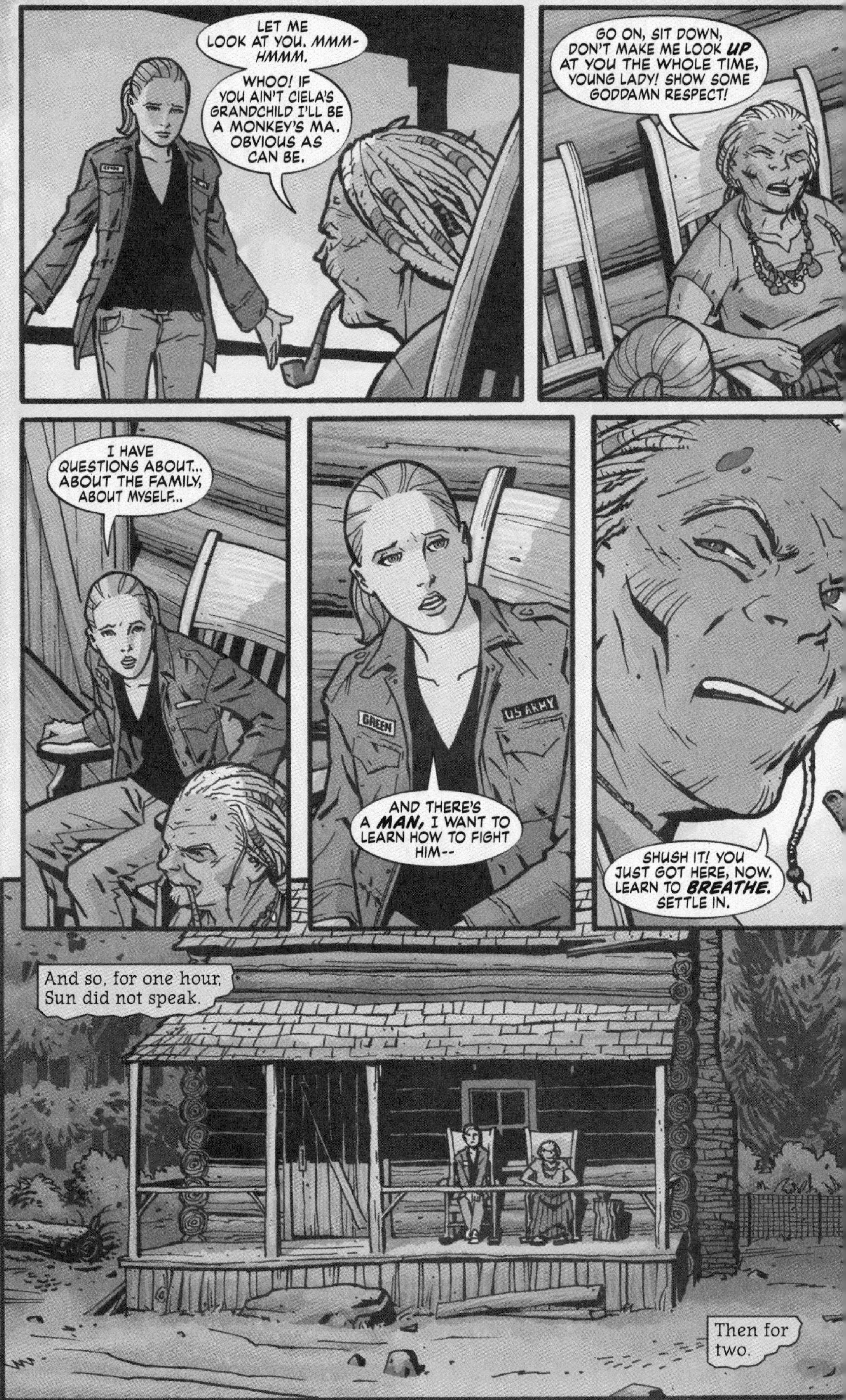

LET ME LOOK AT YOU. MMM-HMMM.
WHOO! IF YOU AIN'T CIELA'S GRANDCHILD I'LL BE A MONKEY'S MA. OBVIOUS AS CAN BE.
GO ON, SIT DOWN, DON'T MAKE ME LOOK UP AT YOU THE WHOLE TIME, YOUNG LADY! SHOW SOME GODDAMN RESPECT!
I HAVE QUESTIONS ABOUT... ABOUT THE FAMILY, ABOUT MYSELF...
GREEN
US ARMY
AND THERE'S A MAN, I WANT TO LEARN HOW TO FIGHT HIM--
SHUSH IT! YOU JUST GOT HERE, NOW. LEARN TO BREATHE. SETTLE IN.
And so, for one hour, Sun did not speak.
Then for two.

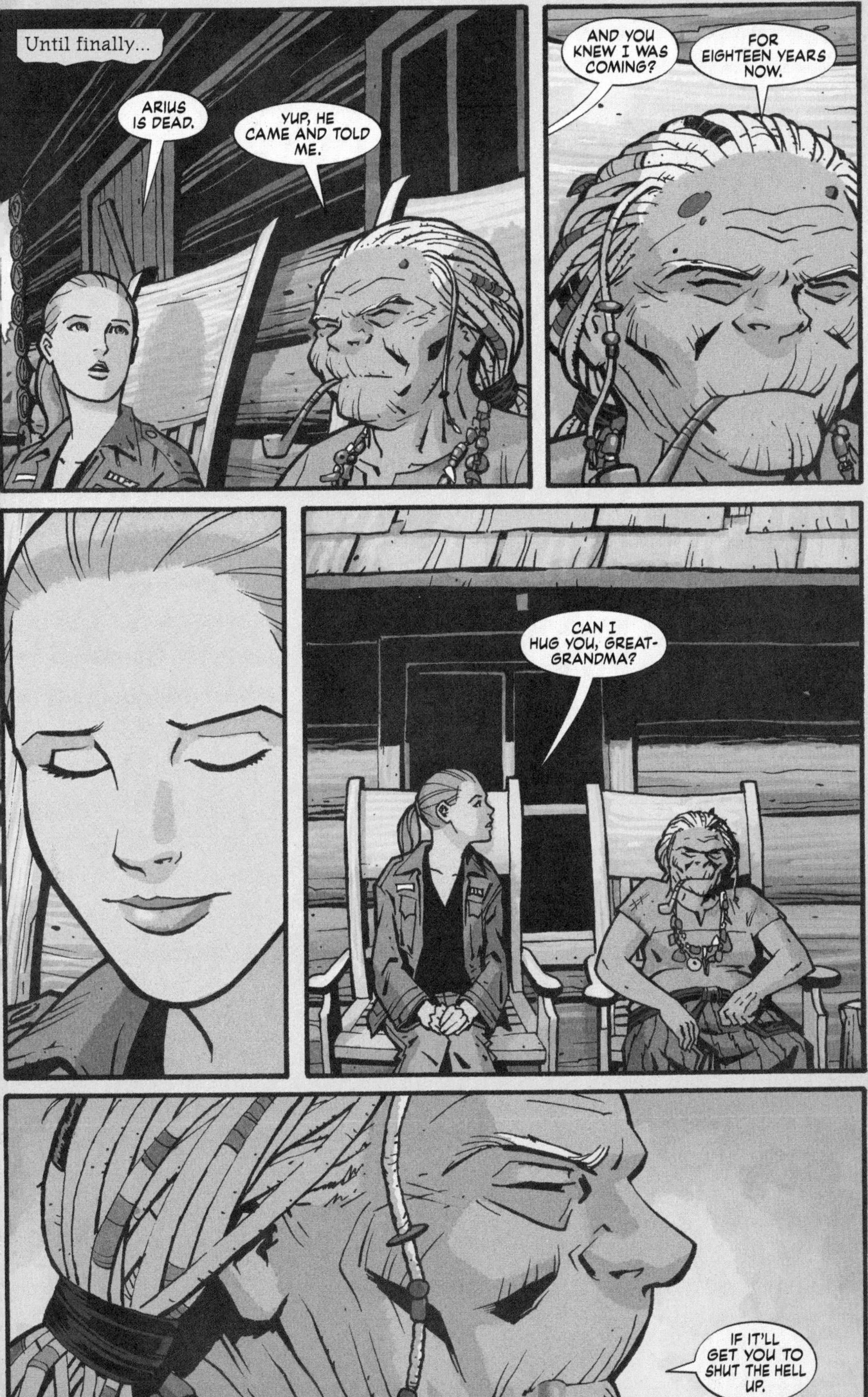
Until finally...
ARIUS IS DEAD.
YUP, HE CAME AND TOLD ME.
AND YOU KNEW I WAS COMING?
FOR EIGHTEEN YEARS NOW.
CAN I HUG YOU, GREAT-GRANDMA?
IF IT'LL GET YOU TO SHUT THE HELL UP.

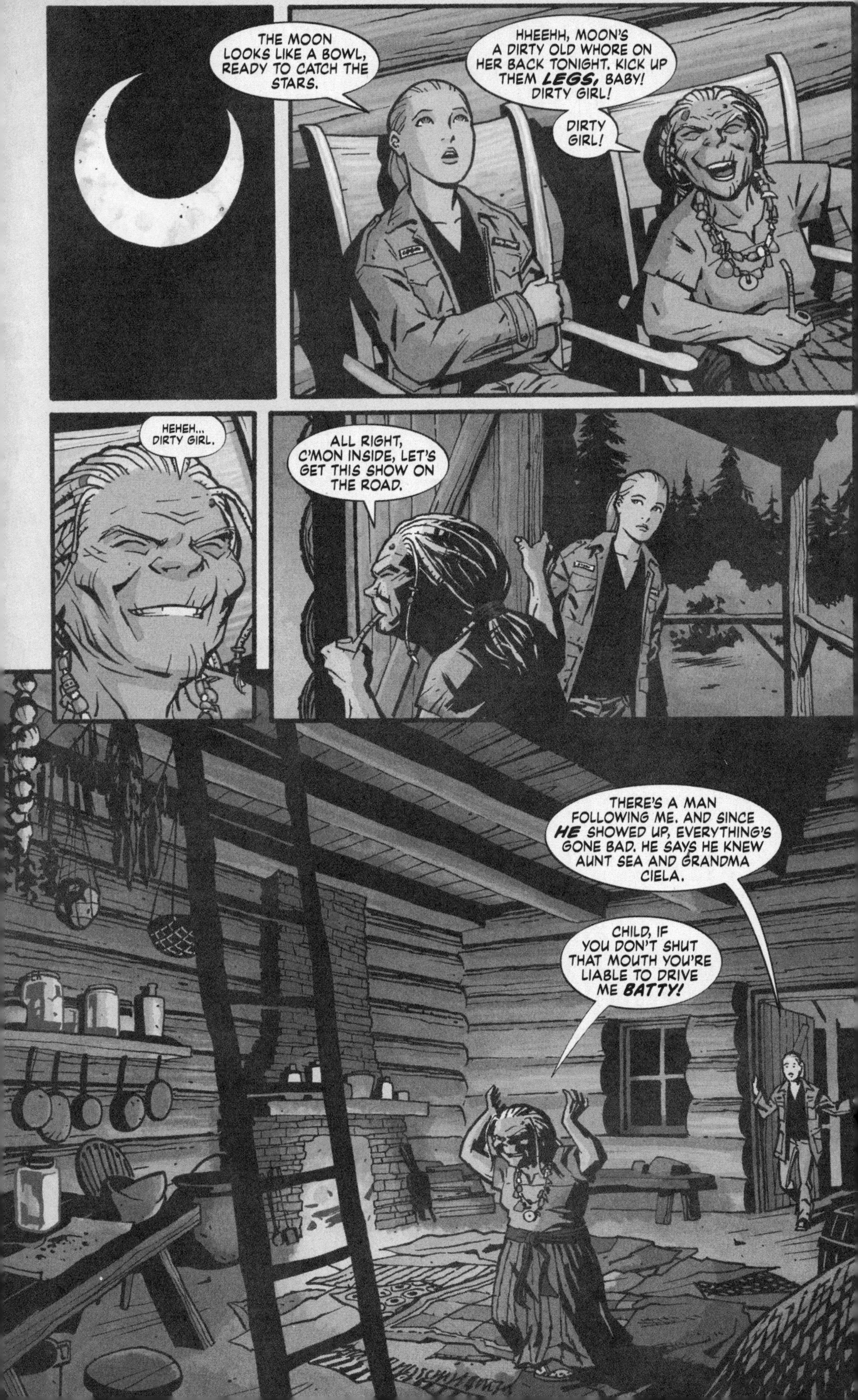
THE MOON LOOKS LIKE A BOWL, READY TO CATCH THE STARS.
HHEEHH, MOON'S A DIRTY OLD WHORE ON HER BACK TONIGHT. KICK UP THEM LEGS, BABY! DIRTY GIRL!
DIRTY GIRL!
HEHEH... DIRTY GIRL.
ALL RIGHT, C'MON INSIDE, LET'S GET THIS SHOW ON THE ROAD.
THERE'S A MAN FOLLOWING ME. AND SINCE HE SHOWED UP, EVERYTHING'S GONE BAD. HE SAYS HE KNEW AUNT SEA AND GRANDMA CIELA.
CHILD, IF YOU DON'T SHUT THAT MOUTH YOU'RE LIABLE TO DRIVE ME BATTY!

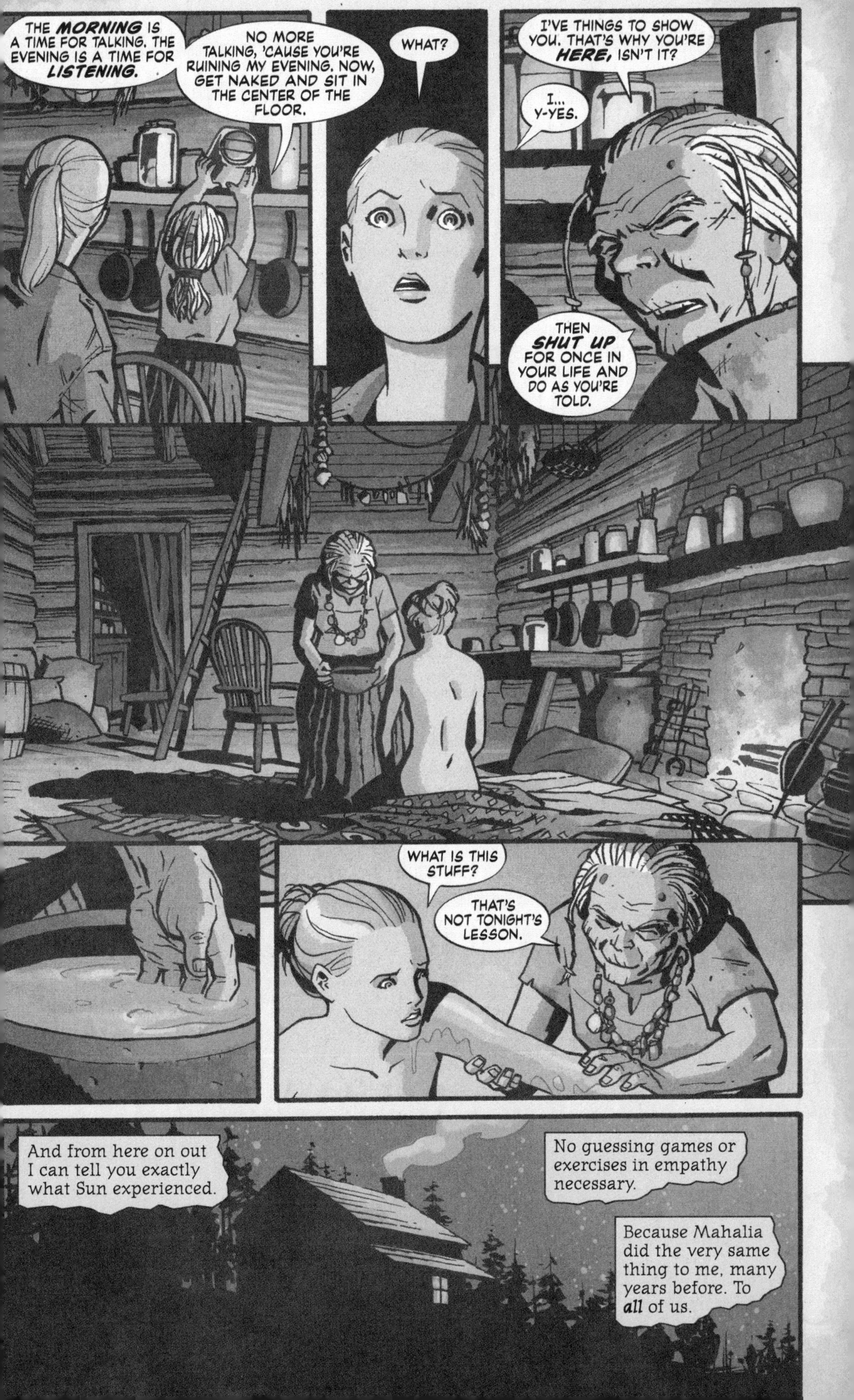

THE **MORNING** IS A TIME FOR TALKING. THE EVENING IS A TIME FOR **LISTENING.**
NO MORE TALKING, 'CAUSE YOU'RE RUINING MY EVENING. NOW, GET NAKED AND SIT IN THE CENTER OF THE FLOOR.
WHAT?
I'VE THINGS TO SHOW YOU. THAT'S WHY YOU'RE **HERE,** ISN'T IT?
I... Y-YES.
THEN **SHUT UP** FOR ONCE IN YOUR LIFE AND DO AS YOU'RE TOLD.
WHAT IS THIS STUFF?
THAT'S NOT TONIGHT'S LESSON.
And from here on out I can tell you exactly what Sun experienced.
No guessing games or exercises in empathy necessary.
Because Mahalia did the very same thing to me, many years before. To ***all*** of us.

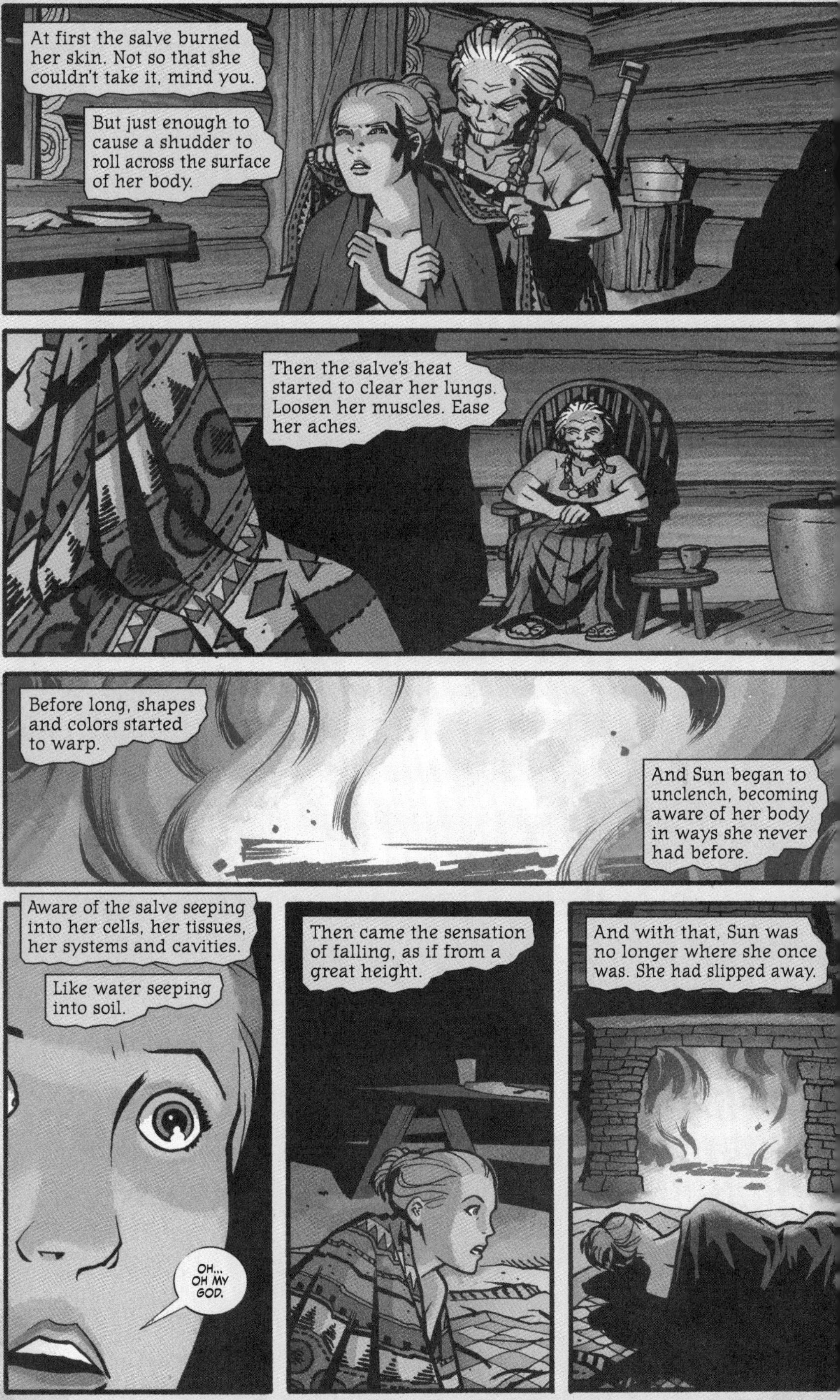
At first the salve burned her skin. Not so that she couldn't take it, mind you.
But just enough to cause a shudder to roll across the surface of her body.
Then the salve's heat started to clear her lungs. Loosen her muscles. Ease her aches.
Before long, shapes and colors started to warp.
And Sun began to unclench, becoming aware of her body in ways she never had before.
Aware of the salve seeping into her cells, her tissues, her systems and cavities.
Like water seeping into soil.
OH... OH MY GOD.
Then came the sensation of falling, as if from a great height.
And with that, Sun was no longer where she once was. She had slipped away.

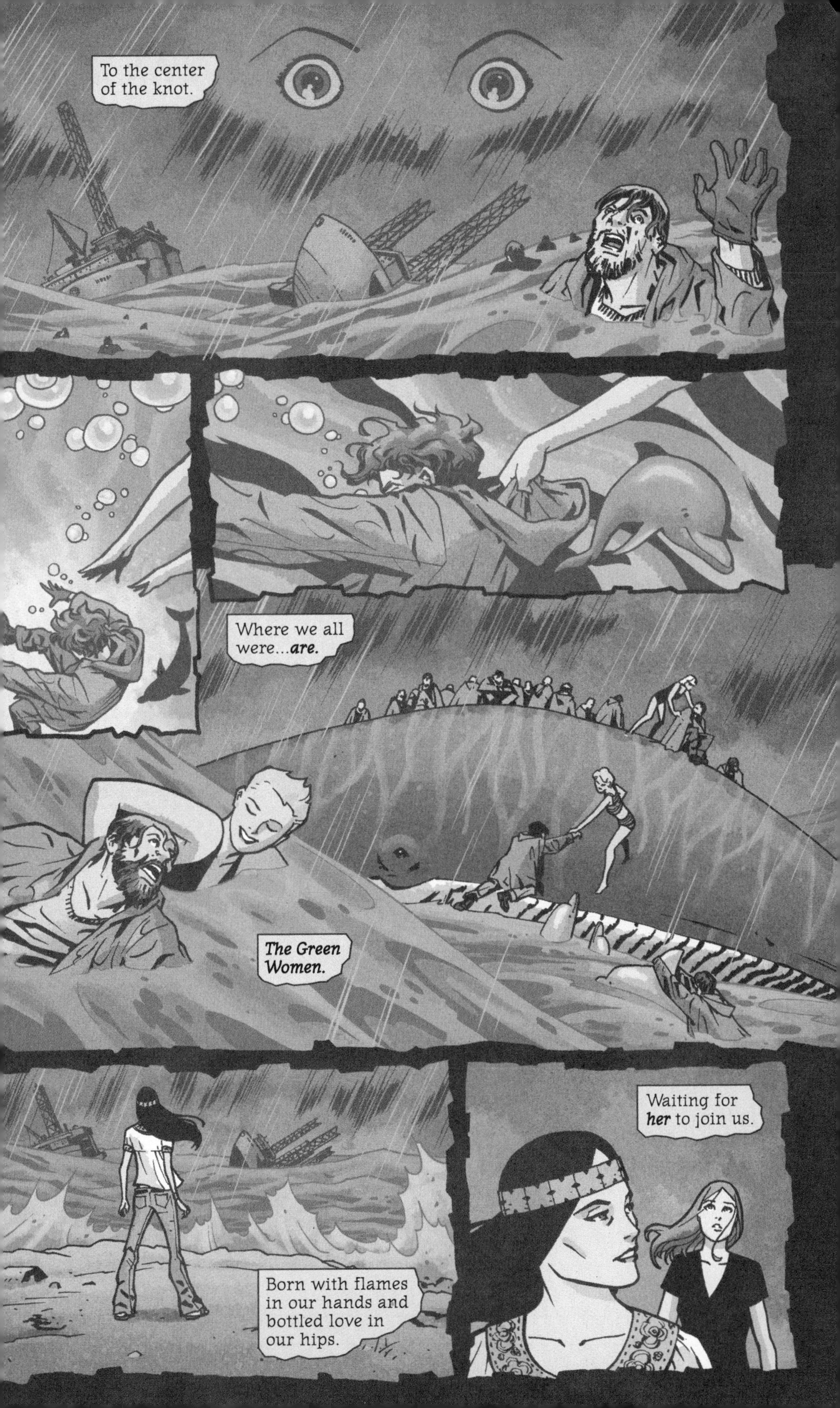

To the center of the knot.
Where we all were...*are.*
The Green Women.
Born with flames in our hands and bottled love in our hips.
Waiting for *her* to join us.

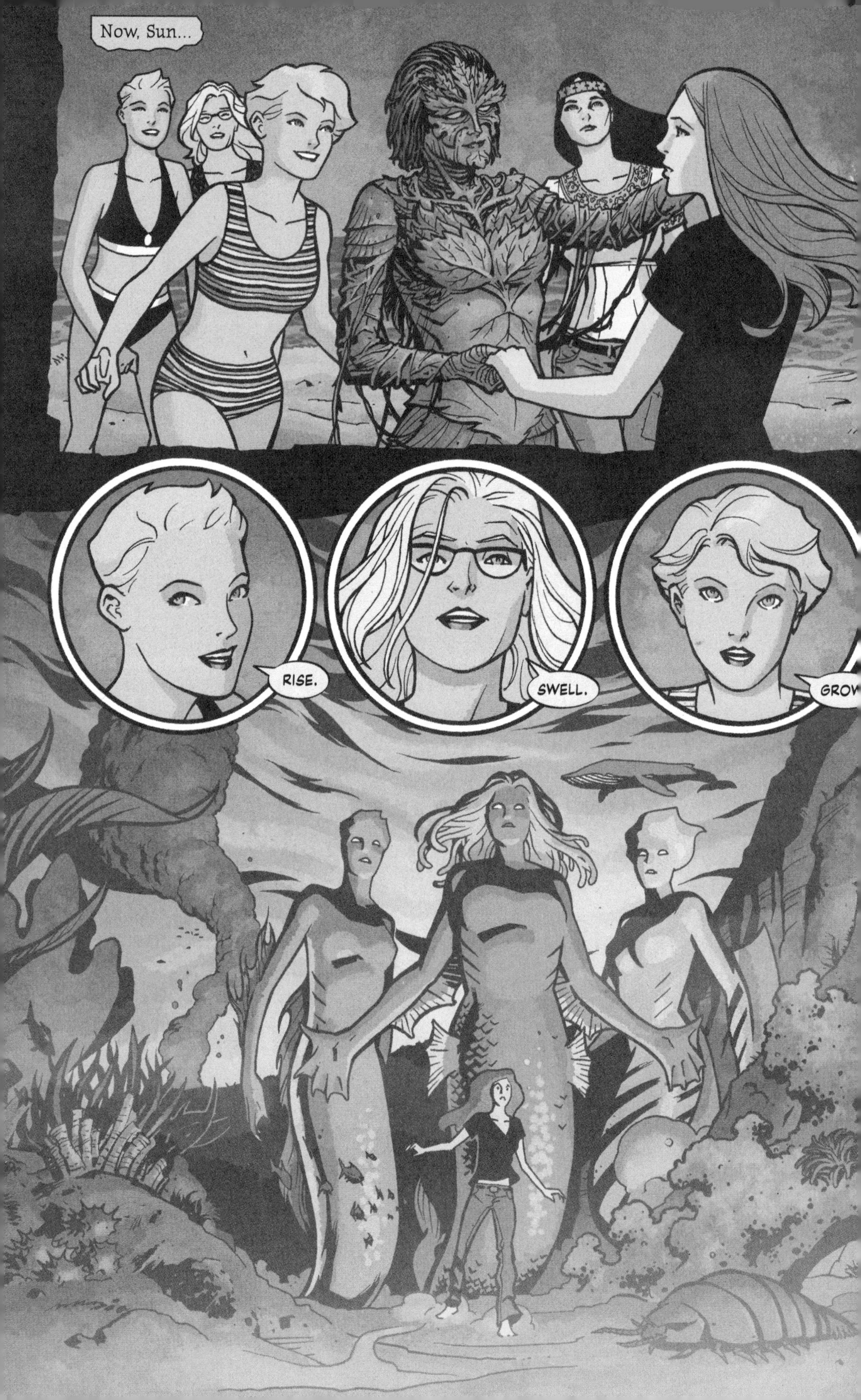
Now, Sun...
RISE.
SWELL.
GROW

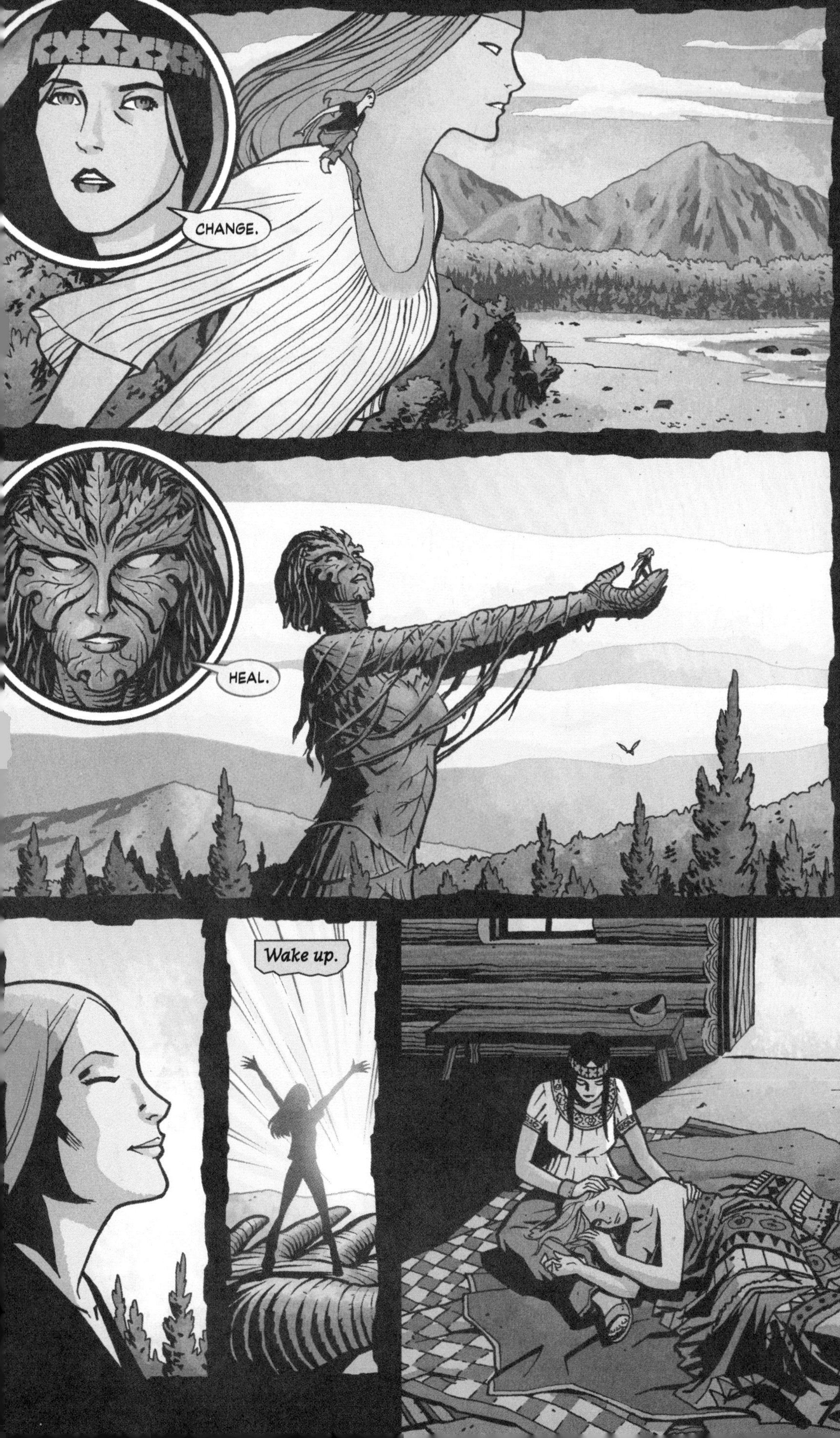
CHANGE.
HEAL.
Wake up.

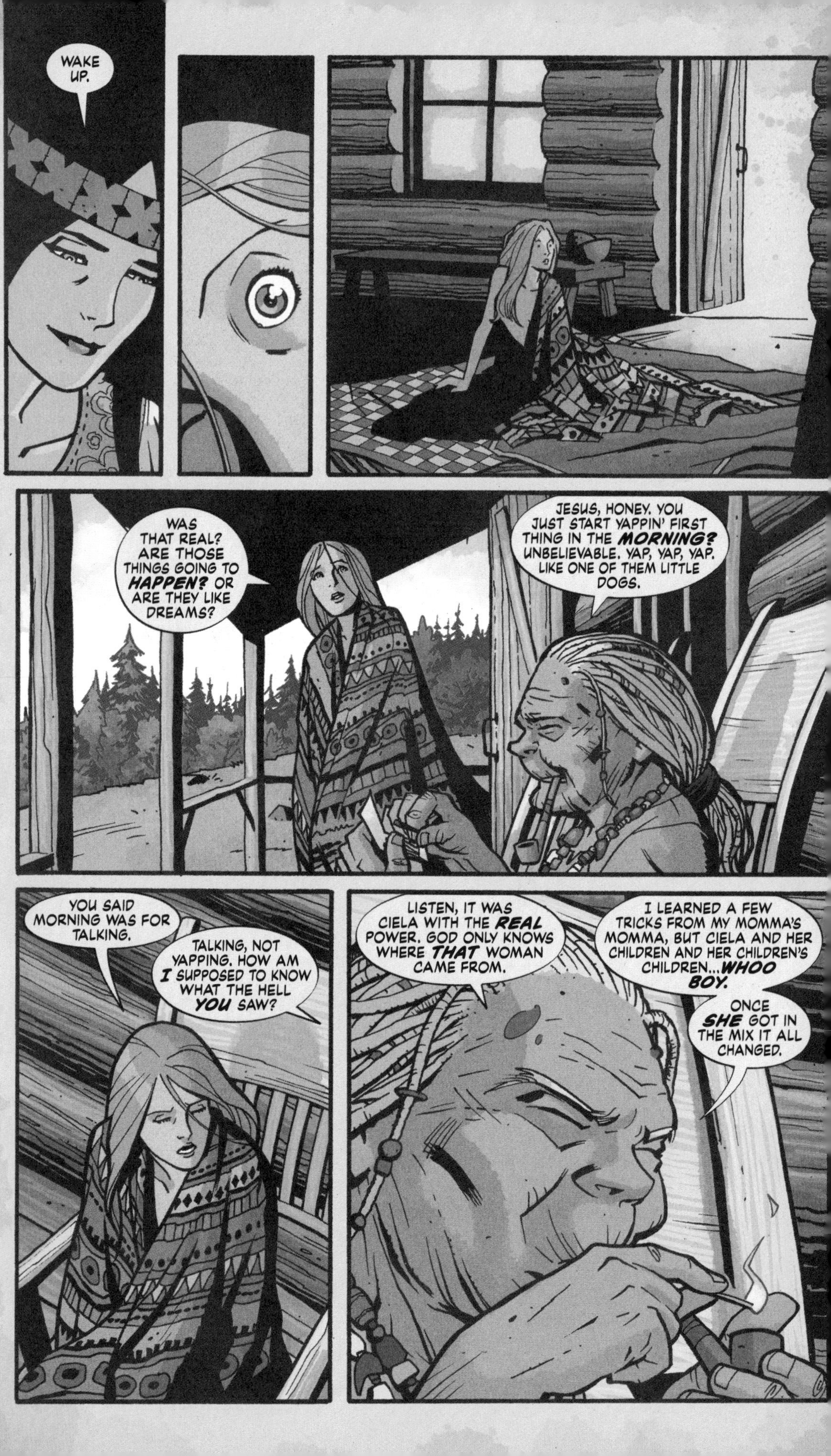
WAKE UP.
WAS THAT REAL? ARE THOSE THINGS GOING TO HAPPEN? OR ARE THEY LIKE DREAMS?
JESUS, HONEY. YOU JUST START YAPPIN' FIRST THING IN THE MORNING? UNBELIEVABLE. YAP, YAP, YAP. LIKE ONE OF THEM LITTLE DOGS.
YOU SAID MORNING WAS FOR TALKING.
TALKING, NOT YAPPING. HOW AM I SUPPOSED TO KNOW WHAT THE HELL YOU SAW?
LISTEN, IT WAS CIELA WITH THE REAL POWER. GOD ONLY KNOWS WHERE THAT WOMAN CAME FROM.
I LEARNED A FEW TRICKS FROM MY MOMMA'S MOMMA, BUT CIELA AND HER CHILDREN AND HER CHILDREN'S CHILDREN...WHOO BOY.
ONCE SHE GOT IN THE MIX IT ALL CHANGED.

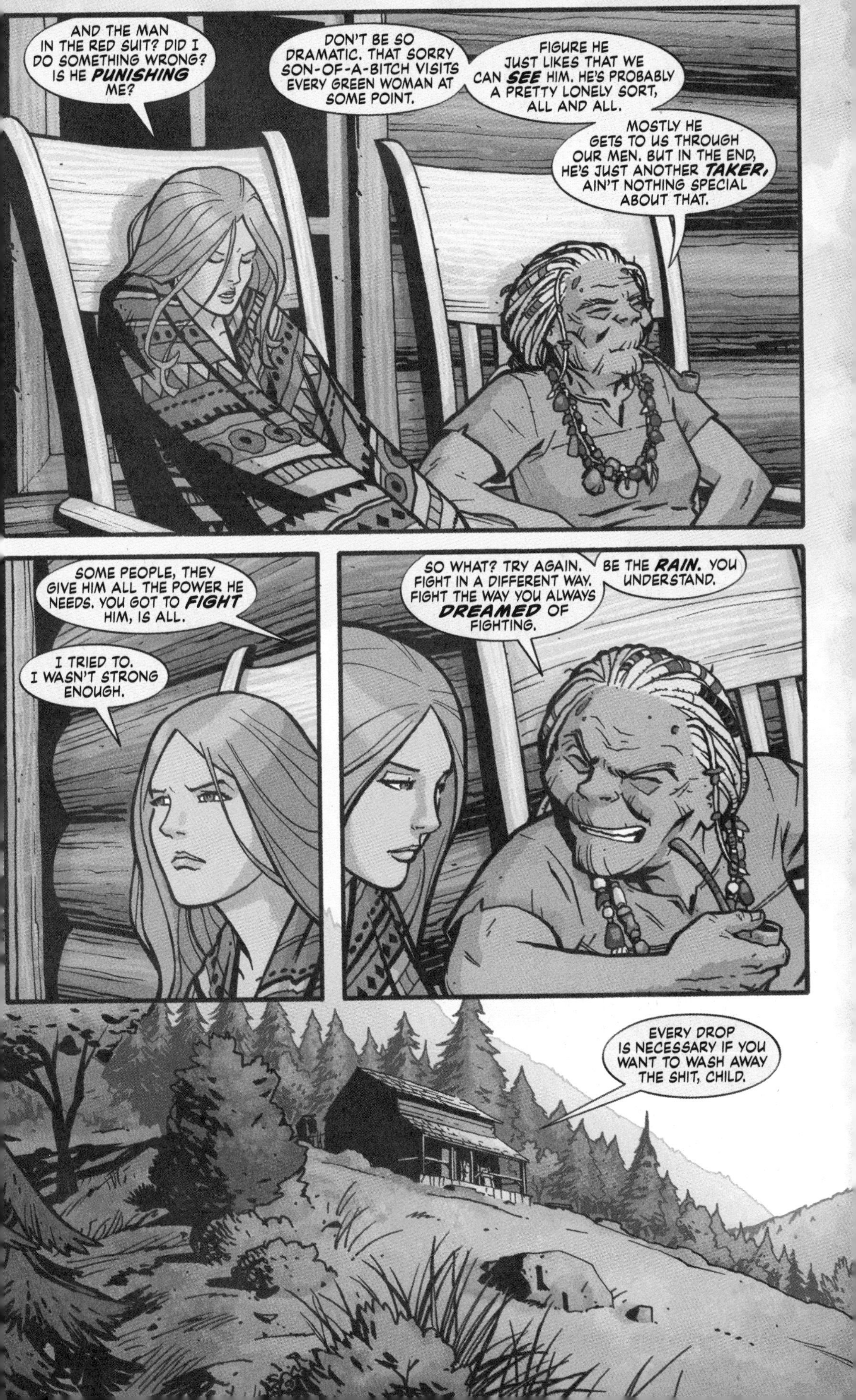
AND THE MAN IN THE RED SUIT? DID I DO SOMETHING WRONG? IS HE PUNISHING ME?
DON'T BE SO DRAMATIC. THAT SORRY SON-OF-A-BITCH VISITS EVERY GREEN WOMAN AT SOME POINT.
FIGURE HE JUST LIKES THAT WE CAN SEE HIM. HE'S PROBABLY A PRETTY LONELY SORT, ALL AND ALL.
MOSTLY HE GETS TO US THROUGH OUR MEN. BUT IN THE END, HE'S JUST ANOTHER TAKER, AIN'T NOTHING SPECIAL ABOUT THAT.
SOME PEOPLE, THEY GIVE HIM ALL THE POWER HE NEEDS. YOU GOT TO FIGHT HIM, IS ALL.
I TRIED TO. I WASN'T STRONG ENOUGH.
SO WHAT? TRY AGAIN. FIGHT IN A DIFFERENT WAY. FIGHT THE WAY YOU ALWAYS DREAMED OF FIGHTING.
BE THE RAIN. YOU UNDERSTAND.
EVERY DROP IS NECESSARY IF YOU WANT TO WASH AWAY THE SHIT, CHILD.

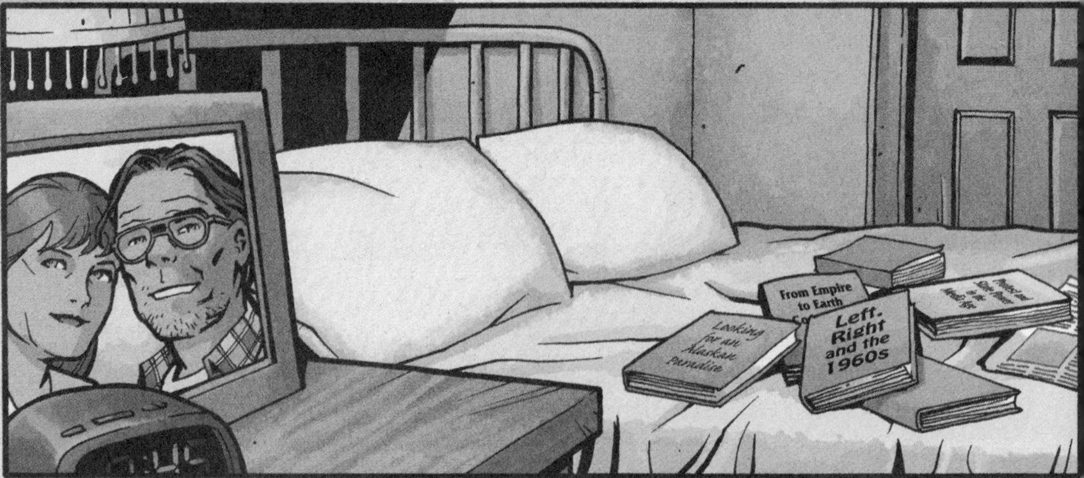
From Empire to Earth
Looking for an Alaskan Paradise
Left, Right and the 1960s

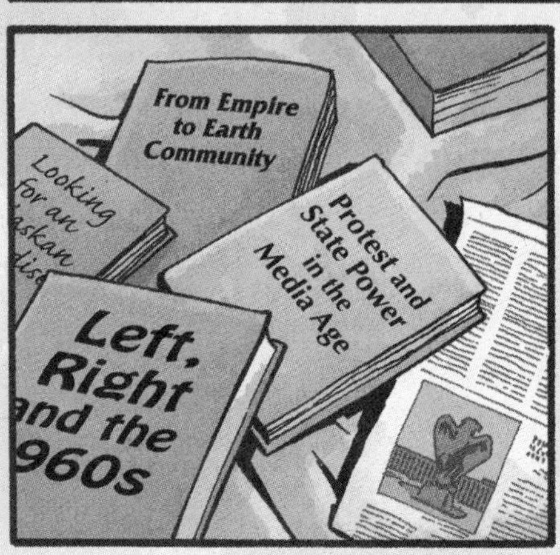
From Empire to Earth Community
Protest and State Power in the Media Age
Left, Right and the 1960s

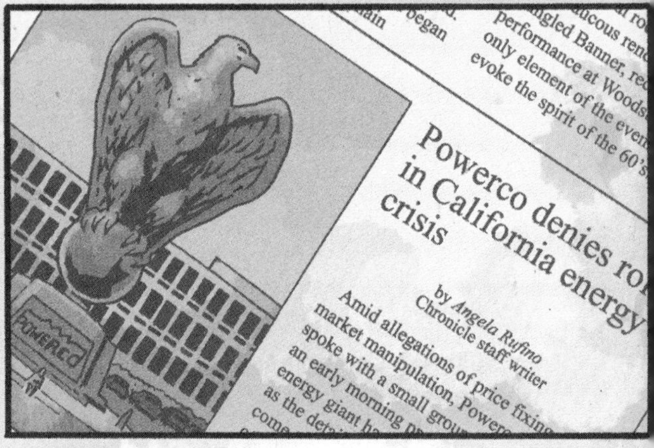
performance at Woods
only element of the even
evoke the spirit of the 60's
Powerco denies ro
in California energy
crisis
by Angela Rufino
Chronicle staff writer
Amid allegations of price fixing
market manipulation, Powerco
spoke with a small grou
POWERCO

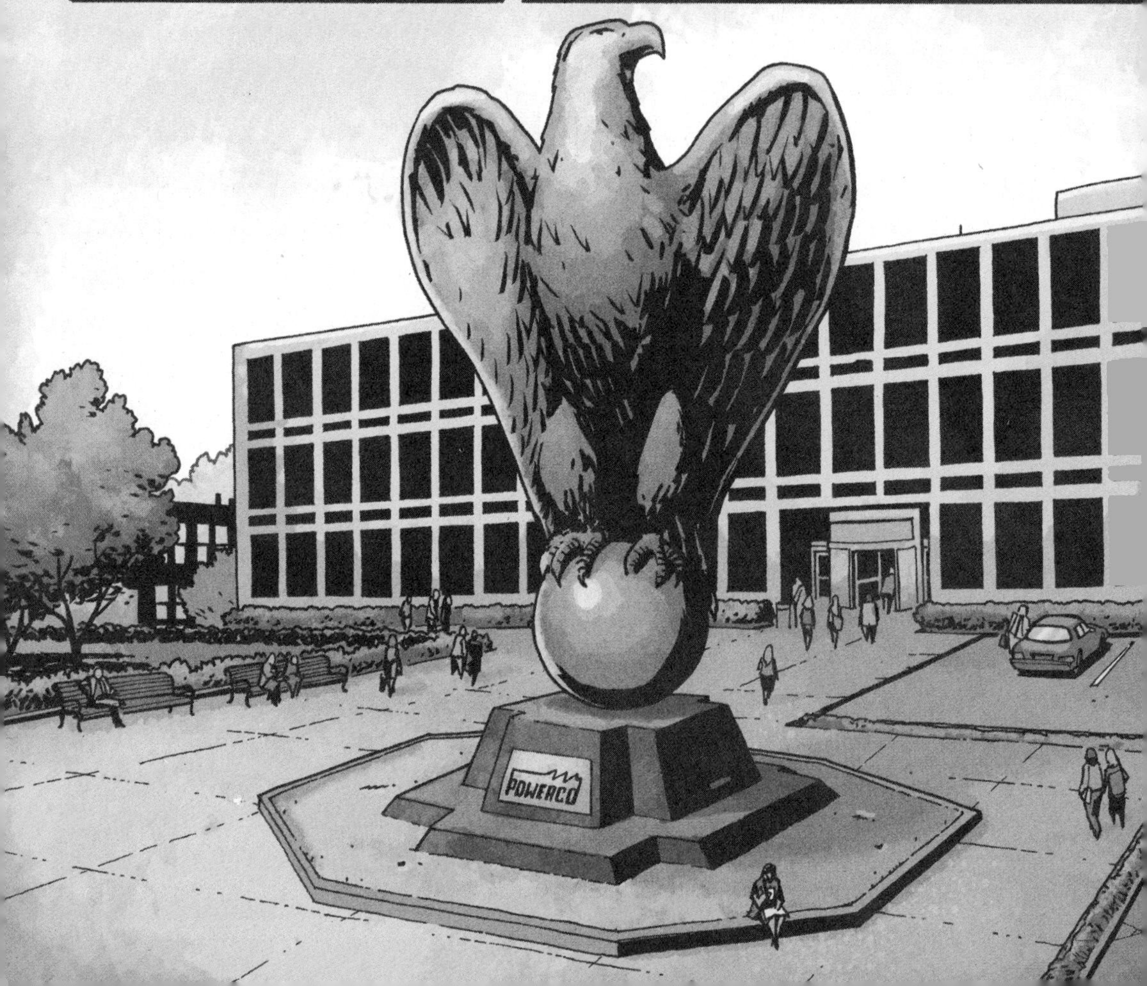
POWERCO

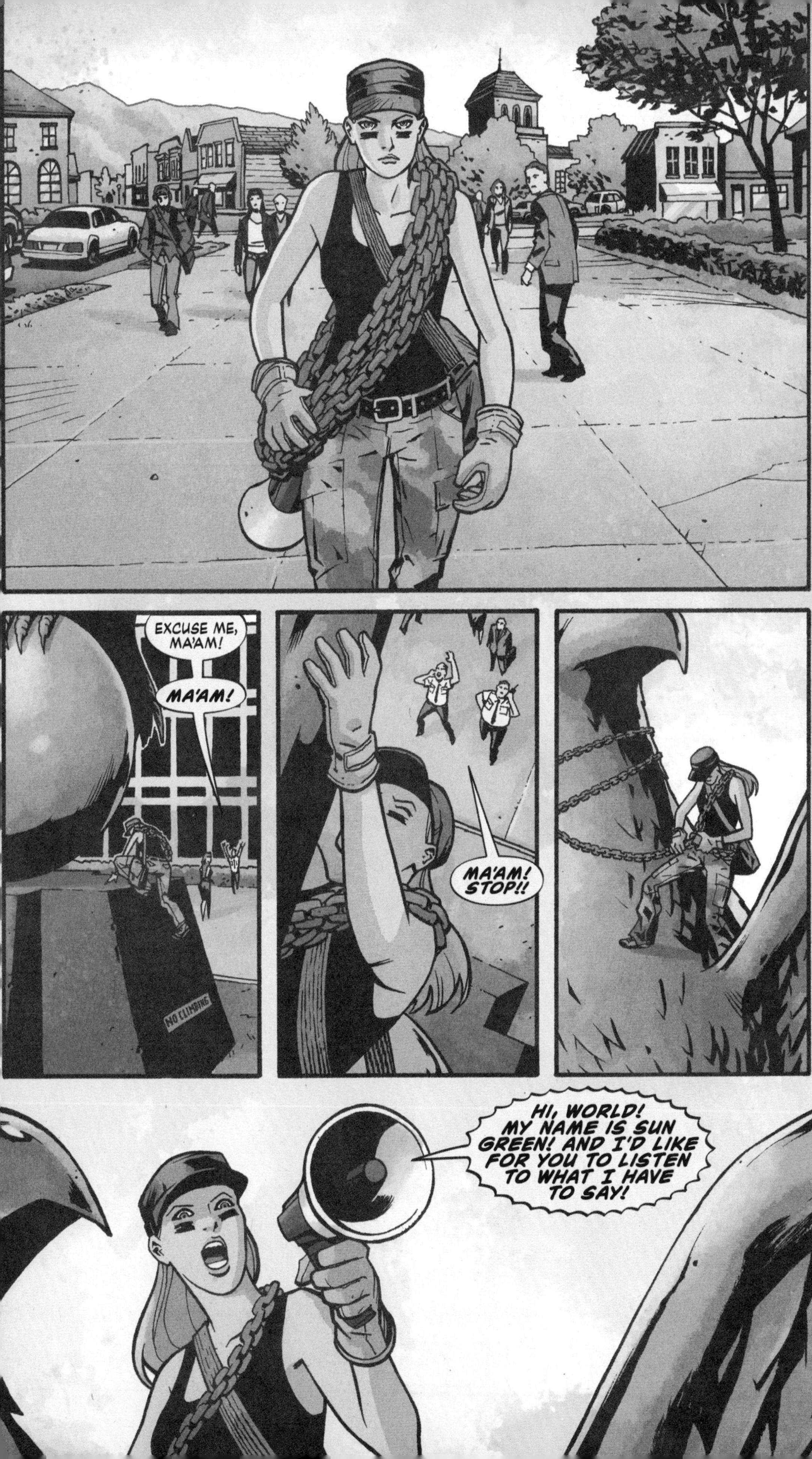
EXCUSE ME, MA'AM!
MA'AM!
NO CLIMBING
MA'AM! STOP!!
HI, WORLD! MY NAME IS SUN GREEN! AND I'D LIKE FOR YOU TO LISTEN TO WHAT I HAVE TO SAY!

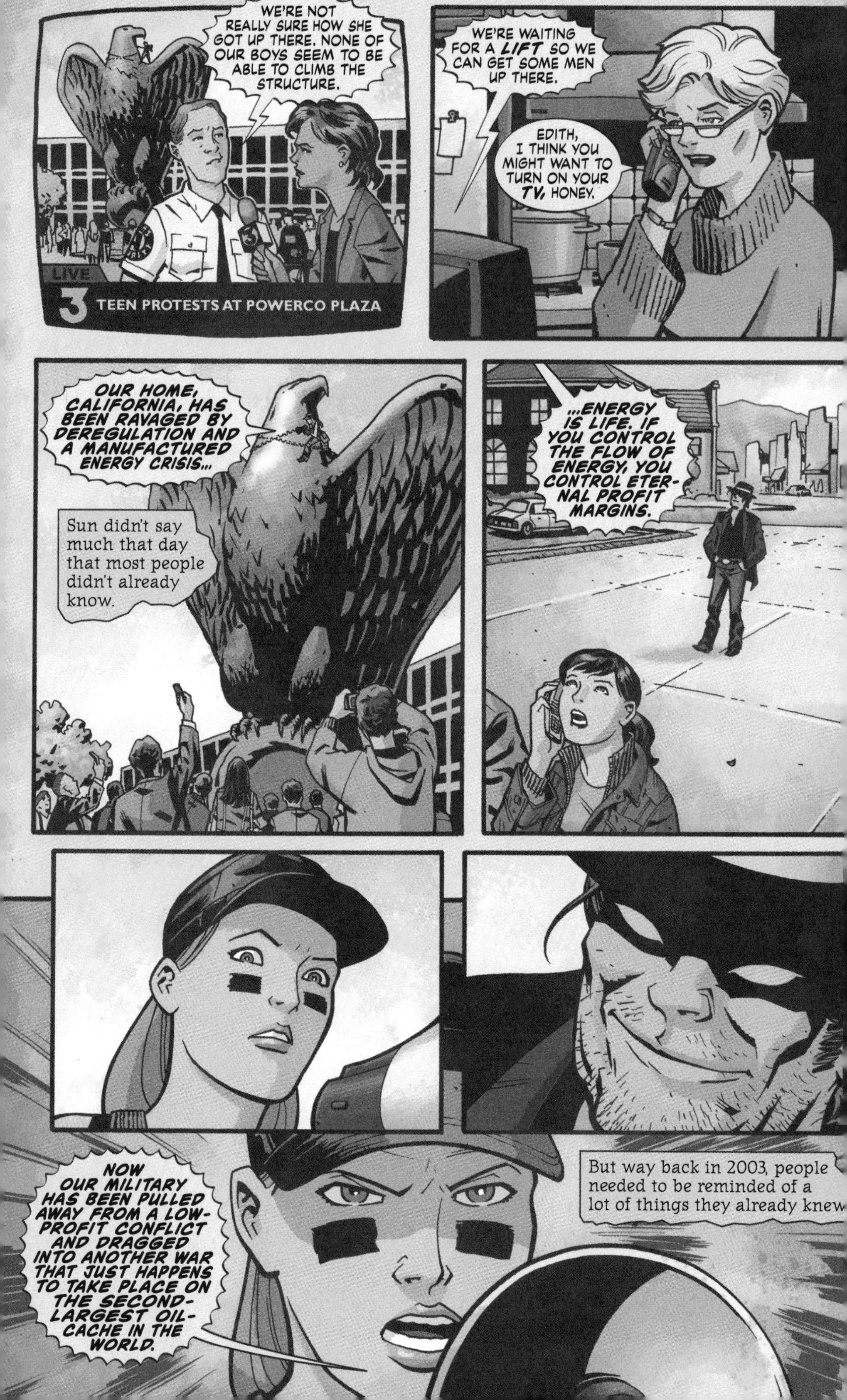
WE'RE NOT REALLY SURE HOW SHE GOT UP THERE. NONE OF OUR BOYS SEEM TO BE ABLE TO CLIMB THE STRUCTURE.
LIVE
3 TEEN PROTESTS AT POWERCO PLAZA
WE'RE WAITING FOR A LIFT SO WE CAN GET SOME MEN UP THERE.
EDITH, I THINK YOU MIGHT WANT TO TURN ON YOUR TV, HONEY.
OUR HOME, CALIFORNIA, HAS BEEN RAVAGED BY DEREGULATION AND A MANUFACTURED ENERGY CRISIS...
Sun didn't say much that day that most people didn't already know.
...ENERGY IS LIFE. IF YOU CONTROL THE FLOW OF ENERGY, YOU CONTROL ETERNAL PROFIT MARGINS.
NOW OUR MILITARY HAS BEEN PULLED AWAY FROM A LOW-PROFIT CONFLICT AND DRAGGED INTO ANOTHER WAR THAT JUST HAPPENS TO TAKE PLACE ON THE SECOND-LARGEST OIL-CACHE IN THE WORLD.
But way back in 2003, people needed to be reminded of a lot of things they already knew

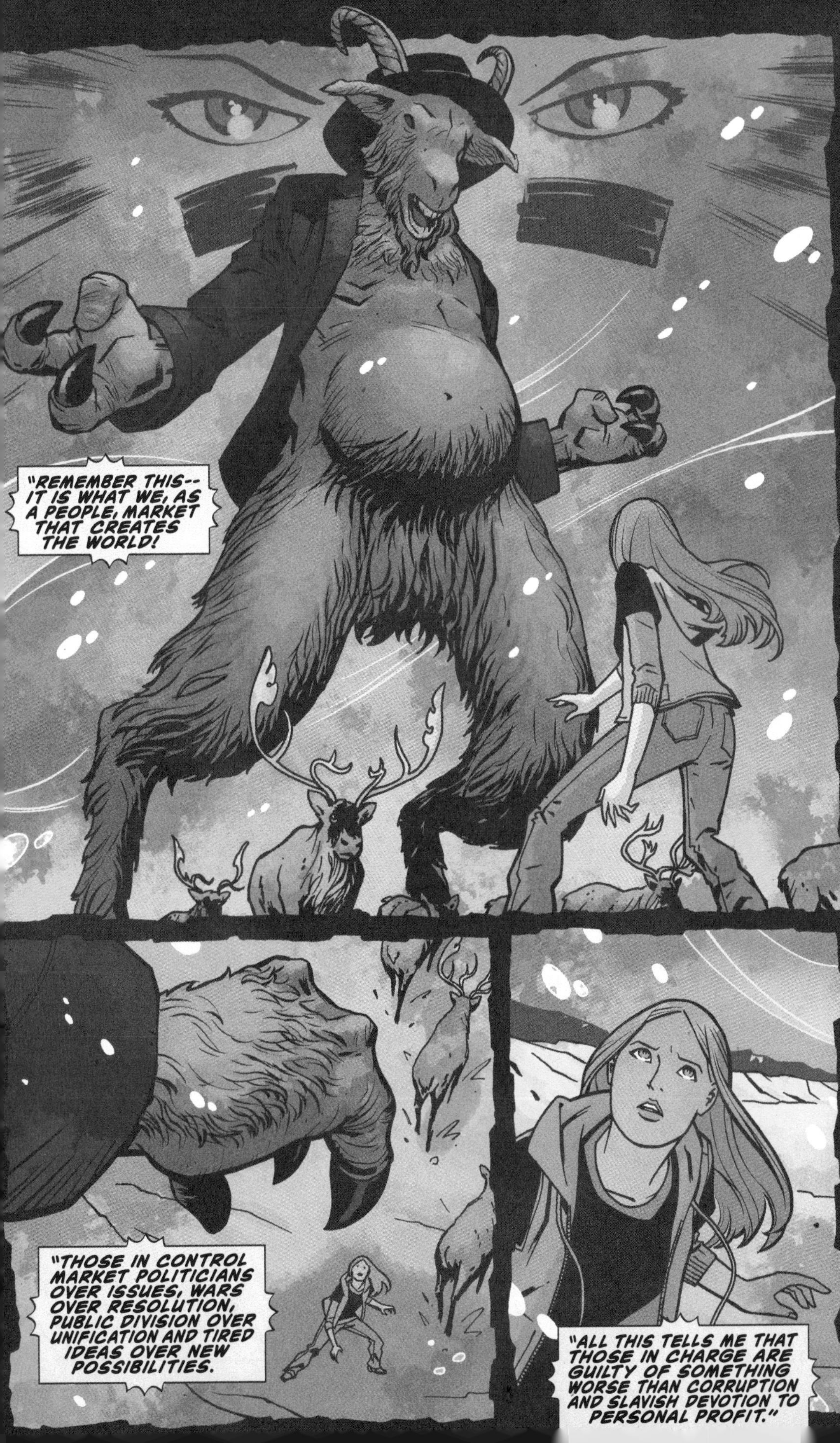
"REMEMBER THIS-- IT IS WHAT WE, AS A PEOPLE, MARKET THAT CREATES THE WORLD!
"THOSE IN CONTROL MARKET POLITICIANS OVER ISSUES, WARS OVER RESOLUTION, PUBLIC DIVISION OVER UNIFICATION AND TIRED IDEAS OVER NEW POSSIBILITIES.
"ALL THIS TELLS ME THAT THOSE IN CHARGE ARE GUILTY OF SOMETHING WORSE THAN CORRUPTION AND SLAVISH DEVOTION TO PERSONAL PROFIT."

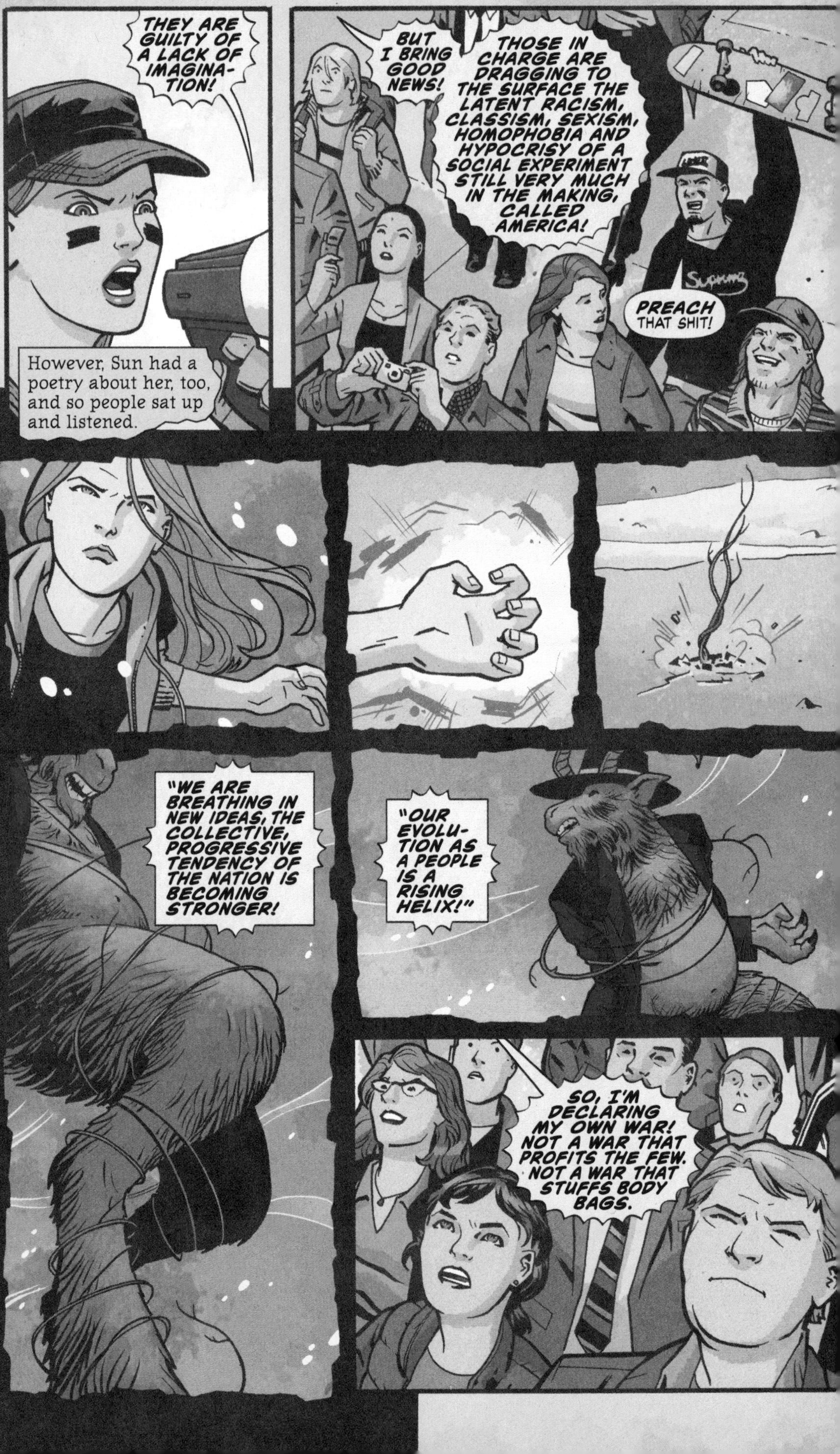
THEY ARE GUILTY OF A LACK OF IMAGINATION!
However, Sun had a poetry about her, too, and so people sat up and listened.
BUT I BRING GOOD NEWS!
THOSE IN CHARGE ARE DRAGGING TO THE SURFACE THE LATENT RACISM, CLASSISM, SEXISM, HOMOPHOBIA AND HYPOCRISY OF A SOCIAL EXPERIMENT STILL VERY MUCH IN THE MAKING, CALLED AMERICA!
PREACH THAT SHIT!
"WE ARE BREATHING IN NEW IDEAS, THE COLLECTIVE, PROGRESSIVE TENDENCY OF THE NATION IS BECOMING STRONGER!
"OUR EVOLUTION AS A PEOPLE IS A RISING HELIX!"
SO, I'M DECLARING MY OWN WAR! NOT A WAR THAT PROFITS THE FEW. NOT A WAR THAT STUFFS BODY BAGS.

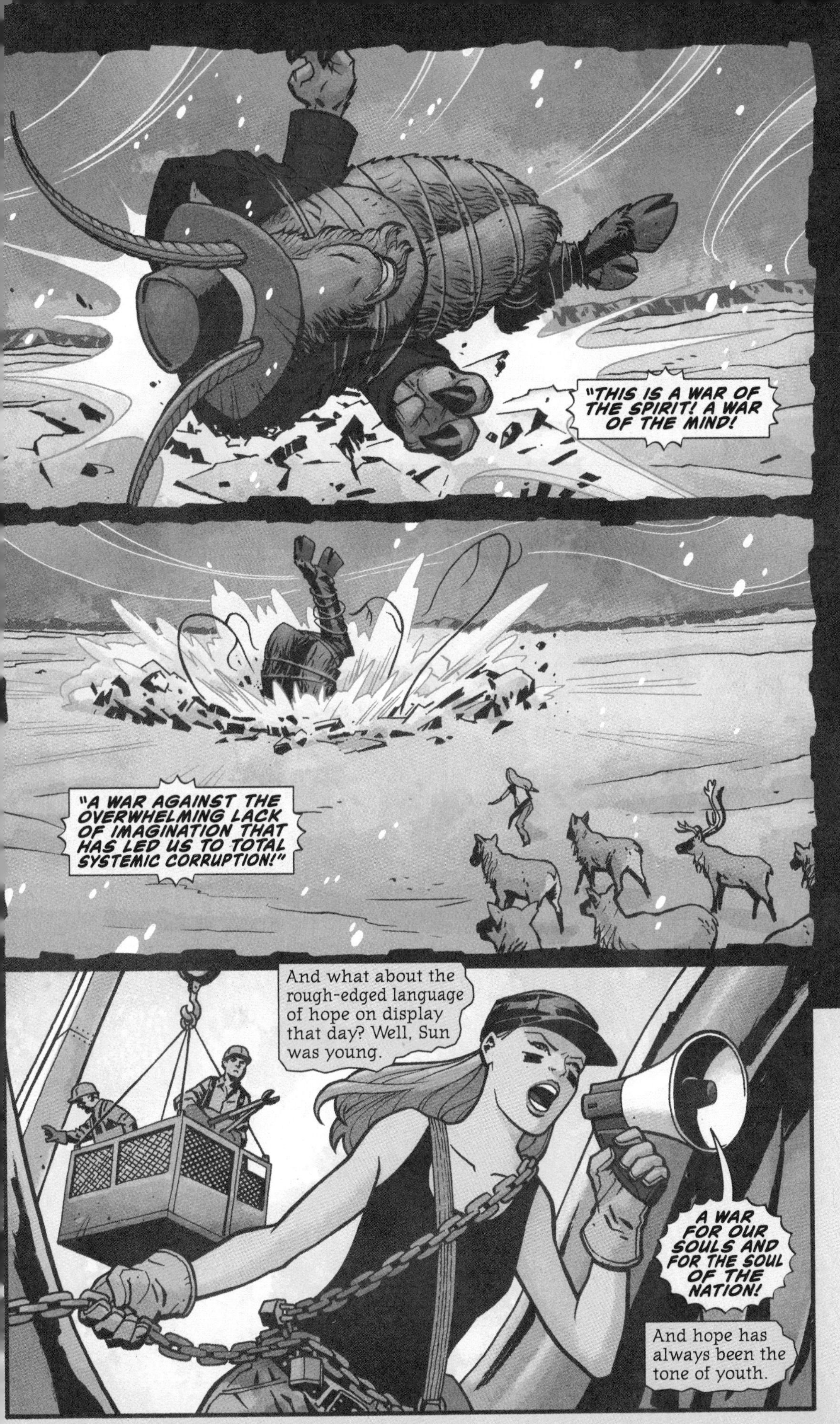
"THIS IS A WAR OF THE SPIRIT! A WAR OF THE MIND!
"A WAR AGAINST THE OVERWHELMING LACK OF IMAGINATION THAT HAS LED US TO TOTAL SYSTEMIC CORRUPTION!"
And what about the rough-edged language of hope on display that day? Well, Sun was young.
A WAR FOR OUR SOULS AND FOR THE SOUL OF THE NATION!
And hope has always been the tone of youth.

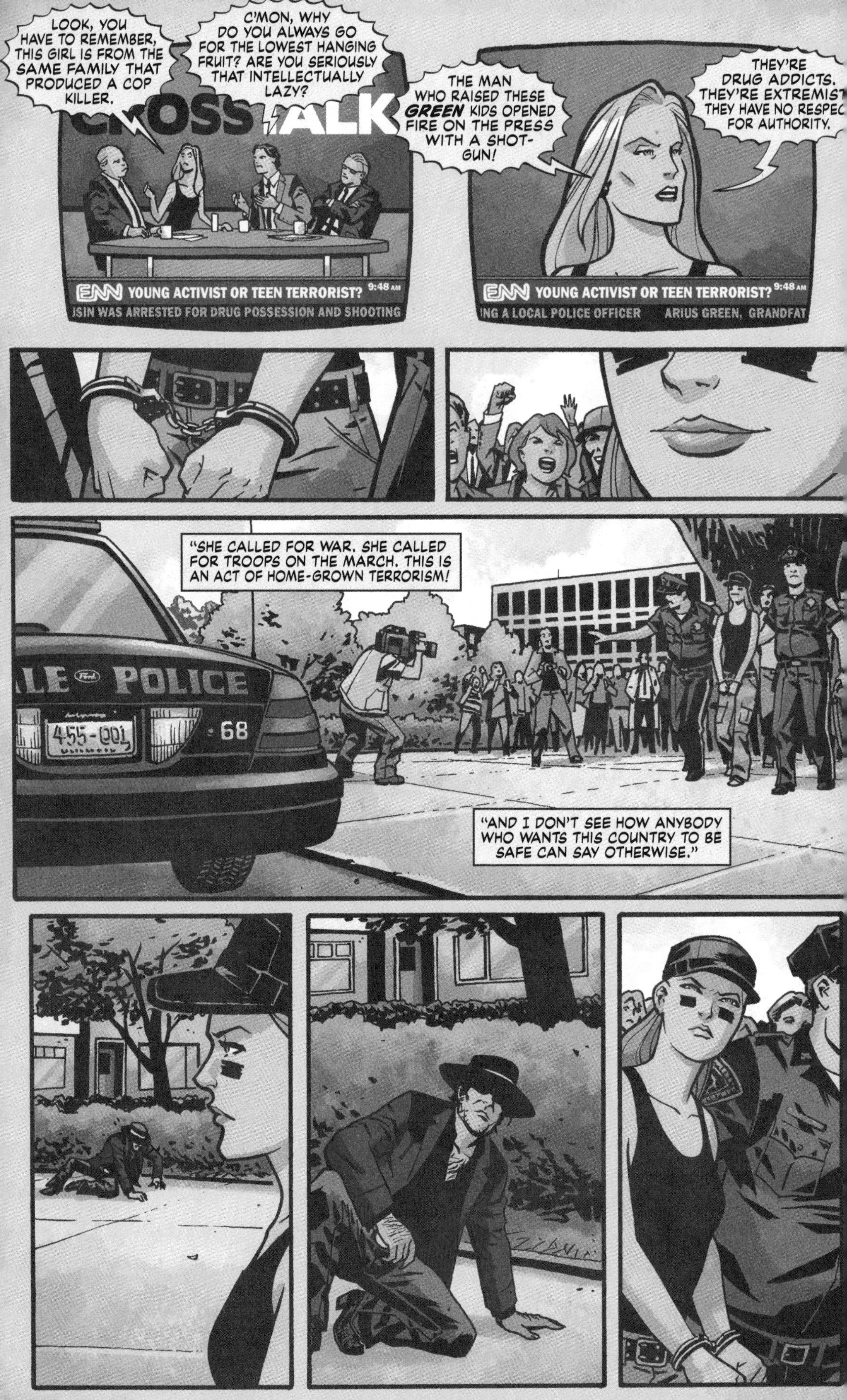
LOOK, YOU HAVE TO REMEMBER, THIS GIRL IS FROM THE SAME FAMILY THAT PRODUCED A COP KILLER.
C'MON, WHY DO YOU ALWAYS GO FOR THE LOWEST HANGING FRUIT? ARE YOU SERIOUSLY THAT INTELLECTUALLY LAZY?
ENN YOUNG ACTIVIST OR TEEN TERRORIST? 9:48 AM
ISIN WAS ARRESTED FOR DRUG POSSESSION AND SHOOTING
THE MAN WHO RAISED THESE GREEN KIDS OPENED FIRE ON THE PRESS WITH A SHOT-GUN!
THEY'RE DRUG ADDICTS. THEY'RE EXTREMIST THEY HAVE NO RESPEC FOR AUTHORITY.
ENN YOUNG ACTIVIST OR TEEN TERRORIST? 9:48 AM
ING A LOCAL POLICE OFFICER ARIUS GREEN, GRANDFAT
"SHE CALLED FOR WAR. SHE CALLED FOR TROOPS ON THE MARCH. THIS IS AN ACT OF HOME-GROWN TERRORISM!
POLICE
455-001
68
"AND I DON'T SEE HOW ANYBODY WHO WANTS THIS COUNTRY TO BE SAFE CAN SAY OTHERWISE."

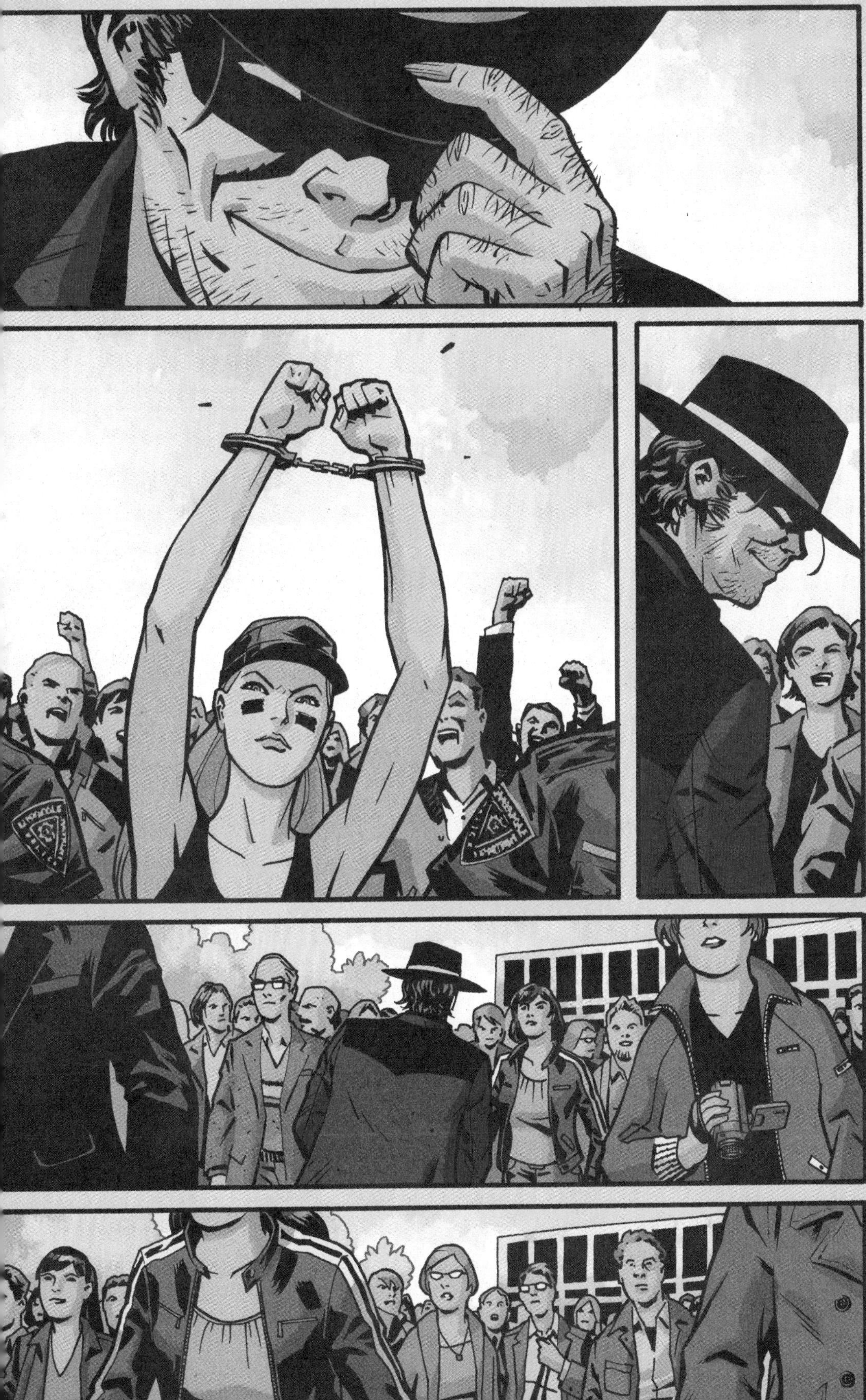

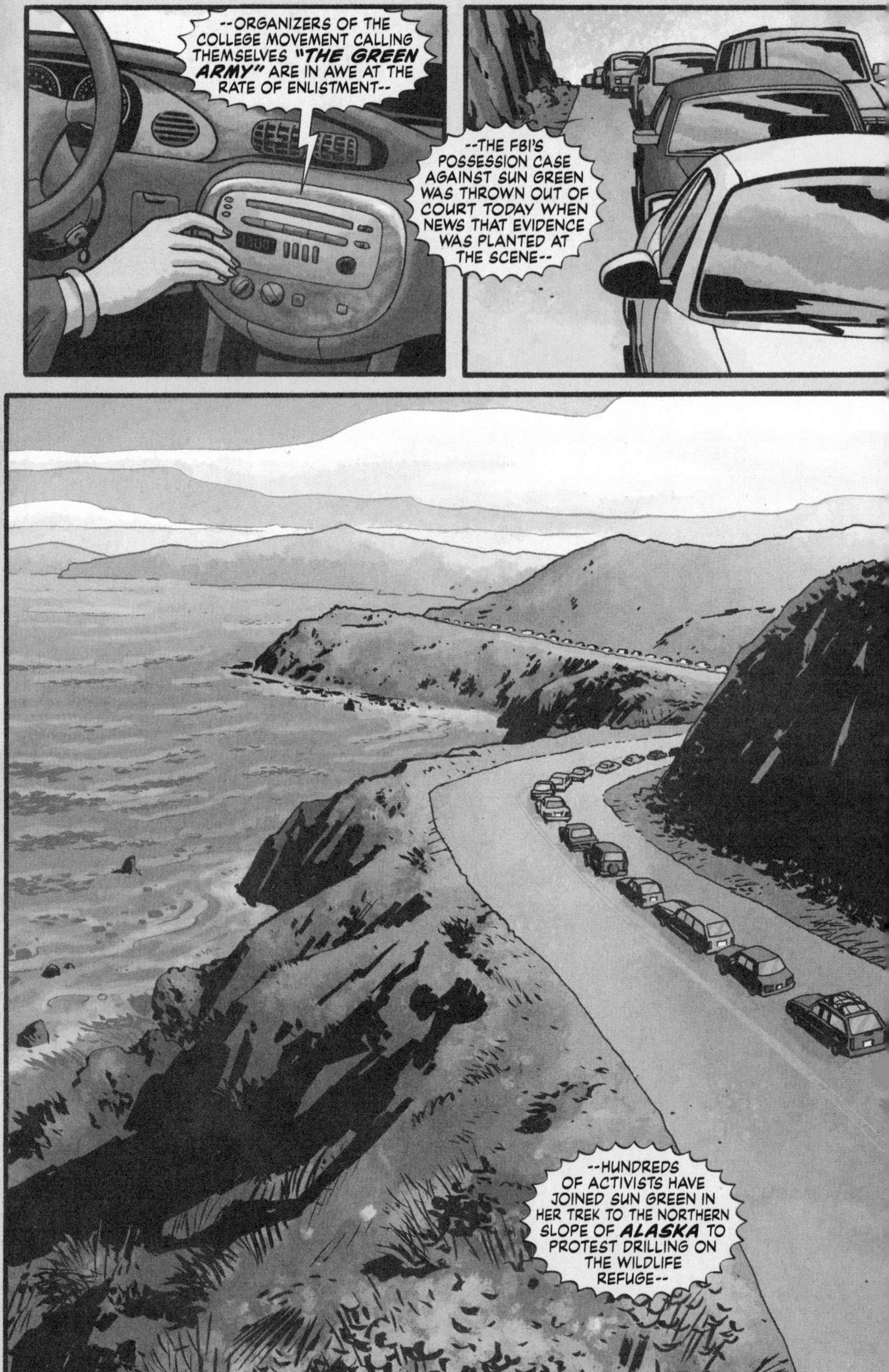
--ORGANIZERS OF THE COLLEGE MOVEMENT CALLING THEMSELVES "THE GREEN ARMY" ARE IN AWE AT THE RATE OF ENLISTMENT--
--THE FBI'S POSSESSION CASE AGAINST SUN GREEN WAS THROWN OUT OF COURT TODAY WHEN NEWS THAT EVIDENCE WAS PLANTED AT THE SCENE--
--HUNDREDS OF ACTIVISTS HAVE JOINED SUN GREEN IN HER TREK TO THE NORTHERN SLOPE OF ALASKA TO PROTEST DRILLING ON THE WILDLIFE REFUGE--

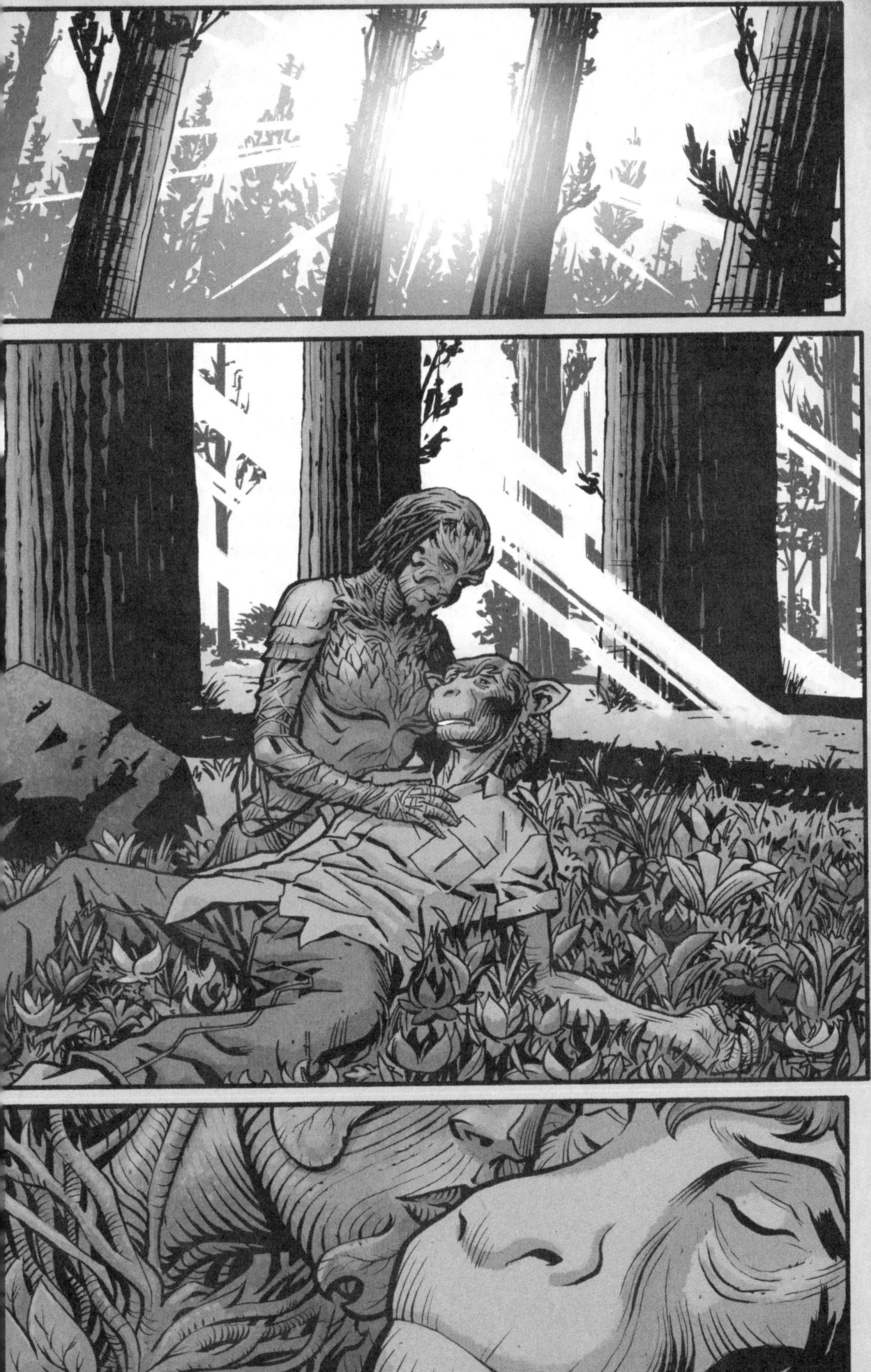

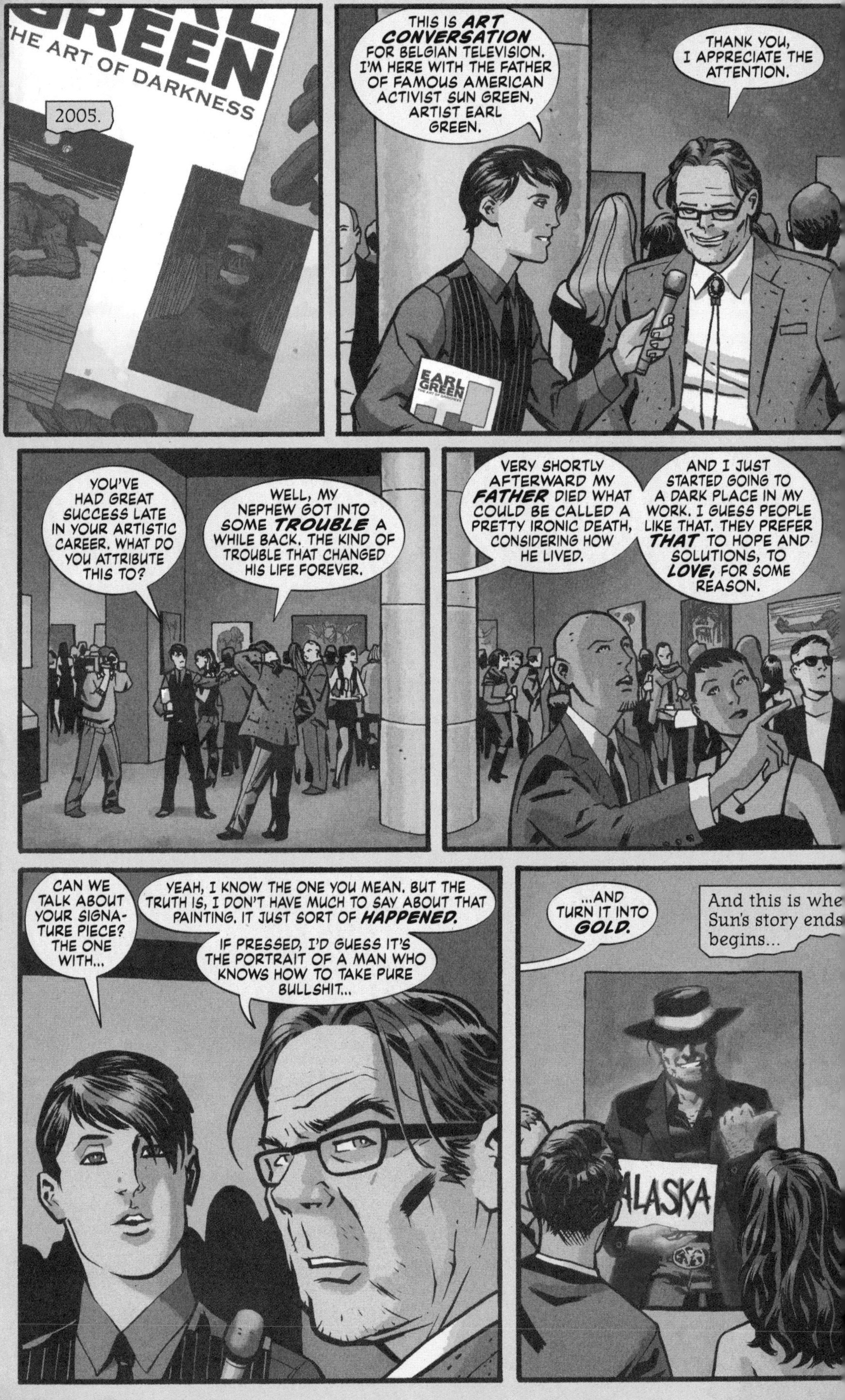

EARL GREEN
THE ART OF DARKNESS
2005.
THIS IS ART CONVERSATION FOR BELGIAN TELEVISION. I'M HERE WITH THE FATHER OF FAMOUS AMERICAN ACTIVIST SUN GREEN, ARTIST EARL GREEN.
THANK YOU, I APPRECIATE THE ATTENTION.
EARL GREEN THE ART OF DARKNESS
YOU'VE HAD GREAT SUCCESS LATE IN YOUR ARTISTIC CAREER. WHAT DO YOU ATTRIBUTE THIS TO?
WELL, MY NEPHEW GOT INTO SOME TROUBLE A WHILE BACK. THE KIND OF TROUBLE THAT CHANGED HIS LIFE FOREVER.
VERY SHORTLY AFTERWARD MY FATHER DIED WHAT COULD BE CALLED A PRETTY IRONIC DEATH, CONSIDERING HOW HE LIVED.
AND I JUST STARTED GOING TO A DARK PLACE IN MY WORK. I GUESS PEOPLE LIKE THAT. THEY PREFER THAT TO HOPE AND SOLUTIONS, TO LOVE, FOR SOME REASON.
CAN WE TALK ABOUT YOUR SIGNATURE PIECE? THE ONE WITH...
YEAH, I KNOW THE ONE YOU MEAN. BUT THE TRUTH IS, I DON'T HAVE MUCH TO SAY ABOUT THAT PAINTING. IT JUST SORT OF HAPPENED.
IF PRESSED, I'D GUESS IT'S THE PORTRAIT OF A MAN WHO KNOWS HOW TO TAKE PURE BULLSHIT...
...AND TURN IT INTO GOLD.
And this is whe
Sun's story ends
begins...
ALASKA

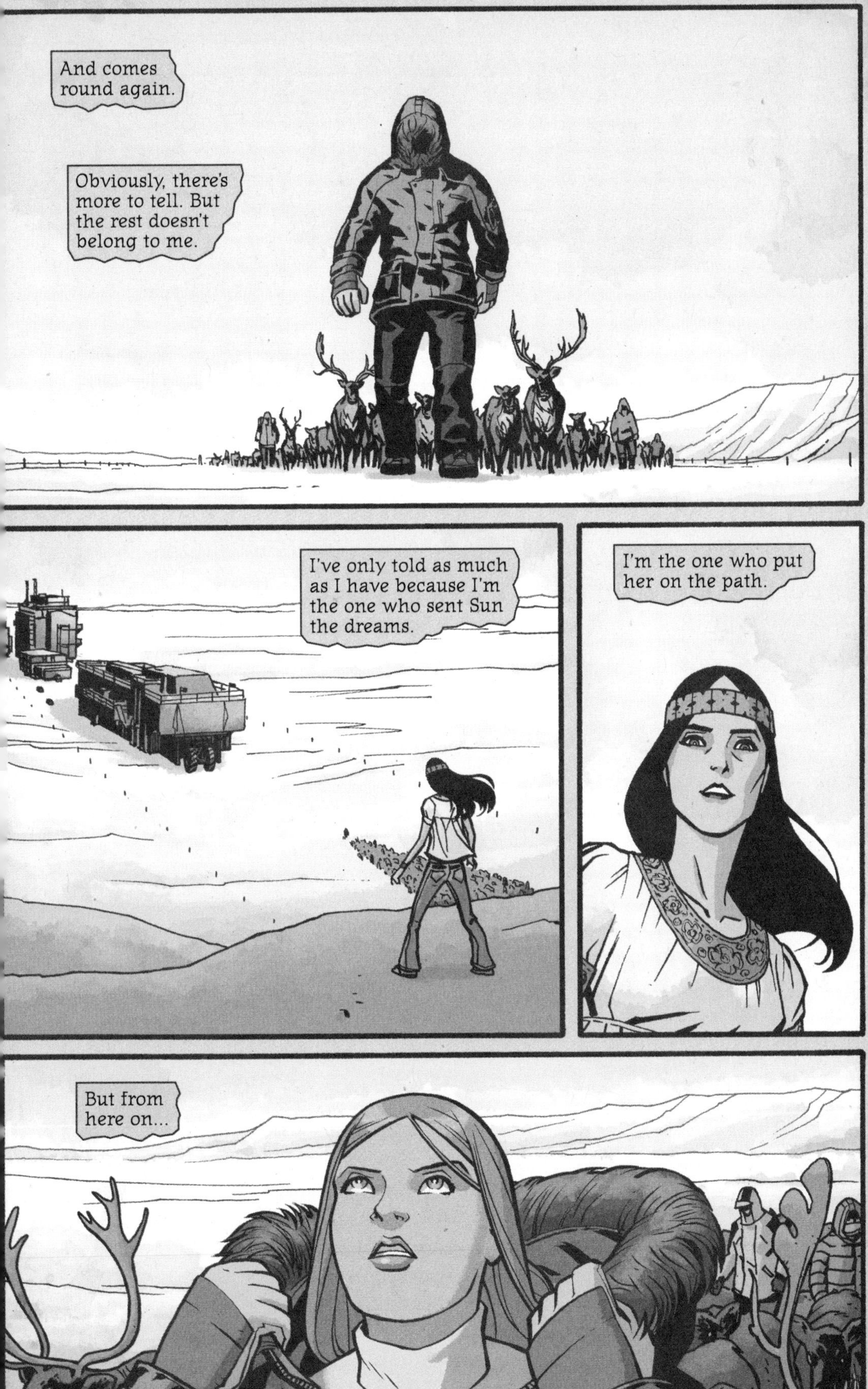
And comes round again.
Obviously, there's more to tell. But the rest doesn't belong to me.
I've only told as much as I have because I'm the one who sent Sun the dreams.
I'm the one who put her on the path.
But from here on...

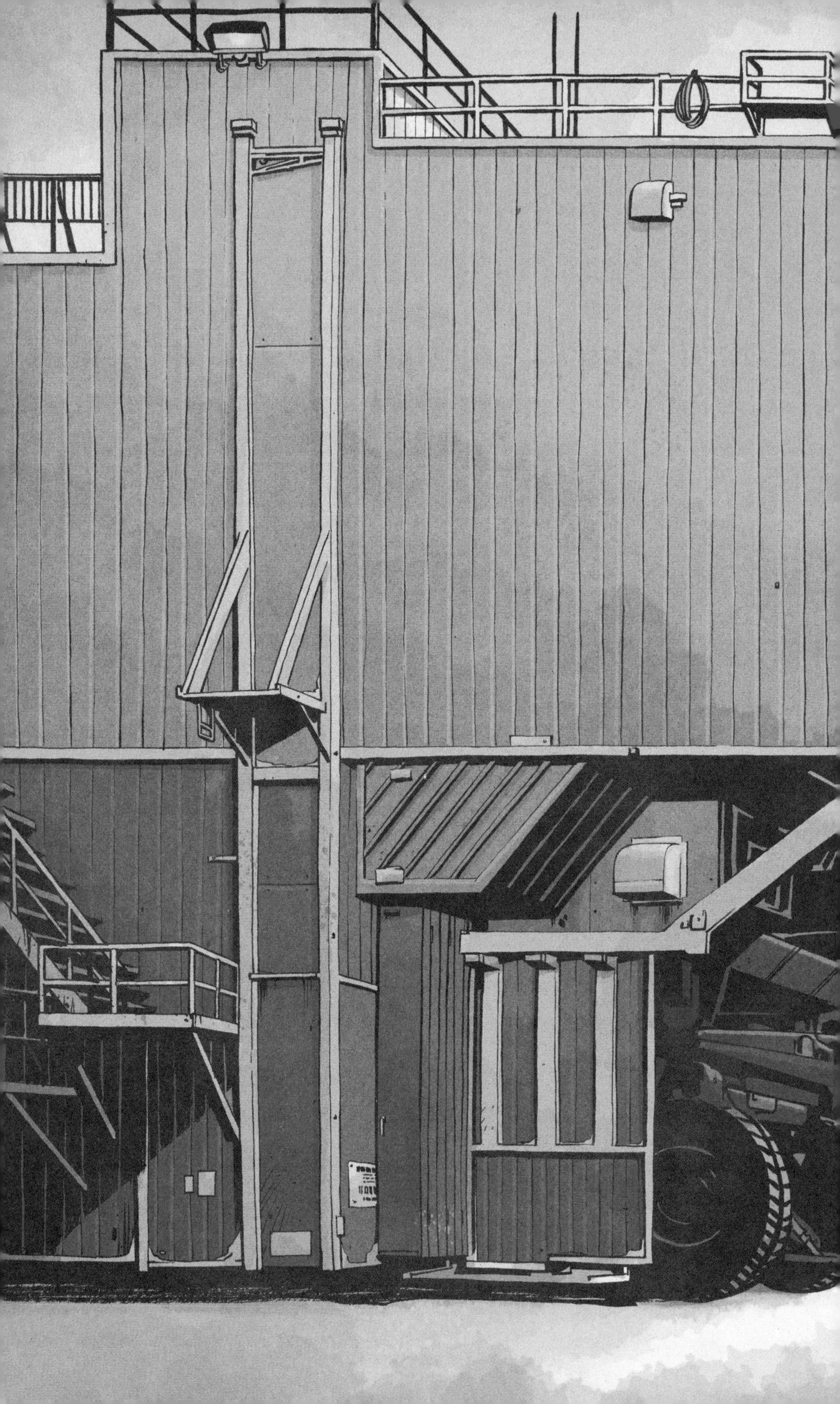

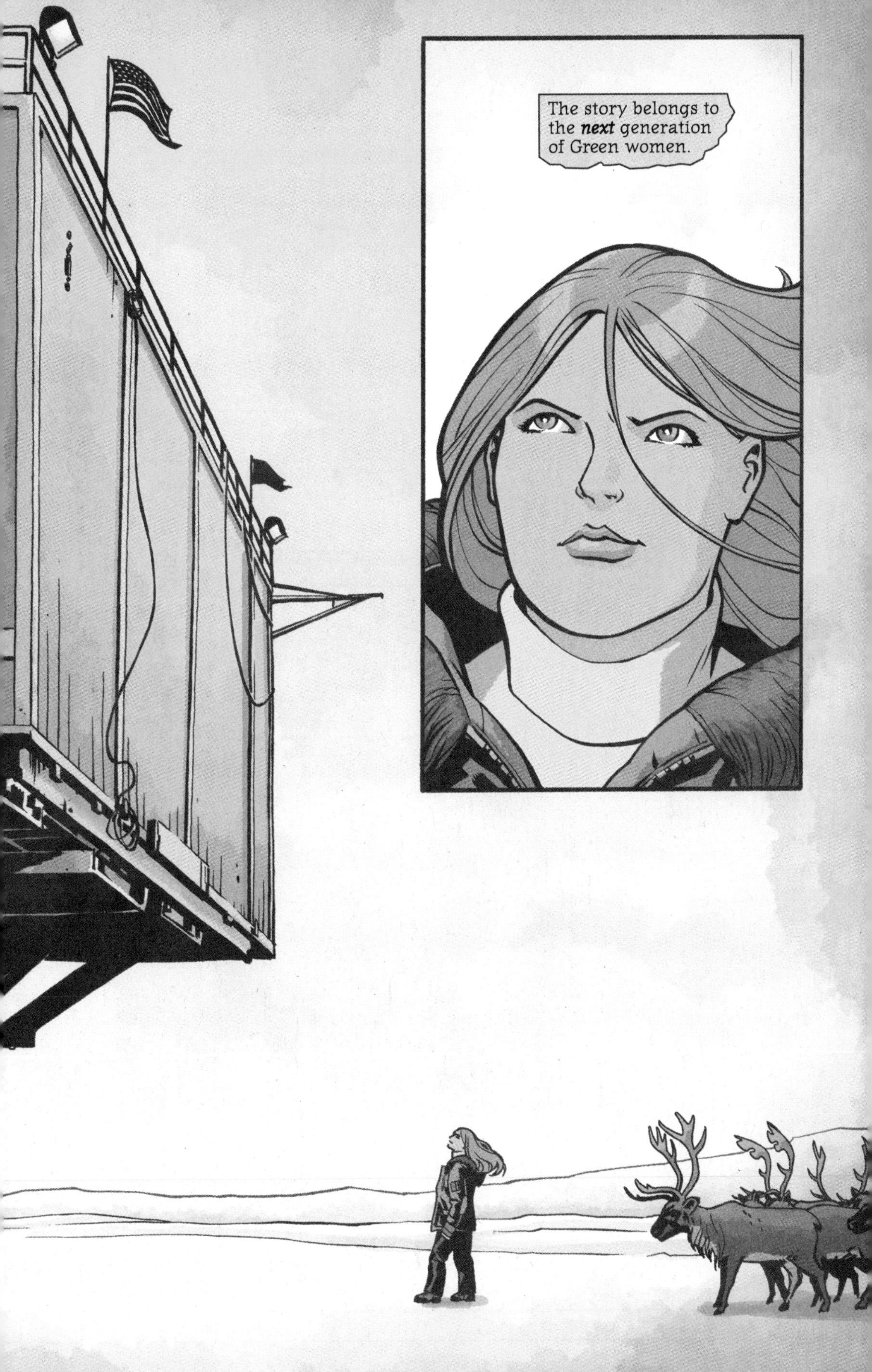
The story belongs to the *next* generation of Green women.

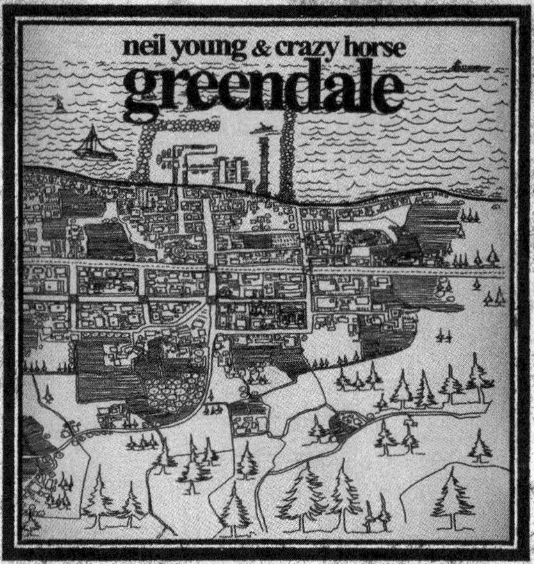
neil young & crazy horse
greendale

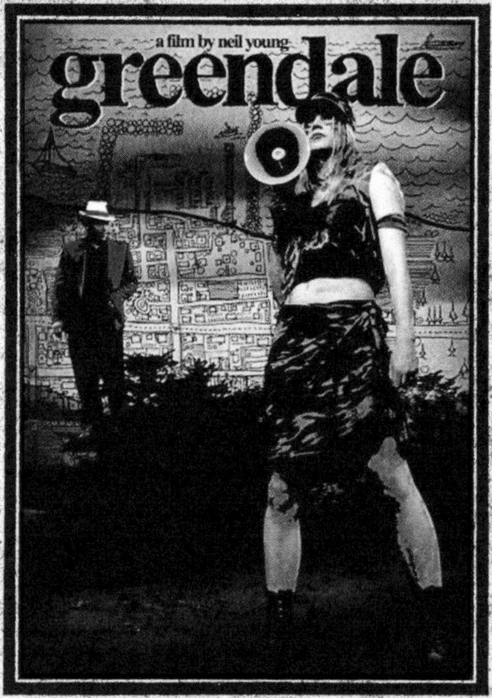
a film by neil young
greendale

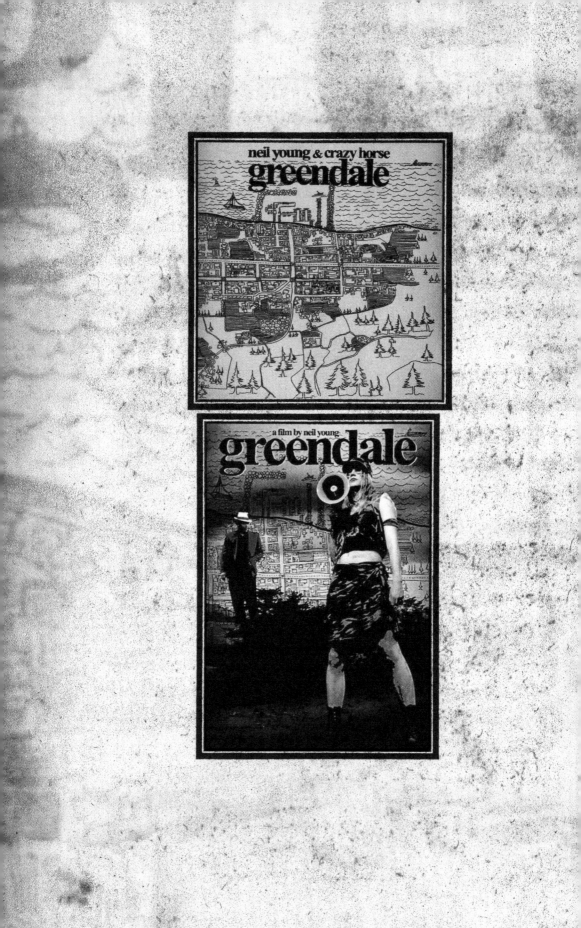

a little love and affection
in everything you do
will make the world a better place
with or without you

Some stories are so personal and important that we cannot let them go. Time passes, details are embellished, and the narrative shifts to accommodate a new audience. But the heart of the story, what is most private and profound about it, remains unchanged.

The tale of a tragic event and its effects on three generations of an American family, Neil Young's *Greendale* was conceived as a "musical novel" — a 10-song rock opera, set in the eponymous fictional California seaside town. Based on the saga of the Green family, the "audio novel" has been compared to literary classics such as Thornton Wilder's *Our Town* and Sherwood Anderson's *Winesburg, Ohio* for its complexity in exploring small town, America. When the concept album debuted in 2003, *Rolling Stone* ranked it as one of the year's best.

But Neil Young's vision would extend far beyond what ten songs could contain. The fictional town and its population would inspire a live rock opera and multimedia tour. That, in turn, would lead to a companion book, as well as a feature-length film directed by Young himself under his pseudonym Bernard Shakey. The movie would win raves of its own, being described as "hauntingly memorable" by Elvis Mitchell of *The New York Times* and "a triumph" by J. Hoberman of *The Village Voice*. These would inspire still more creative efforts, with an off-Broadway musical in 2008 and finally the VERTIGO graphic novel in 2010.

What is unchanged about *Greendale* in all its incarnations is that it remains Neil Young's singular statement of environmental, political and personal responsibility as told through the restless characters of a small Southern California town, with the teenage Sun Green at its center. A young woman finding her voice and using it to face the mounting injustices of the world around her. But even more, it is a call to arms for each and every one of us in the "real" world.

Neil Young is a singer-songwriter, guitarist, activist and film-maker. He was inducted into the Rock and Roll Hall of Fame in 1995 for his solo work, and again in 1997 as a member of Buffalo Springfield. He has directed four movies under the pseudonym Bernard Shakey, including *Journey Through the Past*, *Rust Never Sleeps*, *Human Highway* and *Greendale*. He was also one of the founders of Farm Aid and remains on the board of directors.

Joshua Dysart has done work for nearly every major comic book publisher. He is co-creator and writer of the cult hit comic book series *Violent Messiahs*, and is most recently known for writing *Unknown Soldier* for which he's received rave reviews from *The New York Times*, BBC, *The Huffington Post* and more.

Cliff Chiang's best known works include *Human Target*, *Batman*, *Green Arrow & Black Canary*, *Doctor 13* and *Grendel*. He began his professional career as an assistant editor for *Disney Adventures Magazine* before joining Vertigo Comics editorial. The Harvard University graduate then went freelance to pursue his dream to be an illustrator. He has since drawn stories for Dark Horse Comics and the ACLU, in addition to DC Comics and Vertigo.

Cover Artist: Cliff Chiang

NEIL YOUNG'S GREENDALE Published by DC Comics, 1700 Broadway, New York, NY 10019. Copyright © 2010 by Young Family Trust and DC Comics. All rights reserved. Greendale names, characters and all related elements, are trademarks of the Young Family Trust. Vertigo is a trademark of DC Comics. The stories, characters and incidents mentioned in this book are entirely fictional. Printed in the USA. First Printing. DC Comics, a Warner Bros. Entertainment Company. HC ISBN:978-1-4012-2698-5 SC ISBN:978-1-4012-2822-4

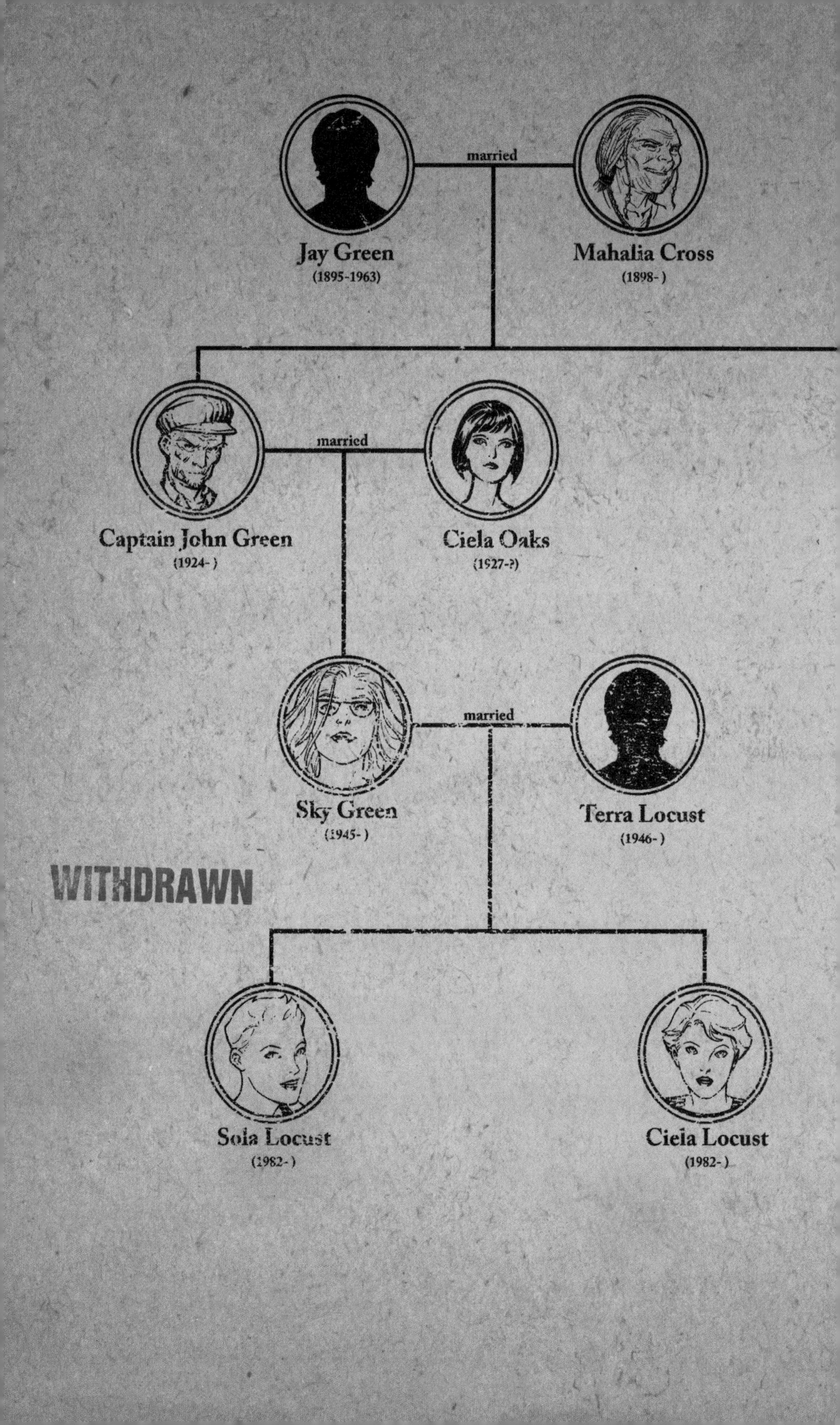
married
Jay Green
(1895-1963)
Mahalia Cross
(1898-)
married
Captain John Green
(1924-)
Ciela Oaks
(1927-?)
married
Sky Green
(1945-)
Terra Locust
(1946-)
Sola Locust
(1982-)
Ciela Locust
(1982-)